POSTMODERN PLATOS

CATHERINE H. ZUCKERT

Postmodern
PLATOS

Nietzsche
Heidegger
Gadamer
Strauss
Derrida

THE UNIVERSITY OF CHICAGO PRESS
CHICAGO AND LONDON

Catherine H. Zuckert is professor of political science at Carleton College.

The University of Chicago Press, Chicago 60637
The University of Chicago Press, Ltd., London
© 1996 by The University of Chicago
All rights reserved. Published 1996
Printed in the United States of America
05 04 03 02 01 00 99 98 97 96   5 4 3 2 1

ISBN (cloth): 0-226-99330-2
ISBN (paper): 0-226-99331-0

An earlier version of chapter 1, "Nietzsche's Rereadings of Plato," appeared in *Political Theory* 13, no. 2 (1985): 213–33, copyright © 1985 by Sage Publications, Inc. Reprinted with permission.

Library of Congress Cataloging-in-Publication Data

Zuckert, Catherine H., 1942–
    Postmodern Platos : Nietzsche, Heidegger, Gadamer,
Strauss, Derrida / Catherine H. Zuckert.
        p.   cm.
    Includes bibliographical references and index.
    ISBN 0-226-99330-2.—ISBN 0-226-99331-0 (pbk.)
    1. Plato.   2. Philosophy, Modern—19th century.
3. Philosophy, Modern—20th century.   4. Postmodernism.
I. Title.
B395.Z78   1996
190—dc20   95-35118
                                                          CIP

Contents

Acknowledgments

I would like to begin by thanking the organizations that made it possible for me to complete this study: Carleton College, the National Endowment for the Humanities, the H. B. Earhart Foundation, the Social Philosophy and Policy Center at Bowling Green State University, and last, but by no means least, the Lynde and Harry Bradley Foundation. Without their support I could never have written it.

Certain individuals have also helped. Jacques Derrida graciously granted me an interview in Paris in July 1993 to discuss his reading of Plato. Michael Davis, Michael Gillespie, Mary P. Nichols, and Vickie Sullivan were kind enough to read and comment on parts of the text. The readers for the University of Chicago Press suggested ways in which the manuscript could be improved. The editors of *Political Theory* granted me permission to reprint parts of "Nietzsche's Re-reading of Plato."

Most of all, however, I want to thank my husband Michael. Not only did he generously share his ideas and reactions in discussing the contents and argument of this book; he also carefully read, reread, and commented upon each chapter. I find it hard to imagine what, if anything I would have done without the combination of affectionate support and intelligent criticism he has bestowed upon me and my work for many, many years. Words fail to describe gifts born of love.

Introduction

Postmodern Platos

A lfred North Whitehead once quipped that all philosophy is a footnote to Plato. That is the problem, according to the thinkers treated in this volume; the scholarly apparatus has gradually covered over and so obscured the original. These thinkers all see themselves engaged, therefore, in an excavation project, seeking to uncover the original character of philosophy in new, emphatically nontraditional studies of Plato.

The repeated returns to Plato inaugurated by Friedrich Nietzsche do not represent exercises in antiquarian history, however. On the contrary, when Martin Heidegger, Hans-Georg Gadamer, Leo Strauss, and Jacques Derrida follow Nietzsche in seeking to discover what philosophy was originally like, they reread Plato in an attempt to reconceive the character of the Western tradition as a whole.

I call these thinkers "Postmodern Platos" for two reasons. First, I am arguing that their understanding of Plato is a central, if not the defining, factor in their thought as a whole. When these thinkers return to Plato to find out what the character of philosophy originally was, they understand themselves to be inquiring into the roots of their own activity. Their interpretations of Plato thus constitute essential parts of their own self-understanding.

The second reason I refer to these thinkers as "Postmodern Platos" is that they look back to the origins of philosophy from an explicitly "postmodern" position. That is, they return to Plato and ask what the character of philosophy was at its origins explicitly on the basis of a conviction that modern rationalism has exhausted its promise and its possibilities.[1] They are all seeking a way of making a new beginning, of moving beyond "modernity" to something better, by articulating a new and

1

different understanding of the distinctive characteristic of "the West."

These thinkers are not interested so much in what Plato meant to his contemporaries as they are in what his work has meant and still can mean for later generations. Explicitly reading Plato in light of subsequent history, four of the five authors deny that it is possible to understand Plato as he understood himself. Later generations necessarily read the dialogues in terms of a different context. In the following analyses, I have not sought, therefore, either to confirm or to deny the validity of their readings by comparing their claims with the original texts. I do not mean to say that their interpretations are entirely irrelevant to an understanding of Plato. On the contrary, I suspect, no one who has read their interpretations will ever read the dialogues themselves in quite the same way. Convinced that philosophy is and ought to be understood to be a distinctive form of human activity, all five of these thinkers raise questions not only about the truth of the doctrine of the "two worlds" usually associated with Plato—the world of the eternal, unchanging ideas in contrast to the sensible, changing world in which we live—but also about the attribution of that doctrine to Plato. To support such an unconventional understanding, these thinkers present new, extremely challenging readings of the dialogues. (The fact that these postmodern thinkers return to Plato and present new readings of the dialogues suggests that they are not quite so anti-Platonic or antirational as their partisans and foes in the current "cultural wars" sometimes suggest.) The following analysis of the readings Nietzsche, Heidegger, Gadamer, Strauss and Derrida give of Plato is, nevertheless, primarily a study in contemporary political philosophy. It is not a work in classics or a study of ancient philosophy as those fields are ordinarily understood.

Why did these thinkers conclude that we need to reconceive philosophy? Why did they go back to Plato? Nietzsche provides an explanation of the genesis of this line of inquiry in his first book on *The Birth of Tragedy.*

Philosophy had traditionally been understood to consist in the search for wisdom or knowledge. Hegel claimed to have brought this search to an end by developing a real science or knowledge; but Hegel's claim to be able to explain everything that had or could happen—at least in principle—did not prove to be credible to any of his successors. Returning to Kant's argument that we cannot know the "things-in-themselves," Nietzsche thus concluded that the two-thousand-year-long search for knowledge had culminated only in the knowledge that we could not know. But, he asked, if philosophers had not been acquiring knowledge all that time, what had they been doing? What kind of activity was philosophy if it could not result in the acquisition of knowledge? Nietzsche looked back to the origins of philosophy, as traditionally understood, in Plato in search of an answer. He thought that he might find the source of a different understanding of philosophy in Plato for two reasons. First, unlike his student Aristotle and his successors, Plato did not write treatises in which he presented positions and argued for them in his own name; he wrote dialogues that are in many ways more like dramas than traditional philosophical discourses. Nietzsche's turn back to Plato in search of a new understanding of philosophy thus led him to reopen the question of the relation between philosophy and poetry or art. Second, Nietzsche observed, the "hero" of most of the Platonic dialogues, Plato's teacher Socrates, himself claimed only to know that he did not know. Socrates apparently knew something at the beginning of the history of philosophy that had become apparent again only at the end.

In a series of rereadings of Plato, I argue in chapter 1, Nietzsche never determined completely to his own satisfaction what Socrates or Plato knew. But, he came to suspect, either Socrates or, more probably, Plato sensed, even if he did not admit it to himself consciously, that philosophy did not consist simply in the formulation of arguments and doctrines. On the contrary, philosophy was a way of life; indeed, philosophy constituted the only form of human life that was truly satisfying and, as such, could be affirmed to be worthwhile in and of itself.

True philosophers are legislators, Nietzsche proclaimed; philosophy is the most spiritual form of the will to power. Rather than finding or discovering an intelligible order in the cosmos, philosophers have projected order and intelligibility upon it. Once human beings recognize they have been the only sources of order and meaning in the world, they will seek to do consciously and intentionally what they have done heretofore unknowingly. They will seek to impose their own order and values—worldwide. During the next century or two, he thus predicted, we will see the rise of "great politics" in the form of a competition between ideologically defined "superpowers" for world domination.

Nietzsche correctly diagnosed the political crisis of the twentieth century, Martin Heidegger concluded; but Nietzsche was mistaken about its source. Philosophers had never merely legislated or imposed an order on the cosmos; they had simply articulated the order or truth that was disclosed at their particular time and place. *The* truth disclosed at Heidegger's own time and place was that the history of philosophy had come to an end; it had come to an end in the thought of Nietzsche, whose doctrine of the will to power represented the working out of the furthest possibilities of the thought that had originated in Greece and was most decisively articulated in its peak, the doctrine of the ideas and the corresponding notion of education described in Books VI and VII of the *Republic*.[2]

Whereas Nietzsche first presented the life and death of Socrates as the "vortex of world history" and later emphasized the Platonic notion of the philosopher-king as the precedent for his own understanding of the philosopher as moral legislator (*BGE* 211), Heidegger argued that Plato's articulation of the original understanding of being as 'idea' unintentionally gave rise to an historical development or disclosure of 'the truth of Being'. That historical development proceeded in stages through the medieval scholastic notion of beings as having the source and ground of their existence in ideas in the mind of God, to the modern philosophical conception of being as that which could be clearly and distinctly represented to the mind of man. This Cartesian notion of being, in turn, provided the foundation for mathematical physics—and, we might add, genetics or microbiology—which currently threaten to deprive the world of all intelligibility by making not only all things but also human beings themselves into formless 'standing reserve' to be technologically transformed at will.

Like Nietzsche, I argue in chapter 2, Heidegger sought to overturn or invert the Platonic teaching with regard to the relation between philosophy and poetry. Where Plato emphasized the need for poetry to serve philosophy, Heidegger concluded, like Nietzsche, that poetry is both purer and more primary. But by 'poetry', Nietzsche and Heidegger had in mind very different activities. Whereas Nietzsche emphasized the creative character and effects of the poet's art, Heidegger thought it consisted primarily in the articulation of a particular 'world' as that world appeared to a particular people, living at a certain time and place, and speaking a particular language.

Heidegger's student Hans-Georg Gadamer objected to both the particularistic and the eschatological character of his mentor's final vision. If human existence were truly as open or essentially historical, as Heidegger maintained, Heidegger contradicted his own fundamental insight when he began writing about an end of history. Although ancient Greek philosophy was not explicitly or properly speaking historical, Gadamer concluded, Plato's notion of the Idea of the Good and Aristotle's conception of *phronēsis* or practical reason provided a better foundation for a truly historical, that is to say, open-ended, nondetermined, and hence essentially free understanding of human existence than Heidegger's conception of a fateful dispensation. Where Nietzsche and Heidegger both tried to overcome Platonic "metaphysics" in different ways, I argue in chapter 3, Gadamer thus attempted to revive Platonic philosophy in an explicitly historical form.

As Leo Strauss wrote Gadamer in an exchange of letters concerning *Wahrheit und Methode*, his thought moved from a common beginning point in an almost entirely opposite direction. Rather than seeking either to critique or to revive the traditional, Christian or Neoplatonic understanding of philosophy, he sought a different, if not altogether new understanding of ancient rationalism by studying the works of the medieval Jewish scholar Maimonides and his teacher, the Islamic philosopher Farabi. Whereas Nietzsche, Heidegger, and Gadamer all read the dialogues in terms of the Neoplatonic Christian tradition that emphasized the importance of the ideas, Strauss's study of Farabi led him to suspect that both the theory of the ideas and the Platonic doctrines concerning the soul might be mere public teachings. In chapter 4 I argue, Strauss's discovery of "Farabi's Plato" gave him a new understanding of the history of philosophy. It also led him, as I show in chapter 5, to seek to discover the character of "primitive" as opposed to traditional Christian Platonism by looking at what Nietzsche called "the problem of Socrates" in its original context, by comparing the depictions of the first political philosopher to be found in the works of Aristophanes, Xenophon, and Plato. And the new, more original view of Socrates to which he came, I argue in chapter 6, led Strauss to a new understanding of the Western tradition as a whole, an understanding he sketches in his final work entitled *Studies in Platonic Political Philosophy*.

I had to spend more time and space explicating Strauss's views than those of the preceding, more famous authors for two reasons. In the first place, the medieval Jewish and Islamic writers or tradition through which Strauss approached Plato are much less well known than the dominant traditional Christian or Neoplatonic reading. It was necessary, therefore, to explain them or at least Strauss's use of them in more detail. Second, partly as a result of his reading of these medieval authors, Strauss presented his "studies," particularly of ancient authors, in a rather unconventional manner; like Farabi's *Philosophy of Plato*, they appear to be mere summaries of the works in question. In order to indicate the basis of the rather controversial conclusions to which Strauss came, I had to report something about the accounts, that is, the implicit analyses, he presented of the works of Aristophanes, Xenophon, and Thucydides as well as of Plato. There is very little secondary work on the "late Strauss" to which I could refer readers.[3]

Whereas Strauss explicitly tried to save Western rationalism from the Nietzschean-Heideggerian critique, I argue in chapters 7 and 8, Derrida has just as explicitly attempted to extend that critique even further. He does not want to destroy the "history of metaphysics," he explains in *Of Grammatology*, so much as to move beyond it—on the basis, and therefore preserving some "traces," of the tradition out of which his own work comes. In "Plato's Pharmacy" he suggests that not only Plato's depiction of Socrates' death but also his metaphysical teaching about the idea of the Good in the *Republic* was designed to serve ethical and political ends. Careful reading of the dialogues shows that their explicit teachings are systematically undercut. Like Nietzsche, Derrida suspects that Plato himself may have been aware of the difficulty. There was nothing he could do, however. An author does not and cannot control the meaning of his text. As Derrida shows more fancifully in *The Post Card*, we cannot recover, restore, or reconstruct anything or anyone as it was. Nor can we control anyone or anything's future fate. In *Khora*, he argues, there has been a certain instability or "doubling" of meaning within the history of philosophy from the very "beginning" in Plato. Heidegger was mistaken, therefore, to think that "history" had an identifiable beginning or end. What we have in the history of philosophy is, rather, a series of different accounts that have some common elements, but that all also leave something out. We should beware of taking any version of the story to be simply authoritative. Plato put forth his ethical and political doctrines, because he was afraid of anarchy. But, Derrida suggests, two-thousand-years' experience with philosophy suggests that the danger arises more from excess rationalization than from skeptical questioning; rather than endanger political and other forms of order, philosophy has supported it. By showing how philosophy deconstructs itself, he hopes to subvert any attempt to establish a total(itarian) regime.

Gadamer, Strauss, and Derrida are probably best known as proponents of different ways of reading texts called hermeneutics, secret teaching, and deconstruction. But all three authors emphatically deny that what they have attempted to do is to propound a method of reading or interpreting the writings of others. In the introduction to *Truth and Method*, Gadamer states, "The understanding and the interpretation of texts is not merely a concern of science, but obviously belongs to human experience of the world in general. The hermeneutic phenomenon is basically not a problem of method at all."[4] In his correspondence with Gadamer, Strauss observes:

> It is not easy for me to recognize in your hermeneutics my own experience as an interpreter. Yours is a "theory of hermeneutic experience" which as such is a universal theory. Not only is my own hermeneutic experience very limited—the experience which I possess makes me doubtful whether a universal hermeneutic theory which is more than "formal" or external is possible. I believe that the doubt arises from the feeling of the irretrievably 'occasional' character of every worthwhile interpretation.[5]

Likewise, in his "Letter to a Japanese Friend," Derrida insists that "Deconstruction is not a method and cannot be transformed into one."[6]

In this book I have attempted to show that all three thinkers develop their distinctive modes of reading as a part of a larger project. They have been responding to the challenge posed by Nietzsche and Heidegger's contention that philosophy as it has been practiced in the West is no longer possible. Whether philosophy has come to an end, all three of these commentators see, depends at least in part on what one thinks philosophy was from the beginning; to discover what it was, they thus all go back to Plato. Gadamer concludes that philosophy is not the sort of activity that has an end. In his critique of the "radical historicists," Strauss concedes that philosophy may come to an end, but he argues that this end is not necessary or fated. Derrida suggests that the question whether philosophy has come to an end cannot be answered by philosophers, but it is *the* question they or we need to address.[7]

As Derrida reminds his readers by prefacing his statement of the question with a quotation from Matthew Arnold about Hebraism and Hellenism, the question of the character and status of the Western tradition is complicated by the fact that it is not simply a matter of philosophy. What we call the West is an amalgam or at least a result of a combination of philosophical inquiries with ideas derived from Scripture; and these two sources differ, at least apparently, both in their origins or principles and in their content. One of the questions that has faced all of Hegel's successors has been the extent to which these two elements can or have been merged. Whereas Nietzsche, Gadamer, and Derrida argue that they have necessarily been combined, although in very different fashions for fundamentally different reasons, Heidegger and Strauss both insist that reason and revelation have been and ought to remain completely separate. (Strauss criticizes Heidegger, indeed, for incorporating biblically derived ideas into his purportedly nontheological "thought.")[8] All five of these thinkers have been primarily concerned with philosophy, however; that is the reason they have all gone back to Plato to discover what philosophy originally was.[9]

The question of the effects or influence of philosophical inquiry becomes particularly dramatic in relation to politics. Socrates himself was accused, tried, and convicted of a capital crime by the city of Athens and perished as a result. Later philosophers, especially of the so-called Enlightenment, tried to show that, rather than threatening fundamental democratic beliefs and institutions, the pursuit of knowledge and its popular dissemination provided the only firm basis for free government. As part of their critique of modern rationalism, Nietzsche and Heidegger both presented devastating critiques of liberal political philosophy. As a result, their thought became implicated, more or less directly, in Nazi politics. Persuaded by the critique Nietzsche and Heidegger gave of mod-

ern rationalism and of the need, therefore, to reconsider the adequacy
and status of the modern philosophical critique of the ancients, Gadamer,
Strauss, and Derrida have all pursued the line of thought set out by
Nietzsche and Heidegger with particular attention to its political effects.
Their responses to or extensions of the Nietzschean-Heideggerian critique of the tradition can be characterized, indeed, in political terms as
liberal, conservative, and left. All end up endorsing forms of liberal democracy, but the grounds of that endorsement and the vision of liberal
democracy each presents differ radically from the others as well as from
the traditional justification of liberal democracy in terms of the protection of rights.

But, I conclude, the differences among these thinkers are not exclusively or fundamentally political. They concern the character of human
existence, the kind of knowledge we can have and the extent to which
we can control our fate. Whereas Gadamer argues that human life is
essentially historical, which is to say, progressively and essentially open-
ended, both Strauss and Derrida argue, for somewhat different reasons,
that history has no necessary direction or character. Human beings can
never entirely control their destiny, because the world is not completely
intelligible or rational; there is something always and essentially *alogos*.
That is the reason political order can never rest simply or solely on the
truth. Human beings are free, both Gadamer and Derrida maintain,
because their existence is open-ended and, therefore, undetermined.
Heidegger and Strauss argue, on the contrary, that the preservation of
humanity, in almost any sense, depends on our recognizing the limitations or determinate character of human life. More specifically, they suggest, human beings will not remain human, if they do not recognize the
existence of something above and beyond them—what has traditionally
been called 'god' or the 'gods'. Agreeing that human beings cannot have
certain knowledge of the whole, all five of these thinkers nevertheless try
to show the consonance between philosophy and the findings of natural
science.[10] But, precisely because they recognize that human beings can
never have full knowledge, all of Nietzsche's successors also agree on the
need to check or control technology. They disagree very much, however,
on both the means and the rationale. Whereas Heidegger hopes that human beings will turn away from technology when they recognize the
danger it poses and begin to cherish the earth, Gadamer and Strauss advocate practical, political control and direction. Agreeing with Heidegger
that techno-science gradually invades all spheres of endeavor, Derrida
denies that such control is possible. The only way to respond to the danger of complete "rationalization" of life is to show the problematic character of rationality itself, that is, to submit it to an internal critique. These

thinkers' disagreements about the practical significance of science in the modern world thus remind us the continuing salience of the questions Socrates first posed to his predecessors: Do students of nature think they already understand the human things? Do they really think human beings can know the character of the whole? Do they think they can use their knowledge of the way in which things come into being to produce heavenly things like wind and rain, or will they be satisfied merely with knowledge?[11]

One

Nietzsche's Rereadings of Plato

Philosophy has traditionally been understood to be the search for wisdom. But, Nietzsche argued in his very first book on *The Birth of Tragedy*, with Kant that search culminated only in the "knowledge" that we cannot know. What, then, should we make of this apparently sisyphean endeavor that has distinguished the West? In attempting to answer this question, Nietzsche reexamined the origins of the Western philosophical tradition in the work of Plato and his peculiar "hero," Socrates—not just once, but repeatedly. During the course of his life's reflections, Nietzsche came to suspect that Platonic doctrines like the idea of the Good and the immortal soul constituted public teachings that Plato himself did not believe and that differed markedly from Plato's understanding of own activity or philosophy properly understood. To the extent to which later philosophers built on the Platonic theory of ideas, they built on a falsification, a "noble lie" or *mythos*, that Plato intentionally fabricated not merely to protect philosophy from persecution but to give philosophy political influence. If Nietzsche's suspicion is correct, Western philosophy since Plato has proceeded on a misperception of its own origin and essential nature and must, therefore, be radically reinterpreted in light of its political origins and goals.

Nietzsche's rereadings of Plato are thus important, first, because they raise questions about the adequacy of the traditional understanding of philosophy and its historical development. Nietzsche would lead us to read not only Plato but all of Plato's successors in a most untraditional way.

Second, Nietzsche's reinterpretation of Platonic philosophy brings out the affirmative conclusion of his own reinterpretation of Western philosophy and makes it more concrete. If there is no incorporeal, eternal, unchanging "truth," all meaning, wholeness, or completeness must assume a particular, emphatically corporeal and historical form: That is, it occurs and can only occur in an individual human being. As the only form of self-fulfilling human activity, philosophy represents the only possible source of justification for all other forms of human life. Plato offers perhaps the only example of such a life besides Nietzsche himself. Nietzsche's challenge to the traditional understanding of philosophy is both more radical and more positive than Martin Heidegger suggested when he emphasized Nietzsche's critique of otherworldly ideas or "metaphysics."[1]

Third, Nietzsche's rereadings of Plato explicitly raise the question of the proper relation between politics and philosophy. According to Nietzsche, Plato intentionally hid the true nature of his own activity behind the skeptical, plebeian mask of Socrates and his nihilistic metaphysical doctrines in order to have a political effect. Does political philosophy necessarily involve dissimulation, if not lying? Does Nietzsche himself escape the need for public teaching only by giving up all concern for the fate of the many nonphilosophers, that is, by giving up politics altogether?[2]

Nietzsche did not come to his new reading of Plato immediately. But, even in the lectures he gave as a young professor of philology, he presented Plato as the writer who had formed our vision of what it is to be a philosopher, full of desire for knowledge and wonder at the beauty of the cosmos. "Imagine that the writings of Plato had been lost, that philosophy began with Aristotle; we would not be at all able to imagine this ancient *philosopher* who is, at the same time, an artist."[3] However, in opposition to the scholarly consensus at that time, Nietzsche did not think that Plato was simply a philosopher or an artist; he thought that Plato was a political activist. To effect political reform, Plato saw he needed to educate a new ruling class. By founding the Academy, he hoped to change the world entirely!

Interested in the author as much as in his writings, Nietzsche spent as much time in these lectures discussing those people who had a formative effect on Plato—Kratylus (a Herakleitan), Socrates, and the Pythagoreans—as he did on the dialogues and the arguments to be found in them. Since these lectures were delivered over a four-year period, from 1871 to 1874, their relation to the discussion of Socrates and Plato in Nietzsche's first book on *The Birth of Tragedy out of the Spirit of Music*, published in 1872, is somewhat unclear.

In *The Birth of Tragedy* Socrates is the major figure. He is—or was—the "vortex or turning-point of so-called world history," who corrupted "the typical Hellenic youth," "the divine Plato."[4] Socrates destroyed the tragic insight with his demand that everything be intelligible, but he created a new illusion to replace the tragic insight—the illusion that man could not only attain knowledge but also correct his existence with the knowledge he attained. Plato merely followed Socrates in making poetry subservient to philosophy.

Socrates destroyed tragedy, according to Nietzsche, through his explicit teachings.

> Consider the consequences of the Socratic maxims; "Virtue is knowledge; man sins only from ignorance; he who is virtuous is happy." In these three basic forms of optimism lies the death of tragedy. For now the virtuous hero must be a dialectician; now there must be a necessary, visible connection between virtue and knowledge, faith and morality.[5]

As a student of Socrates, Euripides tried to make tragedy intelligible; but as he himself finally admitted in *The Bacchae*, it was an impossible task. Tragedy could not be made logical, because tragedy reveals "the contradiction at the heart of the world"—that all things exist only as particulars, that all suffer from their particularity or limits and therefore try to overcome them, but that all thus destroy themselves by destroying the limits which define their particular form of existence. Since tragedy revealed the truth about existence, that everything is always becoming, the emergence of philosophy appeared to be an extremely problematic phenomenon to Nietzsche. The self-proclaimed search for "the truth," understood to be the eternal, unchanging order, arose only the basis of a denial of the truth!

As the destroyer of tragedy, Socrates appears to represent an essentially negative, critical, and hence destructive force. Claiming to have no knowledge himself, he only asks questions; he is "the only one who acknowledged to himself that he knew *nothing*."[6] The key to the character of Socrates is "the wonderful phenomenon known as 'the *daimonion*'.... This voice, whenever it comes, always *dissuades*"; it never prompts the philosopher to act.

Yet, Nietzsche observes, the image of Socrates presented in the Platonic writings had a definitely positive, preservative rather than negative or destructive effect.

> For if we imagine that whole incalculable sum of energy used up for this world tendency had been used *not* in the service of knowledge but for the practical, i.e., egoistic aims of individuals and peoples, then we realize that in that case universal wars of annihilation and continual migrations of peoples would probably have weakened the instinctive lust for life to such an extent that suicide would have become a general custom . . .—a practical pessimism that [has been] in the world wherever art did not appear in some form—especially as religion and science.[7]

By initiating the search for knowledge, Socrates gave human beings a new reason to live.

Post-Kantian students of philosophy now know that Socrates and the philosophic way of life he represents constitute an illusion; the search for knowledge culminates only in the knowledge that we cannot know. However, the source or nature of this illusory search for knowledge is not so clear.

> Socrates might be called the typical *non-mystic*, in whom . . . the logical nature is developed as excessively as instinctive wisdom is in the mystic. But the logical urge that became manifest in Socrates . . . displays a natural power such as we encounter to our awed amazement only in the very greatest instinctive forces. Anyone who, through the Platonic writings, has experienced even a breath of the divine naivete and sureness of the Socratic way of life, will also feel how the enormous driving-wheel of logical Socratism is in motion, as it were, *behind* Socrates, and that it must be viewed through Socrates as through a shadow.[8]

Socrates himself seems to be aware of the instinctive or non-conscious source of his activity, when he insists on his divine calling.

Indeed, Nietzsche observes, at the end of his life Socrates himself suspected that there was something missing in his own activity. "As he tells his friends in prison, there often came to him one and the same dream apparition, which always said the same thing to him: 'Socrates practice music'." So in prison, Socrates finally composed a prelude to Apollo and turned a few Aesopian fables into verse. "Perhaps—thus he must have asked himself—. . . there is a realm of wisdom from which the logician is exiled? Perhaps art is even a necessary correlative of, and supplement for science?"[9] Socrates himself thus pointed toward the need to complete or complement philosophy with art. The disjunction between poetry and philosophy so strongly urged in the *Republic* was, Nietzsche concluded, ultimately false.

Explicitly calling for the emergence of a "Socrates who practices music,"[10] in his first book Nietzsche does not pay much attention to the author of the new form of art which makes Socrates its dialectical hero—Plato. If Socrates himself was utterly amusic, Plato admittedly was not. Did Plato not represent the fusion of philosophy with poetry that Nietzsche sought? This question proved more difficult for Nietzsche to answer over his lifetime than would first appear.

In *The Birth of Tragedy*, Nietzsche presents Plato merely as Socrates' student. Convinced by Socrates that poetry was irrational, but unable to eradicate his own poetic instincts entirely, Plato sought to avoid the criticism of art he himself leveled in the *Republic*, "that it is the imitation of a phantom and hence belongs to a sphere even lower than the empirical world . . . [by] endeavoring to transcend reality and to represent the idea which underlies this pseudo-reality."[11] Socrates' demand that the world be (made?) intelligible was much more important than Plato's particular attempt to describe or imagine an intelligible world. If philosophers had been satisfied even with refuting the purported "knowledge" or the doctrines of their predecessors, Socrates would not have had such a powerful, life-preserving influence, because the philosophers would quickly have discovered the sisyphean character of their endeavor. It was not the disproof of competing visions but the attempt to discover an intelligible order that prompted people to ever renewed effort; that is, it was the nature of the activity and not the particular results that made philosophy such an attractive way of life. Plato did not influence later men so much through his "theory of ideas" as through his presentation of philosophy as the only satisfying way of life in his portrait of Socrates. In *The Birth of Tragedy* Nietzsche did not criticize Plato so much for inventing the "other world" of the ideas, therefore, as he did for making poetry merely ancillary to philosophy.

The attempt to discover an intelligible order was based on an illusion, the illusion that there is an order to be discovered existing independent of man. As an illusion or myth, the rationalism Socrates represents constituted an artistic creation. It was not Plato who created the new illusion, however, but Socrates himself.

Socrates did not exercise such great historical influence through his explicit teaching or even as a living example of the philosophic way of life as he did through his death.

> The image of the *dying Socrates*, as the human being whom knowledge and reason have liberated from the fear of death, is the emblem that, above the entrance gate of science, reminds all of its mission—namely, to make existence appear comprehensible and thus justified; and if reasons do not suffice, *myth* has to come to their aid in the end.[12]

Not Plato, but Socrates was the real historical actor or influence, because Socrates engineered his own death.

> Being thoroughly enigmatical, unclassifiable, and inexplicable, he might have been asked to leave the city, and posterity would never have been justified in charging the Athenians with an ignominious deed. But that he was sentenced to death, not exile, Socrates himself seems to have brought about with perfect awareness and without any natural awe of death.[13]

Deeds are more persuasive than words. Socrates' life may have been based on an illusion, but his life itself was not illusion. Socrates was the first, not merely to produce a new vision, image, or illusion, but to act it out and thus to make it a living reality. But Socrates remained a problem for

Nietzsche, because the significance of his intentionally seeking his own death was unclear. Did he knowingly create his own myth through deeds rather than speeches? Did he understand the limits of the *logos* he was wont to celebrate in dialectical conversation? Did philosophy involve intentional deception, even self-deception?

In his first book Nietzsche indicated that there was something veiled or deceptive in the Platonic dialogues and hence in the entire philosophic tradition which followed. But Nietzsche had not yet identified either the nature of the deception or the reasons for myth-making. In writing *The Birth of Tragedy*, Nietzsche was still very much influenced by Arthur Schopenhauer and Richard Wagner. He thus subordinated philosophy, which he equated with "science" as the search for knowledge in general, to art, which he described in terms of "metaphysical comfort" or "relief." He did not long rest satisfied with this view of philosophy, science, or art.

In an incomplete and therefore unpublished manuscript on *Philosophy in the Tragic Age of the Greeks*, written one year after *The Birth of Tragedy*, Nietzsche recognized that philosophy did not commence with Socrates. If the decisive break in Western history occurred with Socrates, it could not then be accurately described simply as the emergence of rationalism or science in contrast to the preceding poetry of generative chaos. In this manuscript Nietzsche gave a very praising account of "pre-Platonic" philosophy; he not only distinguished philosophy from poetry and science, he also showed how it encompassed and yet was superior to both. He now identified the decisive break not with Socrates but with Plato.

Philosophy began with Thales' apparently absurd statement that water is the primal origin and womb of all things. In seeking the origin, philosophy resembled the poetry which preceded it; but philosophy expressed its central thought in an entirely different, nonallegorical, nonmythical manner. The difference in expression reflected a substantive difference of fundamental importance. To express one's thought in images is to see or to conceive of the world anthropomorphically. Thales declared that not man but water was the truth and the core of things. As a scientist and in contrast to the poets, Thales sought truth without regard to the human consequences. "Aristotle rightly says that 'What Thales and Anaxagoras know will be considered universal, astonishing, difficult and divine, but never useful, for their concern was not with the good of humanity'." Pre-Platonic philosophy was characterized by a scientific stance which was essentially amoral.

As the search for knowledge, general and undifferentiated, science is completely nonselective. Science thus needs to be directed, regulated, or "tamed," by philosophy, which seeks knowledge only of the most important things. Since what is regarded as important is changeable, philosophy must begin "by legislating greatness." The scattered empirical observations Thales made did not justify his grand generalization. "What drove him to it was a metaphysical conviction which had its origin in a mystic intuition. We meet it in every philosophy, together with the ever-renewed attempt at a more suitable expression, this proposition that 'all things are one'."[14] Insight into the fundamental unity of all things constitutes the distinctive act of the creative imagination of the philosopher who, unlike the poet, seeks not merely to express his own vision but to encapsulate reality or the truth.

Philosophy properly speaking cannot take its bearings from the interest, concern or good of a part, like human happiness, because the whole cannot be subordinated to a part without distortion. If all existence is particularistic, however, the truth can be perceived and literally incorporated only in a particular form of existence. The "truth" can never, therefore, be adequately expressed as a doctrine; words (and, hence, concepts) are inadequate. Although pure or pre-Platonic philosophy does not take its bearings from human needs and desires, it does have an emphatically human meaning. Comprehending the essential unity of all things, the philosopher rather self-consciously sees himself as the image or expression of the whole. The philosopher does not so much lose himself in contemplating the cosmos, as he finds his own distinctive identity as the sum or abbreviation of the whole. Taken in themselves, all philosophic "truths" or doctrines constitute errors; they merely represent one man's vision or experience of his own existence. They are true only of and for him. Philosophic doctrines should not therefore be studied so much as arguments, opinions or even visions, as they should be celebrated as signs of supreme individuality: "So this has existed—once, at least—and is therefore a possibility, this way of life, this way of looking at the human scene" (Preface).

Philosophy can only, indeed must be understood as a particular way or form of life. It is *the* form of life that encompasses the whole. This is why Nietzsche emphasized Socrates rather than Plato in his early writings; Socrates represents philosophy as a way of life much more than as a doctrine like the theory of ideas.[15]

Beginning with Plato, philosophy lost its unifying ability. Instead of penetrating to the core of existence, Plato attempted to mediate among the several preexisting doctrines and variety of psychological types that produced these doctrinal differences.

All subsequent philosophers are such mixed types. . . . What is far more important, however, is that the mixed types were founders of sects, and that sectarianism with its institutions and counterinstitutions was opposed to Hellenic culture and its previous unity of style.

Although pre-Socratic philosophers had no such intention—Nietzsche observed that they lived very much aloof from their community or people—each served to reinforce the unity of Hellenic culture by giving that unity a new expression or interpretation. "Beginning with Plato, [however,] philosophers became exiles, conspiring against their fatherland."[16] Nietzsche did not explain the source of the division, what we might call the politicization of philosophy, in this manuscript. In *Daybreak* he suggests that the politicization occurs when philosophers try not merely to discover an order or the unity of all things but to rule or order other men.

Nietzsche's understanding of philosophy was not complete or entirely coherent in this early unpublished manuscript. Although he said that all philosophy, including pre-Platonic philosophy, began by legislating what is important, he did not develop the meaning of this legislation. Nietzsche made the conjunction of order with rule or legislation (a conjunction suggested by the Greek word *archē*) explicit in his later teaching of the will to power. Likewise, in his later works, he associated philosophy as an ordering and hence a valuing activity preeminently with Plato, because Plato taught that the idea of the Good is *the* ruling principle of the whole. Insofar as they taught the existence of a cosmic order, Nietzsche later suggested, pre-Socratic philosophers were also moralistic. Plato simply made the conjunction of intelligibility and morality more explicit.

In the *Untimely Considerations* he published immediately after *The Birth of Tragedy*, Nietzsche called for a new educational system (*Bildung*, usually translated culture, but better understood in terms of the formation of character) in explicit contrast to Plato. The distinctive characteristics of modern men were very much products of the scientific search for knowledge that commenced with Socrates, if not with Thales. We have collected so much information about past ages and cultures that we have lost all sense of ourselves. In order to discover ourselves and therein the source of all this scientific endeavor, we have to free ourselves from the past and hence from the scientific tradition itself; but we can use science itself to do so! Collecting information about the past may serve to preserve the effects of past efforts; but when ancient pieties become oppressive, collecting information may also serve to destroy the authority of the past by showing the origin of past thoughts and acts in violence and error.

> It is always a dangerous process. . . . Since we happen to be the results of earlier generations, we are also the results of their aberrations, passions and errors, even crimes; it is not possible quite to free oneself from this chain.[17]

Nietzsche made his reasons for studying the tradition, particularly for returning to its origins in Greece, especially clear in "Of the Use and

Disadvantage of History for Life." We are products of that tradition; this is the great modern historical insight and virtue. To understand ourselves, we must understand the tradition; but the tradition does not make sense in its own terms. To understand it or ourselves, we must therefore free ourselves from past understandings or pieties.[18] Like Plato we have to criticize previous thinkers; we are, after all, descendants of the Platonic tradition, and we cannot change the fact that we descend from it. But as modern thinkers, we can, indeed, we must, be more honest and scientific than Plato.

Plato thought a just and rightly ordered society had to be founded on a "necessary lie."[19] People must believe that they were shaped for their particular function in society before they were born, that is, by nature. The necessary lie is, then, that social order reflects a natural order. If social order does not rest on a natural order, as Plato's insistence on the necessity of lying suggests, if perhaps there is no natural order at all, all actual orders have been based on ignorance, error, deceit and violence.

Nietzsche did not pause in this early essay to consider the implications of Plato himself admitting that the just society must be founded upon a lie. Instead Nietzsche devoted himself in his second positivistic period to exposing the errors or ignorance at the basis of all previous moral and philosophic doctrines. He wished to see human beings form or educate themselves on the basis of the truth. In his middle period, Nietzsche thus appears to be more scientific than Socrates, whereas Plato appears to be more poetic than Nietzsche. Like Nietzsche in *The Birth of Tragedy*, Plato believed that the perpetuation of human life requires illusion or art.

"Philosophy severed itself from science," Nietzsche states in *Human All Too Human*, "when it put the question: what is the knowledge of the world through which mankind may be made happiest? This happened when the Socratic school arose."[20] Nietzsche's observation of the severing of philosophy from science appears to be critical of the Socratic school, because it suggests that with Plato if not with Socrates, philosophy becomes less honest and hence less rigorous as it becomes more moral. If the truth must be embodied, however, philosophy does not simply decline when it acquires a more explicitly human focus. Rather it becomes more self-conscious.

Philosophy did become more deceptive, if also perhaps more interesting, according to Nietzsche, when it became explicitly moralistic. When philosophers sought knowledge of the conditions of human happiness rather than knowledge simply and in general, they might well have concluded that deception or illusion was a condition of human happiness, as Nietzsche himself urged in his own earlier analysis of art. Plato did. But, if it was merely a necessary *lie* that social order rests upon nature, philosophers deceived others, if not themselves also, when they presented themselves simply as scientists seeking knowledge of the natural order who justify their vocation by observing that such knowledge is useful. Useful for what, and to whom, Nietzsche asks.

In fact, Nietzsche concludes in his preface to *Daybreak,* philosophers never "found" the truth, because that was not what they were really seeking.

> Why is it that from Plato onwards every philosophical architect in Europe has built in vain? . . . How false is the answer . . . "because they had all neglected the presupposition for such an undertaking, the testing of the foundations, a critique of reason as a whole." . . . The correct answer would rather have been that all philosophers . . . , even Kant . . . were apparently aiming at certainty, at "truth," but in reality at *"Majestic Moral Structures."*[21]

One cannot give philosophy a solid foundation with a critique of pure reason, that is, by establishing the possibility of knowledge through an examination of the operation of the human mind. One has to ask, why seek knowledge at all? That question points, of course, to an answer beyond knowledge itself. Science or knowledge has no inherent value or existence apart from human beings, Nietzsche argues in both his early and his late writings. Mind does not exist apart from or independent of body and hence cannot be understood as an independent entity.

In *The Gay Science* Nietzsche thus revises his account of the origin of knowledge or the historical development of philosophy and science.[22] Human beings acquired their first concepts or ideas through an error of their senses which suggested "that there are enduring things, that there are equal things, that there are things, substances, and bodies, that a thing is what it appears, that our will is free, that what is good for me is also good absolutely." These errors were formulated and perpetuated because they proved useful to people; they helped preserve the species. "It was only very late that the deniers and doubters of such propositions came forward."

Because our senses lead us to err, doubting the evidence of the senses constitutes an important intellectual advance. Because "knowledge" always presupposes life, however, knowledge can never be affirmed in complete abstraction from the requirements of life.

> The exceptional thinkers like the Eleatics, who . . . advanced and maintained the antitheses of the natural errors, [thus] believed that it was possible also *to live* these counterparts: it was they who devised the sage as the man of immutability, impersonality and universality of intuition . . . ; they were of the belief that their knowledge was at the same time the principle of *life.*

Not Plato but the Eleatics first posited the world of eternal, unchanging, perfectly intelligible 'being'. It was they who first attempted to escape the unsatisfying, never entirely intelligible flux of the sensual world into the pale, cold world of pure intelligibility. But to do so, they had

> to *deceive* themselves concerning their own condition; they had to attribute to themselves impersonality and unchanging permanence, they had to mistake the nature of the philosophic individual, deny the force of the impulses in cognition, and conceive of reason generally as an entirely free and self-originating activity.

With the development of more philosophic probity and skepticism, such people (which is as much as to say such philosophic self-deception) became impossible.

Plato's attempt to mediate among the competing doctrines thus appears to be a necessary development, a higher stage of philosophic self-consciousness, not merely a decline as in Nietzsche's earlier manuscript.

> The human brain was gradually filled with such . . . ferment . . . [that] the intellectual struggle became a business, an attraction, a calling, a duty, an honor: cognizing and striving for the true finally arranged themselves as needs among other needs.

Nietzsche tends to associate the search for knowledge as a vocation with Socrates. Without referring to any specific examples, in *The Gay Science* he notes two crucial aspects or effects of the new intellectual calling:

> From that moment, not only belief and conviction but also examination, denial, distrust and contradiction became *forces;* all "evil" instincts were subordinated to knowledge . . . and acquired the prestige of the permitted, the honored, the useful, and finally the appearance and innocence of the *good*. Knowledge thus became a portion of life itself, and as life it became a continually growing power.

The questioning of the evidence of the senses that emerged with Parmenides led to the questioning of moral judgments, because people came to redefine what is permitted, honored, useful—in sum, what is good. The pre-Socratics did not really understand the nature of their own activity. Despite his continuing praise of Herakleitus, Nietzsche does not advocate a return to pre-Socratic philosophy.[23] We are left rather with the problem he consistently associates with the myth of Socrates: "Now that the impulse to truth has *proved* itself to be a life-preserving power. . . , how far is truth susceptible of embodiment?"[24]

Plato did not invent the doctrine of the intelligible world. Rather he saw that this doctrine or postulate constituted a necessary condition for maintaining the only life truly worth living. As the first to reconceive philosophy as the definition of human happiness, Plato and his hero-teacher Socrates perhaps understood more of what they were doing than their successors. Socrates and Plato saw that no human action is disinterested; they taught that all men, philosophers perhaps preeminently, seek their own conception of what is good.[25] Nietzsche doubted that Plato believed his own doctrines. "Is Plato's integrity beyond question? [We] know at least that he wanted to have *taught* as absolute truth what he himself did not regard as even conditionally true: Namely, the separate existence and separate immortality of 'souls'."[26] Plato taught what was necessary to maintain philosophy as a way of life.

Plato understood the dangerous character of philosophy. He saw that it threatened the psychic balance of the philosopher himself as well as the established conventions of his community. To have sufficient faith in oneself, to destroy the old order with confidence that one can replace it with a better, a philosopher needs to be, or at least needs to appear to be, a little mad.[27] "Plato has given us a splendid description of how the philosophical thinker must within every existing society count as the paragon of all wickedness: for as critic of all customs he is the antithesis of the moral man."[28] Perceiving the necessary tension between philosophy and established society (or the polity), Plato recognized the need for the philosopher to disguise the radical nature of his activity. The division between the philosopher and his fatherland to which Nietzsche first referred in his unpublished manuscript resulted from the philosopher's desire, the "political drive" Plato himself says that he was filled with, to establish a new order in the place of the old.

In Plato, the philosopher thus appears to be a legislator, not only for others, as in the *Republic* or in Sicily, but also and more importantly for himself. Both Socrates and Plato advocated such a strict, absolute, indeed tyrannical rule of reason, because they both felt themselves in need of such order; their senses were so strong and chaotic.

> When the physiognomist had revealed to Socrates who he was—a cave of bad appetites—the great master of irony let slip another word which is the key to his character. "This is true," he said, "but I mastered them all." *How* did Socrates becomes master over *himself?* "The impulses want to play the tyrant; one must invent a *counter-tyrant* who is stronger."[29]

Likewise Nietzsche observed:

> The charm of the Platonic way of thinking, which was a noble way of thinking, consisted precisely in *resistance* to obvious sense—evidence—perhaps among men who enjoyed even stronger and more demanding senses than our contemporaries, but who know how to find a higher triumph in remaining masters of their senses—and this by means of pale,

cold, gray concept nets which they threw over the motley whirl of the senses—the mob of the senses, as Plato said.[30]

Nietzsche did not criticize Plato for attempting to bring order to his own life or that of others, but for disguising the true nature of philosophy as legislation. From his early unpublished manuscript through his later writings, Nietzsche consistently presented "legislation," that is, the declaration of the highest values, as *the* proper work of the philosopher. He recognized that there is a comprehensive kind of philosophy which gathers together and orders all existing knowledge, the kind that he first associated with the pre-Socratics; this is also the way he characterized the thought of Kant and Hegel. *"Genuine Philosophers, however, are commanders and legislators; they say, 'thus it shall be!'* . . . This 'knowing' is *creating,* their creating is a legislation, their will to truth is—*will to power."*[31] In a note for his book on the will to power, he added, "They alone determine the 'whither' and the 'wherefore', what is useful and what constitutes utility for men. . . . This second kind of philosopher rarely prospers; and their situation and danger is indeed fearful. How often they have deliberately blindfolded themselves." Plato was such a philosopher. He did not merely dissimulate. He deceived himself, "when he convinced himself that the 'good' as *he* desired it was not the good of Plato but the 'good in itself', the eternal treasure that some man, named Plato, had chanced to discover on his way!"[32]

Nietzsche was not always sure Plato deceived himself, however. For example, in *The Genealogy of Morals* he observed:

The whole of history teaches that every oligarchy conceals the lust for *tyranny;* every oligarchy constantly trembles with the tension each member feels in maintaining control over this lust. (So it was in *Greece,* for instance: Plato bears witness to it in a hundred passages—and he knew his own kind—*and* himself . . .).[33]

Nietzsche could not be certain of Plato's self-understanding, precisely because he saw that Plato engaged in public teaching.

Nietzsche did not attempt to give a true reading of Plato on the basis of a careful analysis of the dialogues. Instead, he engaged in a contest with Plato in order to show the true nature of philosophic activity. Rather than look out beyond himself to an other world of eternal being, Nietzsche suggested, the philosopher seeks above all to bring order to his own feelings and perceptions. Overflowing with joy at achieving this order, the philosopher beneficently attempts to help other men overcome their pain and confusion by instituting a rule or order for them as well.

Nietzsche presented his own, true view of the nature of the philosopher in contrast to Plato's deceptive presentation most clearly in *Thus*

Spoke Zarathustra. Although neither Socrates nor Plato is mentioned in Nietzsche's self-proclaimed masterpiece, Zarathustra is clearly intended to supplant Socrates as the image of the *living* philosopher.[34] Whereas Socrates knows only that he does not know and is the gadfly who constantly interrogates others in the marketplace, Zarathustra overflows with wisdom.

> This is my poverty; that my hand never rests from giving; this is my envy, that I see waiting eyes and the lit-up nights of longing. Oh, wretchedness of all givers! . . . Oh, ravenous hunger in satiation! They receive from me, but do I touch their souls? There is a cleft between giving and receiving.[35]

Likewise, whereas Socrates remains always in the marketplace, Zarathustra withdraws to his heights. In terms of Plato's famous allegory of the cave, Socrates is forced to return and remain in the shadows whereas Zarathustra regularly travels the mountain road between the cave and the sunlight.

Like Socrates, Zarathustra recognizes that the people do not understand the philosopher. "Little do the people comprehend the great—that is, the creating," he observes "On the Flies of the Marketplace." "Around the inventors of new values the world revolves: invisibly it revolves. But around the actors revolve the people and fame: that is 'the way of the world'." These actors or showmen persuade people to view shadows as unconditional truths. Pressed to take sides in the shadow-box debate about opinions or 'ideologies', Zarathustra urges, the philosopher must flee to his solitude. He does not flee so much from the danger of political persecution, although Zarathustra recognizes the possibility when the jester warns him (Prologue), as from fear that he will forget himself, and in forgetting himself, lose his humanity.

> The danger of those who always give is that they lose their sense of shame; and the heart and hand of those who always mete out become callous from always meting out. My eye no longer wells over at the shame of those who beg.[36]

Unlike Plato's philosopher who must be forced to descend to the cave, Zarathustra both descends and withdraws from the city out of love, love for man.[37] Recognizing that most people will never understand him, Zarathustra does not speak to them directly except to expose the pretensions of former sages, priests, and politicians. He does not try to persuade people to accept any claim or doctrine; to persuade them would necessarily be to delude them, to convince them of a proposition the grounds of which they do not understand. Zarathustra does not preach or argue, therefore, so much as he sings. Even then, he is ashamed that he must still speak as a poet, because he observes that poets always lie.[38]

Nietzsche himself recognized the necessarily indirect character of the communication between philosopher and reader when he spoke through the mouth of a character named Zarathustra.

> I have not been asked, as I should have been asked, what the name of Zara- thustra means in my mouth, the mouth of the first immoralist. . . . Zara- thustra was the first to consider the fight of good and evil the very wheel in the machinery of things: the transposition of morality into the meta- physical realm, as a force, cause, and end in itself, is *his* work. . . . Zarathus- tra created this most calamitous error, morality; consequently, he must also be the first to recognize it. . . . What is more important is that *Zara- thustra is more truthful than any other thinker.*[39]

As the people cannot understand his words, the most the philosopher can do is to show who he is, a task Nietzsche himself attempted with shocking directness in *Ecce Homo*, where he explained "Why I Am So Wise," and "Why I Write Such Good Books." The truth does not lie any in opinion, doctrine or teaching. Any philosophy which attempts to teach (that is, to persuade anyone of anything) necessarily lies. All previous philosophy, at least all philosophy since Plato, has propagated such lies by teaching that there is an intelligible order by which human beings can orient themselves. As Plato himself shows, political orders are based on moral teachings which in turn rest upon metaphysical claims.

Nietzsche sought to expose Plato's lies, but he did not criticize him for deceiving the people. Nietzsche also saw that the people cannot under- stand the philosopher and that the philosopher needs protection. The dis- guise they have most often assumed, he observed in *The Genealogy of Morals,* is the cloth of the priest.

> Let us compress the facts into a few brief formulas: to begin with, the philosophic spirit always had to use as a mask and cocoon the *previously established* types of the contemplative man—priest, sorcerer, soothsayer, and in any case a religious type—in order to be able to *exist at all: the ascetic ideal* for a long time served the philosopher as a form in which to appear, as a precondition of existence—he had to *represent* it so as to be able to be a philosopher; he had to *believe* in it in order to be able to repre- sent it.[40]

Nietzsche attributed such an ascetic misunderstanding to the Eleatic phi- losophers in *The Gay Science*. He was not sure that Plato so misunder- stood himself. Plato recognized the need for philosophic disguise. Like the priests, moreover, Plato understood that it was necessary to lie in order to rule.

> That the lie is permitted as a means to pious ends is part of the theory of every priesthood. . . . But philosophers too, as soon as . . . they form the

intention of taking in hand the direction of mankind, at once also arrogate to themselves the right to tell lies: Plato before all.[41]

Those who would make others moral, must themselves use immoral means.[42] "It is a mistake to suppose an *unconscious and naive* development here, a kind of self-deception. . . . The most cold-blooded reflection was at work here; the same kind of reflection as a Plato applied when he imagined his 'Republic'."[43] Nietzsche himself calls these the "grand *politics* of virtue, . . . pure Machiavellianism, . . . at most approximated by man. . . . Even Plato barely touched it."[44]

Nietzsche did not criticize Plato for wanting to rule. On the contrary, his Zarathustra comments:

> The lust to rule—but who would call it *lust* when what is high longs downward for power? . . . That the lonely heights should not remain lonely and self-sufficient eternally; that the mountain should descend to the valley . . . who were to find the right name for such longings? "Gift-giving virtue"—thus Zarathustra once named the unnameable.[45]

Nietzsche criticized Plato primarily for his dissimulation. He thought Plato understood the tremendously self-affirmative character of philosophic activity. In explaining "How the 'true world' finally became a fable" in the *Twilight of the Idols*, Nietzsche summarized the first stage: "I, Plato, *am* the truth." Plato did not really teach the existence of another world, so much as he affirmed his own existence. "The true world—attainable for the sage, the pious, the virtuous man; he lives in it, *he is it*."[46]

Whether Plato truly believed his own doctrines or not, his followers did. Thus in the Preface to *Beyond Good and Evil*, Nietzsche attacked Plato as the founder of dogmatic philosophy. "It seems that all great things first have to bestride the earth in monstrous and frightening masks in order to inscribe themselves in the hearts of humanity with eternal demands: dogmatic philosophy was such a mask: for example, . . . Platonism in Europe." Even if it represented a "mask," "the worst, most durable, and most dangerous of all errors so far was a dogmatist's error—namely, Plato's invention of the pure spirit [mind] and the good as such." According to these Platonic doctrines, philosophy consists in the search for knowledge of something beyond man—an immortal, incorporeal, infinite Good, *Geist*, or God—which as the negation of mortality, corporeality, and finitude constitutes the negation of the limits and so the very definition of human existence.

In the Preface to *Beyond Good and Evil*, Nietzsche thus seems to return to his initial view of the relation between Socrates and Plato, when he observes, "as a physician one might ask: How could the most beautiful growth of antiquity, Plato, contract such a disease? Did the wicked Socrates corrupt him after all? Could Socrates have been the corrupter of youth after all? And did he deserve his hemlock?" Nietzsche seems to return to a rather standard view of Socrates as the philosophical skeptic, who knows only that he does not know, in contrast to the author of the theory of the ideas. Socrates appears to be a negative, critical spirit in contrast to the affirmative Plato who propounds a doctrine (be it through the voice of Socrates in the *Republic*).[47]

Nietzsche makes both the nature of the corruption he attributes to Socrates and the difference he now sees between teacher and pupil clearer, when he observes:

> There is something in the morality of Plato that does not really belong to Plato but is merely encountered in his philosophy—one might say, in spite of Plato: namely, the Socratism for which he was really too noble. "Nobody wants to do harm to himself, therefore, all that is bad is done involuntarily. . . ." This type of inference smells of the *rabble* that sees nothing in bad actions but the unpleasant consequences and really judges "it is *stupid* to do what is bad," while "good" is taken without further ado to be identical with "useful and agreeable."

Plato was not merely Socrates' student; on the contrary, Socrates became the mouthpiece or mask of Plato.

> Plato did everything he could in order to read something refined and noble into the proposition of his teacher—above all, himself. He was the most audacious of all interpreters and took the whole Socrates only the way one picks a popular tune and folk song from the streets in order to vary it into the infinite and impossible—namely, into all of his own masks and multiplicities.[48]

Nietzsche also states very clearly in *Ecce Homo* that he does not regard Plato merely as a follower, much less the dupe of Socrates. On the contrary, Socrates is the "front"—or character—used by Plato. As Nietzsche himself "caught hold of two famous and yet altogether undiagnosed types" in the two *Untimely Considerations* he devoted to Schopenhauer and Wagner, to make his case about the problems of education in his time, so he observes in *Ecce Homo*, "Plato employed Socrates."[49] Even in *The Birth of Tragedy* Nietzsche spoke of Socrates as a "shadow" through which or behind which one felt an enormously powerful instinctive force.

Nietzsche consistently distinguished Plato from his teacher Socrates in one and only one respect: Whereas Plato was noble, Socrates was vulgar. Nietzsche distinguished Plato from his popular influence or effect, Christianity, on precisely the same ground. "The fight against Plato or, to speak more clearly and 'for the people,' the fight against the Christianecclesiastical pressure of millennia—for Christianity is Platonism for 'the people'—has created in Europe a magnificent tension of the spirit."[50] By explicitly linking Plato with Christianity, Nietzsche indicated the extent to which his understanding of philosophy in general and Plato in particular had changed from his first treatise. Nietzsche did not mention Christianity at all in *The Birth of Tragedy*, as he himself noted in his later "Attempt at Self-Criticism," whereas in his later work, Christianity often appeared to be the major result or effect of Platonic philosophy.

By associating Plato with Christianity, Nietzsche by no means made a simply negative or critical statement. Whether in philosophic or religious form, Nietzsche insisted, the denial of the value of this life, this world in favor of another is a sign of decadence and weakness. Nevertheless, it has (or can have) beneficial effects. Thus in the Preface to *Beyond Good and Evil*, he urged, "Let us not be ungrateful to it, . . . [for] we . . . are the heirs of all that strength which has been fostered by the fight against this error, . . . The fight against Plato." Ascetic ideals, as he calls them in *The Genealogy of Morals*, the denial of the world of appearance, sensuality, body and finitude in favor of the eternal, the intellectual, the immortal and infinite—in a word, 'God'—have their uses. They have, in the first place, produced the intellectual discipline necessary for the emergence of the philosophy of the future.

> Precisely because we seek knowledge, let us not be ungrateful to such resolute reversals of accustomed perspectives and valuations with which the spirit has, with apparent mischievousness and futility, raged against itself for so long: to see differently in this way for once, to *want* to see differently, is no small discipline and preparation of the intellect for its future . . . ability . . . to employ a *variety* of perspectives and affective interpretations in the service of knowledge.[51]

It was, indeed, in terms of the uses of ascetic ideals (or the doctrine of eternal Being) that Nietzsche ultimately distinguished philosophy from religion.

Whereas most philosophers point to a fundamental distinction between reason and revelation, Nietzsche denied it. Philosophy or reason has instinctual roots, he insisted; there is no mind separate from body and therefore no mind or imagination separate from physiological states. Thought originates in or as a feeling, an insight or hunch of the sort often described as a revelation.

> [Philosophers] all pose as if they had discovered and reached their real opinions through the self-development of a cold, pure, divinely unconcerned dialectic (as opposed to the mystics of every rank, who are more honest and doltish—and talk of "inspiration"); while at bottom it is an

assumption, a hunch, indeed a kind of "inspiration"—most often a desire of the heart that has been filtered and made abstract.[52]

What distinguishes the philosopher from the priest or the poet is not the source of his wisdom, but the stance he takes toward his own existence. Both priests and philosophers are legislators.[53] Whereas the priest teaches ascetic ideals as a reaction against the existing order, as a negation of the value of this life, particularly of his own life, except insofar as he serves to ameliorate the suffering of others, the philosopher embraces ascetic ideals instinctively as the optimal conditions for philosophy.

> What, then, is the meaning of the ascetic ideal in the case of a philosopher? ... He sees in it an optimum condition for the highest and boldest spirituality and smiles—he does *not* deny "existence," he rather affirms *his* existence and *only* his existence.[54]

Plato is the first, the preeminent teacher of ascetic ideals.

Although he often blurred the distinction, Nietzsche did finally separate philosophy from its influence.[55] In the case of both Socrates and Plato, the influence consisted of an illusion—the possibility of correcting human existence with knowledge in the case of Socrates, the positing of another world in Plato—which it is not clear the philosopher himself shared. In his final description of "the problem of Socrates" in *Twilight of the Idols*, Nietzsche thus offered a new interpretation of the philosopher's arranging his own death.

> Socrates *wanted* to die ... ; he forced Athens to sentence him. "Socrates is no physician," he said softly to himself; "here death alone is the physician. Socrates himself has merely been sick a long time."[56]

Nietzsche had come to suspect that "this most brilliant of all self-outwitters" also saw that fighting the instincts can only be a mark of decadence or declining life.

> The ancient theological problem of "faith" and "knowledge"—or, more clearly, of instinct and reason ... is still the ancient moral problem that emerged in the person of Socrates and divided thinking people long before Christianity. Socrates himself, to be sure ... had initially sided with reason; ... what did he do his life long but laugh at the awkward incapacity of noble Athenians who, like noble men, were men of instinct and never could give sufficient ... reasons for their actions? In the end, however, privately and secretly, he laughed at himself, too. ... This was the real *falseness* of that great ironic ... ; he had seen through the irrational element in moral judgments.[57]

Dialectics is the tool of the weak; and Socrates was emphatically common. "Is the irony of Socrates an expression ... of plebeian ressentiment? Is dialectics only a form of *revenge* in Socrates?" Socrates used dialectic to show the inadequacies of other moralities, noble moralities, but he did not really believe his own moral teaching. In *The Birth of Tragedy*, Nietzsche had argued that Socrates embodied the *optimistic* illusion that human beings could come not only to comprehend but also to correct their existence by attaining knowledge. "Knowledge is virtue." But in *The Twilight of the Idols* he suggested that Socrates may have intentionally misled his noble young Athenian auditors. One fears death only so long as one is attached to life. Socrates represented not the first optimist but a more knowing pessimist who concealed the insight or knowledge he had obtained about himself through his own experience. His actions told more than his words. He died without visible regrets or qualms.

Did Plato mislead later philosophers as Socrates misled the Athenian nobles? Did Plato create the basis of a new morality, a new religion, instinctively or unconsciously? Did he fool himself as well? Nietzsche never entirely made up his mind. He did not pause to do a careful analysis of Plato's works to determine whether the ancient philosopher knew he was trying to legislate a new morality for subsequent generations or whether he acted primarily on the basis of an instinct, because he was intent upon superseding Plato.[58] Even if Plato recognized the creative, self-affirming character of his own philosophical activity, he had proceeded covertly. Nietzsche wanted to announce the possibility of the *human* creation of meaning, of a new *superhuman* activity, openly and explicitly.

During his own lifetime, the questions Nietzsche raised about the origins and character of Western philosophy represented preeminently by Plato were largely ignored. Nietzsche' initial attack on Socrates as the destroyer of tragedy aroused the ire of a fellow philologist, Ulrich von Wilamowitz-Möllendorff, who wrote a blistering critique of *The Birth of Tragedy*. Along with Nietzsche's ill health, the reception of his first book effectively finished his scholarly career. He became something of a cult figure as early as 1890, but his work was not taken seriously as philosophy by philosophers.[59]

As his early lectures show, Nietzsche was by no means the first German philologist to raise questions about the relation between Socrates and Plato. But in announcing "the problem of Socrates" Nietzsche was not merely investigating the significance of the dramatis personae of Plato's dialogues or the historical relation between student and teacher. He was asking about the nature and value of philosophy itself. Was the search for knowledge based on an illusion? Was the unavailability of truth a modern discovery, a result of the progressive development of human critical faculties? Or, had Socrates—or his student Plato—recognized that ordinary human life was not worthwhile? Had they perceived this truth from the very beginning, but hidden it with salutary teachings? Had Socrates and Plato believed the moral and ontological doctrines they put forward? Or, had they propagated those doctrines—consciously or unconsciously—to establish the moral, political, and intellectual conditions that make philosophy, the only form of human life truly worth living, possible?

In contrast to his nineteenth-century German idealist philosophical predecessors, Nietzsche was not convinced that history was obviously or necessarily progressive. He did not think that modern people were unambiguously superior—morally, politically or intellectually—to the ancients. On the contrary, he wondered whether the conditions for human greatness still existed. The historical insight, that there was no set, natural order, might provide human beings with an opportunity to exercise unprecedented creativity; but it might also give rise to an unprecedented decline. Because he did not think human beings had essentially improved or that they would inevitably progress, Nietzsche was led to ask whether premodern thinkers had not understood something modern philosophers had forgotten. In particular, he wondered whether philosophy and its history should be understood so much in terms of doctrine or arguments. Should philosophy not, be conceived, rather, as it had been by Socrates and Plato, primarily as a way of life?

In the wake of World War I, when many Europeans had become skeptical about historical progress, and the limitations of logical positivism and neo-Kantian epistemology had convinced most professional philosophers of the problematic character of all knowledge-claims, Nietzsche's questions seemed more salient than they had during his lifetime. In the twentieth century, the questions he had raised about the origins and character of Western philosophy thus gave rise to a new and radical path of inquiry.

Like Nietzsche, Heidegger became convinced as a young professor that philosophy must be understood to have its roots in the concerns of everyday human existence.[60] Like Nietzsche, Heidegger thus urged it was necessary to get beneath or behind the tradition by going back to the Greek origins of philosophy to obtain a new, more original understanding of those roots.[61] Like Nietzsche, Heidegger also insisted that these originally Greek ideas had to be understood historically, in light of their later development and effects. Like Nietzsche, he reminded his readers that we are parts and products of this tradition. We must, therefore, come to understand it, if we are to get beyond or to escape its deleterious effects.

In explicit opposition to Nietzsche, however, Heidegger argued that philosophers had not built "magnificent moral structures." They did not have the power or even the inclination to project their own views onto the world.[62] To be sure, Heidegger admitted, the truth changes from place to place and time to time, because it is historically defined or limited. Like the poets whose visions tend to precede theirs, philosophers articulate the truth as it is disclosed to them in their particular time and place. The differences in the views presented by various philosophers in Western history are not products of their individual wills, however! Nietzsche understood both art and philosophy much too subjectively.

Heidegger's confrontation with Nietzsche in the 1930s served not only to make Nietzsche's thought philosophically respectable.[63] It also left later thinkers with two fundamental questions: (1) To what extent was or had philosophy been an essentially moral activity? (2) To what extent could human beings use the knowledge they gained to control the direction and meaning of their own lives? Following the line of thought initially set out by Nietzsche and Heidegger, Hans Georg Gadamer, Leo Strauss, and Jacques Derrida all returned to examine the origins of Western philosophy in Plato with precisely these questions in mind.

Under the influence of his teacher Heidegger, Gadamer began insisting in the 1920s that Socratic philosophy depicted in the Platonic dialogues constitutes a way of life, not merely the first step in the acquisition of knowledge or science.[64] In direct opposition to Heidegger, however, Gadamer argued, like Nietzsche, that this way of life was essentially moral. In contrast to Nietzsche, however, Gadamer regarded the "noble lie" as merely one of the indications that the description of the "city in speech" was not intended to constitute a blueprint or program to be literally instituted.[65] Gadamer did not, in other words, make the relation between truth-seeking and morality or politics a central concern the way his acquaintance Strauss did.

Unlike Gadamer, Strauss was initially a great admirer of Nietzsche.[66] But, Strauss concluded rather early in his career, Nietzsche was not able to revive ancient greatness as he desired, because the philosopher who argued that Christian morality did not have any basis without the Christian God was himself still attached to a principle of scriptural morality—probity.[67] (Zarathustra is the most truthful philosopher.) In contrast to the late Nietzsche, Strauss thus attempted to recover a thoroughly non-Christian Plato. Rereading the dialogues in light of the commentaries of the medieval Islamic philosopher Farabi, Strauss was also tempted to distinguish Socrates, the philosopher who directly challenged the Athenian nobles, from Plato, the writer who sought to improve political life gradually by reforming the opinions of his readers. But Strauss's later investigations of "the problem of Socrates" made him doubt it was possible to "draw a clear line between Socrates and Plato." This was, indeed, *the* difference between Plato and Nietzsche. "Plato . . . points away from himself to Socrates, . . . whereas Nietzsche points most emphatically to himself, to 'Mr. Nietzsche'."[68]

"It is certainly not an overstatement to say that no one has ever spoken so greatly and so nobly of what a philosopher is as Nietzsche," Strauss observed.

> This is not to deny that the philosophers of the future as Nietzsche described them remind one much more than Nietzsche himself seems to have thought of Plato's philosopher. For while Plato had seen the features in question as clearly as Nietzsche. . . , he had intimated rather than stated his deepest insights.[69]

Although Plato stated that divisions within cities would not end until philosophers became kings, Strauss concluded in opposition to Nietzsche, Plato showed that philosophers would never actually become legislators. Socrates' emphatic withdrawal from public life was emblematic of the enduring tension between politics and philosophy. Although philosophy requires a certain kind of moral restraint or *sophrosunē* on the part of its practitioners, Plato and Xenophon both showed, the foundations and character of philosophical morality are fundamentally different from the origins and supports for political morality.

Wishing to extend Heidegger's critique of metaphysics, Derrida also returned to the question of truth in Nietzsche. Derrida has not been so interested in the problematic character or virtue of truthfulness, however, as he has been in reviving Nietzsche's argument that there is no "truth," there are only differential power relations. Like Nietzsche, in "Plato's Pharmacy" Derrida suggests that Socrates arranged his own death. But, according to Derrida, Socrates did not seek to demonstrate how intrepid philosophers are in the face of death so much as to show that the philosopher was not antagonistic to political law and order. In presenting the life, death, and teachings of Socrates, Derrida concludes, Plato was not trying to reform politics so much as to counteract the anarchy he feared skeptical philosophical questioning would produce.[70]

The contrast between Strauss and Derrida—both in their reactions to Nietzsche's critique of philosophy and their own rereadings of Plato—brings us back to the questions Nietzsche raised in his first portrayal of Socrates. Should philosophy be understood primarily as a way of life, which is to say, as an essentially moral phenomenon? Should philosophical doctrines be regarded primarily as public teachings designed to sustain and protect this way of life? Or, should philosophy rather be seen as an intrepid kind of questioning? Does the philosopher serve, first and foremost, to free people from illusions rather than to produce and perpetuate them? Can these two faces of philosophy somehow be integrated?

Two

Heidegger's New Beginning

Nietzsche was correct, Heidegger thought, when he declared not only that Western philosophy was fundamentally Platonism but also that this "metaphysical" tradition had come to an end.[1] However, in responding to the nihilistic consequences of the end of philosophy by trying to reverse and, then, to overcome Platonism entirely, Nietzsche had maintained the same basic intellectual structure.[2] In order truly to begin again, it was necessary to think the origin through more "originally."[3] Each new stage of Heidegger's own thought thus began with a rereading of Plato.[4]

Although Heidegger's view of Plato changed as he probed more and more deeply into the question of the origin and character of Western metaphysics, he never thought the original understanding would suffice. On the contrary, Heidegger repeatedly returned to Plato as the origin of metaphysics only in order to move beyond it. Following Parmenides, Plato taught that Being was eternal, unchanging, purely intelligible, and, as such, perfectly self-subsistent. In opposition to this traditional metaphysical teaching, Heidegger consistently argued that Being was essentially historical.

Because he thought the conjunction of intelligibility and existence Parmenides initially called 'Being' was historical, Heidegger never tried to understand Plato as Plato understood himself. As he saw it, such an understanding was neither possible nor desirable.[5] If 'being' meant what was present, and what was present could be known only in contrast to, and hence in connection with, past and future, no thing, thinker, or event could be known in itself. Heidegger thus consistently read Plato not merely in the context of his precursors but most emphatically in terms of the consequences of his philosophy as they had been worked out in the history of metaphysics. His readings of Plato reveal more about the development of the 'thought' with which he sought to replace previous philosophy than they do about the dialogues themselves.

FROM PLATO TO TIME

Like Nietzsche, Heidegger first returned to Plato, because modern philosophy had shown that the foundations of human knowledge were extremely problematic. Unlike Nietzsche, however, Heidegger did not conclude that human beings did not have and could not acquire any real science or knowledge.[6]

All the different sciences were defined by their particular subject matter. But, Heidegger observed, the sciences themselves did not give an account of the specific forms of being they examined; they simply took the existence of their subject matter for granted. To provide an account of the basis of the sciences, it would thus be necessary to explain not only the various forms but also the character of being itself.

Being had once been the subject of what had been called 'first philosophy'. But modern philosophers no longer engaged in this fundamental inquiry. They claimed that the meaning of Being was self-evident; as the highest form of being, Being itself could not be defined; as the most general characteristic shared by all the determinate forms of being, being itself had no specific properties. This logical modern approach to the question of Being, which assumes that knowledge consists fundamentally of definitional propositions, has its origins in Aristotle. Like his Greek predecessors, however, Aristotle himself had a different understanding of both the relation of logic or *logos* to knowledge and the character of the question of Being. To investigate the foundations of our knowledge, Heidegger concluded, it would be necessary to recover the questions of Greek philosophy. As he reminded his readers by using a quotation from Plato's *Sophist* as the frontispiece for *Being and Time*, the meaning of Being had been a question for the Greeks.

In his first book Heidegger argued that a certain 'destruction' of the tradition, that is, a radical critique of the accepted version of the history of philosophy and its results or outcome, would be necessary for modern students to rediscover the origins of their own, which is to say, Western thought. But in the part of *Being and Time* he actually published, he did not present such a critique.

Heidegger explained both the reasons for a return to the Greek origins of philosophy and what could be learned from it much more fully in the lecture course he gave on Plato's *Sophist* in 1924–25, two years before he published his masterwork on *Being and Time*.[7] To approach a Greek text, he argued, a twofold preparation was required: philosophical/phenomenological and historical/hermeneutic.

First, it was necessary to recapture the original meaning of *phainomenon* as the self-showing of the being to the one who inquired about it. As he explained in the introduction to *Being and Time,* 'phenomenon' had come to mean the potentially deceptive appearance of a thing in contrast to the reality only later, as a result of the emptying out of the original meaning of the word through repeated use. Edmund Husserl had revived the original understanding of phenomenon with his concept of 'intentionality' in his *Logical Investigations* when he insisted that all inquiry was inquiry about something, that all philosophical or scientific questioning had or presupposed not only a relation to its subject matter but also some acquaintance with it from the outset. Husserl's phenomenology thus constituted an important first step, but only a first step.

As Husserl emphasized at the beginning of the article on "Phenomenology" he asked Heidegger to coauthor for the Encyclopedia Britannica, 'consciousness' is always consciousness of something; as con-sciousness, it is also shared. As the term indicates, the phenomenon of consciousness itself presupposes a fundamental connection not only between the conscious or thinking 'subject' and the perceived 'object' but also among thinking subjects. To discover the nature and foundations of our knowledge, it would thus be necessary to investigate the character of this original connection, the connection Descartes severed in his attempt to provide knowledge with an indubitably firm foundation in the *cogito* taken entirely by itself. But, Heidegger observed, because Husserl 'bracketed' the question of the existence of the phenomena in the world in order to avoid the 'naturalistic fallacy' of the empirical sciences, which took their subject matter as simply "given," he never actually got back "to the things themselves." His phenomenology remained almost entirely within the realm of consciousness. A more historical, hermeneutical approach would be necessary to discover the nature of that pretheoretical experience upon which all subsequent theory was founded.

From his investigations of the origins of modern philosophical concepts like 'phenomenon' in the works of Plato and Aristotle, Heidegger rediscovered the centrality of *legein* or *logos*, not merely as the defining characteristic of human life, but as the way or "place" in which truth was both discovered and concealed. 'Speech' was the original connective between what came to be defined in modern philosophy as subject and object as well as among various subjects.[8] Because speech was the defining characteristic of human life, truth was—or at least could be—disclosed through an analysis of human existence.

As Plato and Aristotle emphasized, however, there are different forms

or kinds of speech (and consequently different forms of human existence), not all of which serve to disclose the truth. Based on the way
things appear and the "received wisdom" of the past, most speech serves
most of the time to conceal rather than to reveal. That was why Socrates,
Plato and Aristotle all thought it was necessary to go back through the
various opinions or *logoi* to get "to the things themselves." As the Greek
philosophers pointed out, moreover, people claimed to have different
kinds of knowledge of speech. Whereas rhetoricians claimed to know and
to be able to teach others how to persuade popular audiences, dialecticians
claimed to sort out true and false statements. There were also sophists,
who claimed they were able to speak about anything and everything
without real knowledge. It was Plato's investigation of the possibility or
grounds of the existence and knowledge of such admittedly false speech
that led him to the revolutionary concept of Being as essentially differentiated and so articulable in *logos* that he presented in the *Sophist* in opposition to the earlier, undifferentiated Parmenidean understanding. Aristotle developed and clarified this Platonic concept in his *Nicomachean
Ethics* by showing that there were different kinds of knowledge or ways
of disclosing the truth, all of which proceeded through *logos* except the
highest, pure contemplation or *theorein* of the beings that always are
by *nous*.[9] Although such knowledge was not simply attainable by human beings, who would therefore always remain like Plato "on the way,"
theory set the standard on the basis of which Aristotle could argue that
knowledge of the things that always are as they are, *sophia* and *epistēmē*,
is higher than knowledge of things that can be otherwise, *phronēsis* and
technē. In his *Physics* and *Metaphysics*, Aristotle showed that knowledge
of the beings consists in an analysis of the different basic kinds of beings
we perceive into their defining principles or intelligible *archē*, as well as
an account of the way in which these beings are constituted by those
principles. But the science of the Being of the beings or first philosophy
consists in the knowledge and articulation of the way in which these different kinds of Being coexist or are present with (in relation to and not
merely alongside of) each other. According to Aristotle, the Being of the
beings is not, then, a propertyless substratum; Being is not and should
not be defined as a kind of being. (That was, according to Aristotle, the
mistake the "ancients" made when they attempted to find the origin of
all the different forms of being in a single element like water, fire, or air.)
By reviving the question of the meaning of Being, as it had first been
posed by Plato and Aristotle, Heidegger thus thought he could avoid the
naturalistic fallacy without bracketing the question of the existence of
the phenomena.

As all readers of *Being and Time* know, Heidegger did not intend merely to revive Aristotelian ontology. By working out the implications of the original Greek understanding of Being as presence, Heidegger thought he was about to achieve an even greater revolution in first philosophy than Plato and Aristotle had effected (vis-à-vis Parmenides).

HEIDEGGER'S LECTURES ON PLATO'S *SOPHIST*

When we seek to recapture the Greek origins of basic philosophical and scientific concepts that over time and with repetition have become self-evident and so empty for us, Heidegger emphasized, we are not seeking anything that is separate from us or simply past. As the source of concepts we continue to use, the Greek origins are still effective in our understanding of the world. An investigation of the origins of our philosophy and science is thus a way of our coming to a better self-understanding. The question remains, however, how we can attain access to this past.

To recapture the significance of Plato's discussion of Being in the *Sophist,* he suggested, it is necessary to go back through Aristotle rather than to proceed as scholars usually do from the pre-Socratics through Plato to Aristotle. First, Platonic concepts have come down to us, traditionally or historically, through Aristotle. The Aristotelian form is the form in which we first encounter and learn them. By proceeding backwards from Aristotle to Plato, we thus retrace the steps, the way we actually acquired these concepts. Second, we will understand Aristotle as he understood himself. Aristotle says that he simply took Platonic concepts, clarified and radicalized them. According to the first principle of hermeneutics, we should, moreover, proceed from the clear to the obscure. Because of its extreme difficulty, Plato was not able to work out all the aspects or implications of the revolution in the meaning of Being he announced in the *Sophist.* If we approach Plato through Aristotle, we are not suggesting that Aristotle was a superior philosopher or that there is an inevitable progress in the development of human understanding. Aristotle would not have been able to clarify and develop Plato's concepts of Being and philosophy, if Plato had not thought them out beforehand as far as he did.

When Heidegger looks at what Aristotle says about the Being of the beings, he discovers that our access to being and the way we deal with it, what defines the being as such and how we come to have such a definition, is what we ought to call knowledge. And what is known, what discloses the being as what it is, is truth. This truth is expressed in a sentence or assertion. Aristotle was the first to say that determinations of truth and falsity are relevant primarily to judgement. This statement is correct, but superficial, if we consider more carefully what the Greeks meant by truth.

The Greek word for truth, *alētheia,* has an alpha-privative; it means, to be disclosed or no longer concealed. As the structure of the word indicates, the Greeks thought the disclosure of the world was something that had to be achieved. The truth was not simply "there." It had to be discovered by people who inquired about the true nature or being of things.

In their natural existence *(Dasein)* human beings discover the truth about things only as far as they need to. They express these initial discoveries in speech or *logos.* But, because people can understand speeches about things in the absence of the things, speech acquires a certain independence from the initial disclosure of the beings in it. Words and sentences are repeated, and people come to orient themselves to the world on the basis of experiences they themselves have never had. As a result of this quasi-independence of speech (which results in what Heidegger calls 'talk' *[Gerede]*), people who seek knowledge about the beings confront not only the original concealment of the nature of the things in the world but also the covering up of things that were originally disclosed in speech by dominant opinions or traditions. To get back to the things themselves, it thus becomes necessary to go back through the *logoi.* This was the task Socrates, Plato and Aristotle all set for themselves; it was also the reason Plato wrote dialogues. Their form was not a product of his artistry or poetry, but a result and reflection of the central character or thrust of his philosophy.

To see that truth is a property of speech or *legein* is to see that truth is not, strictly speaking, a property of the things themselves. Recapturing the Greek understanding of truth or the disclosure of the beings occurring only in and through speech allows us to see that truth emerges in a certain relation between the thing to be known and the being who seeks knowledge of it. Truth does not belong to things or statements, so much as to a certain form of being, the form of being or way of life that speaks: human being. The Greeks were so impressed with the centrality of speech to human life that they defined human being as *zōon logon echon,* life having speech. Speech in and of itself does not give rise to truth, however; in the form of mere talk it also serves to conceal. Living according to the dominant opinions of their time and place *(polis),* Plato and Aristotle saw, most human beings live most of the time far from the truth. Beings disclose themselves only to those who pursue a certain way of life, to those who use *logos* to seek the truth, that is, to philosophers.

Philosophers are not the only human beings, however, who concern themselves primarily with the speeches people make about everything that is. In the Greek *polis,* where the centrality of speech to a distinctively human life was most evident, both sophists and statesmen also claimed to have and to be able to teach the most comprehensive kind of knowledge human beings can acquire by means of *logos*. It was no accident that Plato raised the question of the meaning of Being and its relation to *logos* in a dialogue that begins with the question, are philosopher, sophist, and statesman the names of three different forms of human existence or are they three different names for the same.[10] Whereas most commentators treat the introductory attempt to define the sophist as a dramatic shell, separable from the metaphysical kernel, Heidegger insists there is an essential connection. If it is impossible to say or to think what 'is not', as Parmenides had argued, the existence of the sophist, the man who deceives others by constantly speaking of what is not, would be impossible. It was the concrete, factual preeminence of the sophists in the life of the Greek polis that forced Plato to re-raise the question of the status of the 'is not'.

Both sophists and philosophers claimed to speak about everything that is—the divine or the highest things, what comes to be under the heavens and on the earth, thus the Being of the beings, the affairs of the city, the different ways of life and the different possible forms of knowledge *(technai)*. By showing that the sophist speaks of things that are not as he says they are, the interlocutors disclose the character of the philosopher by way of contrast; his *logoi* are intended to disclose the beings as they are. In seeking the sophist, the Stranger thus announces at 253e8, they have found the philosopher as well. In the sophist and the philosopher the two antithetical potentialities of *logos* are realized in concrete forms of human existence.[11]

In seeking a definition of the sophist, the Stranger and Theatetus agree, they are seeking to come to an agreement about the nature of the being to which the word refers, not just an agreement about what the name means. They are thus engaging in philosophy as it comes into view in the dialogue. The only way we learn what philosophy is, Heidegger observes, is by philosophizing ourselves. We cannot simply name or define the nature of the activity externally.

Before they tackle the extremely difficult case of the sophist, the Stranger suggests they practice the method of determining what something is by sorting it into its *genē, diarēsis,* with an easier, less controversial example.[12] Because the sophist claims to possess an art *(technē)*, they look at an ordinary, everyday artisan—the fisherman. But, Heidegger emphasizes, the example is by no means arbitrary or unconnected to the investigation undertaken in the dialogue as a whole. Plato uses the same method in determining the character of ordinary things and activities in the world that he later applies to Being itself. This continuity of method suggests that Plato saw no fundamental difference in the structure or understanding of the objects. Greek philosophy proceeded on the basis of a naive or natural understanding of being that it did not explicate as such. The word these philosophers used for being, *ousia*, refers first to items of household property, things that are acquired and kept 'ready-at-hand' *(zuhanden)* for the sake of living—or living well. By using *ousia* to mean being, the Greeks showed they understood being as the presence of things which were defined initially in terms of their everyday use.

From Aristotle we learn that *technē* is a kind of *alētheuein* (disclosing of the truth) by means of *logos* in *poetikē* (doing or making). In the *Sophist*, we see, there are two kinds of *technai*. Some involve production, that is, the bringing forth into being of what was not before *(herstellen)*. But other *technai* constitute forms of appropriation, taking things to and for oneself, that can occur either by means of *logos*, as in learning, or in deed, in the form of an attack. (Later in the dialogue, Heidegger points out, we see that the two forms of *technē* are related insofar as a craftsman needs to have an idea of what he is going to make.) Here we see that the first *eidos* of *technē* provides the ground for the second inasmuch as we can only approach what is *vorhanden* (present-at-hand). Appropriation may, but is not necessarily related to *poiēsis*, because some things always are by nature (and thus can be appropriated). We also see that

> *logos* and learning are understood by the Greeks, especially Plato, as a way of appropriating what is present-at-hand. . . . Appropriation in knowledge does not mean taking into consciousness; the object remains standing where it is—present to the knower. . . . To speak about something is a way of appropriating the being as it appears.[13]

Like the fisherman, the sophist appears to be a kind of hunter—of men rather than fish, on land rather than at sea, with *logoi* rather than lines and nets. But, since the sophist promises to give the young men he attracts an education in exchange for their money, he cannot be defined simply as a hunter. He is also a merchant. Traveling from city to city, he sells speeches he has produced himself or those he has heard from others. He is producer, wholesaler, and retailer. The third and fourth definitions of the art of the sophist bring out how completely it is a matter of *logos*: *logoi* are the means the sophist uses to attract students; *logoi* are the "goods" he sells; *logoi* are what he produces and the means he uses to educate. By presenting his students with a variety of *logoi*, the sophist shows them how to attack and defeat the arguments of others. His art can thus be characterized, fifthly, as eristics. Because he shows his students how to refute the opinions of others with elenchtic speeches, the art of the sophist may also be described, sixthly, as a kind of psychic purification. If ignorance is the worst psychic disorder, and the worst form of ignorance is thinking one has knowledge when one does not, the sophist's eristic contradictions can be said to purge his interlocutors of the worst psychic disorder and so, if not to educate, at least to prepare them to be educated. At this point, Heidegger observes, Theatetus becomes confused, because the sophist looks very much like a philosopher. The Stranger thus suggests a last and, it turns out, all-encompassing definition of the sophist: he specializes in *anti-legein* or contra-diction. Contradictions are what he uses to attract youths, they are what he sells. But as contra-dictions, his speeches represent mere images. They appear to disclose what is, but in fact they show what is not. The confusion occurs and the sophist is able to deceive his listeners about the status of what he says, because the name of the image is the same as the name of the thing itself.

The problem the interlocutors have faced in attempting to define the sophist, who is repeatedly said to have many colors and forms, is, Heidegger emphasizes, the problem encountered in any attempt to say what a thing is, that is, to show the unity, the *eidos*, in the manifold of aspects or examples. The definition of the sophist leads, however, to a new and bigger problem. As the existence of artistic images, to say nothing of sophistry, shows, Parmenides' dictum is wrong. It is possible to say and to think what 'is not'. To show how this is possible, a new understanding of both Being and the not becomes necessary.

At first glance, Parmenides would appear to be correct. If *legein* is always *legein ti*, speaking about something, speech about nothing is no longer speech; it is silence. But, as Theatetus observes, in saying that it is not possible to say what is not, Parmenides himself is doing what he declares it impossible to do. He contradicts himself. Such *anti-legein* is not the same as talking about what does not exist. *Mē on* is not the same as *ouk esti*.

In search of a more encompassing notion of being, the interlocutors review past doctrines—ancient and "modern." The ancients gave histories of the way things had come to be; they did not account for the doctrines of others or show why their own was necessary. Those who said that being was manifold could not explain how it was or could be named one; those who maintained that it was one could not explain how or why there could be different forms. Plato's contemporaries tended to argue that being was either sensible or intelligible. Those who argued that it was sensible—to the extent to which they "improved" and were willing to present their position in *logos*—had to deny that "things" like *phronēsis* or justice could be. Those who claimed that being was purely intelligible, an *eidos*, could not explain motion. It is difficult for us to conceive of *nous* in the absence of *psyche* or life (and hence motion), the Stranger observes. The two notions of being might be brought together as forms of *dunamis,* the ability or power to affect or be affected. Both being as that which resists and being as what is perceived purely intelligibly can be known only as present, Heidegger points out. "Plato will make both intelligible as being present-at-hand in the possibility of being with each other."[14]

The phenomenon through which the Stranger brings the two theses together is knowledge. It would be impossible to know anything if everything remained the same, that is, if there were no motion. But knowledge would also be impossible if everything were constantly in motion and so changing. If being is what is known to be such, being must somehow encompass both rest and motion. It must be a third *genos* or *eidos.*[15]

We see the same kind of being together of different elements in *logos*—both in the combinations of vowels and consonants necessary to make up words and in the combination of name and verb needed to constitute the simplest *logos.* The Being of the beings can be disclosed in and through *logos,* because *logos* has the same structure as Being itself.

Just as there is an art or *technē* that tells us how to put sounds together to make music, letters together to make words, and words together to make speeches, so there is an art that enables us to separate out the different *eidē* or *genē* and to see how they are combined. That art is dialectics. Dialectics thus presupposes the *koinonia tōn genōn,* Heidegger emphasizes; it does not establish it. As the presupposition of dialectics, the *koinonia tōn genōn* is the presupposition of the way of life we call philosophy as well.

The Stranger demonstrates the coexistence of the five most general *eidē*—being, rest, motion, same and different—by showing that, as being must encompass both rest and motion, it is not the same as either, but different from both. Ideas must be the same as themselves in order to be; difference, on the other hand, is always *pros ti,* in relation to something else or other. It is not the same, but it still is. In the *heteron,* the Stranger thus finds the meaning of the *mē on,* which characterizes all particular forms of being and, he subsequently argues, the articulation of the beings as such in *logos.*

Just as the character of Being is shown by articulating its relation to, which is to say, its difference from but co-presence with, the other most general *eidē,* so Plato suggests

> Every factual concrete being has a multiplicity of content that can be shown through dialectical consideration in *legein* of this *on,* as being present together in pure *noein.* It is precisely this being together that makes the *on* what it is.[16]

By showing that *mē on* means not total exclusion or negation, but different, other than, Plato shows how negation "involves a purification that has a productive character." By sorting or analyzing the different *eidē* that are present with each other in any specific concrete being, "not-saying" lets the being be seen in its being.

"We have to free ourselves from traditional epistemology," Heidegger observes, "to understand . . . the positive uncovering function negation has in phenomenology."[17] He explains:

> Every "not" in every not-saying, whether expressly in language or not, has, as speaking, the character of showing. Also the empty not, the plain exclusion shows that on which negation is founded, . . . the nothing. That is the meaning of negation in Parmenides. This standing before nothing . . . is thus first in the historical development of our logic. . . . [But] one ought not to be misled into thinking that this empty negation is the nearest in speech.

The understanding of negation as complete exclusion that came first in the historical development of logic arose on the basis of the Parmenidean theory of Being, not from a primary study of the *logos*. Logic is not the root or origin of ontology; on the contrary, logic itself has ontological origins.

> That empty negation which dominated *legein* until Plato did not awaken out of a primary study of *logos*, but on the grounds of the Parmenidean theory of Being. . . . He had identified the ontological meaning of Being with the ontic collection of beings. So far as that happened, only the nothing remained left over for any no-saying.[18]

Plato's attempt to clarify the nature of *logos* in order to define the sophist in opposition to the philosopher led him to clarify the meaning of being, and the insight he gained into the *mē on* provided him with the basis of a new interpretation of *logos*. Because the presence of the beings becomes disclosed in *legein*, "*logos* is the core phenomenon." In attempting to recapture the Greek origins of our own thought, Heidegger emphasizes, we "must put aside the Plato of the schools, who contrasted the sensible world with the supersensible. Plato has seen the world as elementarily as we, only more originally."[19]

"It is no accident that Plato uses the examples of the *eidē* and *grammata*" to show the meaning of Being. There is a

> factual connection. . . . The *onoma* [name] in which the *eidos* becomes visible is itself made up of *grammata* [letters]. . . . The multiplicity of forms are not found next to one another in isolated realms but stand in an inner factual *koinonia: things, visibility of things, word, word sound—*

being, world, distinctiveness of beings, talk, announcement. This is no other than the *universal connection of phenomena, within which man, the zōon logon echon generally is. It is grounded finally in Being-in, the preceding uncoveredness of the world.*

Plato himself did not see this. But, "the task of interpretation is to press through to the underlying connection of phenomena that Plato did not investigate but which was nonetheless real [and so effective] for him. Only so do the grounds out of which he produced his analysis become present."[20]

BEING AND TIME

When Heidegger turned from his study of the Greek origins of philosophy to ask the question of the meaning of Being for himself, he thus began with the understanding he had found implicit in Plato and its basis in *Dasein*. The Greeks had not actually asked the question of the Being of being per se, but that question was included in their search for a being that would give a meaning of Being. Their not asking the question does not mean the Greeks did not have a concept of Being; on the contrary, it shows that the meaning of Being was self-evident for them. They did not think out their implicit understanding of Being as presence *(Anwesenheit)*; "it was what life itself, factual *Dasein* bears in it, so far as all human *Dasein* is explicating itself as well as all being." Heidegger proposed to begin with "this meaning of Being, . . . because the whole problem of time and therewith the ontology of *Dasein* lies enclosed therein."[21] Asking "the question of the meaning of Being" does not involve an abstract inquiry into an empty concept, Heidegger urged in his introduction to *Being and Time*. As he learned from studying the Greeks, the meaning of Being can be determined by giving a phenomenological analysis of human existence. Human being is the only form of being for which its own being is an issue. To determine the meaning of being, one thus needs to interrogate human beings about the meaning of their own existence.

In his own analysis of *Dasein*, Heidegger did not use the terms 'human', 'soul', or even 'living' that he had, in accord with their use by Plato and Aristotle, employed in bringing out the way the Greek understanding of Being was rooted in the character of their everyday existence. Heidegger wanted to distinguish his own, ultimately more historical, understanding, from the more naturalistic understanding that had become traditional. He thus emphasized the spatio-temporal character of the *da* in *Dasein* (which literally means "to be there").

In the "Preparatory Fundamental Analysis of *Dasein*" he gave in Division One of *Being and Time*, Heidegger presented a "phenomenological description" of the structure of human existence he had found implicit in Greek philosophy as 'Being-in-the-world' and 'Being-with-others'. Human beings understood themselves, initially and always, in relation to other things and people. But they did not initially encounter things merely as objects, 'present-at-hand'. They understood the things they encountered first and primarily as 'ready-at-hand' to use. Only when tools did not work as expected did people become aware of the existence and problem of things (present) in themselves. The theoretical perspective or inquiry was secondary, derivative from the initial practical encounter.[22] The practical use of things-ready-at-hand was defined, moreover, in terms of a conception of the meaning, character, and purpose of human life articulated in a language people shared with other beings like themselves. Human existence or *Da-sein* was, in other words, essentially social and intelligent.[23] That was the reason the Greeks had first defined *human* being as *zōon logon echon*. The speech that distinguished human being did not consist merely of a conventionally agreed upon set of signs for things; it was inseparable from the general understanding of 'the world' articulated in it.

Human existence is impossible in the absence of speech or language, the development of which presupposes society. But, Heidegger observed, it is ironically the generally applicable character of everyday 'talk' that prevents most human beings most of the time from understanding the true character of *Dasein*. This was the reason the Greek philosophers thought it was necessary to proceed through the opinions back to the things themselves.

Since things disclosed themselves only to the human beings who asked about them, it was necessary to understand the complex structure and character of *Da-sein*. *Human* beings were and understood themselves to be 'persons', as Kant had pointed out, in contrast to things (ready-at-hand) to be used. But the essentially personal character of human existence was covered over, if not entirely lost, in the impersonal character of everyday talk in terms of the 'they'.[24]

A person could recapture a sense of his existence as fundamentally and essentially his own, however, at least temporarily. By recapturing this 'sense', Heidegger promised, he would come to see the essential temporality not only of his own but of all human existence.

Because Heidegger made explicit the structure of human existence upon which the Greek understanding of Being had implicitly been based, he thought he could go further than the Greeks had in showing what the meaning of Being implicit in *Da-sein* actually was. In Division Two of *Being and Time* he thus argued that the meaning of Being was defined fundamentally in temporal terms.

His argument began with an analysis of a particular mood, which as a mood affected the person's understanding of the entire world. Reflecting on the reasons why she sometimes fell into a general state of anxiety without any specific source or object of fear, an individual would come to realize that this anxiety was rooted in a more or less conscious recognition not merely that she herself (in contrast to the impersonal 'they' of society) was going to die, but that her death might occur at any moment. She did not and would not *necessarily* continue to live. Since she *could* die at any moment, she continued to live only by willing to do so, by choosing, in effect, to project what she had been in the past into the future. Rather than viewing her life 'inauthentically' as something imposed by the accident of her birth and external circumstances, by recognizing that she herself chose to perpetuate it, she could make that life 'authentically' *(eigentlich)* her own.[25] A confrontation with death as her 'own-most' *(eigentlich)* possibility thus showed a person that, as a matter of her own choice, her life was fundamentally free.

Although an individual chose whether to live or die, she was not free to determine all aspects of her existence.[26] By choosing to perpetuate their existence, human beings necessarily 'fell' back into the perspective of the impersonal 'they'. When individuals chose to continue to exist, what they projected into the future was what they had been in the past; and that past was essentially defined by their 'world'—the time, place, and people into which they had been 'thrown' by birth. When individuals took responsibility for their own lives by resolutely projecting them into the future, they did not therefore simply embrace their own fates as individuals, because the 'fate' *(Schicksal)* of an individual was inseparable from the 'destiny' *(Geschick)* of his or her people.

The analysis of *Angst* shows that *Dasein* is essentially undetermined or open, because it is temporally structured. Human beings live by projecting what they have received from the past, the heritage they had acquire at birth, into an unknown future. That is what it means to live over an 'abyss'. Both individuals and peoples have histories *(Geschichte)*, because of the fundamentally temporal structure of human existence. These histories do not consist merely of records of past events or accumulations of factual information. There is always an element of selection; events are recorded with an eye to the anticipated end. In life, and thus in history, that end is projected; its achievement is uncertain. That is why resolve is needed. Human existence is not historically determined. On the contrary, human beings live historically for the same reason they can foresee the possibility of their own death, and that they consequently became concernfully engaged—whether authentically or inauthentically—with the people and things in the world around them: the basically temporal structure of *Dasein*.[27]

In his introduction to *Being and Time* Heidegger suggested that his analysis of the temporal structure of *Dasein* would provide a key to the 'meaning of Being' itself. But in the explicitly incomplete book he ended up publishing, Heidegger contented himself with showing that the original Greek perception of 'being' as 'present' had given rise to an erroneous understanding of time as a series of present moments or 'nows'. Human beings were not able to plan or project into the future, because they were able to measure and calculate such a sequence of moments. On the contrary, they became aware of the passage of time and devised ways of measuring it, because of the fundamentally temporal structure of their existence. What analysis of that structure showed, what was implicit but unthought in the original Greek perception of being as present, was that the present or being is known only in conjunction with past and future.

Heidegger's analysis of *Being and Time* pointed toward a revolution in the history of philosophy. As he reminded his readers in the introduction, the original Greek perception of being as present led to the notion, articulated most clearly by Plato and Aristotle, that the only truly or completely intelligible things were eternally present. What he had shown in his analysis of the fundamentally temporal structure of *Dasein* was that understanding or intelligibility depended, rather, upon finitude! Human beings were able to understand their own lives *(Dasein)* precisely because they had known beginnings (births) and ends (deaths). They were able to extend themselves, to involve themselves in a comprehensive and comprehending fashion in a world of other people and things, *not despite, but because* of the temporal structure of their existence. By thinking through what had remained unthought at the beginning, Heidegger was about to overturn the entire tradition!

Heidegger did not carry out the revolution he anticipated, his later work indicates, because his analysis of the temporal structure of *Dasein* led him to see two additional problems that became the foci of his lectures in the 1930s and early 1940s. First, if being as present exists and is known only in conjunction with past and future, it exists and is known only by virtue of what is absent. As present, being exists and can be understood only in conjunction with non-presence or non-being. Two years after he published *Being and Time*, he turned in "What Is Metaphysics?" to ask about the 'nothing', the question he had argued in his lectures on the *Sophist* had led Plato to a revolutionary new conception of Being as Being-with.[28] And in the 1930s he repeatedly returned to an investigation of the original Greek understanding of truth as *a-lētheia*, literally, that which emerges from oblivion or concealment, because the Greek word seemed to contain an implicit recognition of an intrinsic relation between disclosure or revelation and its concealed source.

Second, if the fundamentally temporal structure of *Dasein* made it essentially and emphatically historical, should there not be a history of *Dasein* or the present-ation of *Sein* in space and time? Although he had concluded that human understanding and existence were essentially historical, Heidegger's phenomenological analysis of *Dasein* in *Being and Time* was itself rather ahistorical. Admitting that particular individuals and nations had different life histories, Heidegger nevertheless proceeded as if *Dasein* had the same structure and produced basically the same kind of self-understanding at all times and places. After *Being and Time*, Heidegger thus turned more explicitly to a study of the history of philosophy as the history of the progressive forgetting and consequent concealing of the irreducibly mysterious character of the ground of intelligibility or being itself.[29]

Heidegger's renewed concern with *a-lētheia* led him to emphasize philosophy, as he had in his lectures on the *Sophist*, because he remembered that beings disclosed themselves as such only to those who asked the Socratic question, What is ... ? In Heidegger's later writings the difference between the philosophers (along with poets, sometimes statesmen, and later "thinkers"), who articulate anew the truth disclosed at their time and place, and the non-philosophers, who live according to inherited opinion, replaces the distinction between authentic and inauthentic existence in *Being and Time*. Because human existence is essentially historical, Heidegger saw, philosophers do not and cannot begin their investigations, as Descartes urged, from scratch. Like all other human beings, philosophers begin with opinions, views or "truths" they have inherited from the past. They disclose new truths by questioning these inherited opinions. There is an inherent connection, even though it often appears in the form of a negation or contradiction, between the truths disclosed in one age and those disclosed in the next. The latter do not represent discoveries of new information or the results of new techniques of analysis so much as the hidden potential, what remained concealed in the tradition until it was brought out by philosophical questioning. In order to make a new beginning, Heidegger himself thus had to inquire into the understanding of Being implicit, but only implicit and so hidden in his own tradition, the philosophical tradition of the West.

FROM PLATO TO NIETZSCHE

Heidegger's renewed interest in exploring the original Greek understanding of *a-lētheia* and the history of philosophy led him back to Plato. But in contrast to his initial exploration of the original meaning of Being in

Plato's *Sophist,* this time Heidegger did not explicitly read Plato in light of Aristotle.

In his famous image of the cave, Heidegger argued both in his 1931 lectures *Vom Wesen der Wahrheit* and in the essay on "Plato's Doctrine of the Truth" he published in 1942, Plato depicted the Greeks' initial experience of *a-lētheia.* Plato's analysis of that original experience had, however, produced a decisive change in the understanding later thinkers had of truth. 'Truth' did not originally refer to the correspondence between word or idea and thing; it referred to that which emerged from hiddenness. Understood as self-showing or disclosure, 'truth' belonged to the beings themselves, not to statements about them. Things disclosed themselves as such, that is, as beings, however, only to human beings; as Plato's image suggested, truth was, therefore, an aspect or event of human existence.[30] Plato also showed that disclosure occurred in stages— which is to say, in time. In his initial lectures *On the Essence of Truth,* Heidegger thus concluded, the original Greek experience of truth was fundamentally historical.[31]

Both in his initial lectures on the "chief images" of Plato's *Republic* and in the essay he himself later published "On the Essence of the Truth," Heidegger pointed out that the 'essence' of truth involved a certain kind of liberation. That liberation did not consist merely in freeing "man" from external restraint or in the lack of internal, instinctive direction traditionally taken to distinguish "men" from animals. As Plato showed, it did not suffice to unchain an inhabitant of the cave; the "freed man" had to be forced to stand up, turn around and face the bewildering light of the fire, and then be dragged up out of the cave into the blinding light of the sun. As Heidegger had argued in *Being and Time,* so he emphasized in his reading of Plato: the freedom of *Dasein* constitutes a *possibility,* not a necessity. Neither man's essential freedom nor the knowledge it makes possible are properties of some preexisting or self-subsisting species. In his reading of Plato, Heidegger emphasizes that the possibility of living a truly human existence is realized only by the very few who become philosophers, and they only realize it with the assistance of other philosophers and the application of force.[32] Left to themselves, Plato indicated, human beings will remain in the cave or, as Heidegger described it, the fallacious, essentially empty realm of everyday opinion. Following others and accepting what was given is easier, safer and more reassuring than raising painful, alienating and unsettling questions.

Questioning everyday opinion is not enough, moreover. Potential philosophers not only have to be forced to look at things as they truly are; they also have to be forced to return to the cave! And in both cases, the initial result is not heightened clarity, but confused vision. Unable to see what is "plain as day" to their companions, Plato suggested, philosophers become objects of ridicule when they are forced to descend. Should they explicitly challenge the truth of their contemporaries' secure convictions, philosophers are also apt to anger their companions and so, like Socrates, endanger their own lives.[33]

Philosophers do not have to return to the cave to correct the opinions of the cave-dwellers, Heidegger insists. Attempts at popular enlightenment à la Kant denied the essential difference, the necessary and continuing opposition, between common opinion and philosophy. Philosophers have to return to the cave to discover the grounds of the opposition between philosophy and common opinion in the temporal essence of both truth and human existence. Wishing to remain in the light, Plato stated, philosophers would "believe they were in the isles of the Blessed."[34] Believing that they had arrived in the realm of unchanging ideas, Socrates suggested in the *Phaedo*, philosophers would think they had emigrated to the afterworld, that is, that they were dead. Such philosophers were oblivious of their own mortality. Failing to recognize the essentially temporal character of *a-lētheia* as that which was previously hidden (or unknown) and would again become hidden in the future when it was forgotten, such philosophers did not understand that hiddenness and unhiddenness were essentially connected as well as essentially opposed. They did not perceive that the cave itself was an 'open space' in which the source of light was not and never would be perceived by most of its inhabitants. They did not see that a philosopher's 'soul' might be turned toward the light and directed so that he became aware of the sources, both artificial and natural, of what was disclosed in it as well as of the light itself, but that as a human being he neither had nor would ever entirely leave the cave and its darkness behind him. Light and dark, concealment and unconcealment existed and only existed in opposition and time.[35]

In arguing that philosophers do not have to return to the cave to help the other people still imprisoned and deluded, Heidegger might appear to ignore the political context in which Socrates proposes both this and the preceding image of the divided line.[36] But in the initial series of lectures he gave on Nietzsche in 1936–37, Heidegger suggested that this "political" context had been misconstrued.[37] The discussion of the proper order of the *polis* in the *Republic* did not culminate in the suggestion that philosophers should become kings to realize some moral conception of justice. In Plato, as in the so-called pre-Socratic philosophers who preceded him, *dikē* referred primarily to the constitutive order of things.[38] Only after and as a result of Plato's work did justice degenerate into a moral concept. Philosophers had to become kings and so determine the order of the city in the *Republic*, because, as Plato explicitly suggested in the *Phaedrus* (249e), human being is distinguished by its relation to Being.[39] Since, as Plato indicated in the cave scene, this relation which constitutes the essence of "man" is realized only in and by philosophers, they alone possess the knowledge requisite to organize a truly human community.

When he finally published his own analysis of "the essence of the truth" separate from his account of "Plato's doctrine," Heidegger obscured the extent to which his own understanding of the truth was based upon his rereading of Plato. The differences between his own understanding of truth and Plato's were, he had concluded, more important than the original similarities. As he observed in his 1936–37 lectures on *Nietzsche*, Socrates' description of the human condition in the cave pointed to, if it did not rest on, the Platonic distinction between the sensible and supersensible intelligible Nietzsche initially tried to invert and then realized must be completely dropped, if Platonism were to be overcome. Following Husserl, in *Being and Time* Heidegger had attempted to get behind or under the modern version of that Platonic opposition between ideal and real in his analysis of *Da-sein* as Being-in-the-world. There is clearly a relation between Heidegger's contention in his own essay "On the Essence of Truth" that there has to be an 'open space' into which something can emerge from unhiddenness to become "visible" to an observer and Socrates' account of the nature of vision in Book VI of the *Republic*.[40] (There Socrates reminds Glaucon, vision requires not only an ability to see on the part of the viewer and visibility as a property of the thing seen but also the light of the sun.) But Socrates proceeds to draw an analogy between the requirements of seeing [in the sensible world] and knowing [in the supersensible, unchanging realm of the intelligible], whereas Heidegger denies that there is initially any difference between the way a thing shows itself (the *phainomenon* or appearance) and the being of the thing. The difference between word or idea and thing (and so the possibility of false opinion or inauthentic speech) emerges over time as the original experience or look that was poetically embodied in a new word becomes lost in the repetitive and conventional use of the word in everyday speech. But, Heidegger now emphasizes, the possibility of that loss of meaning or falsification is rooted in the character of the original experience or 'lighting'. The initial self-showing of the beings tends to distract attention from the light or "space" that makes their self-disclosure possible. Being only discloses itself in the dis-closure of the beings; yet in that very showing, Being itself is covered over and concealed.

Heidegger distinguished his own understanding of 'the essence of truth' from "Plato's doctrine" fundamentally because he saw that a thinker's conception of truth was inseparable from his understanding of Being. Although Plato maintained the original Greek understanding of *a-lētheia* as unhiddenness, Heidegger concluded in the 1930s, Plato's work had nevertheless produced a fundamental change in the conception of truth by associating it with an understanding of being as idea.[41]

Just as Plato retained the original Greek understanding of truth, so his description of being as idea incorporated the original Greek understanding of being as that which showed itself to be present. *Eidos* did not mean concept; it referred to the external form or shape of a thing which revealed what it was. *Idea* likewise referred to that which revealed or showed what a thing was. But by suggesting that these *ideai* were always present (and so timeless), Plato had fundamentally changed the understanding later thinkers came to have of both being and truth. For Plato, unhiddenness was still a property of the beings. But, if the ideas were always present and intelligible, possession or lack of truth depended on whether people turned their attention to these unchanging ideas. Even in Plato, truth thus became a matter of correct *(orthes)* "vision," of the agreement *(homoiosis)* between the content of a person's mind and the beings themselves. Aquinas later concluded that truth was, therefore, a matter of human or divine intellect. At the beginning of modern times, Descartes made it clear that 'ideas' were concepts; truth consisted in the agreement of these concepts with the order of things in the world. As a result of the Platonic interpretation of being as idea, truth thus became a property or characteristic of human thought rather than of the beings themselves. Indeed, as a result of the Platonic association of truth with correct vision rather than unhidden phenomena, "truth" became solely a matter of perspective, as Nietzsche finally declared.

There was, therefore, a hidden path from Plato's reconception of being as idea to Nietzsche's extremely subjectivist declaration that there is no truth, because there is no eternal, intelligible order to be apprehended correctly; there are only the different orders individuals attempt to impose on an ever-changing flux.

> Plato's thinking . . . has begun its unconditional fulfillment in Nietzsche's thinking. Plato's doctrine of "truth" is therefore not something of the past. It is historically "present," but not as a historically recollected "consequence" of a piece of didacticism, not even as a revival, not even as imitation of antiquity, not even as mere preservation of the traditional. The change of the essence of truth is present as the slowly confirmed and still uncontested reality . . . of the history of the world rolling on and on into its most modern modernity.[42]

When he declared that "God is dead," Nietzsche expressed *the* truth of the modern world. Because he had not freed himself from a Platonic conception of truth, however, Nietzsche himself did not properly understand the significance of his own thought. In urging that "truth" was an error, because if everything was always in process of becoming something else, no statement about the nature of anything could remain accurate, Nietzsche had ironically maintained the traditional philosophic conception of truth as correspondence between idea or statement and reality. He retained that traditional understanding of truth, because he ultimately also retained the traditional understanding of Being as sub-stance or substratum.[43] Rather than overcoming Platonism, Nietzsche had brought out the true nature of previous metaphysics and so completed it.[44]

Nietzsche thought that he had overcome the Platonic dichotomy between sensible and intelligible or, in modern terms, real and ideal, by arguing that everything, spiritual as well as physical, was essentially will to power. In the modern world, Heidegger agreed, everything was not merely an expression of, but essentially constituted by, an unlimited will to power. Unrestrained by any belief in God or an independently existing natural order, nations not only sought worldwide dominion in the name of one or another ideological theory of purportedly universal application; they also sought to transform the world technologically to make it more adaptable to human needs and desires. As the explicitly philosophical roots of both "individualist" liberal and "collectivist" communist ideology indicated, both the major political and scientific drives of the twentieth century were products in some sense of the development or history of Western thought.[45] Commonplace, everyday talk about "values" was itself indicative of the political influence or effect of philosophy. Before Nietzsche, people had talked in terms of truth. In modern times, people did not really believe that there was any higher truth outside, independent of, or beyond themselves. "Man" was or was to be made master of the world.

Nietzsche suggested that the "devaluation of the highest values" that produced modern "nihilism" was not merely or necessarily negative, because the destruction of old values was the necessary precondition for the creation of new forms or ways of life. What were values after all but statements setting the conditions necessary not merely to preserve but to enhance a certain form or way of life.[46] What was "life" but a manifestation or form of the "will to power" which seeks only to increase its own sway (or power). Past values had been discredited, because they did not and could not support explicit modern power-seeking. A new kind of "man" was required to achieve the world dominion all modern people desired.⁴⁷ By self-consciously creating their own values as masters and as such openly seeking to impose their own order on the world, "supermen" could provide better justification for human striving—past, present, and future—than any previously available.

Past philosophers had admittedly not understood themselves to be stating values. They thought they were articulating a truth they had discovered. Neither Plato's nor Descartes's philosophy was accurately or aptly stated in terms of values, Heidegger therefore insisted. Nevertheless, in arguing that what they had actually done was to project a value, Nietzsche had disclosed something fundamental about their respective philosophies and therewith about the history of metaphysics as a whole.

Although Nietzsche was very critical of Descartes's famous *cogito*, he nevertheless built on the foundation the French philosopher laid. When Descartes declared *cogito ergo sum*, he was not stating a syllogism nor was he seeking to found knowledge upon logic. He was articulating a new understanding of Being, according to which only those things that could be re-presented *(vor-stellen)* to the mind in the form of clear and distinct ideas were regarded to be intelligible. As a result, the human being or mind became the 'sub-ject' (the locus of sub-stance or underlying reality) before which everything else in the world became an 'object'. Although Descartes's doctrine was, as even Nietzsche saw it, an expression most immediately of his 'will to truth', his work also explicitly had a broader purpose—"to find a philosophy that immediately advances to beings and against them, so that we gain knowledge about the power and effects of [the elements] . . . so as to . . . make us masters and proprietors of nature."⁴⁸ Descartes himself had no doubt that the mathematical order he posited in the world existed or that it did not merely constitute a human construct. Nevertheless, Descartes's thought pointed in the direction of Nietzsche not only by making the human mind the center or ground of the world, but also by explicitly stating that the knowledge resulting from his investigations would serve a broader will to power.

Although it constituted a fundamental modification of, if not break with, the earlier doctrine, Cartesian idealism developed out of the Scholastic version of the Platonic theory of ideas. For Plato, the ideas did not represent mental concepts. On the contrary, they were that through, or by virtue of, which all forms of being were able not merely to show, but to be what they were. Just as the ideas made it possible for different forms of being to be, Plato suggested in Book VI of the *Republic*, so there must be something that made the ideas themselves possible—an 'idea of the ideas', so to speak. And by reexamining Plato's sole presentation of the Idea of the Good, Heidegger saw: (1) What later (after Aristotle) came to be called meta-physics originated in a distinction between the beings (even as a whole) and what was "beyond being," that is, the "ontological difference." (2) In the original articulation of this difference, Being was posited as *the condition* for the existence and intelligibility of the beings. (3) Defined as the idea of the ideas or the 'Being of the beings', Being became identified as that which all beings had in common, itself lacking any particular defining characteristics or properties.

Nietzsche misunderstood the significance of Plato's 'Idea of the Good', because he understood 'good' in later Christian, moralizing terms. To the ancient Greeks, *agathon* meant "useful."[49] Just as things became visible to the human eye only in the light of the sun (which was therefore useful, indeed, constituted a necessary condition for the possibility of vision), so Socrates suggested, ideas or beings became intelligible as such to the mind's eye only in the "light" of the Idea of the Good (which thus constituted the necessary condition for both the *possible* existence and apprehension of being as such). If values constituted the conditions or pre-conditions for "the preservation and enhancement" of other forms of existence, Plato's Idea of the Good was quintessentially a value, although it was not at all moral.

Following Socrates' suggestion, Plato's conception of the Good was later mistakenly identified with God as first cause.[50] But, Heidegger insisted, cause is not the same as condition. A condition may be a necessary pre-condition for the *possible* existence of something else without itself determining or causing the actualization of that possibility. In Socrates' schema, there were three interdependent factors—the mind of the knower, noetic light, and the things known or ideas—none of which could produce being or truth by itself.

By rereading Plato in light of Nietzsche's interpretation, Heidegger thus came to clarify his own understanding of truth and Being in contrast to both the beginning and the end of the metaphysical tradition. In opposition to Nietzsche's insistence that "truth" was an error, Heidegger argued that there was, in fact, truth, and that philosophers had articulated it. In his essay "On the Essence of Truth," he pointed out that beings disclosed themselves as such only to those who inquired about their being. The e-mergence of truth was an essentially interactive process; human beings did not and could not simply project their own desires, perspectives, or orders onto the world. They dis-covered a truth that was there *(da)*. This truth varied from time to time and place to place, but the reason it varied was not simply or solely the spatio-temporal limits of the human being who articulated it. Truth was not a property of human perception or thought; it emerged in the self-disclosure of the beings. But in the self-dis-closure *(a-lētheia)* of beings as beings, there was always something that remained hidden, forgotten or concealed. What was hid-

den was what made it possible for the beings to disclose themselves as
such, the Being of the beings. Because Being manifested itself only in
and through the beings, Being itself could never be directly cognized. In
contrast to the beings, it itself was never present or un-concealed. Because the ground of human knowledge was itself never present or cogni-
zable, all truths, all disclosures of being were necessarily partial. As such,
they were also false. There was and could be no unconcealment, truth, or
dis-covery unaccompanied by concealment, error, and oblivion.

Being itself had been lost or forgotten in its first self-disclosure in
response to the questions of Greek philosophers. Although Greek philosophy originated in a recognition of the difference between Being and the
beings (characteristic not merely of Plato and Aristotle but also of their
predecessors, Parmenides and Heraclitus), these philosophers forgot or
obscured the difference by defining Being as the Being of the beings. As
that which was common to all particular forms of being, Being itself had
and could logically have no distinguishing character of its own. So conceived, Being could never become known or even an object of inquiry. It
was no accident, therefore, that the metaphysical inquiry which originated with Plato and Aristotle concentrated on the beings, on asking
What is ... ? The 'truth of Being' that had and could have become manifest only through the history of philosophy, that is, through the demonstrated failure of philosophy not merely to answer but finally even to
pose the question of the meaning of Being, was not only that human
knowledge or truth was always partial, but also that the ground or source
of human knowledge was and always would be essentially mysterious.

To dis-cover that the ground of human knowledge or Being was never
present did not mean that there "was" no such ground or source of
"light" independent of human beings, as Nietzsche had suggested. It
meant, as Plato indicated with the cave, that human beings lived in a
physically (and, therefore, Heidegger would add, temporally) limited and
defined space or world which was nevertheless partially open and as a
result partially, but only partially lighted. Like Plato, Heidegger suggested that the opinions most people held were mere reflections of the
work of artists or poets who had themselves seen beyond the cave. Unlike
Socrates in the *Republic* but like Socrates in the *Phaedo*, he insisted that
it was not possible for these poets (or any other human beings) to look
directly at the source of light.

FROM PLATO TO HEIDEGGER

Heidegger's prolonged *Auseinandersetzung* with Nietzsche not only led
him to clarify his own understanding of the historical dis-closure of 'the

truth of Being' and its ancient Greek origins. It also led him to a different understanding of Nietzsche; he concurred with Nietzsche's own judgment in the *Twilight of the Idols* that his thought owed more to the Romans than to the Greeks.

> [In] a segment called "What I Owe to the Ancients" . . . he says: "To the Greeks I do not by any means owe similarly strong impressions; . . . they *can* not be for us what the Romans are. . . ." Nietzsche by that time had clear knowledge of the fact that the metaphysics of will to power conforms only to Roman culture and Machiavelli's *The Prince*.[51]

If Nietzsche's thought was more Roman than Greek, his work could not properly be regarded as the completion and disclosure of the hidden potential or essence of Greek philosophy. Heidegger's confrontation with Nietzsche thus led him to yet a third reconsideration and reformulation of the origins of Western metaphysics in Plato.

The year he published "Plato's Doctrine of Truth," Heidegger delivered a series of lectures on *Parmenides* in which he (1) insisted that Nietzsche had taken over a Christianized (which is to say fundamentally Romanized) understanding of the Greeks from Jacob Burckhardt (who was, in turn, indebted for his understanding to Hegel) and (2) suggested that all ancient Greek poets and philosophers—Parmenides and Plato, Homer and Pindar—had essentially the same understanding of *a-lētheia*. The historically decisive change in the meaning of 'truth' had occurred not in Platonic philosophy, but in the translation of the Greek term into Latin, shaped as it was by the Roman experience of war and conquest.[52]

In explicating Parmenides' poem, Heidegger observed, if we regard the goddess "Truth" who shows him the way as a personification of an abstract concept, we claim, in effect, to understand what the Greeks meant by both 'truth' and 'god'. In fact, we understand neither so long as we retain a modern understanding of both. To recapture the original, Greek understanding of truth, we have to attend to the structure of the word itself. The alpha privative suggests that the Greeks understood *alētheia* in terms or even as a kind of opposition.

Derived from *lanthanomai*, *lēthē* refers to that which is concealed (and, no longer present or showing itself, therefore forgotten by men). The opposition the Greeks experienced was thus between the concealed and the un-concealed (to be distinguished, moreover, from the not-concealed. That which was un-concealed was that which had previously been concealed.) The basic opposition the Greeks experienced was not between true *(alethes)* and false *(pseudes)*.[53]

In Latin, *falsum* referred to that which could not maintain itself. As the opposite of the 'false', *veritas* became associated with that which could be maintained—certain, secure, upright. Adopted and transmitted by the Christian popes, this Roman understanding of truth became 'right reason' or 'will'. Secularized by Descartes, the false was conceived as 'error' or an incorrect use of reason, right reason as certainty. And the knowledge obtained through the right use of reason was to be used to secure the conditions for the improvement of human life. Nietzsche completed and so brought to the surface the historical consequences of the Latin translation (and hence transformation) of *alētheia* into the attempt to secure the conditions of human life by obtaining ever more power.[54]

This change in the meaning of truth was accompanied by equally fundamental changes in the understanding of the essential nature of both gods and politics. Like the Hebrew God, Roman deities issued commands; they no longer simply pointed the way like their Greek predecessors.[55] Likewise, whereas the Greek *polis* had been the place at which the truth was disclosed, in Rome politics became identified with the search for power.

To recapture the original understanding of truth, gods, and politics, as well as their inter-relation, Heidegger suggested, it would be useful to reexamine the last Greek saying about *lēthē* in the myth of Er. It was no accident that this statement was to be found at the end of Plato's *Republic*. Greek thought completed itself in Plato (although it found its highest expression in his student Aristotle). Plato's fullest and most far-reaching dialogue dealt with the nature of the *polis*, because the *polis* was *the* site of the disclosure of the truth. That was the reason the dialogue about the essence of political order or *politeia* reached its peak in the "high images" concerning *a-lētheia* and concluded with a saga concerning its origin and limits in *lēthē*.

Polis was the *polos* (pole) around which being-as-a-whole was disclosed to man. As the Greeks saw it, human being was defined by its relation to Being. As the time and place in which Being dis-closed itself to men through the beings, the *polis* constituted the site *(da)* of human existence *(Da-sein)*. Since it was temporally as well as spatially defined and limited, Heidegger emphasized, that existence was essentially historical.[56]

The Greeks called the constitution or order of being-as-a-whole observable from or within the *polis*, *dikē*. As in his earlier explications of Plato, Heidegger emphasized, the conception of *dikē* was not originally or essentially moral. Because the un-concealment of the beings existed only in opposition to concealment, the *polis* itself was always and necessarily characterized by strife. Those who lived according to the constituted order were called just; those who opposed it, unjust. Since such opposition was an unavoidable component of human existence, it could not properly be called immoral. It was, rather, tragic.

Because human existence was temporally and spatially restricted, Plato appropriately concluded the *Republic* by considering what lay beyond, surrounded, and so de-limited or de-fined it. The account of the 'beyond' given in the myth of Er should not be understood in Neoplatonic or Christian terms of an after-life.[57] In Plato's myth, death is portrayed as a place of transition, the 'there' to which a soul must go before beginning another course or period of life 'here' on the surface of the earth.[58] Er calls this place daimonic, but he does not mean that it is inhabited by demons or ghosts. Derived from *daiō*, *daimonic* means that which shows. It refers, more particularly, to the *ungeheure* (literally, the e-normous)—that which shows itself only in and through the normal; that which makes the normal, normal; that which is not abnormal, monstrous or gigantic, but rather all encompassing and natural. *Daimonic* refers, in sum, to the showing of Being in the beings.[59] *Daimonic* refers, therefore, to the same showing or 'look' the Greeks called *Thea*.[60] These 'gods' showed themselves only to the men (poets) who simultaneously named them. (That was the reason, Heidegger suggests, the initial 'sayings' about the Being of the beings, Greek myths, consisted of stories about the gods.)[61]

When Er calls the underworld a daimonic place, he suggests it shows something extraordinary about the character of Being itself. The essence of this place is gathered in the field of *lēthē*. This field, which allows nothing to emerge, is the opposite of *physis*. What the daimonic place shows is that withdrawal and covering are the essence of Being. Being itself never emerges or shows itself as such; it is disclosed only through the withdrawal of concealment that allows the beings to emerge in *a-lētheia*. Being itself is concealed by the very disclosure of the beings through which Being shows itself—only in its ab-sence—by going away.

Before they could reemerge on the surface of the earth, Er reports, souls have to drink from the river *A-mēlēs* (literally, without care) that runs through the field of *lēthē*, and most drink without measure. These souls entirely forget their previous experience; they forget even that they have forgotten. (To know that one has forgotten, Heidegger observed, is not entirely to have forgotten.) They retain no sense of the concealed, essentially mysterious source and foundation of everything that is disclosed or given to them. Only philosophers endowed with *phronēsis* (prudence or fore-sight) drink with measure and so are saved from complete forgetfulness. Sensing the fundamental mystery within themselves as well as without, they ask questions, and in response to their questions, beings disclose themselves.

Er's tale had been saved, Socrates suggested, so that by listening to it, they might be saved themselves. But, Heidegger concluded, although Plato voiced a sense of the saving essence of *a-lētheia*, neither he nor the other Greeks fully understood it. Plato had recognized the strife at the core of *a-lētheia* in his doctrine of recollection. Literally translated, *mnaomai* refers to the summoning or calling forth of a being; *ana-* to maintaining it in the present or its presence.[62] In emphasizing the connection between *logos* and *anamnēsis* (or knowledge as 'recollection'), Plato showed he understood that beings became evident as such only in word. But, Heidegger stressed, in order for the meaning of a word or a being to become evident as such, much less to be re-collected later, there had to be an 'opening'. It was this need for an opening for the truth to emerge that the Greeks had almost entirely missed.

The Greeks could not fully understand or fully appreciate the concealed and in being concealed, preserved and potentially preserving, essence of *a-lētheia*, because they experienced it originally, at the beginning. The beginning announced itself only in having begun. What had begun or originated did not become clear until the process had been completed. What had been concealed as well as unconcealed in the history of the truth of Being could be known only at its end.

However, because the Greeks experienced *a-lētheia* originally, their works contained some hints. In his *Aias* (V, 4, 46), Sophocles observed that everything not only emerges in, but is also eventually concealed by, time, which is not graspable by the calculating.[63] Once time was reconceptualized, beginning with Aristotle, as an infinite series of discrete moments or nows, that original sense of time as an opening or even, as in Plato, space *(chora)* in which Being dis-closed itself in an essentially limited or finite way, was lost. Being and time had never been the same, Heidegger emphasized; they were essentially connected.[64] Like Being, time showed itself only in passing away or withdrawing.[65]

To save or preserve themselves as human beings, Heidegger urged, modern "men" had to regain a sense of the essentially temporal meaning (or, as he now put it, truth) of Being.[66] Human being exists only in relation to Being. And in modern times it has become clear that neither Being nor, consequently, human being has to be. To recapture the meaning of what has become an empty term, Heidegger argued from *Being and Time* onwards, it was necessary to re-collect its original, temporal sense. Understood as presence, being had originally been defined in temporal terms. When that which was truly in being was re-conceived as that which was eternally and hence unchangingly present, the temporal framework or context of the meaning of Being had been lost. To re-collect the temporal essence (*Wesen* or, literally, having been) of Being, he finally concluded, it would be necessary (or at least useful) to re-conceive Being, once again, as *Ereignis*.[67]

To reconceive Being as *Ereignis* meant, first, to recall that it was an event (one of the dictionary definitions of the term). Before philosophers in Greece perceived the conjunction of intelligibility and existence in Being, that conjunction and hence Being did not exist. There was no reason, necessity or ground for this conjunction or perception. It suddenly and inexplicably occurred at a specific place and time. The initial mutually constitutive relation between human being and Being thus began with a 'leap'.[68] The full meaning and consequences of the original apprehension of the intelligibility of being were not evident at the beginning, however; they had to be worked out in time or history. To characterize Being as *Ereignis* did not mean, therefore, that it was an event which happened at a certain moment and then was over.[69]

Being was historical, because the conjunction of intelligibility and existence Parmenides first named Being occurred only in and to human beings whose existence was, as Heidegger had argued in *Being and Time*, essentially historical.[70] *Human* life was constituted by a certain understanding of the intelligibility of beings-as-a-whole (or world).[71] In diametric opposition to Nietzsche, however, Heidegger insisted from *Being and Time* onward that the order, cosmos, or world human beings perceived did not have its origin solely in man. Both the order and the intelligibility of the various worlds in which human beings found themselves at different times and places were given. In the essay "On Time and Being," Heidegger published in the 1950s he thus urged his readers to ponder the awe-arousing, wonder-provoking character of the *es* that *gibt*.[72]

Reconceiving Being as *Ereignis* meant understanding it not only as an historical 'event' but also as an 'ap-propriation' (another dictionary definition of the word) whereby all beings, but most especially human beings, become what they are by being taken up into and by Being.[73] Because Being could only occur or be in and through human being *(Dasein)*, Being could be said to have "used," even to have "possessed," "man." Human beings became distinctively human, which is to say, intelligent, beings, however, only by being "taken up" into the "light of Being."

Being did not have to be. That was *the* truth of Being which had been dis-covered only in modern times. If human beings did not open themselves to Being, the conjunction between intelligence and existence which had given birth to Western civilization would come to an end. The complete obliteration of Being would result in the obliteration of human being as well.

The complete withdrawal of Being into oblivion had become manifest,

Heidegger argued, in the apparently inexorable drive which compelled his contemporaries to transform the world technologically. Technology had come on the scene, to be sure, merely as the practical application of modern science. But, as Descartes had pointed out at the very beginning, modern science itself arose primarily as a form of knowledge which would enable human beings to reconstitute the world so as to make it more amenable to human needs and desires. Both science and technology thus initially appeared in the guise of service to humanity. By reconceiving everything in terms of calculable units of matter (or extension) and motion (or energy), however, modern physics had reduced all particular forms of being into a kind of 'standing reserve' to be transformed at will—humanity included! If every thing consisted, fundamentally, only of a certain quantity of material or energy waiting to be exploited or used, there was no reason to make human being an exception. But if human beings themselves became subject to the transformative technological process which was initiated to serve them, that process itself no longer had any ground, purpose, end, or reason.[74] Although it proceeded on the basis of logical mathematical calculation, the 'essence' of technology was, as Nietzsche had perceived, to be found in a pure, unadulterated, and fundamentally unintelligible will to power.[75]

His contemporaries faced an absolutely fundamental decision. They could proceed with the willful technological transformation; neither Being nor human being necessarily existed. If human beings were going to preserve themselves as such, however, they would have to turn away from the frenzied self-assertion of technological superpower politics and open themselves once again to a new dis-closure of that which was essentially and always beyond human knowledge or mastery, though not impossible to re-cognize in its absence or essential concealment.[76]

HEIDEGGER'S NEW, POETICALLY DEFINED WORLD

Viewing technology merely as a tool, Heidegger believed, most of his contemporaries would unthinkingly persist with it. Only a few appeared to have any sense of the true nature of the modern crisis of humanity and the need to look in another direction. The German poet Rainer Maria Rilke was one of those few. Like Heidegger himself, Rilke had spoken of 'nature', which is to say, the 'Being of beings', in terms of the 'open'. But, Heidegger pointed out in his lectures on *Parmenides*, Rilke followed Nietzsche by associating the 'open' with the essential indeterminacy of infinite becoming. Whereas unconscious plants and animals merged with nature without difficulty, the poet observed, human beings remained alienated from it, because they were always aware of their own impending end or death.[77]

Rilke had accurately located the origin of man's alienation from nature in a rebellion against his own death or finitude in Cartesian metaphysics, Heidegger pointed out in the lecture he gave commemorating the twentieth anniversary of the poet's death several years later. (The alienation did not, we should note, originate in ancient philosophy with Platonism, as Nietzsche had maintained.) By reconceiving everything as an object to be re-presented in his consciousness, "man" had taken a stand over and against everything else in the world as 'other'. But the science with which human beings had tried to master the world in order to relieve their fundamental sense of insecurity served in the end only to heighten it. The preservation of humanity was at risk in the modern world of technological production and commercial exchange as it had never been before. To save themselves, Rilke suggested, human beings would have to turn back from their scientific confrontation with the world to the inner truth of the heart which was, as Pascal had urged in opposition to Descartes, deeper than that produced by the calculating spirit of geometry. Turning inward, human beings would face their own mortality; and accepting that mortality, they would be re-integrated into the world of becoming. By turning inward, they would also recapture the immediacy of sensual perception. Rather than dissolve all specific forms of existence into calculable units, they would once again be able to cherish the particular things and places which constituted their lives as mortals and thus, for the first time, achieve a kind of security in feeling that they were truly at home in the world.

According to Rilke, the poet was the 'angel' (literally, messenger) who announced the urgent need *(Not)* for a turn in destitute times. Because he retained a metaphysical understanding of Being as the Being of the beings, however, Rilke continued to understand both the need and the 'turn' itself in completely subjective terms.[78] *The* poet who, Heidegger thought, understood both the urgent need and the role of the poet in responding to it historically (and thus essentially or properly) was Friedrich Hölderlin.[79]

Hölderlin saw that human beings dwell "poetically . . . on this earth." To say that qua *human* beings people live poetically is, Heidegger explained, to recognize, first, that they inhabit a specific place. Because there is no reason for them to live in this, as opposed to any other habitable location, their existence rests upon an impenetrable 'ground'. The dimensions of human existence are not only spatially defined, however; they are also temporally bounded. The poet shows "man" his "measure," when he looks up into the sky in the hope of receiving lightning signs from the godhead, hidden behind the clouds. Human knowledge of both self and world depend upon recognizing its limits. From a particular place, at a particular time, vision is necessarily restricted; human beings themselves are not, moreover, the source of light.

The interrelation or order of things in the opening created by the interplay of the 'fourfold'—earth and sky, gods and men—is articulated and so exists only in language.[80] As languages vary from time to time and place to place, so do the worlds in which humans find themselves. The poet is able not merely to span, but to articulate the dimensions of human existence, because he is, as a poet, particularly concerned with the use of language. Their concern with language enabled poets like Hölderlin, Stefan Georg, and Georg Trakl to perceive the peculiar problem in modern times, Heidegger observed: words are lacking.[81] Poets can no longer name things as they work in the context of a world and so preserve them, because the gods no longer show themselves. When everything is reduced to mathematically calculable units, there are no longer any particular forms of being through which Being can disclose itself indirectly to "man." There is no longer a spatio-temporally defined world or opening in which he can "dwell."

Whereas Plato ended the *Republic* by reminding his readers of the ancient quarrel between poetry and philosophy, in his late works Heidegger concluded that poetry and thought *(muthos* and *logos)* said the 'same', although in entirely different ways, wholly independently of one another.[82] In suggesting that poets disclosed the truth as well as, if not better than, thought, Heidegger disagreed not only with Plato but also with Nietzsche, who had declared there was a "raging discord" between art and truth.[83]

Nietzsche encapsulated the truth not merely of modern times but of the history of philosophy, when he declared that it was all a product of revenge—revenge against the unstoppable, uncontrollable passing of time. To overcome the spirit of revenge, however, Nietzsche had urged men to will the 'eternal return of the same'. He did not see that such a return could and would be achieved through the techno-scientific reduction of everything to uniform units of infinite extension in an unending series of moments.[84] What was really necessary to overcome human resentment at the unstoppable passage of time, Heidegger urged, was for human beings to embrace their own temporality.

Human beings could reverse the technological drive which threatened them and everything else with extinction only by beginning to think, as they never had before. 'Thinking' did not consist of the science of logic. As Heidegger had argued from the 1930s onward, logic represented the technical reduction of Platonic and Aristotelian modes of reasoning by the schools these philosophers founded.[85] In the fragments of Heraclitus, *logos* originally referred to the gathering together of everything that lay before "men" and 'letting it' appear or 'be' in speech. As Parmenides indicated, however, the articulation of the order of the world that was given did not suffice. "It is useful both to say *(legein) and* to think *(noein)* that Being is." In order for Being to be, it was necessary for human beings to keep the given as given in mind. The original meaning of thinking *(denken)* was, in Greek as in German and English, closely related to thanking *(danken)*. Such thinking did not consist merely in saying something in exchange or response to what was given; it required man to take everything that had been, was still, and would be in the future 'to heart'. 'Memory' had originally referred to such devoted cherishing or thought *(Gedanken)*, which was, in turn, the true meaning of the re-collection *(Andenken)* Plato had argued constituted the essential nature of human knowledge.[86]

To begin to re-collect a world, Heidegger argued, it would first be necessary to turn away from the re-presentation of all things as ideas introduced into modern philosophy by Descartes to enable human beings not merely to use, but to use up all particular forms of existence by transforming them into 'standing reserve' to be exploited for their own purposes. The first step in achieving such a 'turn' would thus be to return to the ancient understanding of philosophy as *theorein* (which Heidegger pointed out in his *Parmenides* lectures literally referred to the look *[oran]* given in response to the look *[thea]* of the god) and *technē* as the ability to let beings show what they actually were (as opposed to techniques of manipulation).

Merely returning from manipulative to a contemplative stance would not enable human beings to re-collect their existence or world, however. Plato did not know 'the thing'; he understood only the idea. Like all the other Greeks he understood phenomena solely in terms of the way in which they appeared in themselves; he did not understand them in use.[87] To see what a thing like a jug was used for—to pour water or, even better, libations to the gods—was to see that a thing existed and only existed as such in relation to the preservation of a certain way of life in a given historical context or world. That world was constituted by an understanding of the relation or order of things embedded in a particular language. The failure of the Greeks to understand the intrinsic relation between "man" and his world is reflected in their having no word for language.[88]

Understanding beings in terms of their idea, Plato presented various forms of being as objects made by a craftsman according to a mental model.[89] His "idealism" led not only to the Christian 'onto-theological' notion of God as the supreme maker but also, eventually, to the modern scientific attempt to re-make everything according to human notions. "Instead of 'object' [Gegenstand]—as that which stands before, over against, opposite us," Heidegger urged,

> We use the more precise expression "what stands forth" [Herstand]. In the full nature of what stands forth, a twofold standing prevails. First, standing forth has the sense of stemming from somewhere, whether this be a process of self-making or of being made by another. Secondly, standing forth has the sense of the made thing's standing forth into the unconcealedness of what is already present.[90]

Although Plato sought to dis-cover beings as they were in themselves and not to transform them, his formulation of the goal of philosophy or knowledge in terms of ideas contributed to the modern homogenization of all forms of being into mathematically calculable standing-reserve to be transformed at will, because it led later thinkers to ignore the spatio-temporal definition or limits of the intelligible world. Rather than merely seeking to contemplate beings like the Greeks, Heidegger thought his contemporaries needed to come to understand things in terms of their historical origin and context.

In opposition to the empty, infinitely expanding universe ordered by abstract, intellectual concepts that had been posited by Western philosophy and science, Heidegger urged his readers to adopt an explicitly historical understanding of Da-sein. Unless they recognized the temporal and, consequently, fundamentally mysterious essence of intelligible existence or Being, human beings would not take what was given to heart as such. Only on the basis of an explicitly poetical, antiscientific understanding of the world would they cherish and preserve all things in their complex practical interrelations rather than seek to transform them, both theoretically and practically.

Compared to the dehumanizing alienation and exploitation, standardization and pollution characteristic of contemporary industrial society, Heidegger's homey world initially looks very attractive. Upon reflection, however, we see that his turn away from the technological results of metaphysics leads him to embrace an entirely tradition-based world.[91] Founded on explicit denial of the existence of any eternal or universally valid truths, this world would have no philosophy or science. There would be no moral principles applicable to human beings as such, although there would be mores or customs.[92] Although thought and poetry would be needed to help people recollect the origin and beauty of their way of life, there would, strictly speaking, be no innovation or creation. (Nor would there be much criticism; there would only be devotional appreciation.) Articles of use would be crafted and buildings erected, but there would be no scientific discoveries or technological inventions. Production would occur primarily for domestic consumption; there would be little commerce with (or challenge from) other countries.[93] Rather than a means of calculation, mathematics would once again become a leisured activity *(skola)* as it had been in ancient Greece. Most important of all, there would be no politics in the modern sense. According to Heidegger, the power-seeking we have attributed to human "nature" belongs only to the philosophically defined world of the West.

Heidegger's view of "man" and his world was not always so pacific. In *Being and Time* he argued that the truth had to be "violently wrested" from the impersonal emptiness of everyday speech. Likewise, in his first analysis of "The Origin of the Work of Art," he suggested that its truth emerged in the opening created by the *strife* between earth and world. And in describing the tragic view of human life that arose with Greek philosophy in his *Introduction to Metaphysics,* he argued that the essential character of both human life and cosmos was disclosed through the violent opposition between the *technē* with which "man" challenged the constituting order *(dikē)* and the over-powering force with which it finally subdued him.

Heidegger came to see, however, that emphasizing both the historical character of human existence and the foundation of all order in force brought his own thought rather close to Nietzsche's teaching that everything was essentially will to power and that all forms of order were merely human projections. There was a fundamental difference between the positions of the two German philosophers, but it took Heidegger some time to work the grounds and implications of that difference out. Nietzsche's suggestion that human beings could, consciously or unconsciously, impose whatever order they wished on the world contradicted all human experience. It also required Nietzsche, contrary to his own protestations, to posit a subject not merely separate from, but at least potentially superior to, all other forms of objective existence. In opposition to both notions, in *Being and Time* Heidegger argued that human beings understood their existence only in terms of a world, in which they *found* themselves, into which they were thrown, which they did *not make.* Discovering the ultimately groundless character of their own *Dasein*, they might resolutely project their past into an unknown future. What they projected was not their own creation, however; it was the way of life they had acquired from the people with whom they lived, a people who had, in turn, inherited their understanding and practices in the form of customs and, especially, language from their ancestors. Given its historical structure, that way of life would inevitably change in the future;

but the direction or character of the change was not and never would be under human control.

In the 1930s Heidegger generalized the relation of essential opposition, mutual dependency between "man" and his world he had described in *Being and Time* to the truth about the whole produced by the 'ontological difference' between Being and the beings. By pointing out the unbridgeable cleft or abyss at the core of all intelligible existence, Heidegger thought that he had finally overcome the tendency of all previous metaphysical philosophy to reduce Being to a form-less sub-stance that had been taken to its logical extreme in Nietzsche's doctrine of the will to power. 'Resolution' in the face of an unknown future had something in common with Nietzschean will, Heidegger recognized.[94] Rather than urge supermen to impose their values on the world, however, Heidegger argued that *the* distinctive character of historical human existence lay in its openness to what was and always would be essentially other, unknowable and unconquerable. *The* danger confronting his contemporaries lay in the possibility that they would succeed in transforming themselves along with everything else into mere material to be technologically manipulated at will. In the wake of World War II Heidegger thus stressed the importance of receptivity, 'letting be', and listening rather than commanding, acting, and innovating in order to avoid the destructive consequences of the unlimited search for power Nietzsche had seen was characteristic of the modern world.[95]

Heidegger's thought after *Being and Time* was shaped essentially by his confrontation with Nietzsche.[96] That opposition comes to light in their different understandings of philosophy, in general, and of Plato, in particular, as its founder. Whereas Nietzsche argued that philosophy consisted fundamentally of moral legislation and suggested that Plato with his philosopher-kings and their noble lies constituted the example par excellence, Heidegger presented both Plato and Nietzsche as thinkers who best articulated the truth of Being as it appeared at their respective times.

The increasing passivity of Heidegger's reaction to the will to power leads us finally to ask: Just as Nietzsche failed to overcome Plato, because in reversing Platonism, Nietzsche maintained the same intellectual structure, did Heidegger not fail to overcome Nietzsche by simply opposing or reversing him? Convinced that Heidegger's initial objection to Nietzsche was correct, that the order human beings perceive in the world is not merely or solely their own unconscious construction, projection, or creation, even though it is disclosed in an historical fashion, later commentators like Hans Georg Gadamer, Jacques Derrida, and Leo Strauss have questioned Heidegger's account of the history of philosophy, its beginning in Plato and its conclusion in Nietzsche. They have challenged Heidegger's assertion that philosophy was originally neither moral nor political. In maintaining that philosophy was and continues to be essentially moral or political, however, they have had not merely to reconceive the nature of philosophy. They have also had to redefine the meaning of both morality and politics. Heidegger did, therefore, inaugurate a new beginning, if not exactly the kind of new beginning he himself intended.

Three

Gadamer's Path

From Heidegger to Plato

Hans-Georg Gadamer generously recognized his intellectual debt to Martin Heidegger both frequently and explicitly. For example, when *Plato's Dialectical Ethics* was reissued in 1982, he explained in the foreword:

> Although the researches of Paul Natorp, Nicolai Hartmann [and] Julius Stenzel..., Werner Jaeger, Karl Reinhardt, and Paul Friedländer ... stood behind his initial effort..., he felt himself to be the first reader of Plato who sought to approach a classical text in the spirit of Husserl's phenomenological motto, "to the things themselves." That he dared to do so was a result of the influence Martin Heidegger had exercised on him during his Marburg years.[1]

Gadamer had been particularly impressed by Heidegger's reading of Aristotle; at the time, he later admitted, he did not understand that in giving his thorough, highly original and apparently sympathetic interpretation Heidegger was merely laying the foundation for a radical critique.[2]

Pursuing his own studies of Plato and Aristotle, Gadamer gradually separated himself from his mentor. In the preface to *The Idea of the Good in Platonic-Aristotelian Philosophy* he thus stated:

> The philosophical stimuli I received from Heidegger led me more and more into the realm of dialectic, Plato's as well as Hegel's. . . .[3] In the background was the continuous challenge posed for me by the path Heidegger's own thought took, and especially by his interpretation of Plato as the decisive step toward "metaphysical thought's" obliviousness to being *(Sein)*. My elaboration and project of a philosophical hermeneutics in *Wahrheit und Methode* bear witness to my efforts to withstand this challenge theoretically.[4]

Although Gadamer acknowledged that "Heidegger's description and existential grounding of the hermeneutical circle . . . constitute[d] a decisive turning point" in the development of his own 'philosophical hermeneutics' or 'historical dialectic', he recognized that his own understanding of both philosophy and history was fundamentally different.[5] Having concluded that philosophy had come to an end in Nietzsche, Heidegger had gone back to its origins in Plato to discover the sources of the limitations of metaphysics so that he could overcome them. Gadamer's reading of Plato had convinced him, on the other hand, that

> Philosophy is a human experience that remains the same and that characterizes the human being as such, and that there is no progress in it, but only participation. That these things still hold, even for a civilization like ours that is molded by science, sounds hard to believe, but to me it seems true nonetheless.[6]

This understanding of philosophy led him to disagree with Heidegger about the fundamental character of politics, history, art, and language as well.

PHILOSOPHY AS A WAY OF LIFE

GADAMER'S DEPARTURE FROM HEIDEGGER

Gadamer's initial analysis of *Platos dialektische Ethik* in the habilitation thesis he wrote under Heidegger's direction clearly bore the marks of his mentor's influence.[7] In the person of Socrates, Gadamer emphasized, Plato presented philosophy not as a doctrine or theory so much as a form of human existence.

> Plato's dialogues are as little philosophical treatises as the elenchtic disputes which made Socrates half laughable, half hateful to his contemporaries. They are first grasped in their own intention if they are understood as introductions to the existence-ideal of the philosophers, the life of pure theory.

Like Heidegger, and unlike Nietzsche, Gadamer insisted there was no fundamental difference between Socrates and Plato.[8] In his dialogues, Plato attempted to recapture in word what Socrates achieved in deed.

> Plato taught a philosophical ethic as little as a philosophical discipline. That makes Plato a Socratic and Socrates the form in which Plato expressed his own philosophical intention. His literary works repeat the completely unliterary, undogmatic existence of Socrates in literary form.[9]

Like both his predecessors, Gadamer thought the philosophic way of life represented by Socrates revealed the fundamental character of human existence as a whole. Just as Heidegger urged that human being exists and can be understood as such only in relation to Being, which always remains beyond it, so Gadamer pointed out, in Socrates Plato presents philosophy as the search for wisdom, never the possession of it.[10] In Plato *philo*-sophy is, nevertheless, shown to constitute the highest possibility of human existence. "That means, however, that human being is not enclosed within itself."[11]

Like Heidegger, Gadamer concluded, Plato (in contrast to Aristotle) understood the essentially open-ended character of human existence. "Platonic philosophy . . . not only conceives itself as on the way to conception [rather than as the clarification of concepts] but also knows man as one underway and in between."[12]

In opposition to Heidegger, however, Gadamer's study of the Platonic dialogues, in general, and the *Philebus*, in particular, convinced him that there was no decisive break between man's original, more practical or concernful involvement with things in his world and fundamentally detached, theoretical observation of things in themselves.[13] On the contrary, Gadamer urged, the major point of the Socratic dialogues is to show that human beings need to know what is really and truly good—in order to be able to satisfy their everyday desires and concerns. As Socrates points out in the *Republic* (505d), people may be satisfied with the appearance of nobility or justice; but no one wants what is only apparently good. In direct opposition to Heidegger's insistence that there was nothing ethical or moral about Plato's Idea of the Good, Gadamer argued, this metaphysical concept emerges directly out of the practical concerns dramatized in the Socratic dialogues. Rather than represent a break from man's concernful circumspection of (or involvement with) his world, theory constitutes a necessary extension of it. Contrary to his mentor, Gadamer thus concluded, both the doctrine and the practice of philosophy as originally presented by Plato are essentially ethical. As Plato shows in each and every dialogue, the pursuit of wisdom has a formative or educational effect.

Both the essentially open-ended and ethical character of Platonic philosophy are reflected, Gadamer observed, in its dialectical form. Whereas in *Being and Time* Heidegger declared that the dialectic was a "philosophical embarrassment" which had fortunately been quickly superseded by Aristotle,[14] Gadamer thus argued that dialogue was an essential feature not merely of philosophical inquiry but of human social life as well. Indeed, as Hegel saw, it formed the core of human historical existence.

Heidegger never fully appreciated the meaning of Plato's Idea of the

Good, Gadamer later suggested, because he read Plato too much in terms of Aristotle's critiques. In the *Nichomachean Ethics* Aristotle faulted Plato's Idea of the Good because it failed to provide human beings with practical guidance in making decisions, that is, because it severed theory from practice. In the *Metaphysics* he faulted Plato's theory of the ideas in general for unnecessarily separating the idea from the thing. (In a sense, Gadamer observed, Heidegger extended both criticisms to the history of philosophy as a whole.)[15]

Aristotle did not misunderstand Plato, Gadamer insisted. In attempting to clarify Plato's conceptions, however, Aristotle transformed Platonic philosophy understood as the search for wisdom into metaphysics and a science of ethics. As a result, both Plato's understanding of the way in which the practical concerns of human life pointed toward an investigation of that which would always remain beyond them, that is, Plato's understanding of the essentially open-ended character of human existence, and Plato's sense of the "light" in which and through which beings were disclosed as such, were lost.[16] To recapture an original, pre-theoretical view of human existence as it was illuminated by philosophy it was not necessary, as Heidegger had urged, to turn to the pre-Socratic philosophers, tragedians, or Homer; such a view was to be found in Plato—and only in Plato—because in his depiction of Socrates Plato rooted philosophical investigations in the concerns of everyday practical life.

On the Relation between Theory and Practice and the Primacy of the Good

Responding to the Aristotelian criticisms that shaped Heidegger's (mis)-understanding of Plato, Gadamer observed, Aristotle often over- or even misstated the positions of others in order to make his own argument clear.[17] Careful consideration of Plato's articulation of the Idea of the Good in the *Republic* as well as his exposition of the ontological grounds of the theory of ideas in "later" dialogues like the *Sophist* and *Parmenides* shows that he never had the patently absurd concept of a world of ideas existing somehow in complete separation from things.[18]

According to Gadamer, the problematic attempt to date the Platonic dialogues has obscured the substantive development of thought implicit in the relation of the three identifiably different types. In "early" refutational dialogues like the *Laches* or *Euthyphro*, Socrates raises questions about the character and definition of specific virtues like courage or piety without coming to a decisive conclusion about what they are singly, much less how the virtues are related to each other, how they are all somehow knowledge, and so how they are one as well as many. Although these conversations do not generate any specific doctrine, they do perform several very important functions. First, they show how the question of what is truly good for human beings and thus what is good in itself arises from the practical concerns of everyday life. Second, these dialogues demonstrate not only that the given or customary answers to these questions are not tenable, but also that human beings will never know or attain what is truly good until they are shown that they do not actually know (as they think they do) what is good. Like the *Protagoras*, these conversations not only demonstrate the inadequacy of pleasure as a definition of the good; they also illustrate the need for philosophy. Socrates' signal discovery (which distinguished him from the "pre-Socratics") was not merely that human beings claimed to have knowledge they did not possess, but that they recognized their ignorance only when asked to justify themselves. Forced to defend their chosen way of life, they saw such a defense rested on a claim about what is good.[19]

Because Socrates suggests that human excellence consists in some kind of knowledge, the question arises in the *Protagoras* and the *Meno* whether virtue is teachable. Somewhat surprisingly, Socrates concludes in both dialogues that it is not. The point, Gadamer suggests, is that the knowledge required to make good choices does not have the character of an art or *technē* like carpentry, medicine, or navigation—to use examples of which Socrates was fond. The kind of knowledge that makes human beings virtuous has more the character of the *phronēsis*, the practical judgment that Aristotle also contrasted with *technē* in his *Nichomachean Ethics*. In opposition to Aristotle, however, Plato clearly thought this *phronēsis* had a theoretical aspect or component.[20]

In the dialogues of Plato's so-called middle period, Gadamer acknowledges, Socrates clearly assumes a new role. As in the *Republic*, he no longer simply reveals the inadequacies of accepted notions; he puts forward a positive doctrine about the meaning of justice. But in arguing that no polity will be just until it is ruled by a philosopher-king, Plato insists even more emphatically than he had in the "earlier" Socratic conversations that practical wisdom is inseparable from theoretical knowledge.

As in the early, elenchtic dialogues, Gadamer emphasizes, so in the *Republic*, the discussion begins with a question about what is good in human life: why should a man be just? To answer this question, Socrates suggests, they have to determine what justice is; and in Book IV, he characteristically concludes that like the other "Platonic" cardinal virtues, justice consists in a kind of knowledge.[21] At this point no mention is made of "the good." Only when Socrates proceeds at the end of Book VI to ask what sort of education philosophers will need in order first to bring the just polity into being and then to maintain it does he introduce the Idea of the Good.

The presentation of the Idea of the Good in the *Republic* is problematic, however, for three different reasons. First, as Socrates emphasizes, his interlocutor does not understand what he is talking about. Glaucon expects the knowledge rulers need to possess to have the character of a *technē*—general rules which are applied to particular circumstances on the basis of experience. But, as Socrates makes clear in the image of the divided line, the Idea of the Good does not have the character of a *technē*. Because knowledge of the Good is what is presupposed by all arts or forms of learning—they must ultimately be good for something—the Idea of the Good constitutes the last, although the most important knowledge human beings can attain; and they can attain it, apparently, only through an examination of the unexamined presupposition of all other forms of knowledge.

Second, at the end of Book VI, the relation between what would appear to be a purely theoretical understanding of the Good-in-itself and the practical responsibilities of rulers remains perfectly unclear. That relation is the major point of the famous cave scene which shows that, to a man who has experienced both, the theoretical life is clearly preferable to the practical. Philosopher-kings return to the cave only because they are forced to. The question nevertheless remains, what is it about the possession of purely theoretical knowledge that makes a philosopher singularly qualified to rule? The answer, Gadamer suggests, is to be found by reflecting on the character of the education Socrates recommends in the following discussion. Although knowledge of mathematics is useful for waging war, as Socrates reminds Glaucon, the purpose of the mathematical education Socrates now describes is not primarily utilitarian. Its function is rather to turn souls from sensory involvement to contemplation of the purely noetic. This turn—the importance of which Heidegger stressed in his reinterpretation of this famous section of the *Republic*—is important not only for epistemological but also for ethical reasons.[22] Only those things which always remained the same could be known, Plato recognized. And only those human beings who adhered steadfastly to, by seeking knowledge of, things which always remained the same would be able to resist the flattery of sycophants, because they would not be satisfied with mere opinion, they would only value truth. In Socrates' description of the mathematical education of the guardians, the requirements of morality and knowledge (or ethics and science) are thus perfectly conjoined.

THE GROUNDS AND LIMITATIONS OF SOCRATIC DIALECTIC

What kind of knowledge was it, however, that the guardians were to seek? As Socrates made clear, the guardians' mathematical training was only preparatory. Having learned (in contrast to the Pythagoreans) to distinguish the eidetic structure of mathematics from its material use and manifestations, the guardians were prepared to ascend from calculations of the logical consequences of certain basic ideas like equality to a dialectical investigation of the nature and relation of the ideas themselves. The investigation of the ideas themselves had to be dialectical, Gadamer suggested, because as Plato argued more explicitly in his "late" work, the *Sophist,* that which always remained the same as itself (corresponding to his earlier definition of an idea or being) could only be known as 'same' in contrast to the different. If that were the case, single ideas could not be recognized or known as such in themselves; they could be known only in relation to others. Whereas Socrates had said in Book VI that, as the source of both intelligibility and being, the Idea of the Good was beyond being, in Book VII he thus spoke of the Idea of the Good as the 'idea of the ideas', that is, as the eidetic structure or articulation of the ideas that made them what they were, purely intelligible. Because no idea was intelligible in itself apart from that unifying structure, Plato made clear in the *Parmenides,* Being could not be understood simply or consistently as one or as many.

For Plato as much as for Heidegger, Being was inseparable from, and did not manifest itself except and indirectly through, the beings. But in Plato this insight did not result, as it had in Heidegger, in a down-playing of ethics as a subfield of metaphysics. On the contrary, Plato's insight into the inescapable and continuing grounds of possible confusion led him to stress the importance of intention or attachment to the good-in-itself (as opposed to acquiring the power to achieve it) which he dramatized in his depiction of Socrates.

Because ideas were intelligible only in relation or opposition to one another, Plato saw, any single proposition or claim could be refuted. The ontological ground of the possibility of philosophy was, in other words, necessarily and always a ground for the possibility of sophistry as well. Externally viewed, he showed in the *Sophist,* the philosopher and the sophist were virtually indistinguishable.[23]

Because he began by refuting his interlocutors, Socrates was easily mistaken for a sophist. The difference between Plato's hero and his predecessors lay in their respective intentions. Whereas the sophists sought to establish their superiority by refuting their opponents and Eleatics like Zeno attempted to refute their critics by demonstrating the contradictory consequences of their assertions, Socrates engaged others in dialogue in order to come to an agreement and thereby bring out the truth about things.[24] Because differences in intention are neither visible or audible as such, it was impossible to show the difference between sophistry and philosophy except by dramatizing the different effects in the life of Socrates.[25]

In the autobiographical account Socrates gives of the development of his own thought in the *Phaedo,* he stresses the importance of intention and his almost single-minded insistence on discovering what is good. As a youth, Socrates admits, he had engaged in the materialistic analysis of nature characteristic of the so-called pre-Socratic philosophers. But he found all attempts to explain things by analyzing them into their component parts unsatisfactory, because he saw no such analysis could ever explain *why* things were as they were. Hearing that Anaxagoras taught that mind *(nous)* was the ultimate cause of everything, Socrates hoped that he had at last found an answer. But he discovered that Anaxagoras also explained all forms of existence in terms of an unending series of relations or differences. The question, why, could only be answered with a statement or argument showing that it was good. For example, Socrates observed, it was impossible to explain solely on the basis of an analysis of his old flesh and bones why he remained in Athens to take his punishment rather than fleeing to Megara without taking account of the reasons why both he and the Athenians thought it good for him to stay.

As a result of his discovery of the primacy of the Good, Socrates turned from the physical investigations characteristic of his predecessors to the examination of the *logoi* for which he became famous. But, Gadamer insists, this turn from the study of the things themselves to an examination of what was said about them did not represent a stepping back or settling for a second best. Socrates' turn to the *logoi* arose from his perception that as ever changing and changeable, sensory perceptions were per se unintelligible. To make sense of the world, we have to discover the things or aspects which stay the same; and, he saw, the enduring similarities among things are captured and expressed first and foremost in words.

As Socrates recognized in his conversation with *Theatetus,* there was a difference between the name and the thing. (This difference was responsible for the gradual emptying out of meaning in everyday speech, according to Heidegger; and Gadamer's analysis in *Plato's Dialectical Ethics* was written under Heidegger's direction.) Nevertheless, Gadamer insisted, because sensory perception was essentially transitory and relative, Socrates thought human beings had no choice, if they wanted to discover an intelligible order, but to investigate the soundness of their opinions by comparing their understanding of the meaning of things (i.e., words and arguments) with those of others. The agreement Socrates sought was not, therefore, merely between word and thing; it was primarily an agreement between the human beings taking part in the conversation about the way in which they viewed the things they confronted.[26] There was always potentially a difference between word and thing and hence an opportunity for mere conventional agreement on the meaning of words as well as sophistic contradiction. In putting forth the idea as an hypothesis, Socrates was not, as Heidegger suggested, introducing a correspondence theory of truth. In seeking the intelligible grounds of the persistent similarities we perceive, Socrates was attempting to come to an agreement with others about the truth of things as Heidegger had defined it, that is, how they appeared in light of a shared understanding of the whole.

The dialectical investigations in which Socrates engaged his interlocutors were both literally and in principle unending. Because, as Plato made clear in "late" dialogues like the *Sophist*, *Parmenides*, and *Philebus*, the ideas themselves could be known only in relation, if not opposition to each other, any single proposition or claim could be refuted. Its truth depended upon its place or position in a larger context. The finitude of human existence and hence knowledge made it impossible, however, for any individual to consider all the possibilities simultaneously and so to comprehend the whole. Each claim, especially concerning the whole or what is good in itself, thus had to be reconsidered, with new interlocutors in different contexts. In contrast to both Nietzsche and Heidegger, Gadamer, therefore, initially thought that Plato's depiction of Socrates' mode of proceeding was much more significant than any doctrine that might result.

PHILOSOPHY AS THE BASIS OF COMMUNITY

If the purpose of Socratic dialectic was to bring people to agree on the same view of things, Socratic dialogues not only depended upon but also themselves constituted a certain kind of community. Not surprisingly, then, Gadamer's initial study of *Plato's Dialectical Ethics* led him during the next decade to undertake a more extensive examination of the dialogue in which Socrates himself investigates the grounds and character of the best possible human community.

In both "Plato and the Poets" (1934) and "Plato's Educational State" (1942) Gadamer argued that Plato's *Republic* should not be read as a programmatic statement for practical political reform. Both in his autobiographical *Seventh Letter* and his most famous dialogue Plato insisted that a just polity would become possible only when philosophers became rulers, because a philosophic education is *the* prerequisite for political reform. To act in politics, he observed in the *Seventh Letter*, it is necessary to have allies. But he saw, all the men and cities around him were hopelessly corrupt. To bring a better form of polity into existence, it would be necessary to form or reform a group of people to constitute and govern it. He himself thus turned away from direct political action to writing dialogues. The primary purpose of these dialogues must, therefore, be understood to be educational. "One misses the full seriousness and importance of [Plato's] requirement [that philosophers become kings] if one takes the projected educational program and ordering of the state literally." In the *Republic*, Socrates himself describes the political association outlined there as existing only "in *logos*." It "is a state in thought, not any state on earth. Its purpose is to bring something to light and not to provide an actual design for an improved order in real political life."[27]

In the *Republic* Socrates proposes to look at justice "writ big" in the city in order to be able to see it better "writ small" in the individual. All the political institutions described in the *Republic* merely represent means of discovering the nature and proper ordering of the various elements of the individual soul (which is, strictly speaking, invisible and, therefore, not merely difficult, but literally impossible to see). This utopia is never presented as a plan for practical political reform. The evolution of the "city in speech" serves rather to reveal the forces within human beings that give rise to their distinctively political existence.

> The "city of pigs" . . . [with] which Plato [begins] . . . in which peace and pacifism are automatically present because each in doing what is right and necessary for all does what is just . . . is no genuine ideal for mankind. . . . Since it is without history, it is without human truth.

Precisely because they are not content with satisfying their physical needs, Plato shows, human beings are not merely natural creatures. They continually reach out and attempt to transcend the limitations of their bodily existence and present circumstances. Their desires bring them into conflict with one another and the need for warriors which arises as a result of that conflict gives rise to a "new, specifically human phenomenon: political existence."[28]

In contrast to the residents of the first, vegetative state, the warriors are not said to be suited by nature to practice one and only one art. Their skill is neither uniform nor productive. On the contrary, Socrates shows, to be effective guardians, human beings must have two-sided natures and two different kinds of ability. They must not only be willing and able to fight; they must also know whom to fight (and for what). They must be able to distinguish friend from foe (and right from wrong). In other

words, they must be both spirited and philosophic. The two-sided education Socrates proposes in "music" and gymnastics is designed to achieve
a balance between these two apparently opposed tendencies.

> It is the goal of education to . . . keep the human being from becoming
> either a tame herd animal (a slave) or a rapacious wolf (a tyrant). For the
> potential of the human being to be a human being among other human
> beings, in short, to be a political being, depends upon this unification of
> the philosophical and martial nature in him.

Although Socrates is, strictly speaking, describing the education of the
guardians, the problem they represent constitutes the problem (and thus
points to the definitive character) of human existence as a whole.

> This potential for political existence is not given to man by nature, for even
> if both these elements are natural and necessary, man becomes a political
> being only insofar as he resists the temptations of power (Cf. Alcibiades,
> Republic 492 ff.). This means, however, that he must learn to distinguish
> the true friend from the false one and what is truly just from flattering
> appearances. It is philosophy which makes such distinguishing possible, for
> philosophy is loving the true and resisting the false. Thus philosophy is
> what makes man as a political being possible.[29]

Rather than political order and freedom constituting the precondition for
the development of philosophy, in the Republic philosophy is thus shown
to be the necessary precondition or means of achieving a just political
order.

Since the purpose of Socrates' sketch of the city in speech is to show
what justice is and why it is choiceworthy in and of itself for an individual, we are not surprised to see that the order of the three classes in the
city becomes the model or a reflection of the proper ordering of the three
parts of the human soul and that justice consists in each performing its
function. What is more surprising is to see that the conversation does not
end with the seeming answer to the question at the end of Book IV, but
that the conversation continues with the question whether justice so defined is actually possible. It continues, although Plato does not say so
explicitly, because the question as to what justice means has not been
fully answered.

> Plato himself noted the preliminary nature of his extrapolation from the
> classes in the state to the parts of the soul (435d). . . . The description of
> the philosophical education of the rulers which follows is indeed the elabo-
> ration of a point in the pedagogical program of the state which had re-
> mained ill-defined. . . , but in essence it is much more than that.[30]

Because the parts of the soul (like the classes of the city) naturally tend
to separate and oppose each other, justice can be established and main-

tained only by a person who sees the order, that is, the proper relation of the parts to the whole, and acts on the basis of that knowledge to institute and preserve it. If they are to be just, rulers must, therefore, become philosophers.

Because the relation between the parts and the whole is by no means obvious or self-evident, it requires a certain kind of art both to see it and to enable others to see it as well. That was precisely the character of the art Plato himself practiced.

> It is fundamentally impossible to say what the true philosopher is without first focussing . . . on that which the philosopher *sees*. Even the description of a philosophical education is not possible without simultaneously experiencing this philosophical education as the directing of one's vision to "true being."[31]

By describing the philosophical education through which a just city can be brought into being, Socrates provides Plato's brothers Glaucon and Adeimantus with such a philosophical education; and by describing Socrates' conversation for his readers, Plato provides them with such an education as well.

Plato's dramatization of Socrates' conversations might seem to fly in the face of the radical critique of poetry Socrates gives in the *Republic*. But Gadamer argues, "the critique of poetry here is simultaneously a justification for Plato's writing."[32] If we read the *Republic* carefully, we see that Socrates did not, in fact, banish all poetry from his city. Poets who did not present corrupting images of gods and men, poets who did not seek to deceive their auditors with their imitations would be allowed. Plato's dialogues were designed to achieve the educational function works of the muses or "music" traditional Greek poetry failed to perform. The problem with older poetry was not simply that it did not inculcate virtue because it presented its auditors with bad examples by showing both gods and men acting in an immoral fashion. (In criticizing Homer for presenting corrupting images, Socrates was merely echoing the criticism of previous poets and philosophers.) By depicting acts of passion as the subjects of noble tragedies or hilarious comedies, Plato suggested in Book X, Greek poets had deceptively claimed knowledge they did not have—not only of the gods and life after death, but also and more immediately of the human soul, that it was essentially desirous and fearful rather than rational. These poets had taught, in effect, that virtue and happiness were always opposed. By arousing their audience's sympathies for the suffering of their heroes, they encouraged their listeners to lose themselves in the imagined feelings and adventures of others rather than to seek self-knowledge and the self-control or self-government, the justice, in other words, such knowledge makes possible. Claiming to acquire their knowledge through inspiration or intoxication, the poets themselves set a bad example of self-forgetfulness.

As Plato observed, "the only poetry which withstands his criticism is hymns to the gods and songs in praise of good individuals." There is still an element of fictional imitation or representation, but in such poems

> Neither the one who praises nor the one before whom the praise is made is forgotten. On the contrary, in praising we articulate the standards in terms of which we understand and evaluate our existence. In essence, then, the song of praise in the form of poetic play is shared language, the language of our common concern.[33]

Poetry educates by reminding people of the moral commitments, the sense of a common good or ethos which binds them together as a community. Where no such unifying ethos or commitment exists, as in the corrupt regimes with which Plato saw himself surrounded (or that in which Gadamer wrote his two essays on the *Republic*), "when justice remains only as an inner certitude in the soul and is no longer to be clearly identified with any given reality, and when knowledge of it must be defended against the arguments of a new 'enlightened' consciousness, a *philosophical discussion* about the true state becomes the only true praise of justice."[34]

Just as such a philosophic discussion constitutes the precondition for political reform, so speeches which induce people to engage in philosophical discussion constitute true poetry. In the *Laws* the Athenian Stranger (whom Gadamer takes to be Plato's spokesman par excellence) thus describes the preludes he drafts to prepare citizens to obey the laws as *the* true poetry.

Although the Platonic dialogues represent real people in conversation, Gadamer concludes, they are not simply philosophical dramas of which Socrates is the hero, nor do they attempt merely to replicate something that happened in the past. The purpose of Plato's depiction of Socrates is to introduce his readers to philosophy. Since philosophy cannot, strictly speaking, be imitated, but only engaged in, there is always something ironic and playful about the depiction. The conversations "say something only to him who finds meaning beyond what is expressly stated in them and allows these meanings to take effect within him."[35]

Gadamer did not explicitly say anything about the relevance of his analysis of Plato's *Republic* to the Nazi regime in which he wrote it. It is not too difficult, however, to see the implicit critique.[36] If philosophical inquiry constitutes *the* only basis of a true community, the regime then in power in Germany was clearly unjust. In "Plato's Educational State,"

Gadamer pointed out the way in which Socrates' response to Thrasyma-chus constituted a critique of power politics simply: "A justice which is postulated and advocated using mere power as its rationalization cannot suffice to explain why what is based on power is valid as *just* and not merely as what is coerced."[37] The entire educational scheme suggested in the *Republic* was intended to show the need to check the temptations of power with philosophy. Rather than justify a totalitarian regime, as Karl Popper later argued, Gadamer thought that the *Republic* demonstrated the necessity of founding political community on a continuous and open inquiry. Having shown that the educational scheme Socrates sketches should not be taken literally as a proposal for political reform, he concluded that it does not represent "authoritative instruction based on an ideal organization at all; rather it lives from questioning alone."[38]

Gadamer remains true to Heidegger in emphasizing the priority of the question (as opposed to the answer or doctrine). The differences not only between the readings of the *Republic* the two German philosophers gave during the same tumultuous wartime years, but also between their understandings of the relation between philosophy and politics are, nevertheless, striking. In his lectures in the early 1930s "On the Essence of the Truth" Heidegger insisted that *agathon* meant useful and that there was, therefore, nothing at all moral about Plato's chief idea; Gadamer continued to maintain that Platonic philosophy was essentially ethical. In the infamous *Rektoratsrede* he delivered in 1934 Heidegger argued that academic freedom was based on an erroneous, superficial conception of both science and liberty and that university education should be subject to political direction and control. In the paper he delivered the same year on "Plato and the Poets," Gadamer argued that open-ended free inquiry, philosophical dialogue constituted the foundation of all true community. Making education subject to political control would undermine the basis of decent politics. Heidegger joined and remained a member of the Nazi party; like his Plato Gadamer stayed out of politics and engaged in philosophical education.[39] Finally, whereas Heidegger suggested that Platonic metaphysics was the origin of the untrammeled will to power celebrated by Nietzsche and embodied in the Nazi regime, Gadamer presented the same philosophy as a necessary antidote to the temptations of power politics.

Neither Heidegger nor Gadamer even noted the connection between *Zucht und Zuchtung* Nietzsche emphasized in the *Republic*. On the contrary, Heidegger criticized the "biologistic" reading of Nietzsche propagated by official Nazi ideologists like Alfred Bäumler; Gadamer treated the breeding proposals in the *Republic* as examples of the exaggerations meant to show the dialogue did not constitute a program for practical political reform. Both Heidegger and Gadamer ignored the content of the "noble lie" in which Socrates suggested it would be good to convince citizens that some were born with better "blood" than others, that is, that the different classes in the city were actually different races. Neither paid any attention to Nietzsche's further contention that in pointing out the need for philosopher-kings to propagate such lies Plato indicated that his own philosophy did not consist so much in a search for truth as in moral legislation.

Gadamer did not think that their obvious political differences were any reason for him to question the Heideggerian framework in terms of which he continued to read Plato. In response to some of the political critiques of his teacher, he observed, "The existential analytic does not, with respect to its own intention, contain any existentiell ideal and therefore cannot be criticized as one (however many attempts may have been made to do so)."[40] What led Gadamer to revise his understanding of the argument in *Being and Time* and to become more self-conscious of the philosophical foundations of his own hermeneutics were Heidegger's lectures on "The Origin of the Work of Art."

ART, HISTORY, AND LANGUAGE

Although the lectures Heidegger gave on "The Origin of the Work of Art" in 1936 were not published until 1954, copies of them circulated widely in Germany much earlier. Like many other students of the early Heidegger, Gadamer was surprised by the 'turn' in his mentor's thought.

In raising the question of the meaning of being, Gadamer observed in an introduction he later wrote for "The Origin of the Work of Art" (which Heidegger himself recommended to readers as giving an important clue to his later writings),[41] Heidegger had intended to show that being could be defined only within the horizon of time. "But his goal of thinking being as time remained so veiled that *Being and Time* was promptly designated as 'hermeneutical phenomenology,' primarily because self-understanding still represented the real foundation of the inquiry."[42] Arguing that the conception of Being as presence characteristic of traditional metaphysics was derivative from the essential temporality of Dasein, Heidegger suggested that the metaphysical notion represented a narrowing abstraction from the concrete, finite, historical *reality* of human existence itself. But this new approach had certain problems or lacunae. As Oskar Becker pointed out,

> Various forms of being that are neither historical nor simply present-at-hand have no proper place within the framework provided by the herme-

neutical phenomenon of self-understanding: the timelessness of mathematical facts, which are not simply observable entities present at hand; the timelessness of nature, whose ever repeating patterns hold sway even in us and determine us in the form of the unconscious, and finally the timelessness of the rainbow of art.[43]

By applying a Heideggerian framework of analysis to Plato's account of the beautiful in the *Philebus* in part 2 of *Platos dialektische Ethik*, Gadamer may have thought he was merely extending it.[44] The extent to which Gadamer had diverged from the path of his mentor's thought becomes obvious, however, if we compare Gadamer's apparent endorsement of Plato's critique of the poets in the paper he gave in 1934 with Heidegger's 1935 lecture on art. Whereas Plato faulted the poets for merely imitating human passions and so presenting an essentially false view of the possibilities of human existence (by excluding the possibility and promise of dialectical philosophy), Heidegger criticized the Platonic view that art consisted merely of imitation. On the contrary, he insisted, "Art is the becoming and happening of the truth," and that, "the nature of art is poetry."[45]

Responding to the challenge posed by this famous 'turn' in Heidegger's thought, Gadamer became much more self-conscious about the philosophical foundation and character of his own hermeneutics. Explicating and defending his own interpretative stance more than two decades later in *Truth and Method*, he stressed its Heideggerian roots. Like his mentor, in Part I Gadamer argued that works of art exemplified the way in which truth was disclosed. Explicitly basing his argument on Heidegger's analysis of Dasein in *Being and Time*, in Part II Gadamer also insisted that all human knowledge was essentially historical. Finally in Part III he concluded, again following Heidegger, that truth was communicated by language as opposed to *logos*. Nevertheless, we shall see, in each case Gadamer also explicitly modified Heidegger's approach on the basis of his own earlier studies of Plato.

Upon examination, Gadamer's argument in *Truth and Method* turns out, indeed, to be a somewhat muted, but nonetheless fundamental critique of Heidegger.[46] Some of the differences are clear from the very beginning. First, whereas Heidegger emphasizes the difference between his 'thought' and the 'metaphysics' which had originated with Plato, Gadamer stresses the elements of continuity. Thus in the *Letter on Humanism* he wrote after World War II Heidegger explicitly distances himself from traditional humanism, whereas Gadamer begins *Truth and Method* with a chapter on the significance of the humanistic tradition. "Heidegger would probably feel a lack of ultimate radicality in the conclusions I draw," Gadamer ruefully concedes in his introduction to the second edi-

tion of *Truth and Method*,[47] Rather than emphasize the nihilistic consequences of the culmination of metaphysics in total technocracy,
he admits, he attempts to bring out the richness of accrued meaning in
the tradition. Instead of bringing philosophy to an end, he wants to
preserve it.

Gadamer's own emphasis on the continuity of the tradition does not,
like Husserl and Heidegger's phenomenology, merely "enlighten the
modern viewpoint based on making, producing, and constructing concerning the necessary conditions to which that viewpoint is subject. . . .
It limits the position of the philosopher in the modern world." Recognizing the essential finitude of human existence, Gadamer insists, a philosopher should not take on the role of Cassandra; he should, on the contrary,
recognize the limits of his own powers.

> What man needs is not just the persistent posing of ultimate questions,
> but the sense of what is feasible, what is possible, what is correct, here and
> now. The philosopher, of all people, must, I think, be aware of the tension
> between what he claims to achieve and the reality in which he finds
> himself.

Rather than recognize the essential limits of human existence in opposition to a Nietzschean will to power, in Heidegger "the will of man is
more than ever intensifying its criticism of what has gone before to the
point of becoming a utopian or eschatological consciousness." Gadamer's
own "hermeneutic consciousness seeks to confront that will with something of the truth of remembrance: with what is still and ever again
real."[48] His more modest understanding of the character and powers of
philosophy is truer to Heidegger's original insight into the significance
of human temporality and finitude than Heidegger's own later thought.

Implicitly following Heidegger's analysis of the essence of the truth,
in *Truth and Method* Gadamer argues that truth does not consist merely
in an agreement between word or idea and thing. Truth emerges from
the disclosure or presentation of being(s) in relation to one another in a
world to a receptive or open human being. Truth is not an enduring possession or property, therefore, but an event (Heidegger's later word for
Being).[49] Each such event has consequences, moreover; it affects the understanding, which is to say, the self-understanding and hence the very
essence of the human being to whom the truth occurs. Like a play, a past
truth or insight can be re-presented to (and so re-conceived by) a present
audience, but its meaning will never be the same because both audience
and time are different. But, Gadamer insists, since the difference in each
and every re-presentation (which presupposes a re-appropriation, that
is, an attempt to make the truth one's own merely by understanding it)

is a result of earlier presentations, the difference between the first or original presentation and later re-interpretations of it does not, as Heidegger had maintained, result merely in loss of meaning or an opposition between an original (authentic or *eigentlich*) experience or poetic "saying" and a later, customary (inauthentic) repetition of the external form of expression.[50]

In arguing that drama could serve as a model of the way in which truth was disclosed to man, Gadamer obviously departed even further from Plato than from Heidegger. Rather than disguise themselves or merely imitate characters in the "real" world, Gadamer now argues, both playwright and actors completely submerge their own identities in presenting another, the completely self-contained world of the play to their audience. This world becomes present for and to the audience, however, only if they, too, lose or forget themselves in their everyday existence by concentrating on the matter at hand. This self-forgetfulness does not have the corrupting effect attributed to it in "Plato and the Poets." On the contrary, Gadamer suggests in a brief and provocative interpretation of the famous cathartic effect of tragedy in Aristotle's *Poetics,* having seen a person suffer more than he or she could possibly expect or deserve, the audience comes away with a "tragic pensiveness." Watching a tragedy does not involve "a temporary intoxication from which one reawakens to one's true being." It arouses a sense in each member of the audience of the fundamental character of his or her life: "What is experienced in such an excess of tragic suffering is something truly common. The spectator recognizes himself and his own finiteness in the face of the power of fate."[51]

Nevertheless, Gadamer emphasizes, there is still something fundamentally Platonic (and, therefore, not purely Heideggerian) about his understanding of art. If a play exists as a play only in being presented, it continues to exist only in re-presentation. Although each and every reproduction is different, there is an enduring core that remains recognizably the same. Whereas in "The Origin" Heidegger argues that a work of art loses its meaning when it is removed from its original location, Gadamer admits that there is a loss when a statue from a temple is put into a museum, but he insists it still retains some of its original meaning. (How else could Heidegger recapture it?)

The truth we perceive in a work of art has something essentially in common with what Plato called *anamnesis* (recollection), Gadamer suggests. The skill or technique displayed in a work of art is always a secondary consideration in our appreciation of it. "What we experience in a work of art and what invites our attention is how true it is—i.e., to what extent one knows and recognizes something and oneself."[52] In recognizing something for what it is, we do not see it as it appears in its everyday existence. We see something more; we recognize its essence or idea as Plato would have it. That idea is not identical with any particular manifestation; it appears only in abstraction or freedom from the particular circumstances. It exists, indeed, only in being recognized.

Works of art are able to reveal the essence of things, because they are imitative. "In imitating, one has to leave out and to heighten." Because imitation involves simplification, there is always a difference between the original and its likeness. "As we know, Plato insisted on this ontological distance . . . between the copy and the original; and . . . placed . . . art as an imitation of an imitation, in the third rank." But, "operative in artistic presentation is recognition, which has the character of genuine knowledge of essence; and . . . Plato considers all knowledge of essence to be recognition."[53]

Art was understood to be imitation, so long as truth was understood to consist in knowledge of the essence. When Descartes changed people's understanding of knowledge, their appreciation of art also became subjectivized. "Once the aporias of this subjective turn in aesthetics have become evident to us," Gadamer argues, "we are forced to return to the older tradition." Heidegger also criticized the modern understanding of art as an expression of subjective experience or *Erlebnis,* but he did not think we should return to the older understanding. On the contrary, his analysis of art constituted an important step in his discovery of a new understanding of truth. In the analysis of art with which he begins *Truth and Method,* we thus see, Gadamer explicitly combines Heideggerian and Platonic insights in such a way as to distance himself more than might initially appear from his mentor. He defends such a combination of present and past thought in the next section as a 'fusion of horizons'.

Using the truth of the work of art as a model, in Part II Gadamer argues that knowledge (or, literally, a science) of human existence cannot be achieved using the methods of natural science; it can only be acquired hermeneutically. Although he explicitly bases his argument on Heidegger's analysis of *Dasein* in *Being and Time,* Gadamer's explication of hermeneutics is quite different. (The difference is underlined, indeed, by the fact that Heidegger completely drops any explicit concern with hermeneutics after *Being and Time,* whereas for Gadamer it retains its central importance.)

Ever since Kant, Gadamer observes, German philosophers had recognized that the techniques of natural science were not adequate for attaining an understanding of human, historical existence. However, those who rejected Hegel's argument that history constitutes the self-realization of reason had not been able to devise another model of knowledge. In *Being and Time* Heidegger overcame the difficulty previous historical thinkers had encountered by showing that understanding was not something people incrementally acquired over time; understanding was an essential characteristic of human existence; science was merely a derivative mode of this primordial being-in-the-world. Heidegger's analysis of the temporal structure of *Dasein* as a projection of the past into the future showed, moreover, that the notion that scientific observers should be purely disinterested, objective, and free from prejudice as well as the notion that truth can be established only by experiments which can be replicated (i.e., in which the particular circumstances, time and place were irrelevant) were fundamentally false to the essential character of human existence.

By recasting the projection of the past into the future as the preservation of a living tradition, however, Gadamer changed the effective thrust of Heidegger's analysis dramatically. In *Being and Time* Heidegger had emphasized the thrown character of human existence: each of us not merely finds him or herself in a particular time, place, family, and nation, but his or her entire existence is defined by these external, inherited conditions—about which he or she had no choice and over which he or she exercises little control. Nevertheless, Heidegger argued, human existence is not essentially determined; by analyzing a fundamental mood like anxiety a person would see that he or she continues to exist only by projecting his or her life into the future, that is, that his or her continued existence is fundamentally a matter of his or her own choice. By consciously choosing to perpetuate his or her existence in the face of future uncertainty, he or she can make it his or her own.

By redefining the preconception of the world in terms of which a person defines his or her existence as tradition, Gadamer both intellectualized and generalized it. Heidegger had argued that a person who authentically understands the historical essence of his existence would see that his fate as an individual is indissolubly bound to the destiny of his people or nation. Gadamer argues that scholars who understand that they have an 'historically effected consciousness' will see that their very attempt to understand the past is a product of, and decisively shaped by, the amalgam of philosophy and scriptural religion which constitutes Western history. In contrast to Heidegger's 'resolution', as he explicates it in his *Rektoratsrede*, there is nothing particularly nationalistic about Gadamer's hermeneutics, although they are explicitly European.[54]

To be sure, the immediate focus of the two books appears to be quite different. In *Being and Time* Heidegger set out to analyze the being for whom its own being is an issue to discover what being more generally or at least its 'horizon' is; in *Truth and Method* Gadamer might appear merely to be setting forth a technique for reading texts. Since the purpose of Gadamer's hermeneutics is to enable people to discover the truth of human existence and Heidegger comes, especially in his later works, to define human existence as the *Da* in which the truth of Being occurs, however, the difference in intent and scope is less than it might seem.

As Heidegger and Gadamer both see it, the world in terms of which human beings understand their existence is temporally limited and defined. Their knowledge has an historical horizon which, Gadamer insists, defines a range of vision; it does not merely constitute a limit. As he points out, the character of a horizon is that it can be progressively expanded. Although a person's view of the world is largely given or received from the past, both Heidegger and Gadamer agree, one can make it one's own, one comes to understand it by reappropriating it, as it were, only by distancing oneself from it. Heidegger thus 'de-structs' received tradition, especially in the history of philosophy, to un-cover its original truth, which he hopes can then be reappropriated along with the history of philosophy in a new mode of thinking or e-vent of Being. Rather than submit texts to such violent Heideggerian readings, Gadamer urges his readers to enter into a dialogue with them.[55] He thus explicitly associates his understanding of both the character of, and the need for, a hermeneutical mediation between past and present with his earlier studies of the distinctive characteristics of Platonic dialectics.

As in a Platonic dialogue, the first principle and purpose of a hermeneutical interpretation of a text is to come to an agreement about the truth of the subject matter in question. But to come to an agreement or understanding, one has to recognize the integrity and independence of the viewpoint of the other. One does not understand the past by looking at it solely in terms of current questions and concerns. One must first try to reconstruct the particular situation in which a past text was written; that is, one must try to recapture the question to which the text represents an attempted response. But, Gadamer adds, so long as scholars seek to understand past works solely in their own terms, as their authors and immediate audiences understood them, that is, so long as present readers fail to ask whether these texts contain truths which remain valid for them living today, these readers do not truly engage either the text or themselves. If one is really to learn anything from a text or a person and so to expand one's own horizon, one has to be open to the possibility that the other view is correct and one's own is wrong. To learn from an historical work we have to ask not simply about the meaning of the text in itself but about its meaning for us. We cannot merely interrogate the text about its meaning; we have to let the text challenge us and our preconceptions.

In attempting to identify concerns addressed by a text which no longer constitute pressing issues for us and so produce a distance between past and present, we cannot forget that we possess knowledge of the work's later effect, knowledge its author could never possibly have. We cannot forget that our own consciousness, the understanding with which we approach the text and try to understand it, is itself historically effected. Like Heidegger, Gadamer argues, it is neither appropriate nor possible for later readers to try to understand texts as their authors understood them. Such attempts (which Gadamer associates with Schleiermacher) involve readers in psychological investigations of the authors' emotions and motives which do not, ultimately, establish anything about the truth of what the authors have written or its historical effect. The truth readers discover when they come to understand past texts will necessarily be different than that the authors of the texts in question had in mind, because the context and the questions later readers bring to the texts will necessarily be different. The understanding of an historical text a later reader achieves will, therefore, constitute a fusion of horizons which differs, because it is more encompassing, from both the original understanding of the author and the reader's own previous understanding of himself and his world.

Such a fusion of horizons does not occur solely in scholarly studies of historical texts, Gadamer emphasizes in Part III. It occurs continuously in everyday human discourse. People cannot come to an agreement or have an understanding unless they can express that understanding in words. *"The fusion of horizons that takes place in understanding is actually the achievement of language."*[56] Because language is so intimately associated with our thought, scholars have only recently begun to appreciate the way in which language constantly mediates between past and present in human existence.

Just as interpreters of historical texts tend not to see the way in which they bring their own present concerns to bear on the text until it refuses to conform to their expectations, so speakers and readers fail to see the way in which their language shapes their thoughts until they have to translate. Languages do not have parallel words for the same things, so it is impossible to communicate the meaning of a speech or writing in one language merely by transposing it word for word into another; the translator has to comprehend the meaning in the original in order to restate it in different words.

Nevertheless, Gadamer emphasizes, the fact that works can be translated demonstrates the ability of human reason to rise above linguistic particularity. Although Gadamer follows Heidegger in arguing that human beings constitute their world in and by means of language, he does not agree that these worlds represent fundamentally different, mutually exclusive "dispensations of Being." Nor does he like the late Heidegger think the major epochs or changes in Western history are marked by the translations of basic terms from Greek to Latin and Latin to French. On the contrary, Gadamer observes, we can learn to think in a different language without losing the ability to speak and write in our own; the worlds so disclosed do not remain separate in our minds. They merge in a broader, richer, more complex understanding.

People have not failed to see the formative role of language merely because it is so intimately connected to human thought and consciousness. They have also been misled by an erroneous theory of language, which understands it merely as a set of signs, that can be traced back to Plato. Although Gadamer implicitly criticizes Heidegger's particularistic understanding of language by reasserting a rather Platonic view of the intrinsic universality of *logos*, he does not therefore merely return to Plato's understanding. On the contrary, he suggests, the Christian concept of 'the word'(the *logos* of the Gospel of St. John translated into Latin as *verbum*) as it was developed by medieval scholastic theologians provides a better basis for understanding the fundamental character of human language (and therewith intelligence) than Greek philosophy. Rather than a union of essentially different elements like the Platonic body and soul, the mystery of the incarnation is that the infinite is united with the finite in God's 'word' or intended meaning, as it were, before that word is uttered or made manifest in flesh.[57] The scholastic doctrine brings out the character of the union of eternal truth with human finitude in the word as an event which occurs in time and acquires depth and resonance through repeated later re-presentations. (Gadamer thus incidentally also points to the unadmitted theological source of Heidegger's poetic understanding of language as well.)

There are, of course, fundamental differences between the divine and the human word. Whereas the divine word is one and eternally present, the human word begins merely as a potential which is actualized only over time. Because their minds are finite and both their experiences and thoughts are, therefore, necessarily sequential, human beings have to use many words, whereas the divine word is one. And because human intelligence is finite rather than infinite, no human word or set of words is ever complete. But, Gadamer points out, the incomplete and therefore open-ended character of the human word means that it is capable of acquiring new meaning—without end. What was traditionally seen as a defect by both Greek philosophers and Christian divines proves, upon reflection, to be an inexhaustible source of richness.

Although Plato understood that human thought was discursive, that human beings could not think except in language and that their intelligence was finite, in his dialectic of ideas he suggested that there was an intelligible order existing independent of, over and above language. His model of intelligibility was numerical rather than lingual. Building on this Platonic foundation, later philosophers like Leibniz thus attempted to set forth an artificial, universal, mathematical language which would replicate the intelligible order.

But, Gadamer argues, the notion that languages merely constitute sets of signs corresponding to independently intelligible ideas or things is false to the fundamental character of human existence, which thinkers since Aristotle have perceived is itself distinguished or defined by language.[58] Because human beings are finite creatures who cannot encompass everything that exists in their minds at once, they learn only from experience. Separated from such an experiential base, abstract symbols do not communicate intelligibly to them.

> Knowledge acquired through these symbols is not clear and distinct, for the symbol gives nothing to the senses to perceive; rather, such knowledge is "blind," inasmuch as the symbol is a substitute for a real piece of knowledge, merely indicating that it could be acquired.[59]

As Aristotle saw, human beings develop both concepts and words to express them by perceiving similarities among objects or events. But such similarities need not be generic. As the nominalists later pointed out, the similarities do not necessarily inhere in the things at all; certain communities may perceive a relation or quality among things—in India, for example, cows are sacred—that reflects the community and its standards more than the things per se. By arguing that the perception of similarities was only the beginning of science, which required classification of things according to genus and species as well as logical proofs, Aristotle deprived the natural metaphoricity of language of its original association with knowledge and made it into a matter of mere rhetoric. The study and use of words became artificially separated from the study of ideas and knowledge of things.

When human beings seek to articulate what they are currently experiencing in words, Gadamer observes, they do not consciously seek to subsume the particular thing they see, for example, under some general concept. They concentrate on the particular thing or event—in all its distinctness—and rummage back into their memories to see whether they can find anything similar. Unless such a similarity is grasped and expressed in a word, the past remains inchoate. But once the word is formulated, it acquires a somewhat different meaning with each and every particular use. As can be seen from any fairly complete dictionary, over time this process generates a considerable variety or varieties of meaning that continue to resonate every time a word is used.

Human beings do not use words merely to articulate their own ideas to themselves, moreover; they use them primarily to communicate what they mean to others. In both articulating and communicating, they use words they have inherited from the past, the meaning of which is to be sure extended, but never simply created de novo or entirely altered, through new applications. Because, as Plato pointed out in the *Sophist*, things can be perceived to be similar in some respects only if they are simultaneously perceived to be different in others, single words or relations become intelligible only in the context of others. Every time a word is used it thus "causes the whole of the language to which it belongs to resonate and the whole world view that underlies it to appear. Thus, every word, as the event of a moment, carries with it the unsaid."[60]

Once we perceive the historical way in which language actually operates, we see that Descartes's attempt to ground knowledge on the *cogito* was fundamentally misguided. There is no conscious thought or individual subject (ego) which exists prior to, or independent of, language. Nor is human knowledge primarily self-reflective. Words are not merely the signs or marks with which we keep track of our subjective impressions any more than they are merely reflections or copies of a preexisting order.

> A word is not simply the perfection of the "species" (Lat.), as medieval thought held. When a being is represented in the thinking mind, this is not the reflection of a pregiven order of being, the true nature of which is apparent to an infinite mind. . . . But neither is a word an instrument, like the language of mathematics, that can construct an objectified universe of beings that can be put at our disposal by calculation. No more than an infinite mind can an infinite will surpass the experience of being that is proportionate to our finitude. It is the medium of language alone that, related to the totality of beings, mediates the finite, historical nature of man to himself and to the world.[61]

What is 'given' to human beings to understand, the 'world' into which they are 'thrown', is, Gadamer concludes, primarily articulated in and based upon what was written down and thus preserved for them in the past. Both as past and as written, that world is initially somewhat alien. It may be taken for granted, but it is not understood. Human beings make themselves at home in the world by applying the concepts and terms they have inherited to new and different circumstances. Such a fusion of past and present occurs without people's noticing it each and every time they use language. In the process new meanings, even new worlds are continually generated.

"Being that can be understood is language."[62] Language is not merely

GADAMER'S PATH   95

the 'house' of Being, as Heidegger had maintained; it is not merely the structure in which intelligible existence becomes manifest and is preserved by means of a 'sheltering' limitation.[63] Language itself is the medium as well as the locus of intelligible existence.[64] There is no mysterious source or ground that is in itself unintelligible.[65]

To say that language is the locus of all intelligibility is to see that all intelligibility is essentially historical. That is to say not only that what is intelligible, the worlds in which human beings live, continually and gradually change over time, but also that this intelligibility is always limited or finite.

In disagreeing with Heidegger about language, Gadamer thus necessarily disagrees with his mentor about the character and meaning of history or temporality in human existence as well. Like Heidegger, Gadamer points out that the beginning of a movement or development can be identified as such only in light of its end or completion. But, Gadamer suggests, if history is essentially open-ended, if both past and present are inseparably tied to an unknown future, history cannot come to an end. Everything is and always will be open to reinterpretation. At most history may cease; it will never be completed. Heidegger was not true to his own insight into the essential temporality of human existence, when he began to speak in terms of an end of history and a new beginning. In making predictions about the future course of human history, he was not true to his own fundamental insight into the significance of man's awareness of the finitude of his own existence and the extent of his possible knowledge.

Heidegger did not give an adequate account of the temporality of human existence, because in emphasizing the way in which human beings project their past into an uncertain future, he neglected the present as the moment of integration. Heidegger was correct when he pointed out that human history does not consist of an unending sequence of undifferentiated nows or moments. The fact that the announcement or discovery of each new truth has the character of an event means, however, that it occurs in a moment, the moment when it becomes present; and that truth is preserved, it continues to exist only through repeated re-presentations in subsequent moments.[66] Had Heidegger described what he himself did in studying past texts more precisely, he would not have said that he was de-structing the tradition so much as re-presenting and so re-viving its inherent truth.[67]

Although in *Truth and Method* Gadamer explicitly acknowledges that Plato did not have a properly historical understanding of language (which Gadamer in contrast to Heidegger identifies with *logos*), in his later works Gadamer nevertheless reaffirms Platonic dialectic as *the* source and model of an understanding of the world that takes account of human finitude. In attempting to bring his interlocutors to an agreement not only with their own opinions but also with him, Socrates emphasizes the need for integration which Gadamer also associates with Hegel. The truth emerges only in the *logoi* or discourse, because the parts can only be understood in light of the whole. But in insisting that all agreements must continually be reconsidered, Socrates in contrast to Hegel explicitly recognized the limits of human knowledge.

ARITHMOS, LOGOS, AND THE INDETERMINATE TWO: GADAMER'S PLATO REVISED

Having moved further away from Heidegger, in his later work Gadamer did not associate Socrates' turn to the *logoi* so much with the truth in names or words as with Plato's investigations of the character and intelligibility of number *(arithmos)* and language. In the preface he wrote for *Plato's Dialectical Ethics* in 1967 he explained that when he wrote the book he had not learned the significance of the Greek concept of *arithmos* from Jacob Klein or seen the importance of the unwritten tradition concerning Plato's teaching.[68] Following "Schleiermacher, who was inspired by the Romantics' emphasis on dialogue as such," the emphasis on the "so-called political Plato" by classicists like Wilamowitz, Friedländer, and Hildebrandt, as well as "Natorp's and Hartmann's rejection of any attempt to evaluate Plato's thought as systematic philosophy," Gadamer thought he had pushed "the basic theme of Plato's doctrine . . . too much into the background" by stressing "the dialogical character of Plato's work and the inherent inconclusiveness and open-endedness of the dialogue."[69] The grounds for Socrates' turn to the *logos* and its realization in a search for knowledge (*philo*-sophy), rather than in the possession of science or wisdom itself, were to be found in the doctrine of the one and the indeterminate two attributed to Plato by Aristotle in his *Metaphysics*.

Klein provided Gadamer with a crucial insight in his analysis of "The Concept of Number in Greek Mathematics and Philosophy."[70] For the Greeks, number *(arithmos)* was always a number of something. One was not a number, therefore; the existence of countable units was a prerequisite for the existence of numbers, but the defining characteristic or principle of unity of any given number was different from that of its component parts or units. And, Klein suggested, this distinction between the character of a unity, which was not shared in by any of the parts, but belonged solely to the whole as a whole, and the characteristics shared by the parts, which made it possible to assemble them into a larger whole, provided the key to understanding Plato's theory of the ideas.

Plato's theory was an elaboration of the Pythagorean teaching that everything in the world could be counted.[71] This notion of counting gave rise to two questions which Plato answered more successfully than his predecessors: First, what is the character of things which makes it possible to count them? In what sense are they units submitted to numeration? Second, in what sense is the number of those things or units in itself a unity? The Pythagoreans answered the second question by sorting all numbers (and, therefore, things) into different types—for example, square, cube, prime, perfect, superabundant—each of which they called an *eidos* (idea). The difficulty, Plato saw, was that such types did not explain the differences among the numbers within them. To clarify the way in which a number constituted a unity of many, it was necessary to consider the character of the units more carefully, that is, to pay more attention to question one. If we can count six stars, six oxen, or six apples, the six is obviously independent of the particular character of the stars, oxen, or apples. The units making up the six are pure units, which are not perceived by our senses, but are conceivable only by our intellect. Turning to the second question, Plato saw that each number constitutes a defined or limited set of such units. Klein suggested that this new, completely eidetic conception of number enables us to understand Plato's doctrine of the participation of particular things in the general idea as well.

The question concerning the character of this participation of the particular thing in the general idea is often raised in Platonic dialogues, Klein observed, in conjunction with a question about the relation between one and two. In describing the quandaries that led him to abandon his studies of nature and to adopt the hypothesis of the ideas in the *Phaedo*, for example, Socrates not only mentions his inability to explain how the things he ate could be transformed into blood and bone, that is, the problem as to how anything, he himself, first and foremost, could remain the same in the face of its ever changing material composition. Socrates also relates his quandary as to how one and one could together make something new and different, that is, two. Likewise in *Hippias Major*

> Socrates asks the sophist Hippias whether he thinks that something which is common to two things may belong to neither of them. Hippias contemptuously rejects this suggestion [by arguing]: "If we, Socrates and Hippias, are *both* just or healthy or wounded, . . . then Socrates is just, healthy, wounded, and Hippias is just, healthy, and wounded. . . ." Accusing Socrates of failing to see "the whole of things," the sophist fails to perceive the way in which his objection may be used against his own position. So Socrates responds, "What you say is true but still we *both* are two, whereas you are I are *each* one and not two."[72]

In the *Sophist*, Klein points out, Being is shown to be identical with neither rest nor motion, but is said somehow to encompass both. The difference between this arithmological conception of Being and the Greek concept of *arithmos* was simply that in the latter case the component units were all the same whereas in the former case the components were different. If Plato's theory of ideas meant that things in the world were organized according to genus and species, each of the species could be one (or have one defining characteristic in common) and yet participate in the genus solely as a constitutive element, lacking the distinctive character of the genus or community as a whole.

If the understanding of Being underlying Plato's theory of ideas had this complex arithmological character, both Klein and Gadamer saw, Platonic philosophy did not have the reductive thrust Heidegger had attributed to it.[73] Gadamer went beyond Klein, however, when he suggested that, as Plato showed in his *Theatetus*, *logos* also had this complex arithmological structure.

> Does not the unity of discourse also have a certain determinate property not found in any of its component parts (letters, syllables, words) and is this not exactly the point? At the conclusion of the *Theatetus* the logos or account which purports to explain something by listing its component parts . . . is reduced to an aporia. . . . Either the syllable consists of the collection of its letters or it is an indivisible unit with its own special property. Here, I suggest, the true relationship of the One and the Many, which gives the logos its structure, is made evident in the analogy of the meaninglessness of the syllable and the dilemma with which it confronts us.[74]

Contrary to Heidegger, Plato showed that number and *logos* or language had the same fundamental structure of intelligibility. In each case the parts had to be understood in terms of a whole that was different from its components taken separately.

> When Plato in transforming the Pythagorean apeiron, discovers in the Two a new categorical version of the earlier Pythagorean concept, he does not just use another word; rather he grasps and defines more precisely what the logos is in essence. Using the Two as a basis, he correlates the intelligible world of the ideas and numbers, sense appearances, and the structure of human knowing; he thereby establishes a splendid system of correspondences. For in spite of its indeterminacy, this Two is the principle of all differentiation and all differing, which is to say that it codetermines reality.

The parallel between the arithmological structure or mixture of the cosmos and *logos* is made even clearer in the *Timaeus* where

> the three ingredients of the world-soul are [said to be] Being, Self-sameness, and Difference (37 a b). On the surface of it, that sounds very

odd, for the latter two are . . . *logical* concepts. . . . But logos is of such a nature that whenever anything is meant by it, that thing is meant as identical to itself and, at the same time, as different from other things. Thus Selfsameness and Difference are always present in anything which is and is recognized as what it is.[75]

Both intellection and motion entail differentiation; so Gadamer argues, both the intelligible and the cosmic order exist and can only exist in time as contemplated by the human mind. "Difference is based upon something's differing from something else. But this sort of differing always implies the emergence of differences not present as such in what is at first undifferentiated." Moreover, "differences which have emerged are simultaneously differences which have been brought out. The emergence of differences implies that the differences have been separated from one another so that they emerge *for* something for which they are different."[76] "To be different," Gadamer thus concludes, "is to be *known* as different."[77]

The unending generation of new numbers through the repetitive process of adding one in counting provides the model for understanding not only the motion of the heavenly bodies (on the basis of which, both Plato and Aristotle point out, human beings calculate time) but also the thought process of the human mind itself. The order human beings perceive in the world is not merely a creation or projection of their mind, as Nietzsche argued. There is, however, no perceptible cosmic order apart or separate from human contemplation.

> Plato can hardly be said to have subordinated the realm of ideas to a divine mind like Leibniz's central monad, in which everything is present which *is* . . . . Plato thinks of the finite, searching human being in terms of the latter's *discrepancy* from the knowing God, and that he does has more than religious significance. It bears on the dialectic as well. . . . Human thinking and knowing can never be complete—any more than anything can which exists on this earth.[78]

All order—be it numerical or 'logical'—not merely is perceived to be but *is* sequential (which is as much as to say it occurs in time), because the human mind is finite. It cannot perceive and compare all possible relations, all possible similarities and differences at once. That is why, in Plato's composite principle of unity, the 'two' is said in the indirect tradition coming from Aristotle to be indeterminate.[79]

In his dialogues Plato shows that the same arithmological structure is to be found in many different realms of existence. Its application and meaning vary, however, according not only to the particular form of existence or idea in question but also to the circumstances, the time, place, and character of those who are investigating it.

Plato did not explicitly articulate an historical account of human understanding. But, Gadamer thought, read in light of the "indirect tradition," Plato's dialogues provided an ontological and epistemological foundation for his own doctrine of the fusion of horizons by showing the arithmological relation of all the differentiated parts to an indeterminate, ever expanding whole.

Gadamer's study of the Platonic dialogues thus led him to conclude, like Heidegger, that philosophy is and was an essentially historical activity, if by historical one means not only changing its content over time but also essentially limited in its scope or range by the fact of human mortality. But, where Heidegger argued that philosophy emerged as a result of a certain dispensation of Being in time and would come to an end with that dispensation, Gadamer's study of Plato convinced him not only that this distinctively human enterprise remains essentially the same over time but also that it is essentially open-ended and hence, in principle, unending. Knowledge of the different parts is possible only in terms of their integration into the whole which exists and is perceived at the present moment. That knowledge must be re-presented, re-collected, and consequently re-vised, however, in subsequent moments in light of the expansion of the horizon of human vision and thus the whole that occurs with the passage of time.

THE POLITICAL IMPLICATIONS

Because he emphasized the continuity of the tradition in opposition to Heidegger and Hegel's 'end of history', Gadamer has been accused of being too conservative. But because, like Heidegger, he maintained that truth changes from time to time, Gadamer has also been charged with relativism.[80]

For example, in a well-known review of *Truth and Method*, Jürgen Habermas asserted, "Gadamer is motivated by the conservatism of that first generation, by the impulse of a Burke that has not yet turned against the rationalism of the eighteenth century."[81] Although Gadamer pointed out (correctly) that human beings never observe things objectively without any predispositions but tend rather to understand new experiences in terms of the inherited categories or ways of thinking imbedded in their language, Habermas thought he did not take sufficient account of the critical powers of human reason. There is a difference between an unexamined prejudice and a considered judgment.

Gadamer responded to the conservative charge by pointing out that an attachment to the tradition by no means proscribes change. "Alteration of the existing conditions is not less a form of connection to tradition than it is a defense of existing conditions." On the contrary, "tradition exists only in constantly becoming other than it is."[82]

The problem with Gadamer's tradition-based hermeneutics, according to Habermas, is not merely that such an approach is inherently conservative; it is too idealistic. Human community is not, as Gadamer suggests, based simply on an understanding or agreement about what is good.

> It makes good sense to conceive of language as a kind a metainstitution on which all social institutions are dependent. . . . But this metainstitution of language as tradition is evidently dependent in turn on social processes that are not reducible to normative relationships. Language is *also* a medium of domination and social power; it serves to legitimate relations of organized force.[83]

Because human life is shaped by the desire for domination and economic necessity in the form of the division of labor as well as by mutual understanding, Gadamer was right to object to Hegel's notion of absolute spirit. Human life will never be entirely reasonable or predictable. But, without a regulative standard of disembodied or ahistorical reason, that is, without projecting an admittedly contra-factual community based solely upon propositions to which all human beings would agree, if they were not in one way or another coerced, Gadamer's historicism makes it impossible to object to the reigning order or regime. His hermeneutics are not merely conservative; they are relativistically anti-revolutionary.

Habermas's critique has evident metaphysical origins, Gadamer responds; it rests, ultimately, on a strong mind-body distinction. Insofar as Habermas suggests that the consensus underlying all actual communities is a product of coercion, the effect of his critical reason becomes simply negative, delegitimizing all existing regimes without providing the basis for an actual or realizable community.

> It seems to me a dogmatic prejudice concerning what one means by human "reason" to always speak in such cases of coercive communications, e.g., where love, the choice of ideals, submissiveness, voluntary superiority or subordination have reached a level of stability. . . . I am not able to see how communicative competence and its theoretical mastery in the social sciences are supposed to eliminate the barriers between groups. . . . In this instance "the gentle power of productivity" seems indispensable, and along with it the acceptance of the claim of a completely different type of competence, specifically that of political activity.[84]

The question is, however, whether Gadamer provides an adequate account of *political* existence on the basis of the view, incorporated in the claim of his philosophical hermeneutics to universality, that understanding and agreement are not primarily and originally a way of behaving towards a text acquired through methodical training. Rather, they are the culminating form of human social life, which in its final formalization is a speech community. Nothing is left out of this speech community; absolutely no experience of the world is excluded.[85]

According to Gadamer, the lives individual human beings live are shaped, both internally and externally, mentally and physically, by the communities in which they find themselves. These communities are products of language. Although these languages differ, the fact that an experience has been expressed in one means that it is in principle expressible and so intelligible in another as well. *Nothing is excluded.* In principle, all human beings can agree. The clear need for international cooperation in responding to the environmental crisis produced by a technological will to mastery makes the conditions for the development of such human solidarity better now than ever.[86] In contrast to Habermas, who regards appeals to emotions to be essentially coercive, because they are not purely rational, Gadamer thinks that rhetoric may legitimately be utilized in achieving such an agreement. (According to Gadamer, language is fundamentally metaphorical and the distinction between rhetoric and logic is, therefore, ill-founded.) *The* question is, still, whether persuasion can entirely replace coercion at the basis of human community, as both Gadamer and Habermas hope. On the basis of even more untraditional readings of Plato than Gadamer's, both Strauss and Derrida answer, no.

In maintaining that there are unbridgeable oppositions or alternatives which cannot be adequately expressed, much less mediated by language, both Strauss and Derrida return in different ways to Heidegger. According to both these commentators, neither language nor *logos* encompasses everything; there is something *alogos* which always remains.[87] Although the debate between Gadamer and Habermas has received much more critical attention, the differences between Gadamer, Strauss, and Derrida are more fundamental. Both Gadamer and Habermas agree not only that there are different kinds of reason but also that the kind upon which free human communities is based is in principle universal. In light of the alternatives represented by Strauss and Derrida, Gadamer looks both less conservative and less relativistic than Habermas charges.

Although Gadamer argues in opposition to both Hegel and Heidegger that history does not have an end, he does think it has an irreversible direction.

> The principle of freedom is unimpugnable and irrevocable. It is no longer possible for anyone still to affirm the unfreedom of humanity. . . . But does this mean that . . . history has come to an end? . . . Has not . . . man ha[d] to translate the principle of freedom into reality? Obviously this points

to the unending march of world history into the openness of its future tasks.[88]

Gadamer is fundamentally a liberal. Arguing that history has no necessary direction and that it may even be reversed, both Strauss and Derrida raise questions about the character of human freedom as well.

Four

Strauss's Way Back to Plato

n an exchange of letters concerning *Wahrheit und Methode* Leo Strauss wrote to Hans-Georg Gadamer, "It is strange that there should be a difference between us where you take a stand against Heidegger and I stand for him."[1] As a Jew, Strauss loathed the Nazi politics Heidegger had espoused; and as a student of the history of philosophy, he criticized Heidegger's 'radical historicism'.[2] Although Gadamer had kept a decent distance from Nazi politics, he had explicitly followed the 'path' of Heidegger's thought. But as we have seen, Gadamer disagreed with Heidegger on two crucial points: Because he denied that there was or could be an end to world history, Gadamer concluded that philosophy continued to be essentially the same kind of open-ended activity it had been since Plato. Strauss agreed with Heidegger that philosophy has come to an unprecedented crisis as a result of the historical insight Gadamer himself embraced. According to Strauss, Gadamer's own hermeneutics required him to posit something like an absolute moment in which it became clear, as it had not been clear to earlier thinkers, that all thought is essentially historical and that philosophers can never, therefore, attain the truth in the traditional sense. Thinkers informed by the historical insight would obviously no longer continue to seek truth, that is, to philosophize, as before.

Despite this fundamental disagreement, Strauss observed, reading Gadamer's book meant more to him than reading most books, because it reminded him of his youth in Germany. Both he and Gadamer had studied philosophy at the University of Marburg in the early 1920s; they had attended many of the same seminars and conversed with many of the same friends (e.g. Jacob Klein, Karl Löwith, and Gerhard Krüger).[3] "A certain community of 'background' helped me in understanding your

book," Strauss wrote Gadamer. "As I knew in advance, we have marched
from that common ground in opposite directions."[4]

STRAUSS'S DEPARTURE FROM NIETZSCHE

The difference between Gadamer's path and his own was indicated,
Strauss noted, by the fact that in *Wahrheit und Methode* there is a chapter on Dilthey, but none on Nietzsche. Gadamer had begun his studies of
Plato explicitly under the influence of Heidegger (whose *Being and Time*
contained a lengthy discussion of Dilthey and only a brief mention of
Nietzsche); but it was Nietzsche who had such a formative effect on the
young Strauss.[5]

In a letter he wrote to Löwith in 1935, Strauss stated, "Nietzsche
so dominated me between my 22nd and 30th years [which include his
time in Marburg], that I literally believed everything that I understood of him."[6] By the time he wrote Löwith, however, Strauss had
discovered that he had understood and so agreed with Nietzsche only
in part. Like Nietzsche, Strauss still wanted "to repeat antiquity . . .
at the peak of modernity." But he now thought the polemical character of Nietzsche's critique of modernity had prevented him from
realizing his intention. Approaching the ancients through an immanent critique of modernity on the basis of probity, Nietzsche had distorted the ancient teaching by presenting it in alien, scripturally based
modern terms.

Strauss was led to question the adequacy of Nietzsche's analysis of the
modern crisis as well as his understanding of the ancients by his own
very scholarly, hence relatively calm and unpolemical critique of the rationalism of the Enlightenment. The date at which he says he ceased to
believe "everything" he understood of Nietzsche coincides roughly with
the publication of *Die Religionskritik Spinozas als Grundlage seine Bibel-
wissenschaft Untersuchungen zu Spinozas theologisch-politischen Trak-
tat.*[7] Strauss's study of Spinoza led him to see that the early modern critics of scriptural religion could not prove that revelation was false, because
revelation had never claimed to rest on, or be available to, human reason.[8]
To show that statements in the Bible were contradictory or anachronistic
did not prove that they were not the word, or accurate depictions of the
acts, of an omnipotent and unfathomable God. To show that miracles
were impossible, modern rationalists would have had to give a systematic explanation of everything that had or could occur; and to do that,
as Hegel had seen, they would have to reorganize the world so that it op-
erated according to the principles of their own minds.[9] But this, modern rationalism in the combined form of natural science, progressive poli-

tics, and industrial technology, after the time of Spinoza, had proved unable to do.

In Nietzschean terms, Strauss's study of Spinoza convinced him that God was by no means necessarily or evidently "dead."[10]

> The last word and the ultimate justification of Spinoza's critique is the atheism from intellectual probity which overcomes orthodoxy radically by understanding it radically, i.e., without the polemical bitterness of the Enlightenment and the equivocal reverence of romanticism. Yet this claim however eloquently raised can not deceive one about the fact that its basis is an act of will, of belief, and, being based on belief, is fatal to any philosophy.[11]

Nietzsche insisted that the denial of God was a requirement of intellectual honesty. It constituted a kind of spiritual courage or, in Heideggerian terms, 'resolution' to face the utter meaninglessness of human life and the world. But, if the world had no inherent meaning or order, if there was no truth, there was no source or basis for Nietzsche's obligation to declare it. According to Nietzsche, the intellectual probity that required him to declare that God is dead was a product of the Christian conscience turning against itself. But if there was no God, there was no ground or reason to have such a conscience. Nietzsche's own philosophy was based on the same scripturally derived morality he himself declared invalid in politics once its ground in faith in God had been eroded.[12]

The antagonism to religion characteristic of modern philosophy that Nietzsche had made manifest was not a result simply of the demands of reason, Strauss concluded. The limits of reason established by the modern philosophical critique showed, if anything, that reason could not disprove revelation. Rather than constituting a logical conclusion of reason's turn against reason, modern philosophical atheism rested on an act of will. Modern philosophers chose not merely to admit that they could not explain everything that happened, that they could not show that either the world or human life was entirely rational; rather they insisted that there was no suprahuman, independently existing order or source of morality, because they wanted to improve the human condition. To improve that condition significantly, they thought it would be necessary to manipulate, if not to transform nature entirely. But nature would not and could not be manipulated so long as it was regarded as a product of divine Creation.[13]

Strauss thus began to suspect rather early, as Heidegger was to argue later, that the core or 'essence' of modern philosophy was technological.[14] But, where Heidegger argued that the technological application of scientific principles was a necessary result of a fateful dispensation of 'Being', Strauss saw it to be the result of a fateful choice.

The crisis of modernity was not so much scientific in origin, Strauss began to think, as it was moral and political.[15] The modern attempt to improve and elevate human life had ended, as Nietzsche had so powerfully shown, in its degradation. Once human beings ceased to recognize any suprahuman goals or standards by which their efforts could be judged, they stopped striving for anything beyond comfortable self-preservation. As a consequence, their lives lost all nobility. Yet, as Strauss saw first in Nietzsche, then in Hobbes, and finally in Machiavelli, modern rationalism originated in a desire to recapture the nobility associated with ancient life. Unfortunately, Nietzsche's Caesar, Hobbes's Aristotelian gentleman, and Machiavelli's revival of ancient political virtue all became means of relieving the general human condition and did not remain ends or goals in themselves.[16]

Strauss saw his suspicion that the crisis of modernity had moral and political rather than primarily philosophical roots confirmed, to a certain extent, by the work of one of his contemporaries, Carl Schmitt. As Strauss indicated by appending it to the English translation of *Spinoza's Critique of Religion,* his review of *Der Begriff des Politischen* provides an introduction or transition to his own later thought.

Like Nietzsche, Schmitt was repelled by the flattening effect of liberal toleration on all aspects of human life, but he gave a somewhat different diagnosis of the cause of this modern disease. The goal of modern liberal, humanitarian "politics" was securing peace, which entailed the end of all armed conflict aiming to establish the rule or superiority of some over others, that is, the end of the 'political' as Schmitt understood it. Toleration of differences was *the* major means of achieving peace. Nevertheless, he observed, the attempt to end all armed conflict itself resulted in armed conflict, in a war to end all war. Although it was submerged or hidden by modern liberalism, the political thus inexorably reasserted itself. In reaffirming the fundamental importance of the political Schmitt claimed to be giving a value-free analysis of modern conditions. But, Strauss suggested, Schmitt's fervor—and polemical antiliberalism—belied his claim. He could not and did not claim to know that the world-peace movement would not succeed; he did not want it to succeed, because he believed this form of moral humanitarianism would deprive human life of all seriousness and dignity. If all human activities were treated as if they were equally valid and valuable, no difference was worth fighting, much less dying for; all kinds of human activity became essentially nothing but varied means of entertainment, different ways of making the time pass pleasantly. Schmitt "affirms the political," Strauss concluded, "because he realizes that when the political is threatened, the seriousness of life is threatened. The affirmation of the political is in the last analysis nothing other than the affirmation of the moral."[17]

Schmitt did not recognize the fundamentally moral character of his own stance, because he identified morality with modern humanitarianism. His conception of the political was equally limited and hence flawed. In calling for a resumption of the war of all against all, Schmitt was in effect trying to negate the end of liberalism by returning to its origins in the 'state of nature' posited by Hobbes.

> Schmitt's critique of liberalism takes place within the horizon of liberalism. . . . The critique of liberalism that Schmitt has initiated can therefore be completed only when we succeed in gaining a horizon beyond liberalism. Within such a horizon Hobbes achieved the foundation of liberalism. A radical critique of liberalism is therefore possible only on the basis of an adequate understanding of Hobbes.[18]

Strauss himself turned immediately to write what has become a classic study of The Political Philosophy of Hobbes in which he argued, contrary to Nietzsche, that modernity originated in Hobbes's thought in a moral attitude that "is independent of the foundation of modern science."[19] Hobbes's political philosophy did not have its origins merely or even primarily in his admiration for the natural science of Galileo and Bacon with its potential for relieving man's estate. Hobbes's political philosophy grew out of a new understanding of morality that not merely built on, but literally incorporated, a good deal of ancient political thought, especially Aristotle's analysis of the passions in the Rhetoric. Hobbes first turned to history, especially Thucydides, in an attempt to discover how morality might be made more effective. But further reflections on what had to be done to establish a just political order led him to see that the aristocratic honor he first admired was incompatible with the requirements of justice.

> Originally he considered fear as the main, but not as the sufficient, motive of right behaviour. . . . Later he understands by fear not only the motive for right planning but also the motive of right execution. . . . As fear is thus considered . . . the sufficient motive for the founding of the State, it is impossible to approve any virtues which do not arise from fear, fear of violent death, and whose essence consists in the conquest or denial of fear. . . . Honour, which was originally recognized by Hobbes as the virtue of war alongside the virtues of peace, is finally directly opposed to justice and therefore to virtue in general.[20]

Strauss's study of Hobbes thus convinced him not only that modern philosophy had its origin in a moral concern, but also that the understanding of morality finally put forward was determined not by a judgment of what was moral in itself, but by a desire to effect certain political results.

Strauss succeeded in "gaining a horizon beyond liberalism," however, not so much as a result of his Hobbes study as through his rediscovery of the Platonic politics of the medieval Arabic and Jewish philosophers Farabi and Maimonides.

PLATONIC POLITICS

By arguing that Spinoza and other representatives of the modern Enlightenment could not disprove revelation with reason, because revelation had never claimed to be based on reason, Strauss recognized that he had proved too much; such an argument effectively insulated any form of orthodoxy (or, we might even say, any explicitly irrational commitment) from rational criticism. Seeking an understanding of the world and human life that both admitted its limitations vis-à-vis the claims of Scripture and yet claimed to be based entirely on reason, Strauss turned away from the atheism of Spinoza and Nietzsche to investigate the character and grounds of the premodern rationalism of Spinoza's great predecessor, the medieval Jewish philosopher Maimonides. Strauss's study of Maimonides led him to read the works of Maimonides' teacher, the Islamic philosopher Farabi; and Strauss's studies of Farabi led him to a very untraditional understanding of Plato.[21]

When he wrote his Spinoza book, Strauss later admitted, he had not believed a return to the ancients was possible.[22] There were some obvious objections to an embrace of the premodern rationalism of Maimonides, objections Strauss stated in the form of questions in the introduction to his first study of medieval Arabic and Jewish philosophy:

> Is [the Enlightenment of Maimonides] not the forerunner and model of precisely the moderate Enlightenment of the seventeenth and eighteenth centuries, which was least able to maintain itself? Indeed, is it not in some aspects even more . . . dangerous to the spirit of Judaism than the modern Enlightenment itself? Does it not rest upon the unrestorable cosmology of Aristotle? Does it not stand or fall by such a questionable method of interpretation as allegoresis?[23]

In *Philosophy and Law: Essays toward the Understanding of Maimonides and His Predecessors* Strauss did not even attempt to answer these objections.

Medieval rationalism *was* to some extent even more sharply opposed to revelation than modern rationalism, he conceded. But to understand the radical nature of the opposition was to understand the essential char-

acter of both rationalism or philosophy and revelation more clearly. Islamic and Jewish medieval philosophy had not been properly understood,
because it had been read too much in terms of Christian scholasticism.
Like Christian scholastics, medieval Muslim and Jewish philosophers had
attempted to reconcile reason (which they associated primarily with Aristotelian philosophy or science) and revelation. There was, however, an
important, if not essential difference. Whereas Christians understood
revelation primarily as specifying articles of faith, which philosophy
could be used to defend, Islamic and Jewish philosophers confronted revelation in the form of law, which was not subject to examination by question and answer, but had to be obeyed. Because Christians understood
revelation primarily as a matter of faith, there was always potentially a
degree of separation between Church and State.[24] (Cf. *Matthew* 22:21:
"Render therefore unto Caesar the things which are Caesar's, and unto
God the things that are God's.") Understanding revelation as law, Jews
and Muslims could not advocate such a division. They had to defend philosophy before the law as fulfilling the command to know God. Such
knowledge could be used to apply or even to interpret the law—for example, to reconcile contradictions of the kind Spinoza later highlighted
in his literal reading of the Bible—but both the knowledge and the interpretative activity based upon it had to be kept secret. Although the understanding of revelation as law characteristic of both Judaism and Islam
made these religions much more explicitly antagonistic to philosophy
than Christianity, Strauss concluded, that very antagonism led Islamic
and Jewish philosophers to retain a clearer sense of the essentially private, esoteric character of philosophy than their Christian counterparts.[25]

Where revelation took the form of law, there had to be a law-giver,
who was understood by medieval Arab and Jewish philosophers to be a
man, 'a prophet'.

> If Revelation were *merely* God's miraculous act, it would simply be with-
> drawn from all human comprehension. Revelation is only understandable
> insofar as God's revelatory act is accomplished through mediating causes,
> insofar as it is built into Creation, into created *nature*. If it is to be *wholly*
> understandable, it must simply be a *natural* fact. The means through
> which God accomplishes the act of Revelation is the prophet; i.e., an un-
> usual man, distinguished above all others, but, in any case, a *man*. Philo-
> sophical understanding of Revelation and philosophical grounding of the
> Law thus mean the explanation of prophecy out of the *nature of man*.[26]

In order to tell other people how to live, Maimonides and his Islamic
teacher Farabi argued, the prophet had to know what was right and
wrong; to have that moral knowledge, he had to have knowledge of God,
which, in turn, required him to have knowledge of nature as a whole. In

other words, the prophet had to be a philosopher who, in addition to his knowledge, possessed the ability to communicate that knowledge, or its practical results, to the uneducated in imagistic terms they could understand.[27] Because people did not always listen to reason, even in its most poetic or persuasive form, his speech could not remain mere admonition; it had to take the form of law, that is, of a command backed by force. Farabi and Maimonides' 'prophet' thus amounted to a Platonic 'philosopher-king'. The only (but, as it turns out, very significant) difference was that, where the "city in speech" Socrates described in Plato's *Republic* constituted a novel sketch of a just regime, to be realized, if at all, in the future, the prophet's law had already been delivered. It simply had to be understood and applied.

When the prophet was understood to be a Platonic philosopher-king, revelation or "the law" came to be understood to be an essentially *political* phenomenon. For example, in *The Guide for the Perplexed*, the commandments specifying the way one should treat other people were shown to establish the conditions necessary to maintain a political community; morality was, in other words, shown to be instrumentally good rather than good in itself.

Human beings cannot live, much less live well except in the company of others, but the differences among them make such peaceful coexistence difficult. Like Socrates in the *Republic*, Farabi presented these differences as the basis of a natural hierarchy. Like the Stranger in Plato's *Laws*, however, Maimonides emphasized the need to moderate the extremes in order to secure peace. That is, he suggested that the function of the law is less to establish a certain order or rank than to join the interests of the few with the interests of the many. Further like the Stranger, Maimonides argued that the securing of the "human" goods of the body—wealth, pleasure, glory, victory, or liberty—was not sufficient. "A law which aims only at the well-being of the body or, in other words, a law which has no other end than putting in good order the city and its affairs, and keeping injustice and rivalry from it" achieves only "imaginary happiness." True happiness "consists in the well-being of the soul, that is, in the knowledge, as perfect as possible, of all that exists and above all of the most perfect beings, of God and the Angels." According to Farabi, the perfect city is designed so that at least some of its members will achieve such happiness; according to Maimonides, the achievement of such happiness is the aim of the divine law.[28]

Strauss thought such Platonic politics pointed to a better solution to the contemporary crisis than either Nietzsche's attempt to synthesize master and slave morality or Schmitt's embrace of the one pole in opposition to the other:

In a century which was not considerably less "enlightened" than that of
the sophists and Socrates, where the very bases of human life, i.e., political
life, had been shaken by Chiliastic convulsions on the one hand and, on
the other, by a critique of religion the radicalism of which recalls the free-
thinkers of the seventeenth and eighteenth centuries, Farabi had rediscovered in the politics of Plato the golden mean equally removed from a natu-
ralism which aims only at sanctioning the savage and destructive instincts
of "natural" man, the instincts of the master and the conqueror; and from
a supernaturalism which tends to become the basis of slave morality—a
golden mean which is neither a compromise nor a synthesis, which is
hence not based on the two opposed positions, but which . . . uproots them
by a prior, more profound question, . . . the work of a truly critical philosophy.[29]

Understood as laying down the basic principles or requirements of political order, religious morality secured not only the bodily preservation
and security most people desired but also the necessary conditions for
the development of the intellectual excellence of a few. It was not necessary to choose between the embrace of inhumane cruelty for the sake of
maintaining a notion of difference in rank and the loss of all sense of
what is distinctively human in a "moral" embrace of unqualified egalitar-
ianism.

In *Philosophy and Law*, Strauss thus concluded that Farabi and
Maimonides began with an essentially Aristotelian understanding of the
cosmos and reinterpreted Islamic and Jewish law in light of that understanding in order to establish and preserve the conditions, especially the
moral beliefs, necessary to maintain political order. They presented their
thoughts in a Platonic framework, because they were not willing to follow Aristotle in declaring the theoretical life to be simply superior to
the moral. Like Plato they would force philosophers to descend from the
heights of contemplation to attend to their affairs of their fellows.[30]

Further study convinced Strauss, however, that Farabi's Platonism did
not consist merely in requiring contemplative philosophers to be prophets as well.[31] On the contrary, repeated readings of Farabi's *Philosophy
of Plato* persuaded Strauss that the political framework, that is, Farabi's
description of the perfect city, was intended primarily to protect philosophy from persecution. Farabi's own understanding of philosophy or theory was not, moreover, as Aristotelian or dogmatic as it first appeared.
The view of philosophy which Farabi not only attributed to Plato but also
shared himself was much more skeptical. Both the Islamic thinker and
his ancient mentor thought philosophy consisted in the search for wisdom rather than in its possession.

"Farabi followed Plato not merely as regards the manner in which he
presented the philosophic teaching in his most important books," Strauss

argued in an article he published in a Jubilee Volume for Louis Ginzburg in 1945. "He held the view that Plato's philosophy was the true philosophy."[32]

In his tripartite work on *The Aims of the Philosophy of Plato and Aristotle*, Farabi argued that happiness was the aim of human life, according to both ancient philosophers. Since both man's perfection and his happiness consisted in philosophy, and since, as the fate of Socrates made clear, philosophy aroused political opposition, Farabi explained in the central section of *The Aims* devoted to Plato, Plato taught that it was necessary to seek a city different from the cities which existed in his time: the city in speech of the *Republic*. It might appear, therefore, that Farabi's Plato was essentially political. But, Strauss argued, a second look showed that Farabi's Plato did not limit the subject matter of philosophy to the just and noble things, as had Socrates. Farabi's Plato put forth his political proposals as a means—and solely as a means—of preserving the conditions for the pursuit of theoretical knowledge.

Both Plato and Farabi presented theoretical philosophy in a political framework, because

> The philosopher who, transcending the sphere of moral or political things, engages in the quest for the essence of all beings, has to give an account of his doings by answering the question, "why philosophy?" That question cannot be answered but with a view to the natural aim of man which is happiness, and in so far as man is by nature a political being, it cannot be answered but within a political framework.

Indeed, Strauss argues,

> One must go one step further and suggest . . . that *sophia* and *sophrosyne*, or philosophy (as the quest for the truth about the whole) and self-knowledge (as realization of the need of that truth as well as of the difficulties obstructing its discovery and its communication) cannot be separated from each other.[33]

Platonic philosophy thus initially appears to be very Socratic.

Nevertheless, Strauss points out, having stated that Plato teaches that human perfection consists in philosophy, but that it must be supplemented by something else, presumably the royal art or knowledge of the best way of life, Farabi then says that Plato "teaches that philosophy does not need to be supplemented by something else in order to produce happiness." Rather than constituting an equal and independent kind of knowledge, the philosopher's concern with moral and political matters turns out to be merely instrumental, a way of establishing the conditions under which he can pursue his primary theoretical concerns.

Farabi's student Maimonides later suggested in the introduction to his

Guide that philosophers use such contradictions to indicate their true opinions to those able to understand them. Farabi presented philosophy in a Platonic or political guise rather than stating straightforwardly and unambiguously like Aristotle that the theoretical life of contemplation constitutes the only truly satisfying form of human life, Strauss suggests, because Farabi was afraid of being accused and condemned of impiety like Plato's Socrates.

To avoid persecution on the grounds of impiety, Farabi did not put forward his true views in his own name. Instead, like Plato he presented them as stated by others. Writing in his own name in the preface to *The Aims,* Farabi distinguished "the happiness of this world" from "the ultimate happiness in the other life." In the central chapter on Plato, however, he silently dropped this distinction.[34] Although Farabi purportedly summarized the *Phaedrus, Phaedo,* and *Republic,* he did not even mention the immortality of the soul. Since Farabi claimed to present "the philosophy of Plato, its parts, and the grades of dignity of its parts, from its beginning to its end," his omitting any topic suggested that Farabi thought it was unimportant or merely an exoteric doctrine. (Farabi was also, Strauss notes, completely silent regarding the ideas.) And "in his commentary on the *Nicomachean Ethics* [in part three of *The Aims*] he declare[d] that there is only the happiness of this life and that all divergent statements are based on 'ravings and old women's tales'."[35]

Farabi could express such impious views without fear of persecution, because as a commentator, he was not explicitly presenting his own views. He did not, however, simply summarize what Plato wrote. Since Plato had explicitly argued for the immortality of the soul and hence some kind of afterlife in the *Phaedrus, Phaedo,* and *Republic,* Farabi was almost "compelled to embrace a tolerably orthodox doctrine concerning the life after death." By choosing to attribute another opinion to the philosopher he most highly revered, "Farabi avail[ed] himself then of the specific immunity of a commentator, or of the historian, in order to speak his own mind."[36]

Farabi attributed his own opinion to his philosophic predecessor not merely to avoid the fate of Socrates or persecution for impiety. He masked his true understanding of the way human beings can attain happiness with a political teaching, because he saw that identifying happiness with theoretical science was "tantamount to closing the very prospect of happiness to the large majority of men." If only for reasons of philanthropy, Farabi was compelled to investigate possible ways of achieving happiness for unphilosophic human beings. He did so by reiterating Plato's suggestion that if philosophers were to become kings, they would secure not only their own but also the happiness of their fellow citizens—in this life. At first he suggested that the happiness of the philosophers themselves also depended upon the establishment of the perfect city. But Strauss emphasizes,

> The real remedy employed in the *Plato* is far more radical: toward the end of the treatise, Farabi makes it absolutely clear that there can be, not only philosophers, but completely perfect human beings . . . in imperfect cities. Philosophy . . . and hence happiness do not require . . . the establishment of the perfect political community.

The "essential implication" is that "in the imperfect cities, that is, in the world as it actually is and as it always will be, happiness is within the reach of philosophers alone."[37]

Because the philosopher necessarily lives in an imperfect political community, he is necessarily "in grave danger." But, Strauss observes, Farabi intimated how the philosopher could deal with his precarious situation by contrasting Socrates with Plato. Because Socrates "limited his investigations to moral and political subjects," Farabi suggested, he had no alternative but "either to comply with accepted rules of conduct or openly to challenge them and therewith to expose himself to persecution and violent death. Plato was fundamentally different." Plato "considered philosophy an essentially theoretical pursuit and . . . his moral fervor was mitigated by his insight into the nature of beings." In treating political questions, he combined "the intransigent way of Socrates," directly questioning accepted opinions as is appropriate for dealing with the political elite, with "the less exacting way of Thrasymachus," gradually undermining accepted opinions with rhetorical appeals to popular passions. As a result,

> The "revolutionary" quest for the other city ceased to be a necessity; Plato substituted for it a much more "conservative" way of action, *viz.* the gradual replacement of accepted opinions by the truth or an approximation of the truth.[38]

The gradual replacement of accepted opinions means their eventual destruction; but, Strauss observes, that replacement "would not be gradual, if it were not combined with a provisional acceptance of the accepted opinions." Farabi says elsewhere that conformity with the religious opinions of one's community is a necessary qualification for a future philosopher.

Strauss's studies of Farabi and Maimonides' commentaries on ancient texts led him to discover the phenomenon he dubbed "persecution and the art of writing."[39] By thinking out the implications of that discovery Strauss came to see that the reasons it was thought impossible to return to ancient rationalism were by no means beyond question.

NONDOGMATIC PHILOSOPHY

Strauss's study of "Farabi's *Plato*" led him, in the first place, to an emphatically undogmatic understanding of the essential nature or character of philosophy itself. Although philosophy had to be presented in a political framework in order to protect it from persecution, that framework or the specific teachings, especially about the nature and foundations of human society, should not be (mis)taken for the activity itself. Farabi distinguished the search for the best way of life from the search for knowledge or the theoretical science of the essence of all the beings. But Farabi did not make what he meant by 'essence' or 'being' altogether clear. The search for knowledge remains viable, of course, only so long as human beings have reason to believe they can acquire knowledge of the intelligible organization of the whole. Understood as a *search*, however, philosophy does not presuppose any specific understanding or doctrine concerning the character of the whole. In particular, it does not presuppose acceptance of the Platonic theory of ideas or Aristotelian cosmology. Strauss had observed "the deep silence of the *Plato* about the *noi*, the *substantiae separatae*, as well as about the 'ideas'." And in concluding the essay he added, "in his treatise on Aristotle's philosophy, which is the sequel to his *Plato*, Farabi does not discuss Aristotle's metaphysics."

> [Farabi's] concept of philosophy is not based on any preconceived opinion as to what allegedly real things are truly real things. He has infinitely more in common with a philosophic materialist than with any non-philosophic believer however well-intentioned. For him, philosophy is essentially and purely theoretical. *It is the way leading to that science rather than that science itself; the investigation rather than the result.* Philosophy thus understood is identical with the scientific spirit "in action," with *skepsis* in the original sense of the term.[40]

Strauss attributed an equally undogmatic understanding of philosophy to Plato himself in a review essay he wrote a year after "Farabi's *Plato*," "On a New Interpretation of Plato's Political Philosophy."[41] And in his later, more thematic works Strauss articulated a similarly skeptical "in the original sense of the term" understanding of philosophy in his own name.[42]

The significance of Strauss's rediscovery of the nondogmatic character of Platonic philosophy becomes clearer, if one views it in light of his early endorsement of Nietzsche's attempt to revive antiquity in the midst of modernity. In *The Birth of Tragedy* Nietzsche had argued that Socrates represented "the vortex of world history," because in urging human beings to seek knowledge he had promised that they could use this knowledge to correct or reform the world and thus find a reason to live.[43] Once

Kant showed it was impossible for human beings ever to attain knowledge of the things in themselves, philosophy could no longer hold out the same promise to redeem life through knowledge. Nietzsche called, therefore, for the emergence of a "Socrates who practices music" to create a new goal to give disillusioned modern men a reason to live.

Strauss now says that, according to Socrates, Plato, and Farabi, the goodness of a philosophic way of life did not depend upon the possibility of human beings' attaining complete theoretical knowledge. Socrates' famous insistence in his *Apology* that his wisdom consisted in his knowledge of his ignorance suggested that he did not think such knowledge was attainable. All he claimed was "that the unexamined life is not worth living, but to make speeches every day about virtue and the other things about which you hear me conversing is the greatest happiness and good for a human being" (38a).[44] Whether or not Socrates ever attained the knowledge he sought, Plato's presentation of his life represented the contention that there was a form of human life which was inherently satisfying. And if that claim could be made good, it constituted a decisive response to modern nihilism. Plato's depiction of Socrates represented, in deed as it were, the proposition that human beings could discover a happy, which is to say good, way of life on the basis of their natural reason alone. To provide a foundation or rationale for morality, it was not necessary to appeal either to a supernatural, divine revelation or to an equally inexplicable historical 'dispensation' of Being or fate. It was necessary, as both Farabi and Maimonides showed, to distinguish morality, as establishing the necessary means, the social conditions and personal traits a human being had to have in order to engage in philosophy, from the more popular or vulgar understanding of virtues as qualities which are good in themselves. When morality became understood, as it had in modern times, primarily as compassion or the selfless serving of others, it became irrational, as Nietzsche argued, insofar as it entailed better (more moral and more talented) human beings sacrificing themselves and their interests for the sake of preserving and promoting the interests of their more narrowly selfish inferiors.[45] Strauss's call for a return to the ancients thus involved, first and foremost, recapturing an understanding or view of a form of human life in itself worth living which, as such, could become the source and justification of lesser, more instrumental forms of human endeavor.

The primary reason people thought it impossible to return to ancient rationality was the evident success of modern natural science. But, if Platonic philosophy did not constitute or presuppose any specific doctrine concerning the character of the whole, the revival of ancient rationalism did not entail "the unrestorable cosmology of Aristotle."[46] Insofar as modern natural science put forward theories understood to be merely the best explanations of current data, subject to revision in light of new findings, there was no necessary disjunction between modern physics and Platonic philosophy *at a theoretical level*.[47] Both involved an ongoing search for knowledge, which entailed the critique of current or dominant opinions, on the part of at least some members of the community. Modern natural science was not and did not understand itself to be purely theoretical, however.[48] Beginning with Francis Bacon, modern natural science had also been presented and justified as a means of relieving man's estate, primarily by his extending his lifespan and making his existence more comfortable.[49] In order truly to improve human existence, Strauss pointed out, modern natural science would have to discover what is truly good for human beings, and modern science neither can, nor claims to, provide such knowledge. As Nietzsche observed, science cannot answer the question, why science? Because it cannot give an account of its own basis and source as a distinctively human activity, modern natural science lacks foundation even as knowledge. As the mere collection and ordering of experimental data, it becomes merely one interpretation among many. The current distinction between philosophy as a kind or source of humanistic interpretations of the world and science as a power generating method or technique of analysis is, Strauss concluded, as destructive of science, ultimately, as it is of philosophy.[50]

A HISTORY BASED ON CHOICE, NOT NECESSITY

The second reason many (including, initially, Strauss himself) thought it was impossible to revive ancient rationality was the history of philosophy. The medieval Enlightenment had given way to, if it had not itself produced modern rationalism. But Strauss saw, if Platonic doctrines concerning the immortality of the soul and the ideas were, as Farabi suggested, merely public teachings intended to preserve the necessary conditions for philosophic activity, it was necessary to review the history of Western philosophy in a new light. To the extent to which modern philosophers like Machiavelli and Hobbes rejected the ancient understanding of politics because of its unrealistic goals, they were reacting primarily to and against the public teaching. Their arguments did not reach the core, that is, the contention that philosophical inquiry constitutes the only truly satisfying form of human life. Both Machiavelli and Hobbes were aware of the pleasures of philosophical activity; they themselves partook in and of them.[51] These modern philosophers did not think, however, that the satisfaction of a few provided an adequate basis for the organization of human life as a whole. On the contrary, they argued, the only effective political science has to be based on the passions common to all. In other words, they made a fundamental choice. Rather than urge human beings to pursue goals few, if any could ever achieve, these philosophers decided it would be better to lower their sights. They urged politicians to take their bearings by what was common rather than what was exceptional in human beings, because if they did, these politicians could more certainly achieve the desired results—peace and prosperity. Insofar as modern philosophy was a result of a choice to pursue lower goals that were more likely to be achieved rather than higher, nobler but more improbable human possibilities, Strauss concluded, the history of philosophy was not a product or reflection of a logical process or necessity, as Hegel had argued. Nor was it the result of a fateful dispensation as Heidegger had maintained.[52]

Once the modern alternative was articulated, Strauss conceded, later philosophy *did* constitute a working out of its logical implications and results.[53] But he maintained his distance from all forms of historicism by arguing, first, that the course of events did not necessarily (or perhaps ever) follow the logic of thought.[54] Nor was the range and content of a philosopher's thought restricted by his historical circumstances; one of the major points of Strauss's analysis of the phenomenon of persecution and the art of writing was to show that philosophers in the past had created a false impression of the conformity of their thought to their times by adapting their form of expression and surface teaching to their circumstances in order to hide and protect their more fundamental freedom of thought.

Insofar as it was a product of choice, Strauss contended, the shift from ancient to modern rationalism did not have the same logic or necessity as Hobbes's correction of the theoretical difficulties in Machiavelli or Rousseau's correction of Hobbes.[55] In other words, the medieval Enlightenment did not lead inevitably to the modern Enlightenment. This contention may, at first glance, be somewhat difficult to understand, because Farabi's account of Plato's replacement of the confrontational way of Socrates with a more gradual, nonrevolutionary reform of public opinion seems to point toward something like popular enlightenment. According to Strauss himself, Farabi's substitution of politics for religion laid "the foundation for the secular alliance between philosophers and enlightened princes" and so "initiate[d] the tradition whose most famous representatives in the West are Marsilius of Padua and Machiavelli."[56] Nevertheless, Strauss argued, in adapting the "Averroist" understanding of the political utility of religion—an understanding Strauss repeatedly insisted was more accurately traced to Averroës's predecessor, Farabi—to Christian circumstances, Machiavelli did not simply draw out the logical consequences of Farabi's premises. On the contrary, he changed both the content and the mode of the public teaching or popular Enlightenment in decisive respects.

In response to political theorists like Eric Vögelin who (following Hegel to this extent) argued that not only modernity in general but also Machiavelli's thought in particular had to be understood as the result of an historical synthesis of biblical notions and ancient Greek rationalism, Strauss pointed out that there was very little distinctively scriptural in the politics advocated by the author of *The Prince* and *The Discourses*. As evidence of his claim, Vögelin had pointed out that Machiavelli called the founders of new modes and orders 'armed prophets'. But Strauss retorted, Machiavelli emphasized the importance of their being armed much more than their being 'prophets'. Although in chapter 6 of *The Prince* he first distinguished Moses from the founders of pagan Rome and Athens, because he followed the word of God whereas they were mere men, in his restatement Machiavelli made it clear that Moses' actions had the same character and thus ought to be understood in the same terms as those of Romulus, Theseus, and Cyrus. Machiavelli's understanding of the founders was based on ancient political practice; it did not require the addition or admixture of a distinctly biblical element.[57] Although Machiavelli claimed that only armed prophets succeeded, Strauss pointed out, he himself claimed to be bringing 'new modes and orders'; and as a philosopher—or mere advisor to a prince—he was an unarmed teacher or prophet like Jesus.[58] The *only* insight Machiavelli took from Christianity concerned the possibility of overthrowing the reigning world order by popularizing a new moral teaching. By secularizing the promise of instituting a new order by spreading "the news," Machiavelli became the founder of the modern Enlightenment.

Like the Averroists, Machiavelli suggested that religion ought to be viewed in terms of its political utility. But, where "Averroists" like Farabi and Maimonides had reinterpreted revelatory texts so as to make them conducive not only to the maintenance of political order but also to the achievement of true human happiness and excellence by the few with the requisite natural abilities, Machiavelli not only openly and directly attacked Christianity for its deleterious political effects but he also explicitly subordinated the theoretical quest for the knowledge of the essence of all beings (that is, nature, especially human nature) to the achievement of a practical, political goal. As Strauss saw it, there were, therefore, two fundamental differences between the medieval and the modern Enlightenment: (1) In order both to support the requirements of justice in earthly communities and to counteract possible popular resentment or despair arising from a realization that most people are barred by nature from the only possible form of a truly satisfying human existence, medieval philosophers refrained from openly disputing what they surreptitiously indicated were rationally unfounded doctrines concerning the immortality of the soul and the afterlife. Whereas medieval rationalists thus tried to minimize popular recognition of the conflict between reason and revelation, the founders of the modern Enlightenment like Machiavelli, Hobbes, and Spinoza brought out not only the deleterious practical effects but also the fundamentally irrational character of the fundamental doctrines of revealed religion. (2) Whereas medieval rationalists taught that moral and political legislation served to establish the necessary conditions not merely for living, but for living well, that is, philosophizing, modern Enlightenment philosophers argued that science was valuable insofar as it helped people satisfy the common bodily desires for comfort and safety more effectively. Whereas medieval philosophers saw practice primarily in terms of establishing and maintaining the conditions for theory, the philosophers of the modern Enlightenment tended to present theory as a means of achieving better practice.

As a result of the fundamental change in the understanding of the relation between theory and practice introduced by Machiavelli, Strauss suggested, later modern philosophers had lost sight of the only form of human life that is truly satisfying.[59] The inversion of the ancient understanding of the relation between theory and practice that occurred when the medieval enlightenment was replaced by modern rationalism was the source of its nihilistic conclusion that there is nothing, especially no form of human life, that is worthwhile in and of itself. Rather than constituting an expansion or correction of ancient philosophy on the basis of ideas derived from Scripture, Strauss concluded, the origins of the modern Enlightenment in the works of Machiavelli involved a severe constriction of the possibilities envisioned. The character of that constriction was indicated by Machiavelli's use of Xenophon, the only ancient Greek author to whom he repeatedly referred. Whereas Xenophon's own works moved between the two poles or possibilities of theory and practice represented by Socrates and Cyrus, Machiavelli took note of only one. He ignored the Socratic alternative, the alternative Strauss himself tried to reintroduce.

FROM ALLEGORESIS TO SECRET TEACHING

The third reason Strauss mentioned in *Philosophy and Law* why people thought a return to the medieval Enlightenment was impossible was that it depended upon such a questionable way of reading as Maimonides' allegoresis. According to the generally accepted understanding Strauss himself employed in his Spinoza book, Maimonides rationalized any biblical statement that did not make sense in itself or was not consistent with others by reading it allegorically.[60] For example, if God were understood to be incorporeal, he could not literally be thought to have spoken to Moses.[61] Strauss's later studies of Maimonides and his teacher Farabi led him to conclude, however, that they were not simply reinterpreting or rationalizing the writings of human beings who claimed to be divinely inspired.[62] Both Maimonides and Farabi used a series of complex devices—including intentional contradictions, numerology, apparent repetitions in which slight changes signal major shifts in the substance or direction of the argument, placing controversial points in the center of discussions where they are least apt to be noticed, obscurity, and brevity to the point of complete silence about relevant topics—to hide their most radical philosophical conclusions or questions from all but the most discerning readers. They concealed their own philosophical skepticism in order to maintain, rationalize, and so improve the moral doctrines to which most members of their communities continued to subscribe. No claim has proved more controversial in Strauss's own work.

Few would deny Strauss's initial observation that philosophers in the past did not write with the protection of the First Amendment and that like Socrates or Galileo they had reason to fear persecution for their views. But fear of persecution is not the only or even the major issue. Enlightenment thinkers like John Stuart Mill and Alexis de Tocqueville argued that those daring enough to articulate unorthodox views encountered even greater, if less obvious pressure to conform to majority opinion in liberal democracies where there was no official persecution of political or religious dissenters.[63] That was the reason they thought it was necessary to do everything possible to protect the individual's freedom of thought. To support the necessary legislation and practices, they argued that complete freedom of expression of divergent views would contribute not only to the full development of individual potential and happiness but also to the common good through the gradual spread of truth or Enlightenment.[64] "The attitude of an earlier type of writers was," Strauss argued, "fundamentally different."

> They believed that the gulf separating "the wise" and "the vulgar" was a basic fact of human nature which could not be influenced by any progress of popular education: philosophy, or science, was essentially a privilege of "the few." They were convinced that philosophy as such was suspect to, and hated by, the majority of men. Even if they had nothing to fear from any particular political quarter, those who started from that assumption would have been driven to the conclusion that public communication of

the philosophic or scientific truth was impossible or undesirable, not only for the time being but for all times.[65]

The difference between the way in which premodern and modern thinkers wrote did not reflect the presence or absence of persecution, therefore, so much as a difference of opinion concerning the extent to which truth can be popularized.

Enlightenment thinkers like Hobbes may have attempted to veil some of their more unorthodox conclusions in order to escape persecution (although, Strauss notes, few such thinkers entirely deceived their contemporaries); nevertheless, they wrote primarily to communicate what they thought was true to their readers. Ancient authors had quite a different understanding of the purpose of philosophic writing. They thought that all anyone could communicate in writing would be an opinion and, as Plato or his Socrates stresses, an opinion is never, even if true, the same as the truth. The only way anyone can discover the truth is by thinking things out for oneself. That is the reason "according to the *Seventh Letter,* as well as according to the *Phaedrus,* no writing composed by a serious man can be quite serious."[66] He knows that he is at most playfully enticing young readers to begin thinking themselves. Such writing is unavoidably ironic, because the author knows he cannot directly express or communicate the truth to the reader even when and if, like Farabi's ascetic, he states it completely openly.[67]

Ancient authors did not think that the truth could be spread in the form of popular opinion simply because they believed most people would never have the time, ability, or desire to apprehend it; it was the problematic character of truth itself that precluded its widespread acceptance. If all human beings could actually ever know was their ignorance, as Plato's Socrates maintained, the truth could not really be stated in propositional form. As knowledge of our ignorance, Strauss explains, "philosophy as such is nothing but genuine awareness of the problems, i.e., of the fundamental and comprehensive problems." To discover what these problems are and why they remain, it is necessary to think out the attempted solutions and to discover what the irremediable defects of each of "the very few typical solutions" are. "It is impossible to think about these problems without becoming inclined toward a solution"; such an inclination could and would be expressed as an opinion or doxa. But "the philosopher ceases to be a philosopher at the moment at which the 'subjective certainty' of a solution becomes stronger than his awareness of the problematic character of that solution."[68]

Plato wrote dialogues and not treatises to defeat any doctrinaire interpretation of his work.

One does not need the evidence of the *Seventh Letter* in order to see that Plato "prohibited" written expositions of his teaching. . . . The prohibition . . . is self-enforcing; everyone who presents such an exposition becomes, to use a favorite Platonic expression, "ridiculous," inasmuch as he can easily be refuted and confounded by passages in the dialogues which contradict his exposition. . . . Plato does not relieve him of the responsibility for discovering the decisive part of the argument by himself. . . . His teaching can never become the subject of indoctrination. In the last analysis his writings cannot be used for any purpose other than for philosophizing. In particular, no social order and no party which ever existed or which ever will exist can rightfully claim Plato as its patron.[69]

Not only can the truth not be directly stated or presented; according to Strauss (and the medieval Islamic and Jewish authors who wrote on the basis of a similar understanding), it would be irresponsible to attempt to do so.

The author of the *Seventh Letter* goes on to say that if the serious teaching were useful for human beings, he would consider it the most noble action of his life to communicate it in writing to "the many"; but, he says, the attempt would not be salutary for human beings, "save for some few who are capable of discovering [it] by themselves by means of slight indication."[70]

As both Socrates in the *Republic* and the Athenian Stranger in the *Laws* observe, the institution and preservation of political society require public agreement on a teaching concerning the highest and most fundamental questions about the gods or nature. To teach openly and unambiguously that no human being can ever know anything for certain about these matters is to destroy the protective atmosphere of authoritative opinion Nietzsche also saw was necessary for the preservation of human life.

According to Nietzsche, the theoretical analysis of human life that realizes the relativity of all comprehensive views and thus depreciates them would make human life itself impossible, for it would destroy the protecting atmosphere within which life or culture or action is alone possible. . . . To avert the danger to life, Nietzsche could choose one of two ways: He could insist on the strictly esoteric character of the theoretical analysis of life— that is, restore the Platonic notion of the noble delusion—or else he could deny the possibility of theory proper and so conceive of thought as essentially subservient to, or dependent on, life or fate.[71]

Ordinary human beings thus had a reason beyond envy to be suspicious of, if not simply to hate, philosophy. Both the interest of the philosopher in the political and economic conditions necessary for his own activity and a just regard for the legitimate interests of others required him to conduct his questioning of received opinion in a way that preserved the salutary prejudices held by most members of his society.

Strauss's critics have charged that his thesis concerning persecution and the art of writing produces arbitrary and ahistorical readings of philosophic texts.[72] To such critics, he responds:

> Reading between the lines is strictly prohibited in all cases where it would be less exact than not doing so. *Only such reading between the lines as starts from an exact consideration of the explicit statements of the author is legitimate. The context in which a statement occurs,* and the literary character of the whole work as well as its plan, must be perfectly understood before an interpretation of the statement can reasonably claim to be adequate or even correct.

If a philosophic text is cogent as it stands, there is no reason to delve beneath the surface. But "if a master of the art of writing commits such blunders as would shame an intelligent high school boy, it is reasonable to assume that they are intentional, especially if the author discusses, however incidentally, the possibility of intentional blunders in writing."[73] To see how a philosopher adapted his teaching to his circumstances, it is obviously necessary to know what those circumstances were, that is, to engage in historical research concerning the context in which a text was written. What Strauss insists is not that historical knowledge is unnecessary or irrelevant—he himself very explicitly engaged in *historical* studies—but that knowledge of the historical context does not suffice to explain the meaning or thought of an author.[74] In response, as it were, to Jacques Derrida's insistence that an author's intention does not and cannot determine the meaning of a text, Strauss points out that we cannot know that our understanding differs from that of the author unless we, in effect, claim to know what his understanding was. The author's understanding is not the only possible understanding or interpretation, Strauss admits; texts look different in different contexts, but all interpretations must begin, that is, presuppose, knowledge of that original understanding.[75] The *belief* that all thought is historically limited or conditioned makes contemporary readers think it is impossible to understand writings of the past as their authors understood them and so destroys the only possible standard or basis of determining what is or is not an historically accurate reading.

Strauss explicitly denied that he provided his students with a method or system for decoding the secret teaching to be found in past texts. At most, he reiterated, observations concerning an author's use of repetition or numbers would provide hints.[76] Ancient authors used such hints to entice readers to think for themselves and so to educate them.

"Education," as Strauss understands it, "consists in reminding oneself of human excellence." Plato suggested that

> Education in the highest sense is philosophy. Philosophy is quest for wisdom or quest for knowledge regarding the most important, the highest, or the most comprehensive things; such knowledge, he suggested, is virtue and is happiness. But wisdom is inaccessible to man, and hence virtue and happiness will always be imperfect. In spite of this, the philosopher, who, as such, is not simply wise, is declared to be the only true king; he is declared to possess all the excellences of which man's mind is capable, to the highest degree.[77]

From studying Plato, we learn that

> We cannot be philosophers. . . , but we can love philosophy; we can try to philosophize. This philosophizing consists . . . primarily and in a way chiefly in listening to the conversation between the great philosophers or . . . the greatest minds, and therefore in studying the great books.[78]

The "overwhelming difficulty" is that the greatest minds wrote only monologues. "We must transform their monologues into a dialogue. . . . We must then do something which the greatest minds were unable to do." Despite his initial modesty with regard to his claim to be a philosopher, properly or Platonically speaking, Strauss thus seems to place himself and his students over and above the thinkers he studies, for he continues, "Since the greatest minds contradict one another regarding the most important matters, they compel us to judge of their monologues." And yet, he emphasizes, "we are not competent to be judges."[79] In order to discover the truth, one must obviously attempt to determine which of the contradictory positions is correct. If philosophy consists primarily in understanding the basic problems, however, it is not as necessary to embrace one of the contradictory positions to the exclusion of the others as it is to study the very best arguments for the competing "solutions" in order to come to understand why none is completely adequate, why the problems remain.

Not surprisingly, Strauss's own work takes the form of the supra-Platonic dialogue he recommends. As Victor Gourevitch has observed:

> Strauss rarely speaks in his own name. Except for Prefaces and Introductions, that is to say except for what might be called public occasions when he is, as it were, compelled to speak in a popular manner, he prefers to appear in the guise of the historian and the exegete. . . . By casting his thought primarily in the form of historical studies that take the entire history of political philosophy for their province, he implies that the relationship between his views and the doctrines he studies is comparable to that between the views of a dramatist and those of his characters.[80]

Rather than clearly articulate a doctrine or propose a "solution" to the modern crisis, Strauss emphasized the alternatives—between the ancients and the moderns, reason and revelation, poetry and philosophy—in order to awaken his readers' sense of the enduring issues or problems.

Because, like Farabi, Strauss availed himself "of the specific immunity of the commentator or of the historian in order to speak his mind concerning grave matters in his 'historical' works," some critics have accused him of secretly teaching Nietzschean nihilism.[81] These critics have failed to notice that Strauss did not slavishly follow any historical example or model. Unlike his medieval predecessors, he did not attempt even seemingly to reconcile reason and revelation.[82] On the contrary, following a long Jewish tradition, he emphasized their opposition.[83] He emphasized the fundamental incompatibility of reason and revelation explicitly in response to the problematic effects of Nietzsche's combining of them, first in his "last virtue" or probity, and finally in the figure of the superman, "Caesar with the soul of Christ."[84]

A philosopher must adapt his writing to his particular circumstances, Strauss observes in *Persecution and the Art of Writing.* "In case the given society is hostile to philosophy, . . . reason advises the philosopher either to leave that society and to search for another society, or else to try to lead his fellows gradually toward a more reasonable attitude."[85] Having fled Nazi Germany to live in the United States, Strauss did not have to fear religious or political persecution of the kind Socrates, Farabi, and even Spinoza faced. He thus found himself free to challenge the reigning schools of thought—and he did. By showing that reason could not disprove revelation, Strauss sought to protect the grounds of popular morality and so the political preconditions for the pursuit of philosophy as well as the grounds for popular hope for happiness in the hereafter from the modern rationalist attack.[86] But, he recognized, the argument he gave to protect revelation proved too much insofar as it protected all forms of irrationalism from a reason-based critique. Strauss was not, therefore, afraid like the Jewish scholar Halevi "to state the case for philosophy with utmost clarity and vigor, and thus to present an extremely able and ruthless attack on revealed religion . . . [because he was unable] to tell whether one or the other of the readers would not have been more impressed by the argument of the philosopher than by the rejoinder of the [Jewish] scholar."[87] Like Socrates, Strauss attempted to make the opinions of his contemporaries more reasonable by showing them that they did not know what they thought they did—that modern science made a return to antiquity—philosophic or religious—impossible, that human life is essentially historical, that ordinary human beings now know more than the most brilliant minds of the past. We have to engage in historical studies, Strauss argued, in order to free ourselves from the historicist prejudices of our age.[88]

> Far from legitimizing the historicist inference, history seems rather to prove that all . . . philosophic thought is concerned with the same fundamental themes or the same fundamental problems, and therefore that there exists an unchanging framework which persists in all changes of human knowledge of both facts and principles. . . . If the fundamental problems persist in all historical change, human thought is capable of transcending its historical limitation or of grasping something trans-historical. This would be the case even if it were true that all attempts to solve these problems are doomed to fail . . . on account of the "historicity" of "all" human thought.[89]

It was not the discrediting of Aristotelian cosmology by modern natural science or a nineteenth-century belief in a necessary course or direction of history that made his contemporaries think a revival of Socratic rationalism was impossible, Strauss concluded. It was their historicist prejudice, their belief that all human thought was decisively shaped and limited by the time and place in which it occurred. Strauss's subsequent studies of the history of philosophy, especially his studies of its ancient, nonhistoricist origins, were intended, above all, to undermine that prejudice.

Five

"Primitive Platonism"
Strauss's Response to Radical Historicism

THE APOLITICAL CHARACTER OF RADICAL HISTORICISM

In order to revive ancient rationalism, Strauss recognized, he had to respond to the dominant schools of contemporary thought that declared political philosophy to be a useless if not, strictly speaking, impossible intellectual quest: positivism and historicism. Taking modern physics as their model, positivists argued that only tautological (analytic or definitional) and empirically verifiable statements could provide scientific knowledge; all evaluative statements were merely expressions of subjective feeling. The resulting distinction between facts and values became widely adopted by social scientists; and in light of that distinction, political philosophy came to be regarded as a meaningless enterprise.[1] The most one could legitimately study was the history of political philosophy, that is, the historical record of the values individuals and nations had held.

It is impossible to describe social and political phenomena accurately without using evaluative terms, Strauss objected; the phenomena themselves are essentially value-laden. To the extent to which social scientists attempt to purge their studies of all evaluative content, they are thus forced either to distort their subject matter or to introduce evaluative measures surreptitiously, without admitting or perhaps even recognizing that they do so.[2] Moreover, in conscientiously attempting to remove all values, especially their own values, from their studies, social scientists eventually come to realize that their own scientific approach is itself a product or expression of the values of Western culture and that there are other cultures with different values and approaches which had to be regarded as equally valid. 'Positivism' necessarily collapses into 'histori-

129

cism'.[3] It is fundamentally this historicism that stands in the way of a revival of Platonic political philosophy in the contemporary world. The fact that human beings have had various beliefs and arranged their lives accordingly at different times and in different circumstances does not in itself prove that no thought is truer than any other or that there is no right or best way of life. The historicist contention that there are no immutable principles intelligible to human beings as such, that is, that the scope and content all of human thought are essentially limited by time and place, cannot be proved solely on the basis of historical evidence; it requires the philosophical critique of reason, prepared for by Nietzsche and completed by Heidegger, "that allegedly proves the impossibility of theoretical metaphysics and of philosophic ethics or natural right."[4]

Strauss's studies of classical political philosophy were intended, first and foremost, to constitute a response to this radical historicist critique.[5] In *Natural Right and History* he urged:

> As long as the issue between historicism and nonhistoricist philosophy is not settled, our most urgent need is to understand that issue. The issue is not understood if it is seen merely in the way in which it presents itself from the point of view of historicism; it must also be seen in the way in which it presents itself from the point of view of nonhistoricist philosophy. This means . . . that the problem of historicism must first be considered from the point of view of classical philosophy, which is nonhistoricist thought in its pure form.[6]

According to the radical historicist critique, all previous philosophy rested on a "dogmatic identification of 'to be' in the highest sense with 'to be always'. . . . The dogmatic character of the basic premise of philosophy is said to have been revealed by the discovery of history or of the 'historicity' of human life."[7] Responding to the major conclusions Heidegger drew from his analysis of *Dasein* in *Being and Time*, Strauss sought to show that Platonic philosophy was originally and fundamentally Socratic, which is to say, undogmatic. Neither Nietzsche nor Heidegger understood the essentially Socratic character of Platonic philosophy, because neither paid sufficient attention to the emphatically political context in which Greek philosophy first emerged.

Husserl had taught both Heidegger and Strauss that science "is derivative from our primary knowledge of the world of things: science is not the perfection of men's understanding of the world, but a specific modification of that prescientific understanding." To explore the foundation (or lack thereof) of human knowledge, it was necessary to recapture the pretheoretical experience from which all later theory was derived.[8] "The horizon within which Husserl had analyzed the world of prescientific understanding was the pure consciousness. . . . Heidegger questioned that orientation by referring to the fact that the inner time belonging to the pure consciousness cannot be understood if one abstracts from the fact that this time is necessarily finite, and even constituted by man's *mortality*."[9]

Although he had gone further than Husserl in actually recapturing man's pretheoretical experience by showing that people did not initially perceive things as such, but that they first understood things as part of a world they shared with others by means of language, Strauss thought Heidegger had not gone far enough. Through his phenomenological description of human existence as 'being-with-others', he had moved beyond the antifactual premise of all modern political philosophy, that human beings are by nature radically asocial. And in his later 'four-fold', he had seen that human life not only is defined by, but also exists only in relation to, that which is above (the gods in the heavens) and below (the impenetrable earth). Although Heidegger had rediscovered the essentially social and religious character of any form of life properly called human as well as the necessarily bounded or closed character of all human communities, he had not recognized the importance of their political organization. Because he identified a people's distinctive way of life with the understanding of the world articulated in their language, Heidegger failed to observe that the sources of conflict within nations were as fundamental and enduring than the differences among them.[10]

Heidegger was unable to recapture the pretheoretical experience that constitutes the basis of all human knowledge, because his discovery that all thought was historically limited convinced him that it was impossible to understand past thinkers as they understood themselves. According to Heidegger, all human thought is bounded both by the past experience that is projected into the present and by unknown future possibilities. One of the problems with the traditional conception of intelligible being and truth as eternal was precisely that it did not allow for unknown future possibilities; it implied that existence had a necessary structure which was essentially static.[11] The traditional conception of intelligible being was thus fundamentally at odds with our experience of human freedom—or openness. But, Strauss objected, Heidegger's notion of historicity also entailed a dogmatic limitation on the possibilities of human understanding, because it excluded the possibility that a political philosopher in the past could have disclosed the truth about human existence— for his time *and ours.*

> It seems as if historicism were animated by the certainty that the future will bring about the realization of possibilities of which no one has ever dreamt . . . whereas non-historical political philosophy lived not in such an open horizon, but in a horizon closed by the possibilities known at the

time. Yet the possibilities of the future are not unlimited as long as the differences between men and angels and between men and brutes have not been abolished.[12]

Examining the emergence of Greek philosophy in its own terms, Strauss found it did not arise in response to some mysterious 'call of Being', nor did it consist essentially in an inexplicable insight into the unity or wonderful intelligibility of the whole. Philosophy arose when human beings began to ask which of the contradictory accounts of the right way of doing things and of the first things handed down from olden times on the authority, ultimately, of the gods was correct. This questioning proceeded in terms of two prephilosophic distinctions based on common experience: (1) the difference between the knowledge of things we acquire from firsthand experience and that related to us secondhand from the past, as tradition or hearsay; and (2) the difference between things that come into being on their own and those which are made. Together these prephilosophic distinctions gave rise to an understanding of the difference between nature and convention, characteristic of pre-Socratic as well as Socratic philosophy, in which nature is regarded as first in all senses—oldest, most fundamental, and most important. In light of this distinction human laws and customs appear to be mere products of agreement or conventions; the first philosophers thus devoted themselves to the study of nature and neglected human affairs.[13]

Only when a philosopher asked, why philosophy? did the human things become of central philosophic concern. To ask why a human being should pursue philosophy is to ask why human beings should devote their efforts to acquiring knowledge rather than power or wealth; it is to ask what is the best way of life. Once philosophy becomes self-reflective, philosophers perceive the need to articulate and defend their own activity in terms of the debate that characterizes politics concerning what goods are most desirable or necessary to obtain and how best to acquire them. Self-reflective philosophy thus necessarily becomes *political philosophy*.[14]

THE PROBLEM OF SOCRATES

"Socrates is said to have been the first who called philosophy down from heaven and forced it to make inquiries about life and manners and good and bad things."[15] To determine what Western philosophy was originally, it thus becomes necessary to address "the problem of Socrates."

Nietzsche had raised the problem, but had not been able to solve it, because he had not distinguished adequately among the three primary sources of our knowledge of the first political philosopher.[16] Nietzsche had leveled the Aristophanic critique at the Socrates of Xenophon and Plato; but the Socrates celebrated by his students differed significantly from the philosopher lampooned by the ancient comedian. Nevertheless, Nietzsche's critique reraised the question, whether the different parts of the Western tradition—particularly the poetry of Sophocles and the rationalism of Socrates—were compatible.[17]

> The problem of Socrates . . . can only be preparatory to "the problem of Socrates" as stated by Nietzsche: The question of what Socrates stood for inevitably becomes the question of the worth of what Socrates stood for. . . . The return to the origins of the Great Tradition has become necessary because of the radical questioning of that tradition . . . that may be said to culminate in Nietzsche's attack on Socrates or on Plato.[18]

In the lectures he gave on "The Problem of Socrates" at the University of Chicago in 1958, Strauss proceeded to examine the three major sources of our knowledge of Socrates; these lectures provide a preliminary version of Strauss's main lines of argument in his later books. Although he published his account of Plato's reply to Aristophanes' critique first in the essay "On Plato's Republic" in *The City and Man* (1964),[19] Strauss's books otherwise follow the lines of thought laid out in the lectures: in *Socrates and Aristophanes* (1966), he gave a fuller account of Aristophanes' critique of Socrates or the case for the need to encompass the philosopher's partial knowledge in a more complete poetic understanding of the human condition; in *Xenophon's Socratic Discourse* (1970) and *Xenophon's Socrates* (1972) he expanded his analysis of the only plausibly historical description; and in *The Argument and the Action of Plato's "Laws"* (1975), published posthumously, he looked in more detail at the only Platonic dialogue in which Socrates does not appear, the dialogue Strauss used in his lectures to correct or modify the radical critique of poetry at the end of the *Republic*. In his final *Studies in Platonic Political Philosophy* (1983), he then turned to ask about the value of the Great Tradition explicitly in light of the Nietzschean-Heideggerian critique.

ARISTOPHANES: THE ANCIENT ARGUMENT FOR THE PREEMINENCE OF POETRY OVER PHILOSOPHY

In his lectures Strauss argued that Aristophanes' comic critique of Socrates in *The Clouds* and Plato's response to that critique in the *Republic, Symposium,* and *Laws* constituted *the* classic statement of "the ancient quarrel between poetry and philosophy." That quarrel became the focal point of Strauss's study of the ancients, because he saw that Aristophanes' comic critique and Plato's acknowledgement of its importance showed that the ancients recognized not only the limits of human knowledge but also the possibility that the search for knowledge would destroy the humanity of the people engaged in it at the very beginning of the history of philosophy; these problems did not become evident solely at the end, as Heidegger maintained.

In *The Clouds* Aristophanes presents Socrates as head of a school in which he and his students investigate the nature of things aloft and under the ground. He also teaches an art of argumentation so powerful that it enables its possessor to defeat any opponent in court. The poet brings out the limitations of both the philosopher's "heavenly" wisdom and his rhetorical skills through the plot.

Socrates' lack of practical wisdom comes to the fore dramatically when we see him tell his would-be student Strepsiades that, contrary to the law of the city which mandates their worship, the Olympian gods do not exist, before the philosopher has examined the old man to determine whether he has the intellectual ability and moral character necessary to study successfully. Socrates does not take even elementary precautions, Aristophanes suggests, because he believes that his rhetorical ability to meet and defeat any argument makes him immune from legal prosecution. Although he is a materialist philosopher, Aristophanes' Socrates believes in the omnipotence of *logos*. He does not see that human beings do not always act logically or legally in a purely public fashion. Like Strepsiades, who burns down Socrates' school at the end, purportedly because the philosopher denied the gods, human beings often act on their own, privately, with physical force rather than persuasive speech, out of passion, without explaining or perhaps even knowing, fully, why they act as they do.

Socrates lacks prudence, Aristophanes suggests, because he fails to recognize his own vulnerability or lack of self-sufficiency. As a philosopher he cares about the eternal truth, not about transitory phenomena. He does not see that he himself is one of those transitory phenomena. Not only is he vulnerable to attack; he also depends upon others to produce both the food he eats and the students with whom he associates. In a word, Socrates lacks self-knowledge; and the reason he lacks it seems to be his extraordinary asceticism. Indifferent himself to both physical suffering and physical attraction, Socrates finds it difficult to understand either why Strepsiades has a hard time concentrating when he is lying in a bed full of fleas or why the old man was led into the burdensome debts he wants Socrates to help him escape.

At first glance Aristophanes' depiction of Socrates thus appears to be diametrically opposed to Xenophon and Plato's. Their Socrates "is a man of the greatest practical wisdom. . . ; he is the erotic man par excellence."[20]

But, Strauss points out, there are disconcerting continuities among the three depictions. Both Xenophon and Plato indicate that Socrates was recognized as a philosophic student of nature before he turned to concentrate on the human things.[21] Although many commentators (including Nietzsche) have been tempted to describe Aristophanes' Socrates as a typical sophist, the philosopher we see in *The Clouds* does not ask to be paid for his teaching any more than the Platonic Socrates. Aristophanes' Socrates is characterized by the same great powers of intellectual concentration, physical endurance, and indifference to bodily attraction that Plato dramatizes in his *Symposium*. In all three primary sources we thus find descriptions of the same distinctive individual. What we see in *The Clouds* might be a caricature of a "pre-Socratic" Socrates; the philosopher we encounter in Xenophon and Plato may be a man who took Aristophanes' criticism—or even friendly warning—to heart.

What *is* clear is that in *The Clouds* Aristophanes presented the first statement of the *problem* represented by Socrates, a statement to which both Xenophon and Plato responded. But to understand Aristophanes' view of Socrates properly, Strauss suggests, we need to look at *The Clouds* in light of his work as a whole. Unlike Strepsiades, the comic poet did not simply object to Socrates' impiety; in *The Birds* he celebrates the overthrow of the Olympian regime by an Athenian pederast who replaced the old gods with a new set of natural deities. The difference between the opprobrium heaped on the philosopher and the glory of the pederast points to the fundamental grounds of the poet's critique. Unlike Socrates, Peisthetairos recognizes that preserving belief in some gods is necessary to establish and maintain political order, which is necessary, in turn, to defend oneself from potential attack.

In all five surviving plays he wrote before *The Birds* Aristophanes dramatized attempts of private people using private means to escape onerous public duties or orders. As he pointed out most emphatically in his characterization of Dikaiopolis in his first play, *The Acharnians*, the natural desire human beings have to attain pleasure and avoid pain is essentially self-regarding. Because the satisfaction of this desire requires the cooperation or assistance of others, people join together. Once joined, however, the self-regarding character of their desires brings them into conflict. To restrain that conflict, people agree on a set of conventions or laws. But, because the natural desires would continue to lead them to evade these conventional restraints in private, out of the public eye, human beings also need superhuman supervisors, judges, and guarantors of their oaths to make their agreements effective.[22]

As Aristophanes shows in both *The Peace* and *The Birds*, the gods are conventional. More than other conventions or products of law, however, the gods lose their effectiveness if their conventional basis becomes widely recognized. To function as superhuman judges and police, they must seem to have wills and powers of their own. Whether they are presented in anthropomorphic form or not, they are, therefore, always associated with natural processes like thunder and the power of chance, which are essentially beyond human control. They acquire some of their power or credibility from their antiquity (as Peisthetairos indicates when he tells the birds they should become gods, because they can claim to have had power of old). By their own admission in *The Birds*, the Olympians are not immortal. As Peisthetairos shows them in action, their continued existence as gods depends upon their being worshipped by men. Just as the preservation of human beings requires gods, so Aristophanes shows, the existence of the gods depends likewise on human beings.[23]

If the preservation of human existence requires belief in or recognition of some kind of divinities, it is neither prudent nor just to proclaim the truth about the gods too openly or directly. This is Aristophanes' most evident criticism not only of Socrates but also of Euripides, who also prays only to Aether, Tongue, and the like.[24]

Aristophanes' deeper-going criticism of Socrates concerns the philosopher's failure to understand the essentially unsatisfiable character of human desire. By acquiring power over all other beings, Peisthetairos might appear to have overcome all restraints on his own desires—we see him eating his own "gods," for example—except his eventual death (which Strauss argues is too serious a subject to be treated in a comedy). But, Aristophanes shows, Peisthetairos continually has to take action against those who would undermine, if not openly contest his rule; to maintain his position of singular preeminence, he cannot allow anyone to become his equal. As a result, he has no friends.[25]

Human desire can never be completely satisfied, Aristophanes shows, because it is essentially complex. To attain the blessings of peace and prosperity, it is necessary to impose conventional restraints both on immediate sexual desire and on its more imaginative poetic expressions. Precisely because human desire is intellectual or imaginative as well as physical, however, it rebels against *all* the constraints put upon it—natural as well as conventional—and projects innovative, if essentially impossible schemes to overcome them. All of Aristophanes' comedies present such schemes—they are, as such, direct expressions of the essentially unlimited character of human eros.[26]

When Aristophanes accuses Socrates in *The Clouds* of lacking prudence and self-knowledge, because he lacks eros, the comic poet accuses the philosopher of not recognizing the inescapable limitations of the human condition and the frustration of human desire that necessarily results. Ridiculously perching himself in a basket hanging above the earth, Socrates thinks he has more in common with the expansive, light element than with the "ephmerals" below. Failing to recognize the limitations of his own existence, Socrates does not feel and so does not understand the desire of others to overcome them. In contrast to the poets, he thus lacks compassion. His indifference to the needs and concerns of others also reveals his failure to take account of the necessary presuppositions or conditions of his own bodily existence. Using his knowledge to steal food and to undermine the family structure which has provided him with these students, Socrates is shown by Aristophanes to be fundamentally unjust.

But, the comic poet suggests, the philosopher's moral failings are ultimately a product of an intellectual error. Socrates does not understand the way in which human nature, although part of nature, is distinctive. Any account of the whole which does not recognize the tensions among the different parts is patently inadequate. In Aristophanes' world there are two primary poles—the elemental and the erotic:

> Socrates asserts the primacy of air or ether; the birds assert for all practical purposes the primacy of Eros. . . . If Aristophanes had been compelled to choose. . . , he would have chosen the birds' doctrine, a doctrine that, with the help of Parmenides and Empedocles, could easily have been stated in philosophic terms. This entitles us perhaps to say that Aristophanes is not opposed to philosophy simply, but only to a philosophy that, disregarding Eros, has no link with poetry.[27]

But Aristophanes did not merely choose. On the contrary, he indicates that the traditional teaching about the primacy of Eros—the birds' theology is very close to Hesiod—is also inadequate. At their own peril, the birds fail to mention air, the element in which they themselves live. They not only neglect the Socratic element; they also fail to explain the nature of the Eros they emphasize.[28] Aristophanes' comic art encompasses both partial views. Because the poet begins with the human and examines it in relation to both what is higher and what is lower, he provides a more accurate picture of the whole. Whereas philosophy is reductive and hence destructive, Aristophanes' poetry not only provides a salutary teaching but also reveals the truth, if in a "cloudy" form, to those able to understand.[29]

XENOPHON: THE RHETORICAL RESPONSE TO ARISTOPHANES

Both Xenophon and Plato respond to Aristophanes' most fundamental criticism of Socrates, that he failed to recognize the difference between the human and the non-human, by showing the philosopher constantly asking, What is ... ? As Strauss emphasizes at the beginning of *The City and Man*, Socrates' characteristic question reflects his perception of the noetic heterogeneity of the whole. In contrast to his "pre-Socratic" predecessors, Socrates does not ask generally, What is being? That is, he does not ask what it is that all things in existence have in common. He inquires, instead, about the distinguishing characteristics of the various kinds of beings and suggests, thereby, that they cannot be reduced to a common denominator.

Socrates was so far from ignoring the difference between the human and the non-human, Xenophon states, that in contrast to all his philosophic predecessors, he restricted his inquiries to human affairs.[30] He asked those who attempted to discover the nature of the cosmos: (1) whether they thought they already had sufficient knowledge of the human things; (2) whether they thought human beings could actually acquire such divine knowledge; and (3) whether they thought they could use such knowledge, if attained, to control natural processes like thunder and rain. Socrates went so far as to characterize these other philosophers as "madmen" who knew no measure, but took things to one or another extreme:

> Some of them believe that being is only one and others believe that there are infinitely many beings; some believe that all things are always in motion and others believe that nothing is ever in motion; some believe that all things come into being and perish, others believe that nothing ever comes into being or perishes. (*Memorabilia* I.1.11–15)

The implication of Socrates' statement is "that according to the sane Socrates the beings are numerable or surveyable; those beings are unchangeable while the other things change, and those beings do not come into being or perish while the other things come into being and perish."[31] What looks like a prototype of the Platonic doctrine of ideas remains *only* an implication. More important than the implied answer is the question and the understanding (or recognition of the partial and only partial intelligibility) of the whole it contains.[32] Socrates' insight into the noetic heterogeneity of the whole is the source of the moderation expressed by his claim only to seek or love knowledge, not to possess it. If the parts of the whole are fundamentally different, we have and can have only partial knowledge. We cannot know the whole or have knowledge per se.[33]

Socrates conceived of his turn to the 'what is' questions as a return to common sense. The world as we first encounter it is composed of a variety of things. And, as Heidegger discovered through his studies of Plato and Aristotle, both the variegation and the interrelations among the things we encounter are captured in speech. "One may say that according to

Socrates the things which are 'first in themselves' are somehow 'first for us'; the things which are 'first in themselves' are in a manner, but necessarily, revealed in men's opinion."³⁴ Socrates' discovery of the noetic heterogeneity of the cosmos thus led him to adopt his characteristic method of investigation or dialectics.

Xenophon and Plato both indicate that Socrates did not discover the noetic heterogeneity of the whole or adopt his characteristic mode of inquiry until he was well into his philosophic career. The Socrates they describe is a philosopher who has learned something the thinker Aristophanes lampooned did not know. But, Strauss observes, "both Plato and Xenophon treat Socrates' 'pre-Socratic' past with great delicacy." Plato's Socrates relates the story of his turn away from investigations of natural phenomena to the study of the *logoi* to his friends only after he is "beyond the reach of those who condemn the study of nature as wicked." Xenophon's account of the change is to be found in his *Oeconomicus*, the dialogue that "describes Socrates' famous turning away from his earlier pursuit, which brought him the reputation of being an idle talker and a man who measures the air . . . toward the study of only the human things."³⁵

Strauss turns to Xenophon to learn the reasons for and character of "the Socratic turn," because of the four sources of our knowledge of Socrates, "Xenophon is the only one who, while knowing Socrates himself, showed by deed that he was willing to be a historian. Hence it would appear that the primary source for our knowledge of Socrates should be the Socratic writings of Xenophon."³⁶

In the *Oeconomicus* Socrates relates a conversation he once had with an Athenian gentleman. The philosopher sought out Ischomachos to ask why he was reputed to be *kalos k'agathos* (the conventional Greek term to describe a gentleman which literally means beautiful or noble and good). Xenophon does not tell us what led Socrates to inquire into the character of the noble. Strauss suggests that it was the comic critique Aristophanes presented of the philosopher in *The Clouds*. As a philosopher Socrates thought that he himself embodied the natural excellence of human beings; but, Aristophanes reminded him, his way of life was not generally regarded to be *kalos k'agathos*. People seemed to use different standards in judging human beings than they did in evaluating animals or inanimate tools.³⁷ Was human nobility, as opposed to excellence or goodness, merely a matter of opinion or convention, rather than nature? Since nobility could not be seen or observed, but was a matter of reputation, the truth about it could be discovered only through an investigation of the opinions people had about it. By asking What is noble?, Socrates thus discovered not only the difference between the human and the nonhuman (and thus the noetic heterogeneity of the whole) but also the need to investigate the natures of the various parts by examining what people said about them, the *logoi*.

As a result of this turn in Socrates' thought, Xenophon shows, the philosopher no longer lacks practical wisdom or is indifferent to the desires of others as Aristophanes charged. On the contrary, in relating the instructions he received from Ischomachos to Kritoboulos, the son of his old friend Kriton, Socrates demonstrates he has as good an understanding of politics and a better understanding of eros than the gentleman farmer.[38]

In *The Clouds* Aristophanes dramatized Socrates' lack of prudence by having him blurt out some of his most blasphemous doctrines before he had examined Strepsiades to see whether the old man would make an apt student. In the *Oeconomicus*, Socrates first interrogates Kritoboulos about his understanding of the economic art. When the philosopher discovers that the young man wants to look fine in the eyes of others without expending too much effort, Socrates stops examining his opinions dialogically and instead relates a speech he once heard from an Athenian farmer about what it takes to gain a reputation as a gentleman.[39] Insofar as Ischomachos suggests that farming is both the most easily learned way to increase one's wealth and the most noble, Socrates' relating of his speech is designed to appeal to Kritoboulos's strongest desires. Like Plato's Socrates, Xenophon's philosopher speaks ad hominem. Like Aristophanes' Socrates, he not only investigates the nature of all things; he is also an accomplished rhetorician. But unlike his earlier Aristophanic incarnation, Xenophon's Socrates does not believe in the omnipotence of speech or *logos*.

Socrates' relating of his conversation with Ischomachos brings out the difference between the way of life reputed to be noble and good and that of the philosopher. First, Ischomachos tells Socrates, a gentleman has to be wealthy. As Socrates reminds Kritoboulos, the needs of the philosopher are minimal, and he has friends who will supply them. A gentleman, Ischomachos informs Socrates, has to train assistants—a wife, stewards, and slaves—to help him obtain and maintain his estate. Both the gentleman and the philosopher are thus shown to be teachers. Inasmuch as Ischomachos and Socrates both instruct their associates to sort things into their different kinds, they may even be said to inculcate the same intellectual discipline. However, the purpose of the sorting in the two cases is very different. Ischomachos shows his wife how to arrange things so that they will be 'ready-at-hand' to use; according to Xenophon (*Memorabilia* IV.6.1), Socrates inquires with his companions about what each of the beings is—in itself.[40] Understanding household management almost entirely in terms of calculations of self-interest, Ischomachos fails to mention erotic attraction in describing the natural division of labor between husband and wife. In both his *Memorabilia* and *Symposium*, Xenophon reminds his readers that Socrates claimed, somewhat comically, to be an expert in erotic matters.[41] Ischomachos regards attempts to "dress things up" to be not merely unjust, but ignoble deceptions. As he objects to his wife's using cosmetics to make herself more attractive to him, so he himself refuses to say anything untrue, even when it would be in his interest. Socrates does not tell lies, but he does adapt both the content and form of his speech to the character of his interlocutors.

Because he succeeded in becoming wealthy without defrauding others, Ischomachos is said to be "noble and good," while the philosopher is "reputed to be an idle talker who measures the air and is reproached on account of his poverty." But, Ischomachos objects, his reputation does him no good. It merely arouses the envy of others, from whose slander he continually has to protect himself (1) by always doing the just thing himself and (2) by bringing to light the injustice of others by accusing them in court.

In *The Clouds* Aristophanes predicted that Socrates would come to harm at the hands of others, because he overestimated the power of *logos* and underestimated the power of *eros*. In the *Oeconomicus* Xenophon responds, people envy and unjustly try to harm anyone who achieves any kind of distinction. There are two and only two possible ways to defend oneself. The first and most common is, like Ischomachos, to amass goods by means of calculation and, then, to secure them by law—the product of an honest agreement or contract, which becomes effective only through the threat of punishment. That is, to engage in politics. The second is, like Socrates, not to seek evident or public goods—the wealth and honor that most people desire (and hence envy)—but to seek the true, but invisible goods of human existence in private in the company of friends. As Xenophon shows more clearly in his *Memorabilia*, a certain mutual attraction or *eros* is necessary to bring friends together, but there is no need of force.[42] Neither form of protection seems to be without cost. Ischomachos constantly has to go to court; as a result, he has no leisure. Socrates spends his days idly conversing with his friends. But, as Xenophon and his readers knew, the philosopher was finally condemned to death by an Athenian court. In his account of the *Apology of Socrates to the Jury*, however, Xenophon shows that Socrates deliberately provoked the jury into condemning him, because he thought it was time for him to die. As the philosopher explained to Hermogenes, at seventy years of age, he could not know when his reason would begin to fade, and he did know that hemlock would be an easy, painless way to expire. Unable to understand the peculiar pleasures or attractions of the philosophic life, Xenophon suggests, the jurors did not convict Socrates because they envied his wisdom; they were angered by his "high-minded" boasting. So long as Socrates restrained his speech, a peaceful accommodation, if not mutual understanding between philosophy and the city was possible.[43]

Unlike Aristophanes' Socrates, who thought he could talk his way out of any court case, neither the gentleman farmer nor his philosophical student have any illusions about the omnipotence of *logos*. On the contrary, Ischomachos tells Socrates, in training stewards to manage slaves, it is necessary not only to praise them for good work and to appeal to their self-interest by promising them a share of the fruits of their labor; it is also necessary to watch them carefully and threaten them with coercive punishment, if they slacken their efforts. One cannot rule human beings by persuasion alone; force is also necessary. The reason, stated generally, is that the appeal to the individual's self-interest, which lies at the root not merely of Ischomachos's household but of political associations simply, consistently undermines both the dedication to the common good or justice and the honesty Ischomachos and the city would inculcate.

The limits of *logos* are not to be observed solely in the requirements of ruling human beings. As Ischomachos indicates in his praise of farming, nature as a whole is not entirely regulated by reason. Little technical skill may be required to till the land, but the size of the harvest is not a reflection solely of the farmer's diligence and self-control.[44] As Socrates points out in his introductory exchange with Kritoboulos, luck or "the gods" also play a role—in the form of unpredictable weather.

Like Aristophanes, Xenophon thus suggests that both the importance of politics and the limitations of philosophy are results of the partial, but only partial intelligibility of the whole. But the self-styled rhetorician pictures both ways of life as inherently more satisfying than the comic poet.

By equating household management with political rule, Strauss observes, in his *Oeconomicus* Xenophon "abstracts from the specific dignity, grandeur, and splendor of the political and the military."[45] Xenophon reminds his readers, however, of a more glorious example of the political alternative in the introductory exchange between Socrates and Kritoboulos. Socrates promises to introduce Kritoboulos not merely to one, but to several, experts in the art of acquisition; and the first such expert he mentions is Cyrus! But, because the Emperor of Persia does not represent an appropriate model for a citizen of democratic Athens, Socrates quickly shifts to relating his conversation with Ischomachos.[46] The limited capacities and condition of his interlocutor in the *Oeconomicus* lead

Socrates to understate the attractions of the philosophical life as well. Socrates does not want to convince someone with as little energy and self-control as Kritoboulos to search for wisdom. In the *Oeconomicus*, the advantages of the philosophical life become apparent only in contrast to the limitations of the political.[47]

In his memoirs Xenophon explicitly defends Socrates not merely from Aristophanes' accusation that he was unjust, but from the public indictment. In strictly legal terms, Strauss points out, the defense is not altogether successful. Responding to the charge that Socrates did not believe in the gods of the city, Xenophon reminds his readers that Socrates was often seen worshipping, both in public and at home. The fact that Socrates went through the motions does not prove he *believed* in the gods of the city, however; impiety is a crime of thought. Responding to the accusation that Socrates corrupted the young, Xenophon emphasizes how unlikely it was for a man of Socrates' known temperance to lead anyone to become drunk or violent. Xenophon does not even try to deny the specific accusation that Socrates led his associates to look down on the laws of Athens, because they mandated the selection of officials by lot rather than on the basis of merit. Nor does he deny that Socrates persuaded his young followers that he was wiser than their fathers. Legality does not necessarily exhaust the meaning of justice, however. To demonstrate that Socrates' justice extended far beyond and above the law, Xenophon spends most of the book showing how Socrates benefitted his companions without harming anyone.

In his description of "the man himself," Xenophon shows that Aristophanes did not understand the character or significance of Socrates' continence, because he had too materialistic an understanding of pleasure. As Socrates explains to the sophist Antiphon, "his continence regarding the pleasures of the body stem[med] from his awareness of a more lasting pleasure, namely, the pleasure going with one's belief that one . . . is growing in virtue." The philosopher's self-restraint did not signify a lack of desire or human feeling, as the comedian thought; it was a product, rather, of the great pleasure he received from learning and sharing that learning with his friends. Compared to this great blessing, all other sources of pleasure paled into insignificance.

Socrates did not prostitute himself by taking money for his teaching, for example, because he wanted to remain free to choose with whom he would speak. If he did not want to engage in a conversation with a particular person, he would—as in all cases when he did not want to give his reasons—refer to his *daimonion*. As Xenophon shows quite clearly in his *Apology of Socrates to the Jury*, such a reference to his *daimonion* did not mean that Socrates himself did not know or could not state the reasons for his actions; he could. What might have seemed to be great boasting on Socrates' part, his claim to have a special divinity, was a kind of dissimulation, designed to hide his superior wisdom and so to spare the feelings of his inferiors—as well as to preserve his own freedom of action.

Socrates' talk of his erotic attraction to the youths whose company he sought was also playful.[48] What Socrates actually did, as in the case of Euthydemos, was to approach young men with the speeches he thought best designed to show them that they lacked knowledge and needed to seek it. If they were persuaded, they then sought his company as a means of achieving wisdom.

Xenophon never shows us an example of Socrates' blissful conversations with a true friend, that is, one who was truly capable of learning. In the place where we might have expected to hear about a conversation between Socrates and Plato (*Memorabilia* III.8, following conversations with Glaucon [III.6], with whom Socrates associated for the sake of Charmides and Plato, and with Charmides [III.7]), Xenophon relates instead a second conversation Socrates had with the hedonist Aristippos. Socrates had embarrassed Aristippos by showing him that rather than freeing him from onerous civic obligations, his status as an alien made him more vulnerable than a citizen would be to both persecution and enslavement. Contrary to Aristophanes' implicit charge, Xenophon's Socrates recognizes that political association is a necessary means of preserving human life, including his own.

Aristippos illustrates the difficulty Socrates faced in general. Rather than acknowledge the philosopher's intention to benefit him by correcting his opinions, Aristippos responds to Socrates' questions by trying to strike back. By asking if Socrates thought anything were good, Aristippos hoped to refute the philosopher by showing that the same thing could be both good and bad or beautiful and ugly, depending upon the circumstances. In order to forestall Aristippos, Socrates maintained that there is nothing good or beautiful in itself, but that things are good or beautiful only for or in relation to some specific end. So understood, Socrates' subsequent discussion of the excellence of houses makes clear, there is no fundamental difference between the good and the useful or the beautiful and the pleasant.

Was there a fundamental difference, then, between Xenophon's more historical Socrates, who denies that there is anything good or noble in itself, and Plato's more poetic, philosophic hero who teaches that there are ideas of the good-in-itself and the beautiful-in-itself? Socrates apparently taught his student Xenophon the difference between the good and the useful as well as the difference between the beautiful and the pleasant, Strauss observes. In the conversations Xenophon reports Socrates had with several artisans and the courtesan Theodote following his encounter with Aristippos he shows that the beautiful is ambiguous: for the beholder, it is precisely that which is good only to look at and has no other use. For the possessor, however, the beautiful can be used to lead others. Socrates used beautiful speeches to persuade young men to seek real virtue or wisdom. The beauty of Socrates' speeches—or, indeed, of Socrates himself—could not literally be seen, however; it could be apprehended only by listening (or ultimately in thought).[49]

Beauty, properly speaking, is a property or product of reason and order. Most people do not understand this, because they cannot detach themselves sufficiently from the sensible to appreciate the purely intelligible.[50] As the reaction Socrates' companions have to the beauty of the courtesan illustrates, people believe in the reality of what they can touch more than in what they merely see, just as they believe in the reality of what they can see for themselves more than what they merely hear from others. By wanting to touch what they see, in practice they confound the beautiful or noble with the pleasant or useful.

To convince young men like Euthydemos that they need to seek knowledge, Socrates had to persuade them that knowledge or wisdom would be a useful, if not indispensable means of satisfying their desires—like Kritoboulos, to look fine in the eyes of others, or like Euthydemos, to rule. Socrates had to present his wisdom or philosophy, in other words, in a practical guise. To be rhetorically effective, he had to conceal the true character of his own activity and object.

Precisely because what is good and beautiful varies, according to the person and his or her circumstances, however, neither goodness nor beauty can be generalized like justice or piety in the form of law. In other words, neither the good nor the beautiful in human life are or can be made to be simply conventional. The questions What is good? and What is beautiful? are, therefore, especially apt beginning points in the search for wisdom. Socrates used them both to attract students and to sort out the apt from the less able.[51]

Xenophon "is very anxious to show that Socrates was good according to the general notion of goodness," Strauss concludes, "and that is perhaps not the deepest level in Socrates."[52] The self-described orator defends Socrates primarily by illustrating the salutary character of his political or Odyssean rhetoric and by understating the extent to which Socratic philosophy threatens the basis of human life, both the city and the family, by raising questions like What is law? and What is god?[53] To discover what was truly dangerous and daimonically attractive about the philosopher, we have to turn to Plato.

PLATO: THE COMPREHENSIVE RESPONSE

"Plato's *Republic* may be said to be the reply *par excellence* to Aristophanes."[54] But like most reactions the *Republic* contains many traces of the
original. As Plato's literal incorporation of passages from the *Assembly
of Women* indicates, his Socrates has essentially the same understanding
of politics as Aristophanes. Like the comic poet, in the *Republic* Socrates
shows that political associations arise naturally out of the requirements
of self-preservation, but that human desires are not exhausted or satisfied
by meeting those requirements. To prevent the conflict attempts to satisfy these extensive desires are apt to provoke, it is necessary not merely
to control what people are taught (especially by poets), but ultimately to
abolish private property and the family as well. There is, Strauss points
out in his lectures, more consonance between Aristophanes' attack on
Socrates and the things we see him teaching in the *Republic*—the problematic moral consequences of the contradictions in the traditional theology, the power of rhetoric, and the right of the wise to rule the ignorant—than one might initially suppose. Just as Aristophanes presents
the realization of common human desires to end war through love and
to institute justice by abolishing the causes of injustice in his *Lysistrata,
Assembly of Women,* and *Plutos* to show why the realization of such
desires is not possible or even altogether desirable, so in the *Republic*
Plato's Socrates shows why it will never be possible to establish a perfectly just polity.[55] In opposition to the comic poet, however, Plato's Socrates indicates that it is possible for an individual philosopher to be both
happy and just.[56]

The major addition Plato's Socrates makes to the institutions proposed
in the *Assembly of Women* is the philosopher-king. This proposal will,
he predicts, appear even more ridiculous than the institutions he took
from Aristophanes; it may even arouse armed opposition. Rather than
undermining political order as Aristophanes had suggested, Plato's Socrates maintains that the rule and only the rule of philosophers will solve
the political problem. He thus not only contradicts the comic poet; he
also apparently disagrees with Xenophon's Socrates, who suggests that
there are two competing definitions of the good life—the political and
the philosophic.[57]

In his "Plato," Strauss observed, Farabi had thus begun by suggesting
that a man needed both theoretical and practical knowledge in order to
be perfectly happy. But, Farabi gradually indicated, the regime proposed
in the *Republic* was designed to stave off popular envy; the philosopher
could live happily minding his own business in an inferior regime. In his
own readings of Plato's two longest, most comprehensive and obviously

political dialogues, Strauss also argues that Plato shows that philosophers would not and could not rule as such. Nietzsche was wrong, therefore, when he declared, *"Genuine philosophers . . . are commanders and legislators. . . ,* e.g. Plato."[58]

The Philosopher-King as the Impossible "Solution" in the *Republic*

In his dialogues, Strauss emphasizes, Plato presents exclusively the speeches and deeds of others.[59] The dialogues must, therefore, be read like dramas in which one never identifies the views of the author with any particular character. It may be tempting to take Socrates as Plato's spokesman; but Socrates is not the only philosopher who appears in the dialogues, and if we take him as Plato's spokesman, we are confronted by the fact that he is explicitly said to be ironic. There is a notable difference between Socrates and his student, moreover; Socrates did not write.

Plato was surely aware of the essential defect of writing Socrates stresses at the end of the *Phaedrus,* that writings say the same thing to all people; his dialogues must thus be understood to remedy this defect. For Plato "the proper work of a writing is . . . to reveal the truth to some while leading others to salutary opinions; . . . to arouse to thinking those who are by nature fit for it."

Like Xenophon, Plato shows Socrates saying different things to different people, first, because such differences are a requisite characteristic of both responsible and effective teaching. But the different teachings presented in the different dialogues do not merely reflect the different characters of the participants in the conversation, nor are they simply matters of rhetoric or persuasion.[60] "Plato's work consists of many dialogues because it imitates the manyness, the variety, the heterogeneity of being. . . . There are many dialogues because the whole consists of many parts." Unlike numerical units, however, the parts cannot simply be added up to constitute the whole.[61]

> The individual dialogue is not a chapter from an encyclopedia of the philosophic sciences. . . , still less a relic of a stage of Plato's development. Each dialogue . . . reveals the truth about that part. But the truth about a part is a partial truth, a half truth. Each dialogue, we venture to say, abstracts from something that is most important to the subject matter of the dialogue.

Insofar as it abstracts from something relevant to the subject, Strauss points out,

> The subject matter as presented in the dialogue is strictly speaking impossible. But the impossible . . . if treated as possible is in the highest sense ridiculous or . . . comical. The core of every Aristophanean comedy is something impossible of the kind indicated.

As Strauss sees it, "The Platonic dialogue brings to its completion what could be thought to have been completed by Aristophanes."[62]

Reading Plato in the context set by Aristophanes enables us to move back from the "tradition of Christian Platonism" to "primitive" Platonism. The differences emerge from a comparison of the descriptions of Socrates by his ancient students and the works of a Christian Platonist, Sir Thomas More, whose *Utopia* is a "free imitation" of the *Republic.* Plato's Socrates is more austere with regard to the pleasures of the body than his Christian follower. (The conversation in *Utopia* takes place after dinner, rather than instead of it.) But he has a less tragic, more comic sense of life. Whereas in his *Dialogue of Comfort against Tribulation* More reminds his readers that Christ wept twice or thrice, but never laughed, Plato and Xenophon's Socrates leaves no example of weeping, but reportedly laughs on his deathbed. The apparently slight literary difference points to a fundamental substantive difference. Comforts—both physical and spiritual—become necessary if life is essentially tragic; if happiness can be attained in this life, however, continence could appear to be the necessary condition and the search for comfort an impediment. *The* secret Strauss thought he discovered by studying Farabi's *Plato* was that Socrates represented the only fully satisfying form of human existence—that is, the attainment of happiness in *this* world—but the open presentation of that fact was apt to provoke popular envy. To show that this was the correct reading, however, Strauss had to look at Plato's Socrates in his own historical context, free from possible distortions introduced by the tension between reason and revelation which shaped, if in different ways, the writings of both Christian and Muslim interpreters.[63]

Reading the *Republic* in light of Aristophanes' critique, Strauss argues that in this dialogue Socrates' arguments abstract, first, from body, but more fundamentally, from eros. The depreciation of eros is not a product or reflection of Socrates' own character, however; it is, rather, as the comic poet himself indicated in plays like the *Wasps, Assembly of Women,* and *Plutos,* a reflection of the anti- or anerotic character of politics. Eros properly understood points to philosophy as the only possible means of its satisfaction. As Socrates suggests in his famous image of the cave, eros can neither be comprehended nor recognized at the level of politics, because it constitutes a desire to transcend the limits of the body which are, ultimately, the limits of politics as well.[64] Socrates' presentation of philosophy in the *Republic* is necessarily distorted by the political setting and subject matter. But once this distortion is recognized, it can be corrected.[65]

"The principle guiding the specific abstraction which characterizes [a]

dialogue . . . is revealed primarily by the setting. . . : its time, place, characters, and action."[66] The setting is what gives rise to and limits, that is,
what literally defines, the conversation depicted. It is what Plato chooses
to show presented as what has happened historically, that is, at least partially by chance.[67]

In the *Republic*, for example, Plato lets us know the place in which the
conversation took place and the names of some of the participants, but
not the precise time. "Yet we are not left entirely in the dark" about
"the political circumstances in which the conversation about the political
principle took place." By setting the dialogue in the Piraeus where Socrates is compelled to speak to a group of ten men, Plato reminds his readers that

> Some years after the conversation, men linked to Socrates and Plato by
> kinship or friendship attempted . . . putting down the democracy and re-
> storing an aristocratic regime dedicated to virtue and justice. Among other
> things they established an authority called the Ten in the Piraeus.

The composition of the two groups of ten is different, however. "Polemarchus, Lysias, and Niceratus were mere victims of the so-called Thirty
Tyrants."[68] By discussing "justice in the presence of victims of an abortive
attempt made by most unjust men [oligarchs unhappy with the excesses
of democracy] to restore justice [by establishing a new regime that turned
out to be a worse tyranny]," Plato prepares his readers "for the possibility
that the restoration attempted in the *Republic* will not take place on the
political plane."[69]

The other two elements of the setting, in addition to time and place,
are the characters and the action. In the *Republic*, Strauss points out,
Socrates' major interlocutor is Plato's brother, Glaucon. "Xenophon tells
us that Socrates . . . cured him of his extreme political ambition. . . . Certain it is that the *Republic* supplies the most magnificent cure ever devised for every form of political ambition."[70]

The explicit question raised in the *Republic* is What is justice? Although Socrates' refutations of the three definitions offered by Cephalus,
Polemarchus, and Thrasymachus in Book I appear abortive, Strauss explains, they point both to a definition of justice and the difficulty it entails. If, as Socrates' refutation of Cephalus's more traditional definition
of justice as giving to each his or her due suggests, justice consists in
giving each what is good for him or her, and if injustice consists, as Socrates' refutation of Thrasymachus is supposed to show, in one part of a
community taking advantage of the other, justice becomes a problem if
what is good for the community as a whole is not good for all of its

members as individuals. Plato's *Republic* shows that this is the case: it would be good for the community if a philosopher ruled, but not for the philosopher himself.

Socrates begins, however, by suggesting that justice in the polity and in the individual must be essentially the same. When Glaucon challenges Socrates to show that justice is choiceworthy for its own sake, Socrates responds that first they have to determine what justice is. To find out, he suggests, they should look for justice "writ large" in a city.

From the perspective of the traditional reading of Plato primarily in terms of his theory of the ideas, Strauss emphasizes, Socrates' mode of proceeding in the *Republic* appears anomalous. Rather than seek the answer to the question What is justice? in an eternal idea of justice in itself, which should be the same not merely in individual and city, but everywhere and at all times, he follows Glaucon's example by looking for it in the coming-into-being of a city, a new city which unlike all others has been established entirely according to nature.[71]

That there is no unqualifiedly natural basis for the city is shown, in deed as it were, by the fact that it has to be founded; cities are products of human making or art. Like Gadamer, Strauss observes that the first "true" city Socrates founds is not humanly satisfying—as Glaucon's passionate protest against the "city of pigs" indicates. By having each person do what he or she does best by nature and exchange the results, this city provides for the necessities of physical preservation. To develop any form of human excellence, however, human beings have to possess more goods or leisure than is necessary simply for their preservation; and in striving to obtain those goods, Socrates suggests, they necessarily come into conflict. Armed guards thus become necessary to defend the city from invasion.[72]

Once a part of the city is armed, it becomes potentially dangerous to the other, unarmed part. The guardians must be carefully educated, therefore, not to misuse their power. But, Strauss observes, "the whole discussion partakes of the character of myth." Unlike Gadamer, who takes the explicitly unrealizable character of the educational prescriptions, especially the "noble lie" in which they culminate, simply as evidence that Socrates is not putting forth a practical program, Strauss thinks the content of the prescribed education is instructive. The difficulties point to the reasons why the institution of a perfectly just regime is impossible.

In *The Clouds* Aristophanes showed that the Unjust Speech defeated the Just Speech by pointing out that, according to the traditional stories, the gods who were supposed to defend justice were themselves pleasure-seeking and unjust. To demonstrate the superiority of Justice to Injustice as Glaucon demanded, Strauss points out, Socrates had to divorce his praise of justice from traditional mythology.[73] He thus begins his account of the education of the warriors with two laws concerning what Adeimantus calls "theology": (1) god shall be said only to cause good; and (2) as an apparent corollary of the first, gods shall not be said to change their shape (*eidos* or *idea*, Strauss notes) or to lie.[74] Adeimantus is troubled by the second, because it suggests the gods cannot rule (which Socrates later shows requires deceit) or, therefore, be just. The "theological" foundation of the just city is, Strauss thus shows his readers, exceedingly problematic.[75]

So is its foundation in nature, Strauss shows in his analysis of the "noble lie" with which Socrates' account of the warriors' education ends. As the need to convince citizens that (contrary to observable fact) they were born from the piece of land upon which they live indicates, no particular people has an unqualified or natural claim to possess any particular part of the earth. (Indeed, it is not clear that any political association that does not include the whole human race has a simply natural basis.) By stating that the founders will also have to convince the citizens, again contrary to easily observable fact, that the different classes have different types of blood, Socrates also indirectly admits that the conventional order in the city does not perfectly reflect a natural order of talent.

Justice proves to be difficult to find in the city they have established, moreover, once Socrates and his associates begin looking for it.

> Justice is said to consist in each part of the city or of the soul "doing the work for which it is best fitted by nature." . . . If each part of the city does its work well. . . , the city is wise, courageous, and moderate and therewith perfectly good; it does not need justice in addition. The case of the individual is different. If he is wise, courageous, and moderate, he is not yet perfectly good; for his goodness toward his fellows, his willingness to help them. . . , as distinguished from unwillingness to harm them, does not follow from his possessing the three first virtues.

The city does not need to be just, whereas the individual does, because the city is self-sufficient, whereas the individual is not.[76]

To maintain the parallel between the city and the individual Socrates has to find the same parts or "natures" in the individual as in the city. But that parallel depends upon an abstraction from the body, because the parts of the individual that parallel the classes of the city are parts of the soul.[77] The body, for the sake of which the city was originally established, is altogether ignored. It is ignored, we discover later in the discussion, because the attachment each individual has to his or her own *bodily* existence is *the* source of injustice.

If justice consists in the good order or health of the soul, it *is* clear that justice is choiceworthy for its own sake, whether or not the individ-

ual enjoys a reputation for virtue or not. By the end of Book IV Socrates
has thus satisfied Glaucon's demand in Book II that he show that justice
is good in itself, without regard to its extrinsic benefits or effects.[78] The
difficulty is that, according to this definition of justice, "only the man in
whom reason properly cultivated rules the other two parts. . . , i.e. only
the wise man . . . can be just . . . and the philosopher can be just without
being a member of the just city."[79]

Justice having been shown to be possible in the individual, but not
so clearly in the city, a new beginning becomes necessary to determine
whether it is possible to found a perfectly just regime. As at the very
beginning of the dialogue, Socrates' companions take a vote and so like a
democratic assembly compel him to serve them, the "many," through a
combination of persuasion and force. But this time, Strauss emphasizes,
Thrasymachus joins them. His joining "the city" is essential, because it
turns out that the possibility of establishing a just city depends, to a great
extent, on the power of his art.

Strauss observes that to his knowledge Alfarabi is the only commentator on Plato who has noted the central importance of Thrasymachus
and his rhetoric for both the argument and the action of the dialogue.[80]
Strauss does not refer to the Muslim philosopher in his published "summaries" of the *Republic* in *The City and Man* and the *History of Political Philosophy*, however; and it is not clear he understands the role of rhetoric exactly the way Farabi did. According to Farabi, Plato combined
the way of Socrates with the way of Thrasymachus to improve the opinions and so the politics of his readers gradually over time. According
to Strauss, in the *Republic* Plato shows that the propagation of salutary
teachings will never suffice to produce an entirely just polity; rational
rule and popular enlightenment will always be limited by the needs of
the body (which Strauss reminds his readers, Aristotle said had to be
ruled by the soul "despotically," that is, not by persuasion but by force).

The explicit reason Socrates' companions will not allow him to end the
conversation by showing that justice is choiceworthy for the individual is
that they want him to explain the "communistic" institutions he said
would be necessary in addition to the noble lie to prevent the guardians
from pursuing their own self-interest at the expense of the common
good. As in *The Assembly of Women* from which Plato literally takes his
proposals, the abolition of private property and the community of women
and children establish justice by removing the fundamental cause of
injustice, the primary attachment rooted in the body each of us has to
his or her own existence.[81] Just as Aristophanes showed that in order to
maintain the equality of condition necessary to end oligarchic oppression
and democratic envy, Praxagora had to impose severe constraints on the

natural preference or eros people have for the young and the beautiful, so in the *Republic* Socrates subordinates eros entirely to the needs of the city. The guardians are to be bred like animals.[82]

There is, however, another way a just city might come into being—by making a just individual, that is, a philosopher, its absolute ruler. Socrates suggests that "the coincidence of philosophy and political power is not only the necessary but the sufficient condition of universal happiness." The communistic institutions that appear to be so contrary to human nature may not be required. But, because they desire only truth and have no interest in either wealth or fame, philosophers will not seek to rule; they will have to be forced. The many will not compel philosophers to take the reins of government unless or until they are persuaded it is desirable for them to do so. That is the function or role of Thrasymachus's art. The difficulty, according to Socrates, is not to persuade the many it is desirable to have philosophers rule; the problem is that once philosophers have seen "the light," they do not want to return to the "cave." But, as the danger Socrates admits philosophers encounter if and when they return to the cave indicates, it is not so much the philosopher's unwillingness to serve their fellow citizens as it is their fellow citizens' passionate attachment to the opinions they have grown up believing and their hatred of those who question and thus appear to discredit these opinions that makes it highly unlikely, if not simply impossible for philosophers to rule. The abstraction from body which characterizes the *Republic* leads not only to a denigration of eros, but also to an overestimation of the power of rhetoric.

Although Socrates finally admits that the just city exists only "in speech," Strauss observes, the fiction of its possibility is maintained throughout the *Republic*. That fiction is necessary to arouse the spiritedness of lovers of justice like Glaucon against the injustice they find not only in existing regimes, but also in themselves. The need to counter their own inner temptation is the reason Socrates goes on, after the depiction of the just regime, not only to sketch the inferior regimes into which it decays, culminating with the portrait of the tyrant, but also to reintroduce the question of the utility and status of poetry.

Although Socrates does not actually provide a better answer to the question What is justice? in the *Republic* than he does to the question What is piety? in the *Euthyphro*, Strauss concludes, he does show us what the source or origin of injustice is—and how it is overcome in or by a few individual philosophers. There will be no just city until a philosopher becomes king, not because philosophers know what is good—in general, much less for each citizen—but because philosophers do not desire the wealth and esteem that lead other men, as Thrasymachus explains, to seek to rule for their own advantage and so unjustly.[83] As in the *Assembly of Women,* so in the *Republic,* a just polity is established primarily by removing the causes of injustice.[84]

As Thomas Pangle points out, Strauss's discounting of the doctrine of the ideas or the knowledge philosophers purportedly need to acquire is the most unusual element of his reading not merely of the *Republic,* but of Plato's works as a whole.[85] "No one has ever succeeded in giving a satisfactory or clear account of this doctrine," he observes. "It is possible however to define rather precisely the central difficulty." Strauss does not state the source of his explanation of that difficulty—the existence of the ideas separate from the things which participate somehow in them—but he gives basically the same critique Aristotle presents in the *Metaphysics* at a place Strauss cited earlier.

Rather than try to explicate what he appears to think is rather obviously an inadequate doctrine, Strauss offers an explanation of the reasons Glaucon and Adeimantus accept it so easily.

> They surely have heard of the ideas . . . many times before. This does not guarantee however that they have a genuine understanding of that doctrine. Yet they have heard still more frequently . . . that there are gods like *Dike* (536b3; cf. 487a6), or *Nike* who is not this victory or that victory. . . , but one and the same self-subsisting being which is in a sense the cause of every victory. . . . More generally, Glaucon and Adeimantus know that there are gods—self-subsisting beings which are the cause of everything good, which are of unbelievable splendor, and which cannot be apprehended by the senses since they never change their "form."

Although Strauss demurs, "This is not to deny that there is a profound difference between the gods as understood in the theology of the *Republic* and the ideas," it is difficult to see what he thinks that difference is. In his discussion of that "theology" earlier he pointed out that Socrates and Adeimantus agree that "the gods are superhuman beings, that they are of superhuman goodness or perfection and that they do not change their form."[86] These gods may not be self-subsisting or subordinate to an idea of the Good, but in light of Strauss's observation in his lectures concerning Socrates' need to separate his just speech from traditional Greek theology, it is hard to suppress the suspicion that Strauss thought Socrates' doctrine of ideas constituted a reinterpretation of a part of traditional Greek theology designed to support justice or at least a decent political order better than the old poetry. Once scriptural religion replaced pagan polytheism in most places in the West, it was no longer necessary to worry about stories about wars among the gods or their unjustly deceiving human beings. Especially in the form of law, more precisely in the First Table of the Ten Commandments as interpreted by Maimonides, scriptural religion encouraged those who were able to seek knowledge of God, that is, to philosophize, while it taught the basic moral requirements of maintaining a decent social and political order in the Second. Strauss's attempt to revive Platonic philosophy did not need to include a defense of that "incredible" doctrine of the ideas. Indeed, his analysis suggests that in criticizing Plato's 'ontotheology', Heidegger and Derrida have mistaken the public teaching for the core.

Rather than constitute a doctrine, Strauss insists, Platonic philosophy was embodied in a particular person, Socrates, because it consisted ultimately in a way of life—the only satisfying way of life. It was this and only this about which Plato fundamentally disagreed with Aristophanes.[87] Poetry that presented philosophy as the best way of life would be allowed in the just city (or speech), Socrates concludes in the *Republic*. Like Gadamer, Strauss points out, Plato's dialogues constitute the example par excellence of such ministerial poetry.[88]

The Conflict between Philosophy and Law in the *Statesman*

As represented by Socrates, Strauss makes clear in his commentaries on the *Minos, Statesman*, and *Laws*, philosophy not only cannot but also will not rule. *The* next-best alternative is rule of law. In the *Statesman* the Eleatic Stranger points out:

> Rule of law is inferior to the rule of living intelligence because laws, owing to their generality, cannot determine wisely what is right and proper in all circumstances. . . : only the wise man on the spot could correctly decide. . . . Nevertheless laws are necessary. The few wise men cannot sit beside each of the many unwise men and tell him exactly what it is becoming for him to do.

As Strauss emphasizes:

> All laws . . . are crude rules of thumb which are sufficient for the large majority of cases. . . . The freezing of crude rules of thumb into sacred, inviolable, unchangeable prescriptions which would be rejected by everyone as ridiculous if done in the sciences and the arts is a necessity in the ordering of human affairs; this necessity is the proximate cause of the ineradicable difference between the political and the suprapolitical spheres.

The main problem with the rule of law is not its generality, however; it is the assumption that these crude rules should bind the wise man as well. As the stranger explains:

> The wise man is subjected to the laws, whose justice and wisdom is inferior to his, because the unwise men cannot help distrusting the wise man, and this distrust is not entirely indefensible given the fact that they cannot understand him. They cannot believe that a wise man who would deserve

to rule as a true king without laws would be willing and able to rule over them. The ultimate reason for their unbelief is the fact that no human being has that manifest superiority . . . which would induce everybody to submit to his rule without any hesitation and without any reserve. The unwise men cannot help making themselves the judges of the wise man. No wonder then that the wise men are unwilling to rule over them.[89]

Demanding that the wise man regard the law as simply authoritative, the unwise will accuse the man who, like Socrates, raises questions about the justice and wisdom of the established order of corrupting the young, a capital crime.

In contrast to Xenophon, Plato's depiction of Socrates suggests that there is an unbridgeable gap between philosophy and politics. The question arises, however, whether Plato himself did not show how that gap could be bridged by means of his poetry in the *Laws*, the only dialogue in which Socrates does not appear.

The Image of the Philosopher as Poetic Legislator in the *Laws*

The best practical solution to the division between the wise and the unwise presented in the *Statesman* would seem to be for the philosopher to convince a legislator to enact a code of law, including provisions for the education of other wise men to administer the laws once enacted. That is precisely what the Athenian Stranger appears to do in the *Laws*. But, Strauss argues, the "city in speech" the Stranger describes is no more likely to come into existence than the city Socrates proposes in the *Republic*.

The *Laws* is the only Platonic dialogue in which Socrates does not appear. Strauss thus begins his account of *The Argument and the Action of Plato's "Laws"* by asking what the relation between the Athenian Stranger and Socrates is.[90] The difference seems to be a matter primarily of the setting—the interlocutors and the place.[91] Because the conversation takes place on Crete where the Athenian is a stranger and the old Dorians with whom he talks have no knowledge of philosophy, he does not confront the same prejudice against philosophers Socrates did in Athens. Whereas Socrates always spoke to or in front of youths, the Athenian talks to two old men. When they begin to react angrily, like the Athenian elders, to his criticisms of their revered institutions, the Athenian reminds them of the

> Dorian law of laws . . . which forbids the young to criticize any of their institutions but stipulates that all should say with one voice that all their laws are fine since they were given by gods. . . ; yet one of their old men may make speeches of this sort when speaking to a ruler and men of his own age, provided no one young is present.[92]

If Socrates had not been so old at the time of his trial, Strauss suggests, he might have gone into exile in Crete. In the *Crito* "the Laws" tell Socrates that

> If he left Athens he would go either to one of the well-governed cities nearby, where he would be utterly discredited by his unlawful escape, or to Thessaly, which is utterly lawless. [They do] not discuss what would happen to him if he went to a well-governed city far away like . . . Crete [which] he had mentioned . . . shortly before. . . . If Socrates had escaped from prison, he would have gone to Crete, where he was wholly unknown and would have come to sight only as an Athenian Stranger.

However, Plato's art was not constrained by the facts of Socrates' life. For example, in the *Menexenus* he has Socrates repeat a speech which mentions events that occurred after his death.[93] There had to be another reason for Plato's replacing Socrates with an Athenian Stranger in his most practical political dialogue, the only dialogue in which the protagonist proposes an actual code of law.

In his commentary Strauss points out that the anonymity of the Athenian extends beyond his name to what he is—namely, a philosopher. The word 'philosophy' does not appear in the dialogue until Book IX in the context of their discussion of how to punish possible infractions of the laws. Not only is philosophy presented as a possible source of infraction, because it brings into question the most fundamental laws concerning the gods. The Athenian's failure to mention philosophy in specifying what the laws ought to be also means he has not made the source and basis of his recommendations clear. He could not—and still persuade the old Dorians to accept them. Their conversations are a model, we learn in Book VII, of the *poetry* the Athenian suggests the legislator ought to use to *persuade* rather than force people to obey. Only at the very end of the dialogue does the Athenian admit, without saying so explicitly, that it will be necessary to abolish the 'Dorian law of laws' to establish and maintain the new regime. In the Nocturnal Council the elders will discuss the foundations of the regime—the nature and unity of the virtues and the arguments for the existence of god—*with young people*. (Strauss points out they may be female as well as male.) The law based on intelligence cannot be maintained solely on the basis of tradition. Rulers of the new regime will have to be philosophically educated, and philosophy necessarily raises questions about "received wisdom" or tradition. By muting that challenge, by depicting an anonymous Athenian Stranger discussing a possible reform of Dorian law with two old statesmen in a private conversation that lasts but a day, Plato presents a poetic picture of possible cooperation between traditional and rational forms of authority he indicates, in the end, can never really exist. The Athenian is not willing to stay to help see his laws enacted; like Socrates' philosopher-king, he would have to be forced to rule. But, if the Dorians kept him and got to know him better, they would see more clearly just how critical he is of their ancestral laws. Their agreement is more apparent than real.

The reason Socrates does not appear in the *Laws*, Strauss concludes, is that he was prevented by his *daimonion* from engaging in politics. In other words, he could not engage in legislative activity without endangering his life. There was an unbridgeable opposition between philosophy, openly represented as such by Socrates, and legislation.[94] That opposition seems, moreover, to parallel the most obvious difference between Socrates and Plato. "The laws proposed in the *Laws* are written." The only other Platonic dialogue that is set outside of Athens is the *Phaedrus,* "which may be said to concern writing." The singular absence of Socrates from the *Laws* leads us to ask whether Plato indicated the way in which he thought the opposition between philosophy and politics could be overcome, by seeking gradually to alter the opinions of one's readers through writing rather than by directly challenging the opinions of the political elite like Socrates.[95]

That was the conclusion to which Farabi had come, Strauss argued in his essay on "How Farabi Read Plato's *Laws*."[96] And that essay provides the key to Strauss's own account. Strauss does not mention or cite Farabi in *The Argument and the Action*. He reminds his readers of the 'Averroist' understanding, however, by prefacing his study with a quotation from the medieval Islamic philosopher Avicenna stating that "the treatment of prophecy and the Divine law is contained in . . . the *Laws*." One of the techniques of esoteric teaching Strauss claimed to have learned from Farabi was leaving out something of central importance to a discussion—like the doctrine of the immortality of the soul from a summary of Plato. By failing to cite Farabi in his own study of Plato's *Laws*, Strauss indicated his disagreement with Farabi's major conclusion.

Like Farabi, Strauss seems to present a mere summary of the dialogue, organized simply book by book, with a brief preface about the indirect character of Plato's writing. But, as Joseph Cropsey indicates in his foreword, repeated rereadings show Strauss's account to be much more than a summary.

According to Farabi, Plato did not think it wise to declare the truth openly to all readers. To illustrate the way in which Plato could nevertheless communicate the truth to discerning readers by stating it baldly in a context which prevented most from understanding, Farabi related a story about a pious ascetic. Threatened with persecution by the rulers of the city, the ascetic dressed up as a drunk beggar, and with clanging cymbals approached the gates of the city. Accosted by the guard, he declared that he was the pious ascetic they were seeking. Thinking the beggar was mocking him, the guard ordered him to pass through. If the ruse were later discovered, Strauss comments, the many would excuse the ascetic, believing he remained true to his character by telling the truth. But, in fact, the ascetic lied in deed. That lie was, however, the necessary condition for his ability to declare the truth safely.

Strauss indicates the importance of the distinction between speech and deed for his own analysis in the title, *The Argument and the Action of Plato's "Laws."* As in Farabi's story, so in the dialogue itself, the action is deceptive. Although the Athenian Stranger appears to be willing to give the Dorian founders of a new colony a code of laws and so to engage directly in political action, he proves in fact willing merely to engage them in a conversation lasting one day.[97] The dialogue concludes with Megillos's announcement that the city they have projected in speech will not work unless they compel the Athenian stranger to become a participant in its settlement, a duty from which the Athenian had excused himself along with Megillos in Book VI (which, if we count the preface, becomes the subject of the central chapter in Strauss's account).[98] The conclusion of the *Laws* is the same as the *Republic:* the establishment of a just city is impossible unless and until a philosopher is compelled to become king.

Like Socrates in the *Republic*, the Athenian in the *Laws* describes a "city in speech." But unlike Glaucon and Adeimantus, Strauss points out, the interlocutors in the *Laws* know nothing of philosophy. The treatment of the city in the *Laws* thus initially appears to be quite different.[99] "In the *Republic*, reason or intellect guides the foundation of the city from the beginning, and eventually rules the city in broad daylight without any dilution or disguise."[100] In the *Laws* the stranger also suggests that best condition for the founding of a city would be a combination of wisdom with tyrannical power.[101] But, since the wise are few and the many strong, he concedes, the just claims of the wise to rule will have to be diluted by the necessity of recognizing the strength or power of the many, that is, by seeking their consent. "[R]ule of law is a kind of rule of the stronger while the rule of wisdom is not."[102] The rule of law may be necessary and even, in light of the probable alternatives, desirable, but it is never entirely right or just. Political, perhaps also philosophical, moderation consists in the "adaptation of wisdom to the opinions of the citizen body or to consent," but moderation is not, according to the Athenian, a virtue in and of itself. The combination of election and lot he proposes for the selection of magistrates does not constitute a just mixture of two kinds of justice or equality.

> According to an old saying, which is true, equality produces friendship, but there is a great difference, not to say opposition, between two kinds of equality. One kind demands that equal honor be given to everyone; this is achieved by lot. . . ; the second kind of equality gives more to the greater and less to the smaller by giving to everyone what is appropriate to his nature, . . . virtue and education. It is the second kind of inequality which . . . is . . . the political right, because it produces for the cities all good things. This implies that the first kind . . . is conventional.

And Strauss concludes:

> There are, then, not two different and conflicting roots or principles of justice, say, freedom and good government; but the single principle of justice must be diluted on account of necessity—the compelling power of the many; . . . a rational society is not possible, unless it be the society ruled by a philosopher exercising tyrannical power. . . . We have here the core of the Athenian's political suggestions.[103]

The way the Athenian presents his political suggestions disguises the difference between the many unwise, who need to be persuaded to consent to the law, and the intellect of the man who alone has a right to declare what it should be. Beginning the conversation by inquiring about the origin of their laws, the Athenian initially presents himself as a student rather than as a teacher of the old Dorians. Even after the Stranger's questions about their institutions convince Kleinias and Megillos that he may have something to teach them, he continues to present the conclusions and effects of philosophical conversations without mentioning philosophy by name. Just as the Stranger's description of Athenian drinking parties (or possibly philosophical symposia like that described in Plato's *Symposium*) in Book I has something of the effect of wine, if vicariously, on his elderly interlocutors, making them a bit more flexible and open to new ideas, so the Stranger's description of the highest Muse without mentioning its name in Book II indicates the way the clarity of the mind of the philosopher must be reduced, as if he too were metaphorically feeling the dulling effects of wine on the sharpness of the intellect, so that his unphilosophic interlocutors can understand him. The harmony thus achieved "between the few wise and the many unwise, the rulers and the ruled . . . is moderation in the highest sense of the word."[104]

Strauss points out several examples of lack of clarity about the most fundamental issues in the Athenian's speech which serve to obscure the difference between the stranger and his Dorian interlocutors. Although he first distinguishes the *logos* which should rule the individual from the law, which is the reason accepted by the city, he later blurs that distinction without his interlocutors' noticing it, as he blurs the distinction between the old and the wise.[105] He is unclear about the question of the origins, the relation between the reverence due parents (or our natural origins) and that due the gods.[106] He blurs the differences among intellect *(nous)*, good sense *(phronēsis)*, and opinion *(doxa)*.

The problems that arise from the Athenian's obscuring the character and source of his own wisdom—that is, the "manifest absence of philosophy"—come to the surface at the end of the dialogue. To institute and preserve the laws he has proposed, the Athenian has to educate successors who share his understanding. The Nocturnal Council is supposed to provide such an education, but the composition of the Council is not made clear.

> Are all its members men each of whom can acquire within his soul science of the subjects in question [the unity and differences among the virtues, the ideas of the noble and the good, and the being and power of the gods]? Are its members potential or actual philosophers? A glance at Kleinias [the Athenian's unphilosophic Cretan interlocutor who will presumably found the colony under his guidance] is sufficient to make one see the pertinence of the question. The heterogeneous composition of the Council makes it impossible to give a simple answer. Hence the Athenian cannot, as Socrates in the *Republic* can, determine the subjects of study and the time to be allotted to each.[107]

When the Athenian suggests that he and Kleinias investigate the question of the unity of the virtues by question and answer, the Old Cretan does not see the point. He does not understand the use or danger of engaging in Socratic dialectics which, Strauss points out, are as absent from the *Laws* as their originator.[108]

Because the Athenian obscures the philosophical foundation of the legislation he proposes, the word 'philosophy' does not appear in the dialogue until Book IX. "Philosophy" is explicitly introduced only in the context of the discussion of penal legislation because, its positive role in the formulation of the law not having been made manifest, it appears only in the form of a questioning of accepted opinions and thus as the potential source of the most heinous capital crime of impiety.[109]

In the *Laws* the tension between philosophy and politics at first appears to be overcome. As Strauss observes in his preface:

> The *Laws* opens with the word "god"; there is no other Platonic dialogue that opens in this manner. The *Laws* is Plato's most pious work. In the *Apology of Socrates* Socrates defends himself against the charge of impiety, of not believing in the gods in whom the city believes. In the *Laws* the Athenian stranger devises a law against impiety which would have been more favorable to Socrates than the corresponding Athenian law.[110]

The Athenian proposes that no capital crime be tried in one day. In the *Apology* (73a–b) Socrates claims that under such conditions, he could

have convinced his judges to acquit him.[111] But Strauss observes toward
the center of his study of the *Laws,* "Whether Socrates would have fared
better in Kleinias' or the Athenian's city than he fared in Athens cannot
be guessed until one knows the Athenian's law regarding impiety and the
prosecution of that crime."[112]

In fact, both the law and the terms of its prosecution turn out to
be unclear. "It is not clear whether a man who believes in the kosmic
gods, . . . without believing in the Olympian gods, is guilty of impiety."
(Socrates might have passed the first test, but could not pass the second.)
The law recognizes that there are different kinds of atheists:

> Some have a character by nature good, hate the bad men, and through
> loathing injustice do not do wrong. . . , while others are incontinent, pos-
> sess powerful memories, and are quick at learning; the man of the first
> kind is likely to be of utter frankness of speech regarding the gods . . . and
> by ridiculing others would perhaps make them, too, impious, if he were
> not punished; the other, . . . full of craft and guile . . . belongs to the class
> of men from which come . . . tyrants, public speakers, and . . . sophists. Of
> these two types the dissembling one (the ironic one) deserves not one death
> or two, but the other needs admonition together with imprisonment.

But, Strauss points out,

> The disjunction made by the law is not complete: what happens to the
> atheist who [like Socrates] is a just man and does not ridicule others be-
> cause they sacrifice and pray and who to this extent is a dissembler? is it
> literally true of him that he deserves not one death or two, i.e., no death
> at all, nor imprisonment? . . . One could say that he will become guilty if
> he frankly expresses his unbelief—but what if he expresses his unbelief
> only to sensible friends? Can one imagine Socrates denouncing him to
> the authorities?[113]

According to the law, the just man is to be imprisoned in the *sophronis-
terion*—the name of which reminds one of the *phronisterion* in *The
Clouds*—for "no less than five years, during which time no citizen may
visit them except the members of the Nocturnal Council, who are to take
care of their improvement; if after the lapse of the five years a man of
this kind is thought to have come to his senses, he will be released; if he
relapses, however, he will be punished with death."

The members of the Nocturnal Council are not to be allowed merely
to profess belief "in the gods as the laws declare them to be and because
the laws declare them to be"; they are supposed to prove to themselves
and others that the gods exist. They will presumably have to raise the
question What is god? and discuss it among themselves. A philosopher
like Socrates might not be apt to denounce a counselor who expressed his

doubts. But what about a non-philosophic counselor like Kleinias? *The difference* between Xenophon's Socrates and the gentleman was that Socrates did not prosecute others for their injustice, whereas the gentleman did. Kleinias appears to believe "in the gods as the laws declare them to be and because the laws declare them to be."[114] How would he like his inability to defend his own opinions to be exposed before the youthful members of the Council? What would become of the fame the Athenian Stranger promises he will gain as founder? It seems likely that the elder members of the Council would finally react to the disruptive effects of the activities of a philosopher among them very much the way the Athenian fathers eventually did to Socrates.[115]

The tension between philosophy and the city does not become fully visible in the *Laws*, Strauss suggests, because "Socrates" is absent. As a result of the dramatic setting, there is no philosopher who arouses the anger of the fathers by explicitly bringing the authority of their opinions into question in front of their sons.[116] As the conclusion of the *Laws* indicates, however, the tension between the philosopher and the fathers can never be entirely eradicated; it is impossible for a philosopher to be a philosopher without raising questions about the validity of inherited views. The tension between philosophy and politics can at most be meliorated, as it was in both Xenophon's and Plato's writings, by the presentation of the philosopher primarily as a *phronimos*, a man of practical wisdom willing to teach potential princes. But, as Plato indicates in his depiction of both Socrates and the Athenian, there are limits on the extent to which the philosopher is willing to dedicate himself to playing such a role.

In contrast to Farabi, who thought the manifest absence of philosophy in the *Laws* suggested the need for the confrontational tactics of the moralist Socrates to be supplemented with the gradual reform of public opinion by the more theoretical Plato, Strauss concluded:

> We are no longer . . . sure . . . we can draw a clear line between Socrates and Plato. There is traditional support for drawing such a clear line, above all in Aristotle; but Aristotle's statements on this kind of subject no longer possess for us the authority that they formerly possessed. . . . The decisive fact for us is that Plato as it were points away from himself to Socrates. Plato points not only to Socrates' speeches but to his whole life, to his fate as well.[117]

As the highlighting of Socrates indicates, Plato's primary purpose in writing the dialogues was not effecting political reform through the gradual alteration of public opinion. Socrates was, after all, *the* philosopher who did *not* engage in political action. As Aristotle points out in his *Politics*, the best possible regime proposed in the *Laws* is ultimately as impossible to put into practice as the "city in speech" of the *Republic*. Plato's primary purpose in writing the dialogues appears, rather, to have been the protection and perpetuation of philosophy by convincing people that philosophy was not necessarily inimical to public order and morality. To persuade the public that philosophy was not inimical to morality, Plato saw, he had to persuade philosophers themselves to moderate their speech. By dramatizing not only the speeches but also the life and death of Socrates, Plato reminded would-be philosophers of the reasons they should not pose certain questions—questions regarding the gods and the soul, that is, questions regarding not only the basis and intelligibility of the cosmos but also the sources of support for justice, both natural and supernatural—too publicly or directly. By keeping himself and his own opinions always hidden, like his teacher Socrates, Plato taught his students, first and foremost, the need for self-restraint.

THE NONHISTORICIST RESPONSE TO RADICAL HISTORICISM

As Strauss reads him, Plato presented "the problem of Socrates" very much in light of its first delineation by the comic poet.[118] By raising questions about the origins or causes of things, Plato shows, the philosopher inevitably provokes the anger of the fathers. This opposition cannot be overcome through the gradual reform of public opinion, because fathers like Strepsiades do not act on the basis of opinion. They react angrily out of a frustrated love of their own.

Farabi provided the vehicle or key to Strauss's more "original" reading of "primitive Platonism," because Farabi led Strauss to question the status of the doctrines concerning the ideas and the soul. By simply ignoring them in his *Philosophy*, Farabi suggested that these doctrines, which were central to the dominant tradition of Christian Platonism stemming from Augustine, and in terms of which both Nietzsche and Heidegger read Plato, were not at the core.

Heidegger was correct, Strauss thought, when he perceived that there was something concealed in the origins of Western philosophy. But Heidegger did not correctly identify what was hidden, or the character of the radical division he also recognized between philosophers and non-philosophers, because he investigated the origins only in the works of the pre-Socratic philosophers and tragedians and did not pay attention to comedy, especially Aristophanes' comic critique of Socrates. Because he followed nineteenth-century scholarship in dismissing Xenophon as a non-philosophic author and so ignored his writings, Heidegger also failed to observe the significance of "the Socratic turn." Like Aristophanes, he accused rationalist philosophy of being essentially homogenizing and reductive. He thought the inherent tendency of mathematical reason to reduce everything to uniform, calculable units had become evident only at the end of history. Because he followed Aristotle in regarding Socrates as merely a moralist and Plato as the "deep thinker," he did not see the way in which Socrates came to embody an understanding of philosophy as the search for knowledge of the whole which is understood to be impossible to achieve because of

> a fundamental dualism which has never been overcome. At one pole we find knowledge of homogeneity: above all in arithmetic, but also in other branches of mathematics, and derivatively in all productive arts or crafts. At the opposite pole we find knowledge of heterogeneity, and in particular of heterogeneous ends; the highest form of this kind of knowledge is the art of the statesman and educator.[119]

Heidegger did not see the way this duality was recognized at the beginning of Western philosophy in the works of Plato, because, again following Aristotle, he understood Platonic philosophy primarily in terms of the theory of the ideas. As Strauss observes, that theory is based primarily on the observation that the intelligible unity of both numbers and the virtues is not visible; stressing their similarity in a certain respect, it obscures the difference between the two forms of intelligibility. The difference is, nevertheless, brought out not only in Aristophanes' critique of Socrates but also in Plato's other philosophic spokesmen's criticisms of the theory. Heidegger did not pay attention to the differences among Plato's philosophic spokesmen, because he did not appreciate the poetic character of Platonic philosophy; he did not fully appreciate the poetic quality, because he did not understand its political roots. He understood the difference or tension between the philosopher and the nonphilosophers primarily in terms of the difference, he first articulated in *Being and Time*, between the original or authentic disclosure of truth and the external, ossified expression of that experience that became emptied out, impersonal and traditional in public opinion over time.[120] Like Plato's Athenian Stranger, Heidegger realized human beings could not live constantly in the face of possible extinction. That was the reason, he thought, they necessarily fell back into the inauthentic view characteristic of society and the false security promised by the bourgeois state. Because he denied the capacity of the philosopher to transcend his time and place, even in thought, because he argued, on the contrary, that the thinker or poet who understood his own-most condition authentically would see that his fate as an individual was inseparably linked to the destiny of his people, Heidegger did not recognize the anger traditional authorities feel for the philosopher who challenges their love of their own and the need, therefore, to take precautions against arousing it. Heidegger did not understand either politics or philosophy "originally" enough, Strauss suggests on the basis of his reading of the non-historicist Plato, fundamentally because he understood human existence too historically.

Unlike Heidegger, Nietzsche was obviously aware of "the problem of Socrates." He was, after all, the first to announce it. By leveling Aristophanes' critique at the Platonic Socrates, Nietzsche showed that he perceived the common elements. Like the nineteenth-century philologists with whom he studied, Nietzsche emphasized the difference between the base, calculating rationality of Socrates and the noble artistry of Plato.[121] In *The Birth of Tragedy*, he contrasted the amusical Socrates, who Plato shows in the *Phaedo* was trying to remedy this defect on his deathbed by setting Aesop's fables to music, with his poetic student. But, Strauss responds, if "music" does not refer so much to harmony and rhythm or the form so much as the content or story of a poem, as Plato indicates in the criticism leveled at poetry in the *Republic*, and if the poet's art consists primarily in knowing what kinds of speeches are suitable to different kinds of people in a variety of circumstances, as the Athenian suggests in the *Laws*, Plato shows that Socrates is a kind of poet—or at least possesses a kind of poetic art—when he shows the philosopher speaking ad hominem to his interlocutors in the dialogues. In his later works, Nietzsche recognized that the asceticism advocated by both Socrates and the priests constituted the ideal condition for the practice of philosophy; but he did not think that either Socrates or Plato or the philosophers who followed them understood that their moral teachings served primarily to preserve the conditions necessary for their own activity.[122] Nietzsche failed to see the difference between Aristophanes' and Plato's Socrates, Strauss suggests in the last sentence of *Socrates and Aristophanes*, because he failed to perceive the difference between philosophical moderation and religious asceticism. As Muhammad b. Zakariyya al-Razi pointed out in his account of Socrates' "conversion," Socrates was initially the ascetic Aristophanes criticizes; his love of philosophy was so great that he subordinated everything else to it. Later, however, he became a father, served in the army, and even attended banquets; that is, he came to recognize the importance of family, politics, and friendship. If, as Socrates argued, both reason and justice teach one should not harm another unnecessarily, to be consistent, one should also not unnecessarily harm oneself. Unlike the medieval monks, Socrates did not mortify his flesh. On the contrary, he was the embodiment of moderation; both because he was naturally inclined to be moderate and because he had acquired the necessary habits during the period of his initial enthusiasm, he regulated his physical desires in such a way as to make him most able to engage in philosophy.[123]

"It is certainly not an overstatement to say that no one has ever spoken so greatly and so nobly of what a philosopher is as Nietzsche," Strauss concludes.

> This is not to deny that the philosophers of the future as Nietzsche described them remind one much more than Nietzsche himself seems to have thought of Plato's philosopher. For while Plato had seen the features in question as clearly as Nietzsche, . . . he had intimated rather than stated his deepest insights.[124]

Nietzsche did not see how close his understanding of philosophy was to Plato's, because he did not understand the character or the causes of Plato's reticence. Nietzsche did not understand Plato as he understood himself, because Nietzsche saw philosophy in terms of "that deepening of the soul which has been effected by the Biblical belief in a God that is holy." He thought that the philosopher must, like the Hebraic prophet, not merely seek, but also tell everyone else, the truth. Nietzsche understood Plato's noble lie to be part of his creative or legislative project. He, the self-proclaimed philosopher of masks, did not see the way Plato's statesman served as a protective mask for his philosopher.[125]

By reading Plato in the context set by Aristophanes and Xenophon, Strauss thought he had been able to recover the "primitive" Plato. What he rediscovered was the connection between Socrates' continence or ascetic morals and his eros, on the one hand, and that continence and his political teachings concerning the virtues of justice and moderation, on the other. These virtues were the focus of Plato's two longest and most comprehensive dialogues, the *Republic* and the *Laws*. Nietzsche replaced these virtues with solitude and compassion.[126] He did not see the need for justice and moderation, because through his portrayal of Socrates Plato had succeeded all too well in convincing his successors that philosophy was useful rather than damaging to the city.[127] Nietzsche did not see the reasons why Socrates, unlike Nietzsche himself, never directly raised the questions What is god? and What is soul? He did not see the reasons that, as Plato's Athenian Stranger argues, the best possible political order depends on preserving popular beliefs in the primacy of both and the need, therefore, for philosophers to offer arguments supporting these beliefs.

Strauss's attempt to revive ancient rationalism, especially as it is represented by Plato's Socrates, consists in an attempt to show the reasons why, contrary to Nietzsche, philosophers should not merely appear, but actually *be* both moderate and just. The sources of their virtue are, admittedly, different from the sources of popular or political virtue. Like Socrates, they know that they do not know. If they are not able to benefit their contemporaries by teaching them the truth, they try not to harm them. Like Plato's Socrates, they may tell stories; they do not, like Nietzsche, directly and unambiguously undermine salutary popular beliefs. Above all, they do not seek to rule.

Six

Reconceiving the Western Tradition

Strauss's *Studies in Platonic Political Philosophy*

ddressing "the problem of Socrates" was preliminary, Strauss observed in the introduction to his book on *Socrates and Aristophanes*, to addressing the question of the worth of what Socrates stood for. In his last book Strauss thus turned to the question of the character and value of the Western philosophic tradition explicitly in the context set by the radical historicist critique.

Commentators have found both the title and the contents of Strauss's *Studies in Platonic Political Philosophy* puzzling.[1] The book appears to be a collection of essays, many of which had been previously published as separate pieces, and few of which explicitly concern Plato or his dialogues. Unlike the collections of essays he published in *What Is Political Philosophy? and Other Essays* or *Liberalism: Ancient and Modern*, the organization is not even simply chronological.

The key to Strauss's last book lies in his announced plan. If we add the introduction and essay on the *Gorgias* he did not live to write, we see that the book was to have seventeen chapters.[2] Strauss's statement on "Jerusalem and Athens," the names of cities which indicate "the broadest and deepest . . . of the experiences of the past . . . [upon which a]ll the hopes that we entertain in the midst of the confusions and dangers of the present are founded," occupies the center.[3] *The* question with which the book is concerned thus appears to be the basis and character of our hopes. In contrast to the philosophers, both medieval and modern, who preceded him, Strauss does not seek to combine these experiences. On the contrary, he wonders

> whether the two ingredients of . . . the modern synthesis, are not more
> solid than that synthesis. . . . Since . . . the two ingredients are in funda-

mental opposition to each other, we are ultimately confronted by a problem rather than by a solution.[4]

The character, to say nothing of the worth, of the Western tradition is a problem, because that tradition constitutes an amalgam of two different, fundamentally incompatible understandings of human beings and the world in which we find ourselves. According to the ancient Greeks, both poets like Hesiod and philosophers like Parmenides and Empedocles, human beings are subject to forces which exceed them in dignity but are by no means simply friendly. Human beings are forced to work, Hesiod shows, because nature does not provide for them adequately. When Prometheus steals fire from the gods to help people relieve their condition, Zeus punishes human beings by sending Pandora to them with her box filled with countless evils. "The evils with which human life is beset, cannot be traced to human sin. . . . There is no divine promise, supported by the fulfillment of earlier divine promises, that permits one to trust and to hope."[5]

Plato seems closer to the biblical understanding. Like the Bible, "Plato teaches . . . that heaven and earth are created or made by an invisible God whom he calls the Father, who is always, who is good and hence whose creation is good." There are, however, important differences between Plato and the Bible: "The Platonic teaching on creation does not claim to be more than a likely tale. . . . The Platonic God does not create the world by his word; he creates it after having looked to the eternal ideas which therefore are higher than he."[6] According to all the Greek philosophers, human beings live in a cosmos which is intelligible to them as human beings, but which does not unambiguously provide support for the requirements of human life, especially the moral requirements of living together in society.[7] According to the Bible, on the other hand, human beings are made in the image of a creator God. As such, they are essentially moral, which is to say, free—as they must be, if they are to choose between good and evil. But the God of whom they are images and who is the ground or source of all that exists is Himself essentially unknowable.

The modern synthesis represents an attempt to combine the rationality characteristic of the Greeks with the morality stemming from the Bible. But, Strauss suggests, the fundamental incompatibility of the two root understandings makes such a synthesis impossible.

The neo-Kantian philosopher Hermann Cohen had argued that the two major sources of modern culture were Plato and the prophets.[8] "What we owe to Plato is the insight that truth is in the first place the truth of science." But "that science must be supplemented by the idea of the good, which to Cohen means, not God, but rational, scientific ethics" and by the prophets. The reason Cohen put forth was that

According to Plato, the cessation of evils requires the rule of the philosophers, . . . of the few men who possess a certain nature. *Plato presupposes that there is an unchangeable human nature.* As a consequence, he presupposes that there is such a fundamental structure of the good human society as is unchangeable. This leads him to assert or to assume that there will be wars as long as there will be human beings.

The prophets provide hope in the face of this bleak prediction. "Precisely because they lack the idea of science and hence the idea of nature, . . . they can believe that man's conduct toward one another can undergo a change much more radical than any change ever dreamt of by Plato."[9]

In the two halves of his *Studies,* Strauss reexamines the two parts of the synthesis.[10] First, he shows that Plato did not propose or promulgate "rational, scientific ethics." Second, he reminds his readers of the difficulties involved in both medieval and modern attempts to combine a rationalist understanding of nature and politics with scripturally based morality.

As a whole, Strauss's *Studies* seems intended to show that the original Platonic understanding of the problematic relation between reason or philosophy and ethical, social, or political practice is superior to any of the subsequent attempts to combine ancient rationality with Scripture-based morality. Although most of the chapters of Strauss's book do not treat the Platonic dialogues per se, he calls them all "studies in Platonic political philosophy," because they all contribute to his overall argument for the superiority of the Platonic understanding to any subsequent mixture of philosophy with prophecy. Even though Strauss admits that scriptural morality is in itself higher and more spiritual than the ancient rationalist understanding of human existence, he suggests that we have no good reason to think that human nature can be transformed or that men will cease fighting wars. The main reason later philosophers tried to achieve an impossible synthesis between ancient rationality and Scripture-derived morality was that shortly after Plato they began losing sight of philosophy as the way of life embodied by Socrates, and began to conceive it rather in more doctrinaire, if not utilitarian terms. Absent a view of the peak, the life of reason appeared to be low and calculating. Seeking to ennoble or beautify human existence, later philosophers embraced biblically derived notions that were not and could not be made consonant with the facts of human existence. They were thus led to advocate radical transformations without having truly rational grounds for them.

PLATONIC POLITICAL PHILOSOPHY

Instead of political philosophy, in the contemporary world we have positivism and historicism. Since, as Strauss had argued previously, positiv-

ism necessarily collapses into historicism, he begins his account of the
need to recapture the ancient understanding with a brief critique of the
philosopher who provides the "hard center" of popularized historicism,
Martin Heidegger.

Heidegger had learned from his teacher Edmund Husserl that, rather
than constituting the perfection of our natural reason (thus providing
the model of knowledge as the positivists and the neo-Kantians thought),
modern science makes us oblivious of the natural understanding of the
world upon which science itself is based. To establish the foundations of
science or knowledge, philosophy must recapture "our understanding of
the world as sensibly perceived prior to all theorizing." Going beyond
Husserl, Heidegger saw that meant "the primary theme is not the object
of perception" (or "phenomenon"), but the "thing as experienced as part
of the individual human context." A thing is not defined merely by its
primary and secondary qualities, but by evaluative characteristics like sacred or profane, which vary from time to time and place to place.

If the definition or constitution of things changes from time to time
and place to place, "one can no longer speak of our 'natural' understanding of the world; every understanding of the world is 'historical'." But,
to declare that all understandings of the world are historical, it is necessary to explain how and why this general understanding becomes possible now, at this particular time and place. Heidegger thus had to articulate something like a philosophy of history, that is, an account of the
progression or stages of history from its beginning to its culmination
or end.[11]

Like Hegel, Marx, and Nietzsche, Heidegger argues that we are coming to the end of history. But unlike previous philosophers of history, he
does not call for any political action to promote the establishment of a
world culture, much less some form of worldwide rule. The attempt not
merely to achieve worldwide dominion, but to conquer or impose man's
will on nature as a whole led not to human supremacy and unqualified
freedom, he saw, but to the destruction of everything that had ever been
called distinctively human.[12]

Like Nietzsche, Heidegger concluded that humanity was radically en-
dangered in the present age. All human greatness had previously grown
out of Bodenständigkeit (rootedness in the soil). Classical Greek thought
had given rise to a kind of thinking, however, that from the very beginning threatened to destroy the rootedness of human existence, and that
potential destructiveness had now become evident in the unlimited and
essentially unlimitable power of modern technology. But, Heidegger suggested, the crisis of the modern age also gave rise to a new possibility.
Philosophers in the past had not understood the limitations inherent in

the rootedness of their reflections in a particular time and space (or place and language). By meditating on the character of its own limits, 'thought' could prepare the way for the first true grounding of human existence as such—on the earth, as such—that would not be restricted the way past philosophy had been to one particular place and people. By initiating a "dialogue between the most profound thinkers of the Occident and the most profound thinkers of the Orient," the late Heidegger hoped to open the way for a "return of the gods," that is, for the emergence of a new world religion.[13]

Heidegger's famous turn away from the destructive consequences of modern techno-science thus led him to embrace "fantastic hopes, more to be expected from visionaries than from philosophers." Although Heidegger initially appears to represent an advance on Husserl, Strauss concludes, Husserl's more sober project of making philosophy into a rigorous science seems more promising than waiting passively for the emergence of a new god or gods to save us.

Husserl admitted it would be a long time before the ideas in terms of which human beings organize their perceptions would be analyzed sufficiently to make a purely rational ethics or religion possible. What Husserl did not appear to understand until the end of his life was that the pursuit of this science might have adverse effects on the *Weltanschauungen* people needed to live by in the meantime. In the 1930s he observed:

> Those who are conservatively contented with the tradition and the circle of philosophic human beings will fight one another, and surely the fight will take place in the sphere of political power. Already in the beginnings of philosophy persecution sets in.[14]

To understand the origins or grounds of the conflict between tradition and philosophy and the reasons that conflict occurs in the sphere of politics, Strauss concludes, it is necessary to go back to the beginning, to recapture the original experience of the conflict Plato dramatized in his depiction of Socrates.

The picture most students have of the ancient conflict between the philosopher and the city is based on Plato's *Apology of Socrates*. But, Strauss argues, in his *Apology* and *Crito* Plato's Socrates presents an explicitly popular and hence somewhat distorted picture of both the character and effects of his philosophy. In these dialogues Socrates presents himself as an innocent victim of political persecution. In fact, Socrates provoked the Athenians to kill him. To discover the true reasons Socrates did not and could not defend himself effectively, that is, to discover the reasons why the tension between philosophy and the city (or the traditional beliefs upon which it rests) cannot be overcome, and that the Husserlian project can, therefore, never be completed, it is necessary to turn to other Platonic dialogues, the *Euthydemus* and the *Gorgias,* as well as to the ancient Greek historians, Thucydides and Xenophon.

In his first speech or defense proper in the *Apology,* Socrates shows that the official charges were trumped up by angry fathers. Unable to answer questions raised by youths imitating Socrates and seeking someone to blame for their own incapacity, his accusers reiterated the old charges against philosophers. This old prejudice might be traced partly to a certain comic poet; but, Plato's Socrates points out, he does not do or study any of the things Aristophanes ridiculed. Nor is it credible, as his new accuser, the poet Meletos, has charged, that, acting in opposition to the efforts of all other citizens, Socrates alone could corrupt the youths of Athens.

Rather than impiously questioning the existence of the Olympian gods like Aristophanes' philosopher, Socrates says he has devoted his entire life to proving the wisdom of Apollo's oracle. By interrogating the men who claimed to have wisdom, he has shown why the oracle declared him to be the wisest; unlike them, he knows that he does not know. Responding to an anonymous interlocutor who asks what Socrates has been doing, if he has not done what his accusers charge, Socrates compares himself to Achilles. Like the epic hero, the philosopher has chosen to risk death rather than abandon the post at which the god stationed him. Neglecting his own affairs, Socrates has devoted himself to exhorting his fellow citizens to virtue. He has acted only as a private citizen and has not gone into politics, because he was forbidden to do so by a certain divine voice. In his defense, Socrates thus presents himself as a "god-fearing" man who has always sought to be just.[15] The conflict between the philosopher and his fellow citizens is, Socrates suggests in his second speech, a product of a misunderstanding he could remedy, if only he had more time. If Athens had a law forbidding one-day trials for capital crimes, he would have been able to persuade the jury to acquit him.

Strauss raises questions about the validity of Socrates' claims, however. First, Chairophon's asking the oracle whether there were anyone wiser than Socrates indicates he had a certain renown for philosophy and had engaged in it before undertaking his oracle-inspired mission. As Aristophanes showed in *The Clouds,* there was a pre-Delphic Socrates with whom Chairophon had investigated the things in the heavens and under the earth (the places in which the gods were traditionally said to dwell). Socrates' claim that he would be able to persuade his fellow citizens of his innocence if he had more time seems to contradict his earlier claim that he had been conversing with his fellow citizens all day long for many years. In fact, Strauss points out, we never see Socrates engaged in a conversation with an ordinary artisan or great politician in any of the other Platonic dialogues.[16] Nor does Plato report any conversation occurring in the agora. Socrates' speeches were more private and less public than he suggests in his *Apology*. That was one reason, perhaps, the ancient prejudice against philosophers persisted virtually unchallenged.

After the jury votes to convict him, Socrates admits that his initial account of his piety was ironic. The philosopher had presented himself as serving the god, because if he had said "that it is the greatest good for a human being to engage every day in speeches about virtue and the other things about which they heard him converse and thereby examine himself and others . . . and that the unexamined life is not worth living for any human being," he would have convinced the jury even less than he did with his seeming dissimulation.

As Xenophon explicitly states in his *Apology*, but Plato only shows in his, Socrates provoked the Athenians into killing him. The "penalty" he initially proposes as an alternative to death is "shocking." His claim that he deserves to be fed and housed at public expense like a victor in the Olympic games assumes that he succeeded in improving the character of his fellow citizens. The fact that they have unjustly accused and condemned him shows that he did not improve their characters any more than the Athenian statesmen—Perikles, Kimon, Miltiades, and Themistokles—he had criticized on precisely these grounds in the *Gorgias* (515b8–516e8). Socrates' claim to need public support is equally faulty; it ignores the fact stressed in Xenophon's *Oeconomicus*, that the philosopher can count on his friends—as Socrates himself reminds his audience, when he subsequently proposes paying a significant fine with their help. By explaining why he does not propose exile, Socrates indicates "there always was an alternative to the death penalty." Socrates chose to die, because he thought it was better than the alternatives. But, "the Platonic Socrates, as distinguished from the Xenophontic Socrates, does not explain his conduct at the trial by his view that in his advanced years it was good for him to die."[17]

By not providing his readers with any information concerning the philosopher's own deliberations or the reasons that persuaded him that he ought to remain and die, Plato made his account of what Socrates said and did into pure drama. We hear what the philosopher said and see what he did, but we are left to infer the reasons why.[18] Comparing himself to a tragic hero, Socrates presents himself in his only public speech as willing to die rather than admit he or his philosophy was wrong.[19] In his *Apology* Plato's Socrates suggests that, like a biblical prophet, he put himself in great danger by directly confronting rulers with their own injustice. In fact, Strauss points out, Socrates himself admits he stayed out of politics until the very end of his life to secure his own preservation. Knowing he was close to death in any case, Plato's Socrates took the opportunity offered by his trial to make a "statement," in deed as much, if not more than in speech, that would convince not only his compatriots but also their descendants that philosophy does not constitute a threat to political order.[20]

Why Socrates provoked the Athenians to condemn him to death is not the only question left unanswered in Plato's *Apology*, moreover. There is also the question of the significance of the difference Socrates emphasizes between the jurors who voted to acquit and those who voted to condemn. In the *Gorgias* Socrates predicted that, if he were ever forced to defend himself and his philosophy in court, his position would be like that of a physician brought before a jury of children by a pastry cook who accused him of not giving them sweets. That is, he treated the *demos* as uniformly hostile to philosophy. In the *Apology* he shows that this is not simply the case. If Meletos had not been joined by Anytus and Lykon, Socrates concludes, he would have been acquitted. Neither the poets nor the people as a whole are the most serious critics of the philosopher; ambitious democratic politicians, concerned particularly about their sons' future, come to light as Socrates' most dangerous accusers.[21]

In the *Euthydemus*, Strauss suggests, Plato shows that Socrates himself was partly responsible for people's mistaking his philosophy for sophistry and thus regarding it as politically dangerous. He intentionally perpetuated the impression that philosophy was a useless endeavor to dissuade fathers of inept sons from pressing him to take them as students.

Like Xenophon, Plato shows Socrates using his *daimonion* as an excuse to do (or not to do) what he wants. At the beginning of the *Euthydemus*, Socrates tells Kriton that his *daimonion* warned him against leaving the dressing room. So he stayed and met, first, the sophists, Euthydemus and his brother Dionysodoros with their students, and then Alkibiades' grandson Kleinias with his train of lovers. By forbidding Socrates to leave, his *daimonion* seems to have imposed the subsequent conversation on Socrates; but, we see, the conversation is far from compulsory. The "divine" sign that gives no reasons appears to mark Socrates' own inclinations; he did not leave, because he wanted to stay and talk to the young men who tend to gather in such places. Readers are reminded of the positive aspect of that *daimonion* or of Socrates' *eros*—his desire to associate with young men as well as his ability to attract them to him—when Kleinias goes immediately to Socrates' side, where after a short deliberation the sophists follow.[22]

Plato also points to the similarity between Socrates and the sophists' teachings at the very beginning of their exchange. Seeking students, the brothers gladly agree to demonstrate their ability to refute whatever is said and to enable anyone else to do the same in a short time. "This power is necessarily identical with virtue," Strauss observes, "if virtue is wisdom and if wisdom in the proper sense—knowledge of the most important things—is impossible."[23] Like Socrates, the brothers show that they are wiser and hence more virtuous than others by showing that those who think they know, do not.

The difference between the sophists and Socrates becomes clear, however, in the subsequent action. The sophists discourage Kleinias from engaging in any further conversation by first refuting his contention that the ignorant learn, by pointing out that the stupid have proved themselves incapable of learning, and then refuting his second contention that it must be the wise who learn, by pointing out that the wise already know. Socrates, on the other hand, encourages the young man to seek wisdom in the protreptic speech with which he responds to the sophists' "playfulness."

The positive effect of Socrates' speech on Kleinias obscures some of its more unsettling implications. When Socrates suggests that a person might need good fortune as well as wisdom, Kleinias is so elated by his newly regained self-confidence that he fails to notice the philosopher's vacillation as to whether wisdom can altogether overcome the power of chance. Nor does Kleinias observe how Socrates' contention that no human virtue or good is useful to its possessor unless he possesses wisdom involves a radical debunking of what Aristotle called moral virtue. According to Socrates' argument, it would be better for an ignorant man to be unjust than to be just!

The drama also covers up Socrates' refutation of the sophists. Having convinced Kleinias that he must seek to be wise, Socrates turns back to the brothers with the question whether it is possible to teach anyone to be virtuous—or wise. Dionysodorus provokes an emotional exchange by asking Kleinias's friends whether they really want to make him wise, because such a wish amounts to a desire to destroy Kleinias as he is. In that exchange the importance of Socrates' observation that, if no one can learn, as the sophists have maintained, no one needs or can learn their "art," gets lost.

In the first half of the dialogue Socrates thus demonstrates his superiority to the sophists both in speech and in deed; but in the second half he appears to be bested. When Socrates resumes his protreptic questioning of Kleinias, they prove unable to identify the kind of wisdom or kingly art that will both produce and enable its possessor to use what is truly good for human beings.[24] The reasons for Socrates' apparent aporia are to be found in the dramatic setting. Socrates is relating this conversation to his friend Kriton, who is looking for a teacher for his son Kritoboulos. By showing that his questioning of Kleinias in the end proved to be fruitless, Socrates discourages Kriton from asking him to become his son's educator. Nor, Strauss observes, does Socrates volunteer when Kriton reminds him of his concern. "Kritoboulos' nature is less fit for the purpose than Kleinias' or, in other words, Socrates' *daimonion* holds him back in the case of Kritoboulos."[25]

Socrates emphasized the elenchtic, aporetic character of his philosophy in order to discourage the fathers of inept sons, like Kriton, from pressing him to take their sons as students (and becoming angry when he refused to serve them and their concerns). As a result, many people were unable to distinguish Socrates' philosophical investigations from the eristic refutations in which the sophists engaged. Plato dramatized the difference, however, in the argument and the action of the first part of the *Euthydemus* as well as in the sophists' comic critique of typical Socratic doctrines like recollection and the theory of ideas. Whereas Socrates claimed to know simply that he did not know, he held out the possibility or hope of attaining knowledge. The sophists claimed, on the basis of a Zeno-like application of Parmenides' argument that one can neither say nor think what is not, to be able to refute any proposition and thus to show that it is impossible to know anything. By not only dramatizing but also having Socrates praise their refutations of his characteristic teachings, Plato shows that both he and his teacher recognized the problematic character of their own doctrines.[26] According to Plato's Socrates, the partial, but only partial intelligibility of the whole gives us grounds both to try to improve our understanding and not to overestimate the power of our intellect. Lacking full knowledge, we are never, as he initially suggests to Kleinias, free from the control of fortune or chance. Nor is it possible, as the sophists suggest, to establish one's preeminence over others simply by besting them in speech. In a world lacking a completely intelligible order, hierarchy cannot be established simply on the basis of *logos;* it requires force.

Contrary to many classicists, Strauss concludes, "Socrates was not the mortal enemy of the sophists nor were the sophists the mortal enemies of Socrates. According to Socrates, the greatest enemy of philosophy, the greatest sophist, is the political multitude (*Republic* 492a5–e6), i.e., the enactor of the Athenian laws."[27] As Aristophanes first warned his Socrates, so Plato's Socrates repeatedly reminds the sophists and rhetoricians with whom he speaks, "intellectuals" are always subject to persecution by unscrupulous democratic politicians who arouse the people against them by accusing them of teaching impious doctrines and so corrupting the young.[28] Interested primarily in his own private affairs, Kriton did not perceive the way in which Socrates put him off.[29] More confident of their own ability and more ambitious for their sons, Socrates' accusers Anytus and Lykon were not so easily fooled. If powerful men like Alkibiades and Kritias found it useful to associate with Socrates, he must have had something to teach them. By denying that he taught anyone anything, Socrates was dissimulating. He also denied them, indeed, all Athenian statesmen, the honor they deserved. However dimly, Socrates' accusers perceived that he was not truly interested in the goals of Athenian politics. Angered by his unwillingness to take them or their ambitions seriously, they charged him with not believing in the gods in which the city believes and of corrupting the young.

By dissimulating, Socrates protected himself from persecution for many years. But, as Kallikles predicts in the *Gorgias*, when the philosopher was brought to court, he was convicted. The fundamental tension between philosophy and politics had not been eradicated. As the vote at Socrates' trial suggests, the people in general are not simply hostile to philosophy; they do not understand what appears to them to be a senseless, even ridiculous activity. But, precisely because people in general never share or understand the philosopher's love of wisdom, unscrupulous politicians can appeal to their fear of the unknown and direct the anger associated with the frustrations of everyday life against these strange individuals, especially in times of crisis.

Since Strauss did not live to write the chapter he planned on the *Gorgias*, we cannot be certain what it would have contained. However, his other writings, as well as a transcript of a class he gave on the dialogue at the University of Chicago which has circulated informally, indicate that he would probably have touched on three topics, corresponding to Socrates' three interlocutors. First, Strauss would have shown how Socrates not only demonstrated his superiority to the much more famous Gorgias in speech, but also how the philosopher warned the rhetorician that he ought explicitly to teach his students to be just as a matter of his own self-interest. By openly teaching ambitious young men how to manipulate democratic assemblies to pass whatever laws they wanted, Gorgias not only encouraged his students to think that they could escape paying him but also and more importantly invited the same assemblies to exile him from their cities lest the rhetorician or his students undermine their regime. Next, Strauss might have commented on the way in which Socrates convinces Gorgias's student Polus that the function of forensic rhetoric is not to help criminals evade punishment, but rather to bring them to justice and so improve them. The problem with this argument is not merely that the criminal who is punished with death—like Socrates him-self—can hardly be said to be improved. The question remains whether punishment can ever improve or "rehabilitate" anyone. In both the *Re-public* (335b) and the *Crito* (40c–d) Socrates suggests that a just man will never harm anyone; like the philosopher, he will only attempt to show him where or how he is mistaken. As Socrates tells Meletos in his *Apol-ogy* (26a), that kind of correction can take place only through a philo-sophical dialogue. Socrates himself does not practice forensic rhetoric, because he does not engage in legislation or judicial prosecution; he does not engage in political action, because he does not think human beings can be improved by law. Strauss would, therefore, probably have stressed the explicit opposition Kallikles draws in the third part of the dialogue between politics and philosophy.

By arguing that rulers prove they are better than others by showing that they are stronger, Kallikles points to the basis of democratic poli-tics—the physical force or power of the many that makes consent neces-sary and purely rational rule impossible. When he accuses Socrates of endangering his own life by not engaging in politics, Kallikles brings the fundamental irrationality of political life to the fore. Political associations are formed to preserve the lives of their citizens, but these selfsame asso-ciations end up placing the lives of individuals within them at risk, be-cause they are characterized by dissension—not only with foreign pow-ers but also internally. Socrates could not prevent himself from being dragged into court by an unjust accuser, even if he were to engage in politics. On the contrary, he reminds Kallikles, the Athenians have proved more willing to accuse and convict their greatest leaders of capital crimes than they have been to persecute philosophers. To preserve themselves and their community, people need legislators to impose order or limits on their unjust desires; but those same unjust desires lead people to re-sent and exile the leaders who serve them.

The conflict between philosophy and politics does not appear to be a product or result of philosophy, therefore, so much as it is a manifestation of the contradictory character and ends of political life itself. In the class he gave on the *Gorgias* in the autumn of 1963 Strauss pointed out that Thucydides' *History* brings out these contradictions. In his *Studies*, we might even say, his "Preliminary Observations on the Gods in Thucyd-ides' Work" constitutes *the* defense of Socrates insofar as it shows that the impiety and corruption of Athenian youths like Alkibiades was a product, not of their philosophic studies, but of the fundamental charac-ter of Athenian politics.[30]

By listing all the references to the gods both in Thucydides' own narrative and the speeches of his characters in his "Preliminary Observations," Strauss shows that in Thucydides' history human beings do not look to the gods to do what they know they can do for themselves. They look to the gods to determine the outcome of events they do not feel able to control. Like the Athenian soldiers watching the battle in the harbor of Syracuse that will decide their fate, they call on the gods when they are encouraged, but fall silent in the despair of defeat. Impiety is not the result primarily of philosophic questioning of tradition or authority; as Thucydides shows, impiety arises out of the same desire for self-preservation (or corresponding fear of death) that gives rise to political associations as well as to piety itself. Impiety is not a characteristic merely of ambitious young men, schooled as both Pericles and Alcibiades were, by philosophers;[31] it infects all human beings—Spartans and Persians as well as Athenians, leaders and followers alike.

Rooted in the fundamental attachment human beings naturally have to their own existence, Strauss suggests in his subsequent study of Xenophon's *Anabasis,* the hopes and fears that give rise to piety and impiety limit the beneficent effect philosophical rationalism can have on practical politics. Socrates' student might appear to combine the practical political wisdom of Thucydides with knowledge of philosophy and so be a greater man than either the historian or his teacher. Like the historian, Xenophon was an accomplished general and orator; he completed Thucydides' *History* in his *Hellenica.* But in his *Anabasis,* Xenophon shows, Socrates had greater practical as well as philosophical wisdom; his teacher understood better than he the limitations the attachment human beings have to their own place on political action.

Although Xenophon was an admiring student of Socrates, he did not always follow his teacher's example or precept. When his friend Proxenos urged Xenophon to go with him to Asia Minor to seek fame and fortune by serving Cyrus, Xenophon asked Socrates' advice. Thinking Xenophon might anger his fellow citizens by becoming a friend of Cyrus, who was thought to have warred zealously together with Sparta against Athens in the Peloponnesian War, Socrates told Xenophon to consult the oracle. However, at Delphi Xenophon did not ask whether he should go on the expedition, but which god he should sacrifice and pray to—to make his journey as good and noble as possible, and to return safely. Unlike Socrates, Xenophon clearly wanted the wealth and glory that go along with political power. Because the Athenian demos would not grant him the recognition he desired, he did not feel any particular attachment to his unjust fellow citizens. He did not see the same need to stay in Athens that Socrates did.

As Xenophon's adventures in Asia Minor show, Xenophon had received a good political education from Socrates. The contrast between Socrates' student and his friend Proxenos, who had been a student of the rhetorician Gorgias, becomes evident early in the *Anabasis*. According to Xenophon, Proxenos wanted

> to acquire . . . a great name and great power and much money, but he was obviously concerned with acquiring those things only in just and noble ways. He was indeed able to rule gentlemen but he was unable to inspire the soldiers with awe and fear of himself; he obviously feared to become hated by the soldiers; he thought that it was sufficient for being and [being] regarded a good ruler that one praise him who acted well and not praise him who acted unjustly (II 6.16–20).[32]

Trusting too much to the power of words, if not oaths, Proxenos was betrayed to the Persians by another student of Gorgias, the Thessalian Menon. After the defeat of Cyrus, Menon invited the Greek commanders to the Persian camp to confer about making peace, and then murdered them. This extermination of the leaders of the Greek army provided the occasion for "the beginning of Xenophon's ascent: through a single speech, spoken at the right moment, and in the right way, he [became] from a nobody a general."[33] During the Greek army's subsequent flight from the Persians across the mountains to the sea, Xenophon demonstrated his ability not only to use words but also to use force when necessary to inspire and control his troops.

Having come to a promising territory where his men could acquire both women and property, and finding that the sacrifices were auspicious, Xenophon was nevertheless frustrated in his desire to found a city. Wanting to return home with the gold Cyrus gave him, a soothsayer told Xenophon's men that their general wanted to stay in Asia and found a city in order to gain a name and power for himself rather than leading them back to Greece as he had promised. Although Xenophon was able both to punish the greedy priest and to convince his men that he was not so foolish as to try to found a city without their consent, he could not overcome their attachment to their native land—even though the soldiers came from different cities and Greece had been torn by internecine war for decades.

Like his teacher Socrates, Xenophon was accused of a capital crime. He was accused of having beaten soldiers from *hybris* on the trip over the mountains, when he had to keep them moving—for their own benefit as well as for the benefit of others. But unlike his teacher, Xenophon was able to convince the jury that he was innocent of the capital crime of which he was charged. He was a better forensic orator. Nevertheless,

Strauss suggests, Xenophon's fate indicates that he was less wise than Socrates, who suspected the Athenians would not be pleased with his leaving the city to serve an enemy. Not only was Xenophon's hope of founding a city frustrated by his men's attachment to their native land; the Athenians also exiled him "because he failed to show that he esteemed his fatherland more highly than Cyrus or Sparta."[34] Xenophon's rhetoric saved him in a trial, but, contrary to his own hopes, he ended up living an entirely private life in exile. The practical wisdom that led Socrates to stay at home and not to enter politics enabled him to continue philosophizing with his friends in Athens until the end of his life.

As Strauss reminds his readers in the essay "On Natural Law" that follows "Xenophon's *Anabasis*," Plato also thought that men's attachment to their own made the establishment of a truly just regime impossible. As Plato hints in the *Republic* by abstracting from it, "the establishment of the best regime is obstructed in the last analysis by the body, the only thing which is by nature . . . wholly incapable of being common." As a result, he points out in the *Laws*,

> Sheer bodily ("brachial") force must be recognized as having a natural title to rule. . . . Political society requires the dilution of the . . . natural right . . . in accordance with which the wise would assign to everyone what he deserves according to his virtue and therefore would assign unequal things to unequal people. The principle governing the dilution is consent, i.e. the democratic principle of simple equality according to which every citizen possesses the same title to rule as every other.[35]

This Platonic understanding of the necessary dilution of natural right by the requirement of consent began to be lost in the works of his student Aristotle. Because he defined natural right in terms of its floor—"the right which must be recognized by any society if it is to last and which for this reason is everywhere in force"—and its ceiling—"the most divine regime," which is "a certain kind of kingship . . . which does not require any positive right," Aristotle no longer recognized a dilution. The requirement of at least the passive consent of the greater body of the citizens was as much a pole or requirement of justice as the rule of the one best man. What is right by nature—the appropriate mixture or balance—is seen to be completely changeable, depending upon the circumstances.

The need to dilute wisdom by the requirement of consent—or, the always imperfectly rational character of political life—became even less clear when the Stoics transformed natural right into a law all human beings are obliged, as rational creatures, to obey. Writing within the context of Christian theology, Aquinas later combined elements of the Stoic natural law with Aristotle's doctrine of natural right; he made the natural law into an intrinsic principle of human action, inherent in man as man, and so "*apparently* paved the way for the conception of 'the state of nature' as a status antedating human society."[36]

Strauss emphasizes the difference between the ancient notion of natural right and the Christian notions of natural law, on the one hand, and the modern notion of natural rights, developed by Hobbes, Locke, and Rousseau, on the other. There was no *necessary* historical development. The modern teaching about natural rights grew out of the principles of modern rationalism enunciated by Machiavelli and Descartes, not directly out of the older teaching about natural law. In contrast to both the classical and the Christian understanding, Hobbes taught that human beings are naturally asocial. But if human beings are naturally asocial, Rousseau saw, they are arational by nature as well. "He found the peculiarity of man in his perfectibility or, more generally stated, his malleability. His successors concluded that the human race is what we wish to make it and that human nature cannot supply us with guidance as to how man and human society ought to be."[37]

The hope that human beings will become better or more moral as a result of a change in their nature does not, Strauss suggests, derive from the prophets. The hopes associated with a transformation of human nature are, rather, products of the development of modern political philosophy.

In his first set of "studies," Strauss thus shows that Cohen was mistaken about both parts of the Western tradition. In his depiction of Socrates, Plato did not put forward a scientific ethics. On the contrary, by showing the need for a dilution of natural right, Plato pointed to the reasons there will never be a purely rational polity, based on purely rational norms. By dramatizing the life and death of Socrates he showed that the "ethics" of the philosopher had their source in his *eros* or desire for wisdom; they were not deductions from some idea of the Good. Because most human beings, like Kriton and Kallikles, do not share that eros, they neither understand the philosopher nor share his notion of the good. Their lives must be organized, therefore, on a different basis than simply the search for the truth. Husserl's hope of finally achieving "in regard to ethics and religion a life regulated by pure rational norms" is no better founded than Heidegger's visionary hope for the emergence of a new god.

The notion that Cohen thought needed to be added to Plato, the idea that human beings can achieve peace on earth by changing their nature, did not arise from the Bible; it arose from modern political philosophy. As Thucydides and Xenophon both showed, most human beings act on the basis of irrational hopes and fears. Since their hopes lead human

beings to attempt impossible, utopian political projects, modern political philosophers like Machiavelli and Hobbes concluded, it was safest
and most effective to build on their fears. They designed institutional
schemes that would direct, if not manipulate human passions to produce
security and prosperity. Combined with the development of a science designed to transform nature to make it more amenable to human desires,
modern philosophy became a means of acquiring power. Nature having
become subject in principle, if not in fact, to human manipulation, there
was no limit. The understanding of philosophy as the only truly satisfying form of human life incorporated in Plato's depiction of Socrates had
been utterly lost.

STRAUSS'S CRITIQUE OF THE MODERN SYNTHESIS

The modern philosophical hope of solving the problems of human existence by transforming human nature found its clearest and most emphatic expression in Nietzsche's call for "man" to be superseded by the
"superman." In light of the multiplicity of cultures, past and present,
Strauss observed in "Jerusalem and Athens," "Nietzsche sought . . . for a
culture that would no longer be particular and hence in the last analysis
arbitrary. The single goal of mankind is conceived by him as in a sense
super-human. . . . The super-man must unite in himself Jerusalem and
Athens on the highest level."[38]

Unable to believe any longer in either the biblical promise of salvation
or in unending historical progress, Nietzsche saw, citizens of the modern
world were in danger of falling into complete disillusionment or nihilism.
They desperately needed someone to show them that there was something to live for, that there was a form of human life that could be affirmed as truly worth living in and of itself. Only a human being of the
highest spiritual powers, combining the inwardness or depth of biblical
morality with the intellectual discipline inherited from the Greeks, could
perform this task.

In *Beyond Good and Evil*, Nietzsche explicitly presents himself "as the
antagonist of Plato, . . . the most beautiful growth of antiquity (Preface)
whose strength and power was the greatest which hitherto a philosopher
had at his disposal." Nietzsche did not see how much his 'philosopher of
the future' resembles Plato's Socrates, because he read the dialogues in
terms of the traditional distinction between Socrates, the rational moralist, and Plato, the theorist of the ideas. "According to the preface to *Beyond Good and Evil* Plato's fundamental error was his invention of the
pure mind and of the good in itself. From this premise," Strauss observes,
"one can easily be led to Diotima's conclusion that no human being is

wise, but only the god is; gods do not philosophize." But in the penultimate aphorism of *Beyond Good and Evil*, Nietzsche suggests in his eulogy of "'the genius of the heart'—a super-Socrates who is in fact the god Dionysos— . . . that the gods too philosophize." Neither they nor human beings possess wisdom but must rather seek it, because the universe is not simply or entirely intelligible. If this is Nietzsche's critique of Plato, Strauss suggests, Nietzsche may not have read Plato carefully enough. "Diotima is not Socrates nor Plato, and Plato could well have thought that gods philosophize."[39] What or who is considered divine depends upon the answer to the question What is god?, a question, Strauss emphasizes, that is never explicitly raised in the works of Xenophon or Plato. If gods represent a desirable way of life, free from the sources of pain and injustice in human existence, Plato might have thought Socrates was a god. Socrates was distinguished by his *daimonion*. (The Greek word for happiness is *eudaimonia*, literally, well-daimoned or blessed.)

"When in the ultimate aphorism of *Beyond Good and Evil* Nietzsche underlines the fundamental difference between 'written and painted thoughts' and thoughts in their original form," Strauss observes, "we cannot help being reminded of what Plato says or intimates regarding the 'weakness of the *logos*' and regarding the unsayable and a fortiori unwritable character of the truth (Ep. VII 341c–d, 342e–343a)."[40] As Nietzsche himself emphasizes elsewhere, Socrates was the philosopher who did not write. Because he read the dialogues in light of the Aristotelian-Christian emphasis on the importance of the ideas, Nietzsche did not perceive the way in which Plato recognized not only the incompletely intelligible character of the cosmos that made it possible only to seek knowledge, not to possess it, but also the way that striving or eros beautified or ennobled the philosopher, in his depiction of Socrates.

Rather than seek to revive Platonic philosophy, Nietzsche thus called for the emergence of a new kind of philosophy. To prepare the way for its emergence, he saw, he had to get rid of the "prejudices" of the older philosophers, especially the belief that they could discover an order or truth existing independent of the human mind or will in "nature" or "things."

All systems of order or ideas are products, Nietzsche declared, of the will to power.[41] His thesis about the will to power constituted a creative act of interpretation, he admitted; but he regarded this apparent objection as a confirmation of his proposition. This thesis enabled him not only to deny that there is any inherent order, but also to combine or integrate past philosophic and religious accounts of the meaning of the world into one comprehensive theory.

Nietzsche suggested that his "doctrine of the will to power—the whole doctrine of *Beyond Good and Evil*—was in a manner a vindication of God."[42] But this vindication was initially atheistic. Nietzsche understood the holy God of the Old Testament to be a human creation as much as the gods of the old Greeks. 'Free spirits' had to show that the biblical God was an illusion or human creation, because such a showing constituted the precondition for the emergence of philosophers of the future, who will self-consciously legislate or give value to everything that is. The skeptical debunking of all past understandings by these free spirits appeared, however, to be a transitional stage—or, as in the organization of the first part of Nietzsche's book, the necessary link—between philosophy and religion that provided the ground for their ultimate integration.

> Could atheism belong to the free mind as Nietzsche conceives of it while a certain kind of non-atheism belongs to the philosopher of the future who will again worship the god Dionysos. . . ? This ambiguity is essential to Nietzsche's thought; without it his doctrine would lose its character of an experiment or a temptation.[43]

Strauss does not, however, follow out Nietzsche's attempt to reintroduce a new "tempter" god. He simply refers to "an important ingredient, not to say the nerve, of Nietzsche's 'theology'" to which he has no access, but which "has been worthily treated by Karl Reinhardt in his essay, 'Nietzsche's Klage der Ariadne'."[44]

Insofar as Nietzsche's call for the emergence of a philosophy of the future depends upon the revelation of a new god, Strauss suggests, that call does not rest on, nor is it ultimately accessible to, reason. Like Heidegger's proclamation that "only a god can save us," Nietzsche's evocation of Dionysus is more appropriate to a visionary than to a rigorous thinker. Rather than comment on Nietzsche's reinterpretation of the Christian mystery, Strauss confines himself to pointing out the difficulties in Nietzsche's nontheological account of the vindication of human suffering by philosophers of the future. Past philosophers claimed to find the basis of morals (and therein a definition of the good life) either in nature or in reason, Nietzsche observed. But as an arbitrary, compulsory limitation on human desire, morality constitutes a tyrannical imposition contrary to both nature and reason. It is impossible to have a philosophical ethics or science of morality of the kind Cohen thought Plato had founded. As Nietzsche points out, "rationalist morality . . . consists primarily in the identification of the good with the useful and pleasant and hence in the calculation of consequences. . . . Its classic [representative] is the plebeian Socrates." Insofar as both Socrates and Plato teach that reason shows human beings the best way of satisfying their desires and so achieving happiness, they "are guided by . . . not only reason but instinct. . . ; the instinct is more fundamental than reason."[45] The "instinct" that gives rise to religion, social morality and philosophy is, Nietzsche argues, the will to power.

Instinct is close to nature. Morality can be understood to be natural, Nietzsche thus suggests, if by 'nature' we refer to a predatory instinct or desire to dominate. But this instinct is hardly recognized, much less fostered in contemporary Europe, where "the herd instinct of obedience which is now almost universally innate and transmitted by inheritance" has become dominant. The degradation associated with the fear of pain and indiscriminate compassion characteristic of modern life in both liberal democratic and socialist regimes can be overcome, therefore, only by leaders who understand that there is nothing necessary or, strictly speaking, by nature. As the necessary condition for all human order and achievement, cruelty, too, must be willed.

> The leaders who can counteract the degradation of man which has led to the autonomy of the herd, can however not be merely men born to rule like Napoleon, Alcibiades and Caesar. They must be . . . the new philosophers who teach men the future as dependent on a human will in order to put an end to the gruesome rule of nonsense and chance which was hitherto regarded as "history."

True history "requires the subjugation of chance, of nature (*Genealogy* II.n.2) by men of the highest spirituality. . . . *The subjugation of nature depends then decisively on men who possess a certain nature.*"[46]

"While Nietzsche's turn from the autonomous herd to the new philosopher is in perfect agreement with his doctrine of the will to power," Strauss observes, "it seems to be irreconcilable with his doctrine of eternal return: how indeed can the demand for something absolutely new . . . be reconciled with the unbounded Yes to everything that was and is?"[47] The connection is to be found in the demand that the philosopher of the future bear "the weight of the responsibility for the future of men" *(das grösste Schwergewicht).*[48] By self-consciously creating values for himself and others, the philosopher knowingly creates an end or purpose for the history that was hitherto nothing but the rule of non-sense and chance. By giving past history a purpose or goal that can be affirmed to be worthwhile, the philosopher of the future makes it possible to will its repetition—eternally.

Does not the philosopher of the future thus make human life reasonable as well as "natural" and even moral by giving it a purpose or end? The creation of new values on the part of the philosopher of the future is, Strauss responds, a free act. It is not a necessary result; it is not the product of evident and universally valid insights or reason; it is an act of will on the part of an individual with a certain nature, "something unteachable 'deep down," that leads him to try to impose his own order and meaning on the whole.

> As we have observed, for Nietzsche nature has become a problem and yet he cannot do without nature. Nature . . . has become a problem owing to the fact that man is conquering nature and there are no assignable limits to that conquest. As a consequence, people have come to think of abolishing suffering and inequality. Yet suffering and inequality are the prerequisites of human greatness (aph. 239 and 257).

To preserve human greatness, suffering and inequality can no longer be taken as given or imposed; "they must be willed. That is to say, the gruesome rule of non-sense and chance, nature, . . . the whole present and past . . . [must be] willed as a bridge to the future." There is no inherent reason to affirm the value of human life or history; as an act of will on the part of a few human beings who have something deep down in them, the affirmation is ultimately irrational.

Nietzsche did not attempt to disprove his antagonist Plato, Strauss concludes, so much as he sought to surpass him in strength or power.[49] Plato "points away from himself [to Socrates] whereas Nietzsche points most emphatically to himself, to 'Mr. Nietzsche'."[50] Nietzsche's doctrine of the will to power could be understood to be a reflection of his own will to excel.[51]

Nietzsche's insight into the limitations of human knowledge should have led him to conclude, like Plato's Socrates, merely that he knew only that he did not know. Nietzsche wanted more, however; he wanted to show that human suffering was not merely inevitable, but that it was justified. He thought such a justification could be found by showing that all past history constituted the necessary condition for the emergence of an unprecedented form of human greatness. By combining the two apparently opposed forms of human excellence from the past, the political and philosophical rationalism of the ancient pagans with the spiritual inwardness and compassion of biblical morality, his philosophers of the future would surpass anything seen or imagined hitherto.

But, Strauss indicates in his examination of the "plan" of *Beyond Good and Evil*, the two parts of Nietzsche's synthesis do not successfully cohere. It is not clear whether the philosophical critique that undermines faith not merely in God, but in reason as well, establishes the conditions for the emergence and worship of a new god, Dionysus—in which case human life continues to acquire meaning from a supra-human source—or whether the philosophical critique itself constitutes the way in which human beings endowed with a certain nature learn how to impose their will on all others. In either case, one might say, Nietzsche's teaching involves a kind of return to nature, but that nature is amoral, essentially changeable and irrational. It lacks the distinctive characteristics of both the Greek and the biblical traditions. Rather than combining the antagonistic excellences of the past, the modern synthesis threatens to destroy both roots of the Western tradition.

In contrast to both Nietzsche and the German idealists, who had explicitly incorporated a great deal of Christian theology into their philosophy, Strauss reminds readers of his *Studies* in the three "notes" on Maimonides that follow his "note" on *Beyond Good and Evil*, the medieval Jewish philosopher recognized the fundamental and irreconcilable tension between reason and revelation. Understanding the extent to which Greek rationalism was not merely alien, but antagonistic to Scripture, Maimonides nevertheless covertly introduced reason into his interpretation of the sacred law for two reasons—to make it possible for the Jewish people once again to become an independent polity and to protect philosophy from persecution.

In his *Guide of the Perplexed*, Maimonides argued that the fundamental issue dividing the adherents of the law from the philosophers— whether the world has a beginning in time or is eternal—could not be definitively answered. In case of doubt, he suggested, it was better to follow the teaching of the Torah. Yet in his explication of the law in the *Mishneh Torah*, a more practical and explicitly Jewish as opposed to philosophical work, Strauss observes, Maimonides based his proof of God's existence on the philosophers' contention that the world is eternal! In practical matters like the interpretation of the law, Maimonides apparently thought it was wise to appeal to the greatest extent possible to reasons accessible to human beings as such rather than to rely simply on authority or a literal reading of the word of God as it had been handed down. In his *Book of Knowledge*, Maimonides thus

> introduced philosophy into the Holy of Holies by as it were rediscovering it there. Since philosophy requires the greatest possible awareness of what one is doing, Maimonides cannot effect that fundamental change without being aware that it is a fundamental change, i.e. without a conscious, although not necessarily explicit, criticism of the way in which the Torah was commonly understood.[52]

In his discussion of ethics *(De'ot)*, for example, Maimonides first contrasted the Aristotelian understanding of virtue as a mean with the biblical understanding of piety as extreme humility. Then he reinterpreted the biblical notion in an Aristotelian direction.[53]

Maimonides made the reason he thought it would be politically beneficial to give a rational rather than purely pious interpretation of Torah more explicit in his *Letter on Astrology,* when he observed, "We lost our kingdom since our fathers sinned by turning to astrology, i.e., to idolatry, and neglected the art of war and conquest."[54] Rather than openly criticize the Torah and thus undermine its effectiveness by bringing its wisdom explicitly into question, he reinterpreted its meaning by stressing the places and extent to which the law resembled the teaching of the ancient philosophers. Thus in his *Letter on Astrology,* Maimonides emphasized the agreement between the philosophers and Torah about the overall structure and guidance of the world. There was a difference, he admitted, with regard to particular providence; whereas the philosophers argued that only the general design is intelligible and that the particular outcomes were products of chance, the adherents of the religion of Moses believe that the particular outcome is an expression of the judgment of the Lord, although His reasons may not always be comprehensible to human beings. When he attributed the loss of the kingdom to the failure of the Jewish elders to study the art of war, Strauss points out, Maimonides identified the kind of proximate cause a philosopher would use to explain a particular outcome; he did not refer to the Judgment of God on the failure of the Jews to follow his Law in the right spirit.

Maimonides introduced philosophy into the reading of Scripture not only because he thought it would have politically beneficial effects but also because he thought the philosophers were right about the most fundamental issue dividing them from the adherents of the law. Maimonides did not announce his position openly, however. He merely hinted at it, Strauss suggests in his "Note on Maimonides' *Treatise on the Art of Logic,*" in a work that was written in Arabic and addressed not to his fellow Jews, but to a "master of the legal (religious) sciences," that is, to an Islamic scholar.[55]

Maimonides did not state his agreement with the philosophers openly, because he recognized that, if even a few human beings were to achieve the only truly satisfying form of human existence, they needed to have a political community to support and defend them. To establish and preserve such a community, it was necessary to have a certain amount of agreement on moral principles or laws. Attaining and maintaining such an agreement had become even more difficult in his times than it had been in antiquity, Maimonides suggested at the conclusion of his *Treatise on Logic,* because the universalistic claims of the revealed religions led their adherents to attempt to impose their rule on all others through the establishment of one great nation rather than accept the division of mankind into a variety of nations.[56]

In his *Discourses on the First Ten Books of Livy,* Strauss reminds his readers, Machiavelli restated the Averroist critique of religion Maimonides had taken over from Farabi in an explicitly Christian context. But unlike the original Averroists, Machiavelli did not use this critique to preserve the conditions for the pursuit of philosophy. On the contrary, Machiavelli attempted to effect a(n) (im)moral revolution. Objecting to both the ancient philosophical notion of virtue and the Christian teaching on the grounds that they were practically ineffective and thus produced only imaginary republics, in *The Prince* he proposed an entirely new understanding of *virtu* as the ability to do whatever was necessary under the circumstances to promote one's own self-interest.[57]

The simplest way to judge the character of Machiavelli's teaching as a whole, according to Strauss, is to observe that

> The writer to whom Machiavelli refers and deferred most frequently, with the obvious exception of Livy, is Xenophon. But he refers to only two of Xenophon's writings: *The Education of Cyrus* and the *Hiero;* he takes no notice of . . . the other pole of Xenophon's moral universe: Socrates.[58]

Rather than expanding human horizons as he claimed in his introduction to the *Discourses,* Machiavelli thus constricted them. His introduction of new modes and orders nevertheless produced a massive change or reversal in the understanding of the relation between politics and philosophy. Rather than political order constituting the necessary condition for the pursuit of philosophy by a few, the pursuit of knowledge became a means of establishing and maintaining political order to secure the bodily preservation and comfort of many.

Pure Machiavellianism was, however, morally repugnant. Later modern thinkers thus attempted to ennoble power politics by putting them in the service of principles or ideas derived from the Bible. For example, Strauss suggests, both the writings of Thomas Hobbes and his twentieth-century critic C. B. Macpherson might be said to represent alternative, modern interpretations of the biblically derived notion that *the* goal of political life ought to be the realization of peace on earth. *The* question that ought to be addressed to both the liberals and their critics is whether the end of war constitutes an adequate definition of the good or most desirable form of human life.[59]

Insofar as the modern synthesis of rationalist politics and philosophy with biblical morality arises in reaction to the narrowing of the understanding of the possibilities of human life introduced by Machiavelli, which is to say, the exclusion of the Socratic alternative, that synthesis is based on a misunderstanding of the character and purpose of ancient philosophy. Because biblical moral principles require something like the perfectly free, fundamentally unknowable biblical God as a foundation, Strauss goes on to argue, the attempted synthesis of reason and revelation results in a misunderstanding of the character and basis of biblical morality as well.

In his "Review of J. L. Talmon's *The Nature of Jewish History—Its Universal Significance*," Strauss notes that the conjunction of the universal character of reason with the historical character of revelation has made it difficult, if not impossible, for modern adherents of the religion of Moses to explicate its true meaning. As Talmon points out, the "idea of 'the chosen people' as of a 'holy nation' . . . expresses 'what Matthew Arnold called the Jewish passion for right acting as distinct from the Greek passion for right seeing and thinking'. It is therefore one of the two basic elements of Western civilization." But, Strauss observes, Talmon does not explain why "'the passion for right acting' . . . requires . . . a peculiar nation as its bearer."

Hermann Cohen did provide an account of the peculiar fate of the Jewish people explicitly on the basis of a combination of reason and revelation. But, Strauss argues in his concluding statement on Cohen's *Religion of Reason*, that account points toward the ultimate extinction of his people either, most beneficently, as a result the universal acceptance of the principles of their religion or, as almost happened in fact, as martyrs.

"Cohen had no doubt that in teaching the identity of Reason and Revelation he was in full agreement with 'all', or 'almost' all, Jewish philosophers of the Middle Ages." Like Maimonides, Cohen presented an idealizing interpretation; like Maimonides, he thus began by arguing that the biblical God is absolutely unique, characterized by unity and incorporeality. "Creation is 'the logical consequence' of the uniqueness of the divine being." But, because Cohen understands Creation to be "the immanent relation of God as the unique Being to Becoming, and Becoming is coeval with God," he does not speak of Creation as a free act or a single act in or before time. *The* issue that divided philosophers from adherents of the Torah, according to Maimonides, thus disappears in Cohen's work.

According to Cohen, "Creation is, above all the creation of man. . . . Revelation is the continuation of creation." Like creation, revelation thus becomes continuous and nonmiraculous. There is biblical support for this idealized understanding, Strauss observes, in Moses' extensive speech in Deuteronomy where revelation is presented as not in heaven . . . but as originating in the heart and reason of man, which are indeed God-given."[60] But, as Cohen recognizes, a question then arises about the relation between God's revelation of Himself in and through the creation of 'man' in general and His specific revelation of Himself as the one and only God to the people of Israel in particular.

Because God reveals Himself only in and through human beings, Cohen argues, the relation between God and humanity is a correlation.

Divine action occurs only in or through human action, although the two kinds of action are not simply parallel. Whereas God is Holiness itself, human beings must strive to become holy. Human beings learn the meaning of love and justice—the attributes of divine action that establish the norms for humanity—first by feeling compassion for the suffering of others. Sympathy for the downtrodden is only the first step, however, to knowledge of both humanity and God. Because human beings are all frail and finite as well as free, we all fall short of the ideal. Finding ourselves lacking and sinful, we see we have no right to judge others. Recognizing our own guilt, unable to acquit ourselves, and needing to be liberated from our sin, we turn necessarily to God. He redeems us by providing us with grounds not only to repent of our old evil ways but also thereby to transform ourselves by acquiring new hearts and new spirits. We accept our suffering not merely as deserved punishment, but as a divine dispensation, only when we come to see it as the necessary condition for the development of both the individual self and the race as a whole.

In his *Religion of Reason* Cohen thus presents "the idea of the Messiah and mankind" in light of the need to justify human suffering. Unlike Maimonides, he does not associate the coming of the Messiah with the reestablishment of a Jewish state. On the contrary, he observes, "The Jewish state as one state among many would not point as unmistakably to the unity of mankind as the one stateless people dedicated uniquely to the service of the unique God."

Cohen traces the "the idea of mankind . . . without distinctions like those between Greeks and barbarians or between the wise and the vulgar" to Jewish monotheism; "the unique God is the God of all men." The Stoics had a universal teaching, he admits, but they thought only of individuals. By comprehending all nations, "the prophets became 'the originators of the concept of world history'" through which "mankind" becomes "unified in its highest aspiration" in a never-ending development or progress. The meaning of Israel's election, according to Cohen, is

> to be *the* martyr. . . . The misery of Jewish history is grounded in messianism, which demands humble suffering and hence the rejection of the state as the protector against suffering. Israel has the vocation not only to preserve the true worship of God but also to propagate it among the nations; through its suffering Israel acquires the right to convert them.[61]

Cohen argues that "the Law is either the moral law or is meant to contribute to man's moral education." It is not intended to establish an independent political community. "The survival of Judaism still calls for a certain self-isolation of the Jews within the world of culture and there-

fore for the Law," but only "as long as the Jewish religion stands in opposition to other forms of monotheism."[62] Cohen was, therefore, critical
of Zionism.

What Cohen "said about Jewish martyrdom provided, without his being aware of it, for the experience that the Jews subject to Hitler were
soon to undergo," Strauss observes. "He did not provide what no human
being could have provided, a way of dealing with a situation like that of
the Jews in Soviet Russia, who are being killed spiritually by being cut
off from the sources of Judaism."

In "Jerusalem and Athens" Strauss suggested that "Cohen's thought
belongs to the world preceding World War I." He thus

> had a greater faith in the power of modern Western culture to mold the
> fate of mankind than seems warranted now. . . . Catastrophes and horrors
> of a magnitude hitherto unknown, which we have seen and through which
> we have lived, were better provided for, or made intelligible, by both Plato
> and the prophets than by the modern belief in progress.[63]

Rather than try to combine and so destroy the two antagonistic roots of
the Western tradition, Strauss thus devoted himself to an attempt to revive both—in explicit opposition to each other.

REINTERPRETING AND REVIVING THE WEST

In his *Studies in Platonic Political Philosophy* Strauss showed, first, what
the ancient understanding of the relation between politics and philosophy was and how it had been lost, and, second, how and why modern
attempts to supersede the ancient understanding by combining reason
and revelation had not succeeded. In the process, he presented a new interpretation of the West. Rather than representing the gradual integration of Greek rationality with biblical morality, he suggested, the history
of Western civilization constitutes a series of unsuccessful attempts to
harmonize its two fundamentally incompatible roots. "The recognition
of two conflicting roots of Western civilization is, at first, a very disconcerting observation," he admitted. "Yet this realization has also something reassuring and comforting about it. The very life of Western
civilization is the life between two codes, a fundamental tension." In
opposition to the philosophers who claimed that we have come to an end
of history, Strauss concluded, "there is therefore no reason inherent in
Western civilization itself . . . , why it should give up life. But this comforting thought is justified only if we live that life, if we live that conflict."
Rather than try like Nietzsche to use the tension by shooting for an impossible synthesis, and so release it, Strauss sought to preserve, if not to

increase the tension, by emphasizing the fundamental incompatibility between reason and revelation.

> No one can be both a philosopher and a theologian, nor . . . some possibility which transcends the conflict . . . or pretends to be a synthesis. But every one can be . . . either a philosopher open to the challenge of theology or a theologian open to the challenge of philosophy.

We all ought strive to achieve one or the other form of human excellence—with the recognition that even if we succeed, we will not have achieved all the virtues of which human beings are capable. There is always something beyond. To maintain the conflict between the two roots of Western civilization is to maintain the possibility or ground for human nobility; there is always something more to strive for. Strauss thus showed how it was possible to achieve Nietzsche's fundamental goal.

Strauss's concern with the survival of the West was, then, more than merely academic. The question was whether and in what form human life would persist in the future. Cohen thought the synthesis was superior to the parts, because he had not experienced the tyrannical results of the modern attempt to mold or transform human nature. More disillusioned than Cohen, Strauss concluded that the two component parts of the Western tradition were superior to the synthesis, because both the Bible and ancient Greek rationalism established an extrahuman floor or ground as well as a suprahuman ceiling or limit to human action. According to the ancient understanding Machiavelli implicitly rejected,

> Nature supplies . . . a standard wholly independent of man's will. . . ; one can say that man is the measure of all things or that man is the microcosm, but he occupies that place . . . in an order which he did not originate. . . . Man's power is limited . . . [by] his nature.

The Bible agrees with classical philosophy in this crucial respect.

> According to the Bible man is created in the image of God; he is given the rule over all terrestrial creatures: he is not given rule over the whole; . . . he has been assigned a place: righteousness is obedience to the divinely established order.[64]

As Heidegger had seen, the prospect of technologically transforming everything, including human beings themselves, into 'standing reserve' threatened to destroy humanity itself. But, in contrast to Heidegger, Strauss saw the threat as a result not simply of the development of science or the search for knowledge per se; he traced it, rather, to a misapprehension of the relation between philosophy and politics.

In his introduction to *The City and Man* Strauss observed,

The crisis of our time may have the accidental advantage of enabling us to understand in an untraditional or fresh manner what was hitherto understood only in a traditional or derivative manner. This may apply especially to classical political philosophy which has been seen for a considerable time only through the lenses of modern political philosophy.[65]

Unlike modern Enlightenment thinkers, Strauss's more original reading showed, classical political philosophers did not think that the pursuit of knowledge necessarily benefitted humanity. On the contrary, he repeatedly insisted that

> Classical political philosophy . . . asserts that the society natural to man is . . . a closed society that can well be taken in one view or that corresponds to man's natural . . . power of perception. . . . It asserts that every political society that ever has been or ever will be rests on a particular fundamental opinion which cannot be replaced by knowledge and hence is of necessity a particular or particularist society. This state of things imposes duties on the philosopher's public speech or writing which would not be duties if a rational society were actual.[66]

Strauss's insistence on the importance of recapturing the ancient understanding of the relation between politics and philosophy has obscured the untraditional character of his view of the tradition. The untraditional character of Strauss's thought becomes clearer if we observe that for Strauss, recapturing the ancient understanding of the irresolvable tension between philosophy and politics is the first, but only the first step. By emphasizing the unresolved conflict between philosophy's affirmation of the need to question all authority and the biblical understanding of wisdom as unquestioning obedience to God, Strauss engages in what he himself called "a kind of thought which is philosophic indeed but no longer Greek: modern philosophy."[67] Unlike the Averroists Farabi, Maimonides, or Machiavelli, Strauss never treats biblical religion merely as civil theology. On the contrary, he argues that, in contrast to the pagan theology Plato had to purify with his theory of the ideas in order to support justice, the Bible presents a purely moral understanding of human excellence that can and does compete with the ancient understanding of philosophy as the only life worth living.[68]

Strauss's thought is not, however, simply or unambiguously modern either. Because it presupposes the end or untenability of modernity, it should probably be called postmodern. The crisis of our times, as Strauss understands it, is essentially the crisis of modern political philosophy, which culminates with Nietzsche in the denial that human beings can know what is right or wrong.[69] The crisis of modernity is, then, first and foremost a moral crisis, to which Strauss responds by showing that morality does and can have two different kinds of foundations—as establishing the necessary conditions for philosophy (the achievement of the best way of life) or as the commands and promises of the essentially unknowable, because omnipotent biblical God.[70] What is untenable is the mixing of the two traditions that has been characteristic of the West.

As he made clear in a public conversation he had with Jacob Klein at St. Johns College, Strauss was not primarily a moralist.[71] On the contrary, he emphasized the inadequacy of ancient political virtue as a definition of human excellence, on the one hand, and reminded his readers of the inability of biblical virtue or submission to support a viable political community, on the other. Whether in the ancient philosophical or the biblical context, he argued, the requirements of human excellence and political necessity are ineradicably at odds.

The return to classical political philosophy that Strauss advocated was "both necessary and tentative or experimental." It was undertaken explicitly in light of the modern predicament. "We cannot reasonably expect that a fresh understanding of classical political philosophy will supply us with recipes for today's use," he warned.

> The relative success of modern political philosophy has brought into being a kind of society wholly unknown to the classics, a kind of society to which the classical principles as stated and elaborated by the classics are not immediately applicable. Only we living today can possibly find a solution to the problems of today.

But, he thought, "an adequate understanding of . . . the classics may be the indispensable starting points for an adequate analysis . . . of present-day society in its peculiar character."[72]

Strauss's analysis of the crisis of modern political philosophy convinced him that the foundation of current liberal democracies in natural rights theory was not tenable. But, he observed,

> The theoretical crisis does not necessarily lead to a practical crisis, for the superiority of liberal democracy to communism . . . is obvious enough. And, above all, liberal democracy, in contradistinction to communism and fascism, derives powerful support from a way of thinking which cannot be called modern at all: the premodern thought of our western tradition.[73]

In his *Studies in Platonic Political Philosophy*, Strauss shows the way both forms of premodern thought provide support for liberal democratic political institutions insofar as these institutions are understood to consist essentially in the rule of law based on popular consent. According to Plato, only the person who knows what is good for each and every individual has a natural right to rule. It is not clear whether any human being has or can have such knowledge; the only possibility is the Socratic philosopher, and qua philosopher he or she does not want to rule. The best practical solution that can be expected is the qualification or dilution of the rule of divine intellect by the need for consent.

Likewise, reading *Genesis* in its own terms, in "Jerusalem and Athens" Strauss suggests that the story of the Fall, the Flood, and the giving of the Torah to Moses can be understood to be an account of God's teaching human beings they need to live under the rule of a law, formulated by Divine Wisdom to which they have freely consented.[74] Like Plato, the Bible not only teaches the practical necessity of the rule of law; it also suggests that so long as there are human beings, they will form nations that will war with one another. The reason the rule of law is needed and war is unavoidable is, in both cases, the same. The primary attachment people have, first, to their own bodily existence and, then, to their own families or goods, makes it impossible for individuals, much less groups always to follow the mandates of the divine intellect.[75] Because no one wants to sacrifice him- or herself for others, people disagree about the best way of doing things. They form different factions or camps and, when their differences become severe, they fight. Those who wish to defend their freedom must, therefore, band together.

Neither the biblical injunction to obey unquestioningly nor the prudential Socratic argument concerning the desirability of law-abidingness at most times and places can be directly applied to modern liberal democracies, Strauss emphasizes.[76] These democracies are neither Judaic theocracies nor ancient mixed regimes. They are representative governments; and, as such, they differ in important respects from ancient democracies.[77] Contemporary liberal democrats do not advocate rule by lot or by uneducated masses. They think "that democracy must become rule by the educated, and this goal will be achieved by universal education."[78] The difference between people today and the classics with regard to democracy does not, therefore, rest on a different understanding of justice. Most people today still think "that it is just to give equal things to equal people and unequal things to people of unequal merit. . . . The difference with regard to democracy consists *exclusively* in a different estimate of the virtues of technology."

Universal education is impossible unless the economy of scarcity is replaced by an economy of plenty and that replacement requires, in turn, the freeing of technology from all moral and political control. And it is by no means clear that the emancipation of technology from moral and political control will not produce the disasters or dehumanization the classics implicitly predicted.[79] Unlike Heidegger, however, Strauss did not think his contemporaries could or should give up technology entirely for the sake of cherishing the earth; technology is too important for defense, and defense is an ongoing political necessity.[80] He simply insisted that people should not think technology will solve their problems, that is, overcome the fundamental limitations or contradictions of human existence.

Strauss sought to revive the premodern *understanding* of the tension between philosophy and politics; in marked contrast to Machiavelli, he did not advocate a return to ancient political practice. By reviving the ancient understanding of politics, Strauss hoped, first, to convince both his fellow Jews and his philosophically minded readers they needed to take account of the political preconditions of their more spiritual, transpolitical endeavors. In the twentieth century, both roots or sources of Western intellectual life were threatened with extinction; defensive action was necessary. By reminding his readers not only of the pressing importance but also of the essential limitations of politics, Strauss also sought to show them the character of the transpolitical religious and philosophical alternatives in their pure form. "Even the trans-political cannot be understood as such except if the city is understood," Strauss concluded in his study of "Plato," "and the city is completely intelligible because its limits can be made perfectly manifest: to see these limits, one need not have answered the question regarding the whole; it is sufficient for the purpose to have raised the question regarding the whole."[81]

Since Strauss's death, the value of the Western intellectual tradition he wished to preserve has itself become a political issue. Critics of the racist, sexist, or generally exclusionary character of the great books or the West have drawn extensively on the writings of Jacques Derrida for support. Yet, when we compare Derrida and Strauss, we seem to confront an irony, if not a paradox. By showing that the roots of the Western tradition are fundamentally incompatible, Strauss thought he was preserving the secret core or nerve of its vitality. By revealing a fundamental fissure, cleft, or instability at its roots, Derrida thinks he is showing how the West is necessarily deconstructing itself. To what extent, we are led to ask, do Derrida and Strauss actually have different views of the West, in general, and its Platonic origins, in particular? To what extent do they use similar literary and philosophical insights in different ways, because they have different understandings of politics?

Seven

Derrida's Deconstruction of Plato

At first glance, no two thinkers appear to have less in common than Leo Strauss and Jacques Derrida. Whereas Strauss sought to revive the Western tradition in the face of the radical critique leveled by Nietzsche and Heidegger, Derrida wants to carry that critique even further.[1] Strauss was politically conservative; Derrida's sympathies are explicitly with the left.[2] The first and necessary step in reading any book, according to Strauss, is to understand it as the author did; Derrida is famous for arguing that the author's intention does not control the meaning of the text. Strauss read Plato (as well as, to a certain extent, the subsequent history of Western philosophy) in terms of the age-old quarrel between poetry and philosophy; Derrida denies that there is a fundamental difference between philosophic and poetic texts.[3] Strauss argued that Plato's Socrates represents a way of life, not a set of doctrines; following Heidegger, Derrida treats the history of philosophy from Socrates onwards as the history of metaphysics or 'onto-theology'. Finally, whereas Strauss emphasized the tension between politics and philosophy, Derrida suggests that we ought to regard all attempts to articulate and so establish order—poetic or rhetorical as well as scientific or philosophical—to be essentially political.[4] Strauss and Derrida seem to mean something very different by politics. Whereas for Strauss, the political is defined by its limits—the need for intelligent direction, on the one hand, and the need for consent or recognition of the power of irrational bodily force, on the other—for Derrida, like most other modern philosophers, the political consists primarily in the exercise of power.

In light of these polar oppositions, the similarities between Strauss and Derrida are both surprising and striking. Both trace the origins of their own thought, at least in part, to their experiences as persecuted

Jews. Because both Strauss and Derrida argue that a careful reading of classic texts shows that they have multiple meanings, commentators have characterized the analyses of both commentators as Talmudic.[5] According to both Strauss and Derrida, what an author does not say can be more important than what is said. In the case of Plato, both argue that careful reading of the dialogues shows that all the apparent arguments and doctrines are undercut. Both suggest that the Platonic Socrates let the city of Athens kill him to prove in deed, as it were, that philosophy does not undermine legal order. Both also suggest that the explicit teachings of the dialogues have a political function or purpose. Neither thinks that Plato's philosophy—or that of anyone else—should be understood simply in political terms. On the contrary, both Strauss and Derrida insist that philosophers, in general, and Nietzsche and Heidegger, in particular, should not be judged solely in terms of their political associations or effects; but both Strauss and Derrida also argue that Nietzsche and Heidegger were implicated in the rise of National Socialism.[6] Endorsing some aspects of the radical critique of the tradition by Nietzsche and Heidegger, both Strauss and Derrida seek to avoid the disastrous political results of that critique.[7] Because both Strauss and Derrida find Nietzsche's analysis of the limits of reason to be basically sound, both conclude that everything is not and never will be wholly intelligible; in opposition to Hegel they both argue that there are aspects of things that are not and never will be captured by, or expressible in, *logos*. Finally, in opposition to Nietzsche and Heidegger as well as to Hegel, both Strauss and Derrida argue that there is no necessary direction or end to history.

What Strauss wrote of his relation to Gadamer—that beginning at a common point, they had marched in almost completely opposite directions—could be said even more emphatically of the relation of his work to that of Derrida.[8] Accepting the validity of Nietzsche's critique of the Enlightenment, Strauss and Derrida both concluded that Nietzsche had not taken his critique of modern philosophy far enough. Explicitly seeking an alternative to the self-destruction of reason presented by Nietzsche, Strauss proceeded back by way of Maimonides and Farabi to a highly original reading of Plato that emphasized the need for philosophers to moderate their speech in order to preserve political order. Wishing to prevent the successful imposition of any form of total(itarian) order, Derrida sought to dismantle the claims of 'rationality' and thereby to divert the process of 'rationalization' even more radically than Nietzsche had. In this chapter I will trace the critique of Husserl, Heidegger, and Nietzsche that initially led Derrida to 'deconstruct' Plato. In the following chapter I will then examine the new, more open interpretation not merely of Plato, but of the Western heritage as a whole he proposed on the basis of his initial deconstruction.

FROM IDEAS TO TRACES: DERRIDA'S CRITIQUE OF HUSSERL

Like Heidegger and Strauss, Derrida began his critique of the Western philosophical tradition with an insight he took from Husserl, but developed in a very different direction than Husserl himself did. Heidegger and Strauss embraced Husserl's contention that science is based upon a prescientific experience it covers over or obscures. They thus forgot about the phenomenological reduction and began engaging in historical studies designed to unearth the original experience traditional doctrines had covered up. In his introduction to *Edmund Husserl's "Origins of Geometry,"* Derrida carefully followed the progressive steps or series of reductions involved in Husserl's explanation of the way in which a science like geometry can have a historical origin and yet establish timeless truths to show that the development of such a science presupposes not only language but also writing. To appreciate the role of writing in the production of knowledge is, Derrida argued, to step decisively beyond the boundaries of the Western metaphysical tradition initiated by Plato and so bring it to 'closure'.

In contrast to Plato and Kant, Derrida emphasized, Husserl recognized that ideas are not eternal or simply there—to be discovered or recognized from time to time by some human beings. Ideas are constructed or produced out of the experience of living human beings. Because ideas arise out of lived experience, they necessarily have an historical origin. Inquiring into the origins of geometry, Husserl thus looked back *(rückfragen)* from the fact of the constituted science of geometry to ask, not who were the first geometers or what they did, but rather what were the necessary conditions for the development of that science, what made it possible?

The first of those conditions is the development of 'ideal objectivities' (general concepts which are intersubjectively understood) in language.

> For example, the word *Löwe* [lion] occurs only once in the German language; it is identical throughout its innumerable utterances by any given person [sic]. Thus, the word [mot] has an ideal Objectivity and identity, since it is not identical with any of its empirical, phonetic, or graphic materializations.[9]

But, because words function in this ideal objective way only within specific languages and are thus linked to the factual subjectivity of a certain speaking community or culture, they must be further 'eidetically reduced' to free them of all empirical residues.

> Therefore we cross into a higher degree of ideal Objectivity . . . as soon as
> we pass from the word to the unity of the sense 'lion', from "the expression" to what Husserl calls in the Logical Investigations the "intentional content" or "the unity of its signification." The same content can be intended starting from several languages, and its ideal identity assures its translatability. This ideal . . . is then freed from all factual linguistic subjectivity.

However, even when the concept 'lion' becomes freed from the constraints imposed by a specific language, its ideality is still limited, because it refers to a sensible and therefore fundamentally empirical and continent experience. We encounter a third level of pure ideality only when, as in mathematics, the object or content no longer has any sensible reference.

But Husserl shows that the development of a science composed of such pure concepts nonetheless continues to presuppose language—this time in the form of writing—to free the concepts from possible imprisonment "as fact in a psychological subjectivity—in the inventor's head." So Derrida asks, "Does this ultimate reduction . . . revolutionize Husserl's thought?" The need to write ideas down somewhere outside the mind in order to pass them on from generation to generation raises questions about the possibility or existence of pure, non-spatio-temporal objects of thought. The dependency on writing for the transmission or preservation of such ideas also brings their eternity into question. For, if the "truth" can be transmitted over time only by means of writing, it can also be erased and so disappear.

In his Origins, Derrida admits, Husserl drew no such conclusion. On the contrary, he argued:

> To constitute an ideal object is to put it at the permanent disposition of a
> pure gaze. Now, before being the constituted . . . act which proceeds toward
> the truth of sense, linguistic ideality is the milieu in which the ideal object
> settles as what is sedimented or deposited. But here the act of primordial
> depositing is not the recording of a private thing, but the production of a
> common object, i.e., of an object whose original owner is thus dispossessed.
> Thus language preserves truth.

Once constituted, the idea or truth can survive not only the death of the person who first discovered it, but also, because it can be translated, the death of the language and culture in which it was first announced.

Although science has its origins in the specific experiences of certain individuals and societies or cultures, Husserl argued, the culture that produced science not only differs from but is also superior to all other cultures in the same way its "language" of mathematics differs from and is superior to all others; it is, both in principle and aspiration, universal. Like his student Heidegger, Husserl recognized that science presupposes not only the experience but also a certain understanding or consciousness of sociality, of "being-with" others in a "world." But, Derrida emphasizes, "the world and fellow mankind here designate the all-inclusive, but infinitely open, unity of possible experiences and not this world right here, these fellow men right here, whose factuality for Husserl is never anything but a variable example."[10]

Husserl's account of the history of development of science is open, Derrida observes, at both ends. The origins are recognized and defined in light of the current fact or state of the science, but that state is understood to be progressively, infinitely (!), changing in light of new discoveries. As a history, Walter Biemel observed, Husserl's *Origins of Geometry* is a failure.[11] Husserl did not intend to give a history in the ordinary sense, however; he intended to show the possibility or grounds of such a history. The grounds that Husserl traces out are, nevertheless, problematic.

In his account of the *Origins* Derrida indicates some of the difficulties in the unity (or unities) of 'mankind', 'language' and 'truth', or 'science' that Husserl presupposes. "Within the horizon of this consciousness of fellow mankind, it is 'mature, normal' mankind that is 'privileged', both as the horizon of civilization and as the linguistic community." But how is the mature distinguished from the immature or childish, and the normal from the abnormal or mad? Having abjured essences, Husserl has to appeal to the 'horizon' or limits set not only by the beginning or origins (identified ex post facto from the fact of developed science), but also and most emphatically by its end or *telos*—universal science or rationality. Rather than including all potentially human beings, the end or horizon functions as a limiting, exclusive norm.[12]

"The possibility of a mediate or immediate horizon of universal language . . . [also] supposes . . . that everything is nameable in the broadest sense." But, Husserl himself admitted in *The Phenomenology of Internal Time Consciousness* that "names are lacking" for "the ultimate identity of the constitutive flux of immanent time and absolute subjectivity," that is, for the very ground of the possibility of knowledge. "Can we not say, then, just the opposite of what Husserl said? Are not noncommunication and misunderstanding the very horizon of culture and language?"[13] Finally, the ability of later human beings to retain, recapture, and add to the ideas or truths first articulated by others presupposes the intrasubjective ability of the first to retain and recall ideas he or she had articulated in the past into the 'living present'. Husserl's infinitely expanding science thus presupposes both the distinction and the negation of the distinction between past and present in the infinite expanding and all-encompassing 'living present' of both the individual and the transcendental consciousness in which the ideas are repeatedly brought back into view (or theorized). It also presupposes a certain division within the consciousness—self or transcendental—which can, like science, recognize itself as a unity only by somehow separating itself or a part of itself and looking back at the course of its development or achievements, that is, history.[14]

Derrida brings out the significance of the division in the subject or consciousness and the temporal disjunction required for the representation of the ideas more fully in a subsequent study of Husserl entitled *Speech and Phenomena.* In his phenomenology Husserl thought he had shown the way in which philosophy could become a rigorous science, rather than mere speculative metaphysics, by reducing all the noneidetic, factual, and therefore contingent elements out of man's 'living experience'. In fact, Derrida argues, Husserl's phenomenological critique restored metaphysics to its original purity.[15]

> The unique and permanent motif of all the mistakes and distortions which Husserl exposes in "degenerated" metaphysics . . . is always a blindness to the authentic mode of *ideality,* to that which *is,* to what may be indefinitely *repeated* in the *identity* of its *presence,* because of the very fact that it *does not exist.* . . , whose possibility will permit us to speak of nonreality and essential necessity, the noema, the intelligible object, and in general the nonworldly.[16]

As Husserl himself admitted upon occasion, he only opposed "conventional Platonism."

> When he affirms the nonexistence or nonreality of ideality, it is always to acknowledge that ideality *is* a way of being that is irreducible to sensible existence or empirical reality and their fictional counterparts. In determining the *ontos on* as *eidos,* Plato himself was affirming the same thing.[17]

When Husserl traces his understanding of the ideas to our experience of an internal soliloquy, he thus exposes the basis of the illusion that has ruled the entire history of Western philosophy or metaphysics since Plato.

At the beginning of his *Logical Investigations,* Husserl distinguished two different kinds of signs—indications, which signify by pointing to something else, and expressions, which contain or signify their own contents or meaning. All natural or communicative language is somewhat indicative, Husserl admitted; the sensible, interior experience of one person cannot be communicated directly to another. We use language to induce others to recall similar feelings or thoughts. The notion that we can formulate and share atemporal, aspatial ideas—the subject matter of phenomenology—is based on the experience of internal soliloquy, that is, mentally "hearing" ourselves speak. Since we already know what we know or think, we do not really communicate with ourselves; in such internal soliloquies, the expression and the content are simultaneous and same.

The experience of hearing ourselves say or express what we think *is* the source of *the metaphysical illusion* that there are atemporal, aspatial ideas that can be intersubjectively recalled and repeated—infinitely, Derrida emphasizes. Because what is said is not visible, the means of communication do not seem to erect any physical or even temporal barrier to the sharing or recalling of the same thought. Because we hear ourselves say what we are thinking, we come to believe that others can hear and comprehend the same thoughts simultaneously, without any distorting intermediary. Voice has the physical or spatial effect of making what is interior, exterior; there is no absolute or complete barrier between the mind and the world outside. But, Derrida points out, there *is* still a gap; no communication is completely undistorted or pure. We never really know what is in the mind of another; we only know what he or she expresses. Husserl himself admits that *all* speech is essentially indicative; and that means all speech is irreducibly spatio-temporal. As Husserl conceded in his study of the *Origins of Geometry*, even the most eidetic or formal of the sciences, mathematics, has to be written down, if its concepts are to endure.

Moreover, if we think about what is entailed by having a soliloquy with oneself or in recalling the same idea, discovered in the past, to be repeated or recollected an indefinite number of times in the future, we see that there can be no pure identity of the "self" or "ego" any more than there can be pure simultaneity in the re-presentation of ideas. On the contrary, the turning around or back to look on oneself involved in self-consciousness presupposes a division within the self. Likewise, the recalling or re-presenting of ideas from the past presupposes their previous absence, that is, temporal noncontinuity. By analyzing Husserl's arguments, we discover that we do not and cannot know any self-identical ego or timeless, eternally present ideas. Both the experience we call self-consciousness and our ability to repeat or reiterate ideas we have had in the past presuppose constant differentiation and deferral, a process Derrida describes with the neologism *differance*.[18]

If there is no uniform, self-identical subject or knower and there are no eternally present, unchanging objects of knowledge or ideas, we need to change not merely the concepts, but the entire Platonic schema in terms of which we have understood ourselves and the world. Above all, we need to jettison the Platonic distinction between soul and body. There are no purely mental, unchanging processes or objects of thought. The traditional oppositions between ideal and real, noema and phenomena, being and becoming cannot be maintained. If our awareness of ourselves and things in the world presupposes constant differentiation and deferral, we do not experience anything as simply present. That is, we have never really had any experience of what Heidegger showed has been tradition-ally understood as 'being'.

The discovery of the *differance* not merely underlying, but implicit, in all experience and existence thus brings the history of philosophy or metaphysics to an end, but not in the sense of completion. With *dif-ferance* Derrida thinks he has brought that history to a close—or clo-sure—by showing that the goal of philosophy as understood from Plato to Hegel or even Husserl is impossible to attain. If self-differentiation and deferral is the necessary condition for all cognition, there never is, was, or will be an ideal order that can be produced or contemplated as a whole. There is not even a horizon that temporarily serves to define the perimeter of a world, as Nietzsche, Heidegger, and Gadamer would say, because something is always held back, reserved or deferred.

Rather than understanding our mental activity in terms of the tradi-tional visual metaphor, as a kind of static "seeing," Derrida urges, we should reconceive the character not merely of our mental activity, but of our interaction with things in the world, more dynamically, physically, and historically as a kind of 'writing'. If there is nothing purely intelli-gible, immaterial, eternal, or present—in sum, if there is no being—everything ought to be reconceived as a spatio-temporal mark, leaving or 'trace' of something that is itself no longer there on something that was there before.

RECONCEIVING THE WORLD AS TEXT

In *Speech and Phenomena* Derrida criticized Husserl on the basis of Hei-degger's showing that in the history of philosophy 'being' originally meant presence. But in a footnote, Derrida observed:

> Perhaps it is already apparent that, while we appeal to Heideggerian motifs in decisive places, we would especially like to raise the question whether, with respect to the relations between *logos* and *phone*, and . . . the pre-tended irreducibility of certain word unities [e.g.] *being*. . . , Heidegger's thought does not raise the same questions as the metaphysics of presence.[19]

In a series of essays written around the same time as *Speech and Phenomena*, Derrida thus extended his critique to Heidegger's concepts of 'being', 'truth', and 'man'.

In developing his own notion of the 'trace', Derrida explained in *Of Grammatology*, he drew on the writings of four other authors without simply agreeing with any of them. More specifically, he related

> this concept of *trace* to what is at the center of the latest work of Emmanuel Levinas and his critique of ontology: relationship to the illeity as to the alterity of a past that never was and can never be lived in the originary or modified form of presence. Reconciled here to a Heideggerian intention,— as it is not in Levinas's thought—this notion signifies . . . the undermining of an ontology which . . . has determined the meaning of being as presence and the meaning of language as the full continuity of speech. . . . This deconstruction of presence accomplishes itself through the deconstruction of consciousness, and therefore through the irreducible notion of the trace *(Spur)*, as it appears in both Nietzschean and Freudian discourse.[20]

In other words, in developing his own notion of the 'trace', Derrida used insights he took from Levinas, Nietzsche, and Freud to take Heidegger's critique of metaphysics even further.

In *The Question of Being* Heidegger suggested that we ought to regard the beings we encounter in the world as traces *(Spuren)* of Being that has itself withdrawn into oblivion. Although Heidegger emphasized that Being was never present—it was not a being, but only manifested itself indirectly in and through the beings—he nevertheless suggested that the beings disclosed through the articulation of a world in language were. They were present, however, as beings only to human beings who asked what they were. Because their being thus depended on an essential relation with something else, with "man," they were not self-subsistent. On the contrary, because the ground or reason for the being of the beings was never present or knowable, the meaning of the terms and concepts used to describe the beings was steadily and necessarily becoming emptied out from the moment of their first articulation.

Heidegger's continued use of the term 'being' obscured his insistence on the essentially temporal and hence transitory character of all things and ideas. Rather than reconceive of things and ideas as traces of Being, Derrida suggested, it would be better to speak and write, as Levinas did, of the traces of 'the other', of that which never itself appears and is, therefore, beyond being and knowledge.

Derrida was not persuaded by Levinas's overall critique of Heidegger's fundamental ontology, however. In particular, Derrida did not think the ethical relation between two persons who confront each other face-to-face is more fundamental than the ontological relation between the human being and Being.[21] Recognition of another presupposed an understanding of the other's *being* another, that is, a precomprehension of being, as Heidegger maintained.[22] In contrast to Levinas, Derrida did not distinguish, therefore, between the *trait* of the other to be seen in his face and the effects things had on other things; that is, he did not distinguish between the personal other *(autrui)* and the impersonal *(autre)*.[23] Contrary to Levinas, Derrida insisted that there was no Absolute Other; otherness or difference exists only in relation to sameness, not in itself. As the 'other' of all determinate forms of existence, the 'other' could be said to be in-finite, but it was a negative infinity, not a positive one. The Other could not and should not, therefore, be identified with God.[24]

Levinas criticized Heidegger's ontology because he thought that, like all previous philosophy, it aimed at com-pre-hending everything. Not merely did ontology reduce everything to the same by understanding it as a form of being; it sought to establish total possession and control.[25] Levinas had misunderstood Heidegger's thought, Derrida objected. In an article entitled "*Ousia* and *Gramme:* Note on a Note from *Being and Time*," he thus presented his own critique.[26]

In *Being and Time* Heidegger had argued that the traditional understanding of Being as the Being of the beings deprived Being of any real meaning; it became reduced to a propertyless substratum. Being originally referred to what is present; and as present, 'the meaning of Being' was determined in terms of time. Philosophers following Aristotle had forgotten the original meaning, because they had adopted his vulgar understanding of time as an unending sequence of moments or 'nows'. In fact, Derrida pointed out, if we turn back to the *Physics* (as well as the discussions of time Hegel based on it), we see that both Aristotle and his successors understood time not merely as a series of moments, but as that which also "is not," because it is always in process of becoming what it "is" not, the past or the future. Previous philosophers had not only understood being in terms of time without fully recognizing it; they had also understood time in terms of being. To move beyond a metaphysical understanding, it would be necessary, therefore, to jettison the notion of 'time' along with that of 'being'. Heidegger himself seemed to recognize as much when he ceased writing about the meaning of Being after *Being and Time* and began talking, instead, about the 'truth of Being' and the 'ontological difference'. If 'Being' was that which made it possible for the 'beings' to appear, but which itself never became apparent, Derrida thought, he had expressed Heidegger's thought better than Heidegger himself, when he suggested that everything ought to be regarded as a 'trace' of *differance*, a process of differentiation and deferral that never appeared or could by definition be known in itself.

Just as Heidegger failed to free his treatment of 'the question of Being' entirely from traditional philosophical concepts and language, so Derrida observed in an essay on "The Ends of Man," Heidegger retained elements of the traditional metaphysical understanding of the co-respondent of 'Being'. "*Dasein* is not simply the man of metaphysics. . . ; [it] does not have the form of subjective consciousness, as in transcendental phenomenology . . . [and] is still prior to what the metaphysical predicate 'human' might name." But, *Dasein* is linked by "the name of man . . . to the totality of metaphysics' traditional discourse." For example, in *Being and Time* Heidegger states that, "as ways in which man behaves, sciences have the manner of Being which this entity—man himself—possesses. This entity we denote by the term '*Dasein*'." And, "in both ordinary and philosophical usage, *Dasein*, man's Being is defined as the *zōon logon ekhon.*" So, "*Dasein*, though *not* man, is nevertheless *nothing other* than man."

Although Derrida endorsed "the archeological radicalness of the questions sketched by Heidegger" in his *Letter on Humanism* and insisted that "any metahumanist position that does not place itself within the opening of these questions remains historically regional, periodic, and peripheral," he nevertheless observed that

> The thinking of . . . the truth of Being in the name of which Heidegger delimits humanism and metaphysics, remains as thinking *of* man. Man and the name of man are not displaced in the question of Being such as it is put to metaphysics. Even less do they disappear. On the contrary, at issue is a kind of reevaluation or revalorization of the essence and dignity of man.

By redefining the substance of 'man' as 'ek-sistence' Heidegger did not declare "the humanistic interpretations of man as *animale rationale*, 'as person', as spiritual-ensouled-bodily being . . . false. Rather, the sole implication is that the highest determinations of the essence of man in humanism still do not realize the proper dignity of man."[27]

Derrida pointed out that such a concern for "humanity" was characteristic, according to Nietzsche's Zarathustra, of the higher men, the best men of the past. To move beyond 'man' and the metaphysical understanding of the world with which humanism was necessary associated, it would be necessary to leave this concern behind.[28]

Just as Derrida corrected or extended Heidegger's analysis of the "difference" which not merely underlies but penetrates all things by incorporating some, but not all of Levinas's critique of Heidegger's ontology, so he deconstructed the corresponding Heideggerian notions of 'man' and 'truth' by giving new readings of some Nietzschean and Freudian texts. In *Spurs* he presented an analysis of Nietzsche's writings to show there was no singular entity called 'man' or any single 'truth'.

As Nietzsche reminds his readers, there is a fundamental difference within what is called "mankind." But it is not clear what the character of this sexual difference is or what it means. It is certainly not merely a "biological" or natural difference with regard to procreation; Nietzsche speaks of barren women and of himself becoming "pregnant" with thought.[29] In Nietzsche's texts (or *Spurs*, i.e., traces) the sexual difference has several, multiple meanings, which cannot be comprehended or reduced to one, either syllogistically or dialectically. According to Nietzsche, "women" are concerned primarily, if not exclusively with appearances; they are attractive only at a distance; they do not, therefore, want anyone to come too close. They do not want anyone to learn the "truth" about the deceptive character of their own—and perhaps all—appearances, that they look good or desirable only at a distance. But, that suggests, women themselves do know the "truth." They represent the truth. "Suppose truth is a woman," Nietzsche writes in the preface to *Beyond Good and Evil*. Life is a woman, according to Nietzsche's Zarathustra. As "woman," "truth" is what spurs us on to greater efforts; "truth" is the illusion that keeps us alive. "Woman is but one name for that untruth of truth."[30] But, how can the truth deny itself, its own truth? It cannot be true that there is no truth, if there is no truth. From Nietzsche's texts, we thus learn that the question of "truth" is undecidable.

"Truth" cannot simply be denied any more than it can simply be affirmed. "For just this reason," Derrida concludes,

> There is no such thing either as the truth of Nietzsche, or of Nietzsche's text. In fact, in *Jenseits*, it is in a paragraph on women that one reads "these are only—*my truths*." The very fact that *"meine Wahrheiten"* is so underlined, that they are multiple, variegated, contradictory even, can only imply that these are not *truths*. Indeed there is no such thing.[31]

In *Ecce Homo* Nietzsche distinguishes himself from his writings. The marks a man leaves persist, to be reincorporated or erased, Derrida emphasizes, by the writings of others. In writing, moreover, a person presents only a partial aspect of himself or herself, never the whole. The authorial voice is but one of several possible personae; as Nietzsche stated, he wore many masks. Neither he nor anyone else has a unitary "self." Nor does he or anyone else unambiguously tell the truth. Nietzsche himself explicitly admits that he dissimulates.[32]

For the same reasons there is no truth, only "truths" or traces, Derrida emphasizes, Nietzsche could not control or determine the meaning of his own writings. Heidegger's reading is too narrow, as indicated by his initial identification of the name 'Nietzsche' with the substance of his thought.[33] Nevertheless, Derrida seeks to incorporate Heidegger's argument that Nietzsche's doctrine of the 'will to power' constitutes the completion or end of metaphysics rather than its overcoming into his own reading of Nietzsche.[34] By arguing that there is no intelligible, eternally existing order to be dis-covered, that everything "is" only a mode of the will to power which constantly seeks to increase itself, Nietzsche thought he had shown that philosophers of the future could impose the order and meaning they wanted. But, Heidegger suggested, 'the will to power' is merely the truth of our time, disclosed not simply by the struggle of two ideologically defined "superpowers" for world dominion, but even more fundamentally by the technology they both employ to transform everything into potential energy or power. Heidegger's reading showed that Nietzsche did not fully understand the "truth" of his own writings. Heidegger's reading abstracted, however, from the "feminine" or essentially undecidable character of the "truth" revealed in those same writings. Heidegger understood that the same texts had different meanings at different times; he saw that the author's intentions or understanding did not determine the meaning of his writings which would be disclosed in the future. He did not see that the essential *differance* of meaning in any text was not simply a product of time.

To understand the reasons why an author's intention would never control the meaning of text, it was necessary to turn to Freud. In "Freud and the Scene of Writing" Derrida used the suggestion that the psyche might be metaphorically described as a mystic writing pad to show how a variety of meanings may be continuously, but not intentionally or consciously produced.[35]

Derrida traced Freud's attempts to account for the phenomenon of memory from his *Project for a Scientific Psychology*, published in 1895, to his "Note on the Mystic Writing Pad," written in 1925, to show how he came to conceive of the psyche as an apparatus that operates by means of a kind of unconscious writing. The problem in explaining memory was to show how we can constantly receive new impressions and yet retain 'memory-traces' *(Erinnerungsspuren)*. According to Freud's early, physiological account, we have two kinds of neurones, some perfectly permeable, with which we continue to receive or perceive new impressions, because the impressions leave no traces and take up no space in these neurones, and others which resist external impressions and thus retain a trace of those strong enough or those repeated frequently enough to breach their resistance and open a path *(Bahnung)* along which memory can proceed later. "All these differences in the production of the trace may be reinterpreted as moments of deferring," Derrida pointed out.

> In accordance with a motif which will continue to dominate Freud's think-ing, this movement is described as the effort of life to protect itself by *deferring* a dangerous cathexis, that is, by constituting a reserve. . . . But we must be wary of this formulation: there is no life present *at first* which would *then* come to protect, postpone, or reserve itself in *differance*. . . . It is . . . the delay which is in the beginning.[36]

We are never conscious of the process of breaching or its effects, yet the interweaving of these breaches or traces determines what we remember. Our sense of our own identify depends upon what we remember; and the constitution of this memory is a dynamic process, in which new impres-sions are constantly re-tracing and so deepening earlier "paths" or cross-ing over and so gradually erasing the traces of older impressions in a new pattern or "text."

Freud himself quickly moved away from a purely physiological to a more literally graphic description of the operation of the psyche. A year after the *Project*, he wrote his friend Wilhelm Fliess:

> I am working on the assumption that our psychic mechanism has come into being by a process of stratification *(Aufeinanderschichtung)*; the ma-terial present in the form of memory-traces *(Erinnergungsspuren)* being subjected from time to time to a *rearrangement (Umordnung)* in accor-dance with fresh circumstances to a *retranscription (Umschrift).*[37]

In his later "Note on the Mystic Writing Pad" these strata become associ-ated with the three layers of the toy or tool: an outer layer of immediate perception of the external world in which there are no traces of present or past impressions, like the cellophane cover; a middle layer in which the impressions made by an inkless stylus appear as traces by virtue of contact with the wax layer underneath, and can be erased by separating the upper sheets from the wax base; and the wax base in which traces of previous impressions remain in an increasingly complex web, which determines what will appear or not in the middle as a result of external strokes on the penetrable surface.

If the psyche is constituted by the interrelations of various strata, Der-rida emphasizes, there is no simple subject any more than there is a unity of lived experience in the present. By showing that "the present in gen-eral is not primal but, rather, reconstituted, that it is not the absolute, wholly living form which constitutes experience," Freud poses a formi-dable challenge to metaphysics "in a conceptual scheme unequal to the thing itself."[38]

The metaphor of the writing pad raises a question Freud himself failed

to make explicit—a question concerning the relation or, really, insepara-
bility of the organization of our inner psyche and that of the external
world. We become able to understand the character of the complex operation of our memory only by virtue of the invention of a "supplementary
machine," a writing pad designed to overcome the limits of that same
memory. The invention outlives its cause or source; used metaphorically,
it has unanticipated effects. Only by having an effect or leaving such a
trace, by writing upon the external world, can we come to understand
how we ourselves are constituted or 'written' upon internally. That internal writing or text determines, in turn, the way in which we see and thus
act in the world. We do not and can never entirely control either the
effects of our actions in the world or the impressions we receive of it.
"We are written only as we write."[39] Inner and outer, past and present,
life and death are not, strictly speaking or completely, divisible. They are
both joined and separable, in part, like the sheets of the pad.

"Thus the Freudian concept of trace must be radicalized and extracted
from the metaphysics of presence which still retains it (particularly in
the concepts of consciousness, the unconscious, perception, memory, reality, and several others)." Derrida "never dreamed of taking [Freud's
'metapsychological fable'] seriously, outside of the question which disor-
ganizes and disturbs its literalness."[40] His own notions of the 'archi-trace'
and *'differance'* are neither Heideggerian nor Freudian, he emphasizes.
He uses Heidegger to erase the traces of the metaphysics of presence in
Freud, and Nietzsche and Freud to dissolve the metaphysical notions of
'man' and 'truth' in Heidegger.

In articulating the notion of 'trace' or 'writing' he thinks will finally
bring metaphysics to closure by revealing its limits, Derrida explicitly
and unapologetically uses the writings of his predecessors in ways they
did not intend. If everything "is" only a trace left from the past, it is
impossible to begin de novo à la Descartes, writing on a blank slate, as it
were. According to his own understanding, Derrida has no alternative
but to rewrite existing texts. In writing, an author admits, in effect, the
limits of his own life and understanding. He will die, but his thoughts or
traces will live on—if and only if, those writings are read, if they impress, if they are taken over, com-prehended, which is to say, re-written
in and by another. The re-writing will necessarily differ from the original, because it will be only one of many traces or impressions to be incorporated, reinscribed or crossed over and so erased by the ongoing
dynamic of differentiation and deferral Derrida calls *differance* that underlies all ex-pressions, articulations, and understandings of 'self' or
'world'.

No author can put down his or her entire experience or understanding of the world, if, as Freud suggests, no one is ever fully aware of all that is impressing him or her. At most he or she can attempt to transcribe that experience in linear fashion, piece by piece, logically. But such a transcription is clearly a reconstruction which leaves out, represses, or defers elements that do not fit. No intelligible statement or text can be formulated without empty spaces between the words or traces and around the margins, Derrida emphasizes. But, what lies behind or beneath the spacing and the timing, the differentiation and the deferral, is not merely forgotten or covered over like Heidegger's Being. What has been repressed as a necessary condition for the ex-pression of anything forms a 'reserve', a deferred source of meaning or opposition, upon which a later reader—or writer—can draw. By expurgating the traces of metaphysics or onto-theology remaining in the texts of Heidegger, Levinas, Nietzsche, and Freud, for example, Derrida discloses a hidden potential of which these authors themselves were not fully aware. His readings are explicitly selective. But, he suggests, every reading or writing is necessarily selective. We must re-press or even suppress certain elements or impressions in order to make others stand out.

BACK TO THE BEGINNING: PLATO'S REPRESSION OF WRITING

"Logo-phonocentrism is not a philosophical or historical error into which the history of philosophy, of the West, that is, of the world, would have rushed into pathologically," Derrida concludes in "Freud and the Scene of Writing." It "is rather a necessary, and necessarily finite, movement and structure: . . . in the European form of the metaphysical or onto-theological project . . . of general censorship of the text.[41] Philosophers who argued that the only true objects of knowledge had to be eternal, unchanging ideas had to deny that everything we encounter in the world results from an interweaving or text of essentially transitory traces.[42] This "censorship of the text" did not begin with Plato, Derrida argues in "Plato's Pharmacy," but it received its classic expression and defense in the critique of writing at the end of the *Phaedrus*. Careful reading of that dialogue shows, however, that Plato was forced in the end to admit the effective power of writing. He tried to redefine and redirect it to serve moral and political ends, because he feared the anarchy that might otherwise result.

Following Friedrich Schleiermacher, Derrida observes, many scholars have commented upon the apparent lack of organization in the *Phaedrus*.[43] The "trial of writing" at the end of the dialogue appears to be tacked on to a discussion of eros or rhetoric. In fact, Derrida argues, the discussion of writing is called for from the beginning; it is *the* organizing theme of the work. At the center of the dialogue, after the three demonstrations or speeches, at the beginning of the subsequent discussion of the nature of rhetoric, Socrates comments on the dishonest behavior of the *doxosophoi*, the men who memorize speeches written by others to deliver in the assembly, that is, who pretend to know what they do not actually know in order to gain power for themselves by making law. Socrates' criticism of the *doxosophoi* at the center of the dialogue points forward, of course, to the trial of writing at the end. But it also points back to the beginning where Phaedrus entices Socrates out of the city with a scroll he had hidden under his cloak, a scroll that contains a speech written by Lysias which Phaedrus had hoped to memorize and then deliver as his own. Both at the beginning and the end, Derrida emphasizes, Socrates describes writing as a *pharmakon*, the Greek word that like the English 'drug' can mean both remedy and poison. The description suggests from the outset that there is something problematic about writing. Even when it has beneficent effects, as a remedy, writing constitutes a response to some kind of defect. Also a poison, it can have harmful effects as well. As in the case of a medicinal drug, the effect writing has seems to depend on the art or knowledge of the practitioner. In contrast to his teacher and protagonist, Socrates, Derrida reminds his readers, Plato himself was a writer. But, Plato himself raises questions about the character and status of his writing in his Second Letter where he declares:

> It is impossible for what is written not to be disclosed. That is the reason I have never written anything about these things . . . and why there is not and will not be any written work of Plato's own. What are now called his . . . are the work of a Socrates become [young and beautiful].[44]

The question of writing is definitely not, as it might first appear in the *Phaedrus*, a secondary or supplementary consideration, added at the end to the discussion of the more important themes of eros and rhetoric. On the contrary, Derrida concludes, the question of writing points to the question of the character of Platonic philosophy itself.

What, then, is the critique Socrates makes of writing that may or may not apply to Plato? First, Derrida notes, Socrates introduces his critique by retelling an Egyptian story or myth. By calling it a myth, Socrates admits that he himself cannot vouch for or prove the truth of the events he relates. He was not present; he does not actually know whether or why they occurred. Second, in the myth the inventor of writing, Theuth, presents it to King Thamus as a great aid to memory. But, the king objects, rather than improve memory, writing will destroy it by replacing it. Writing *is* a powerful tool, the king admits, but its power is destructive.

Its power is, moreover, inferior to that of speech. In his gloss on the myth Socrates suggests two reasons for this inferiority. First, the author of a written piece is not there to explain his words by answering questions. Second, writing, as opposed to speech, says the same thing to everyone alike. In their previous discussion of rhetoric, Socrates and Phaedrus had agreed that someone who knew what he was doing would adjust what he said to the particular character and needs of his interlocutor. But, Derrida points out, as the opening scene in the dialogue reminds us, people like Phaedrus can memorize and repeat written words without really understanding them. The same words do not mean the same thing to all people; they have a tendency to become empty sounds. At the end of his critique, Socrates is thus led to admit that there is a beneficent, if playful form of writing that helps people to recollect what they have previously learned—writing on the soul.

In commenting on Socrates' critique of writing Derrida points out, first, that the absence of the source or ground of Socrates' opinions as expressed in the myth is characteristic of his arguments or *logoi* as well. Who or what is the origin or author of Socrates' *logoi*, Derrida asks. Since Socrates claims merely to examine the opinions of others, the author or origin is not Socrates himself. In the *Republic* Socrates suggests that the origin of all being and knowledge is the Idea of the Good. But, he tells Glaucon, he cannot explain this supreme concept or cause to him; he can merely give him its off-spring *(ekgonos)* or interest *(tokos)*, the analogy between the Sun and the Idea of the Good which is then developed into the image of the divided line. One might suspect that Socrates' inability to explain the Idea of the Good to Glaucon is a reflection of Glaucon's inability to understand rather than a reflection of some flaw in the intelligibility of the Good or Socrates' rhetorical ability. But in the *Phaedo*, Derrida reminds his readers, Socrates explains that he himself turned away from an attempt to look at or for the origin and cause of all things in *Nous*, because looking at the source directly was as intellectually blinding as gazing directly at its visible analogue, the sun. Instead, he began examining its reflections in the *logoi*. The origin of the arguments Socrates examines is no more present, Derrida concludes, than the origin of the stories he retells. The distinction Plato introduced between *logos* and *mythos* is thus shown to be problematic in Plato's own dialogues.[45]

So is the distinction he regularly draws between body and soul. Writing is supposed to be merely a tool that produces an external copy of interior thoughts. But, as King Thamus's objection to Theuth's invention indicates, such external, apparently physical activity can and does affect the internal operations of the mind itself. And the effect is contrary to the intention of the inventor or source!

As Derrida shows by comparing Socrates' account with its Egyptian sources, authors cannot entirely control the meaning of their stories any more than inventors can determine the use and effects of tools. Nobody makes things up literally from scratch. To begin with, nobody invents the language he or she speaks and writes. Like Socrates and Plato, moreover, most authors adapt stories they have heard from others. In both languages and stories certain regular structures or patterns can be observed. Both in its Egyptian sources and in the Platonic version, Derrida notes,

> The organization of the myth conforms to powerful constraints. These constraints coordinate as a system certain rules that make their presence known, something in what is empirically partitioned off for us as "Greek language" or "culture," and sometimes, from without, in "foreign mythology." From which Plato has not simply borrowed, nor borrowed a simple element: the identity of a character, Thoth, the god of writing. . . . Plato had to make his tale conform to structural laws. The most general of these, those that govern and articulate the opposition speech/writing, life/death, father/son, master/servant, first/second, legitimate son/orphan-bastard, soul/body, inside/outside, good/evil, seriousness/play, day/night, sun/moon, etc., also govern, and according to the same configurations, Egyptian, Babylonian, and Assyrian mythology.[46]

In both the Egyptian myth and Socrates' retelling, the god of writing is presented as a subordinate, because writing is conceived as a mere copy or imitation of some original thought or speech. But in both accounts, the god of writing also proves to be cunningly deceptive. Seeming merely to be a copy, the (god of) writing actually replaces the original "authority" with something different. Rather than constituting a mere form of imitation that is, as Plato repeatedly emphasizes, inferior to the original, writing produces something new, a document, that replaces and so supplants its origin. The separation of the writing from its source that Socrates suggests makes it inferior to speaking, because the author is not there to explain what he meant, actually gives writing the power to subvert the author, by making it independent of him.

Writing was invented to remedy the failures of human memory; but, as King Thamus objects, writing actually facilitates not memory but memorizing *(hypomnesis)*. By merely repeating the words of others they have learned by heart, students like Phaedrus imagine they have acquired true knowledge when they actually lack understanding. Another remedy or *pharmakon* thus becomes necessary for the failure of the purported cure. And that remedy proves to be another kind of writing!

Although writing does not really improve human memory *(mneme)*, Socrates later admits, it can assist in the process of acquiring knowledge through recollection *(anamnesis)*. Writing can assist recollection, because both writing and recollection involve a certain kind of repetition. An 'idea' is true, according to Platonic doctrine, precisely because it is always the same—in all times, at all places, to all intelligent beings—and so can be recalled (or repeated) infinitely. Writing can help someone make the truly and eternally intelligible 'ideas' once again present to or in his mind, somewhat ironically, precisely because, as Socrates complains (275d), writings always say the same things to everyone.

In the *Laws* (VII, 793b–c) Plato emphasizes the positive aspects of writings' always saying the same things to all people in stressing the importance of *written* laws in maintaining a given political order. To condemn writing per se is, as Socrates himself suggests when the question is first introduced in the *Phaedrus* (257c–258d), to condemn the rule of law also. Yet in the *Crito* we see Socrates remain to die rather than break the law by escaping from jail. Plato cannot take such a negative view of writing, as Socrates' critique initially suggests.

Both the possession of knowledge and the rule of law entail repetition and so, it seems writing. But, Plato suggests, so long as the marks remain external, writing does not suffice. If students like Phaedrus can merely memorize and repeat the words of others without really understanding them, the use of words or signs always entails the possibility that these words will become emptied of their original meaning. So, if human beings can never come directly into the presence of the truly intelligible beings *(ta onta)*, but can only acquire knowledge of them indirectly through words or *logoi*, as Socrates suggests in the *Phaedo* (99d–100a), the possibility of knowledge or philosophy is indissolubly bound up with the emergence of pretended knowledge or sophistry.

Plato indicates that his critique of writing constitutes a part of his ongoing diatribe against sophistry by calling those who learn speeches by heart from written books *doxosophoi*. But, if we turn to the writings of the rhetoricians with whom Plato often associates the sophists, we discover that they also criticize writing for always saying the same thing to all people. When rhetoricians like Gorgias argue that speech is preferable to writing, however, it is not because writing is "a *pharmakon* coming to corrupt memory and truth. It is because *logos* is a more effective *pharmakon*."[47]

Spoken words can "in-toxicate" as well, if not better than written ones; and, as both Meno and Alcibiades testify, Socratic dialogue has such a spellbinding effect.[48] In the *Symposium* (203c–e), moreover, we hear Diotima present a portrait of Eros, "behind [which] one cannot fail to recognize the features of Socrates." He is described not only as ugly, poor, shoeless, sleeping in doorways and spending his whole life in philosophizing, but also as a "fearsome sorcerer *(deinos goes)*, magician *(pharmakeus)*, and sophist *(sophistes)*."[49]

If Socrates is both philosopher and sophist, Derrida concludes, philosophy and sophistry are not truly or simply opposed. Socrates uses sophistic means to counteract sophistic effects. "Socratic irony . . . reverses the *pharmakon's* powers and turns *its* surface over."[50]

The *Phaedo* provides us the clearest example of such an inversion of values when Socrates attempts to persuade his companions that they should not fear death, because philosophy consists in a search for death. The soul can acquire knowledge of the eternal, unchanging ideas only when it becomes separated from the body, that is, only after death. The poison *(pharmakon)* that kills Socrates thus becomes the remedy *(pharmakon)* for his defective ability to learn while his soul is imprisoned in his body.

To say that sophistry and philosophy are inseparably connected, because they both employ the *pharmako-logos*, is not to make them simply the same, however. Where sorcerers and sophists generally exercise their art for their own benefit and promise by teaching it to increase their students' powers to satisfy their self-interest as well, Socrates has to sacrifice himself in order to make his antidote *(alexipharmakon)* effective. To "charm" away the "childish" fears of his companions, Socrates himself must demonstrate the "truth" of his teaching by fearlessly dying himself. His death serves to maintain the effectiveness of both the philosophy the Athenian fathers suspected of threatening all traditional authority and the legal order itself. Through his death the *pharmakeus* Socrates thus becomes a *pharmakos* as well.

Although Plato does not actually use the word *pharmakos*, Derrida argues:

> We do not believe that there exists, in all rigor, a Platonic text, closed upon itself, complete with its inside and its outside. Not that one must then consider that it is leaking on all sides and can be drowned confusedly in the undifferentiated generality of its element. Rather, provided the articulations are rigorously and prudently recognized, one should simply be able to untangle the hidden forces of attraction linking a present word with an absent word in the text of Plato.[51]

A synonym for *pharmakeus*, *pharmakos* has another, more specific meaning that ties it particularly to Socrates. Every year at Athens they led out two such victims *(pharmakoi)* to be sacrificed in order to purify the city of the evil that had infected it.

> The date of the ceremony is noteworthy: the sixth day of the Thargelia. That was the day of the birth of him whose death—and not only because

a *pharmakon* was its direct cause—resembles that of a *pharmakeus* from the inside: Socrates.[52]

Socrates was sacrificed to maintain civic order.

Socrates had to die so that philosophy in the form of the Platonic dialogues and the law—two forms of writing—might be preserved! In writing his condemnation of writing at the end of the *Phaedrus,* Derrida suggests, Plato himself pointed to the reasons Socratic dialectic had to be 'supplemented', that is, replaced, by the Platonic dialogues.

The description of writing as a *pharmakon* points to the broader question of the status of *mimesis,* that is, the relation of copy to original, because along with remedy and poison *pharmakon* also refers to the colors painters use. In complaining that written *logoi* always say the same thing and cannot respond to questions, Socrates compares written texts *(graphema)* to paintings *(homoion zographiai)* which seem to be alive until you question them and find that they remain majestically silent. Both writers and painters deceive their audience insofar as they present the products of a living soul as if they were living or ensouled entities themselves. By questioning these works of art, Socratic dialectic uncovers the deception by revealing the absence of the intelligent or living source.

The absence of the source of life and intelligibility appears to be the defect especially characteristic of images or imperfect copies.[53] But, Derrida has shown, the absence of the origin or author is characteristic of Socratic dialectic itself. Upon examination, he thus concludes, the Platonic distinction between truth and false image, simulacrum or phantasm, cannot be maintained.

In the *Phaedo* Socrates says that he sought knowledge indirectly through an examination of the reflections of the beings in *logoi,* because he could not approach *ta onta* directly without risking intellectual blindness. *Logoi* reflect *ta onta* insofar as they, unlike Being itself, involve differentiation. Plato brings out the significance of this differentiation in the *Sophist* (241d–242a), when the Stranger observes that their talk of false images has involved them in a kind of "parricide." Although his "father" Parmenides taught that it is not possible either to think or to say the "is not," in discussing images they have in fact been talking about something which is not. If human beings can only think through *logos,* contrary to Parmenides' famous doctrine, thinking and being cannot be the same, because thinking involves words, and words entail differentiation, negation or otherness—that is, the "is not."

If Being or even only the beings become intelligible to human beings only through *logos,* Derrida concludes, they become intelligible only in the absence or, even further, the negation or destruction of the source.

Truth and falsity are both necessarily and inseparably characteristic of *logos*, because in revealing the "truth" or presence of the *eidos*, *logos* simultaneously reveals its absence or non-presence. As the Stranger himself observes, the name 'Being' is not the same as Being itself.

If the ex-pression of Being in man through *logos* entails its absence, negation or destruction, Derrida suggests, the communication of the *eidos* or thought from one human being to another entails its separation from, and so, implicitly, the destruction or death of, its author.[54] Although Plato refuses to admit as much, Socrates' speeches can have a lasting effect—they can bear fruit, as it were—only if they are written down. As Socrates himself admits in the *Apology* and elsewhere, his speeches can have a lasting effect only if they are repeated.

If Being is eternal and unchanging, *logos* as a faculty of human beings is clearly not. On the contrary, human speech is evanescent. Occupying but a transitory moment, the present, speech will disappear if it is not written down. Having castigated the written text as an orphan or bastard son whose father has left it defenseless, Derrida observes, Socrates thus concludes his consideration of writing in the *Phaedrus* by describing its legitimate brother, the product of dialectics, as a kind of writing on the soul. But Derrida warns his readers:

> At the moment Plato seems to be raising writing up by turning live speech into a sort of psychic *graphe,* he maintains this movement within a problematic of *truth.* Writing *en tei psuchei* is not pathbreaking writing, but only a writing of transmission. . . . This type of writing must be capable of sustaining itself in living dialogue, capable most of all of properly teaching the true, as it is *already* constituted.[55]

Although Plato appears to acknowledge the necessary conjunction of being with not-being and their co-presence in *logos,* as well as, if only implicitly, the need for writing, he will not admit the 'indecidability' of 'truth' and 'falsehood', 'image' and 'reality', or the necessity of 'play'.

At the very conclusion of the *Phaedrus,* Socrates admits that even writing in its ordinary sense may be useful, to assist a person's failing memory in old age or as a mode of recreation. But in praising play "'in the best sense of the word', . . . play that is supervised and contained within the safeguards of ethics and politics," Derrida argues, "play and art are lost by Plato as he saves them, and his logos is then subject to that untold constraint that can no longer even be called 'logic'."[56]

At the end of his "pharmacy" Derrida thus suggests that Plato presented not only the death of Socrates but also his own more theoretical arguments with an eye to their political effect. Like Strauss he thinks

Plato restrained his "speech" to conceal the more radical challenges philosophy poses to the foundations of morality. But the ways in which the
two twentieth-century commentators suggest that Plato exercised self-
censorship differ considerably.

Unlike Strauss, in his readings of Plato Derrida does not pay much
attention to the differences among the philosophical spokesmen, interlocutors and settings of the dialogues.[57] Nor does he concern himself
much with questions about the gods or soul. Instead, Derrida points out
that, by presenting them in different dialogues, Plato obscures the extent
to which the Eleatic Stranger's argument that everything exists in or as a
nexus of similarities and differences in the *Sophist* undermines Socrates'
"hypothesis" in the *Phaedo* concerning the eternal existence of mutually
exclusive kinds of things or ideas. Nor does Plato make the significance
of Socrates' turn from an investigation of the origin of things to the study
of the *logoi* clear: the search for the origin produces mental blindness,
because it leads to an undifferentiated blank. Being itself is never present
to or for us. We know, at most, the different kinds of beings.

Plato concealed his or Socrates' insight into the non-presence, which
is to say, non-intelligibility of Being in itself or the first cause (the Idea
of the Good), Derrida suggests, because he perceived that this insight
served, for example, in the works of the sophists, to undermine the oppositions between good and bad, life and death, upon which human moral
and political life depend. Plato recognized the interplay of opposites in
the *Sophist*, but, as both Jacob Klein and Hans Georg Gadamer emphasize, he suggested that the differences were, like the virtues, all parts of
a larger whole. Plato did not concede, perhaps even to himself, what his
dialogues show—namely, that *the* necessary condition for the existence
or intelligibility of a differentiated world is the absence, the non-
existence of an ever-present, homogeneous origin or first principle. He
did not see, therefore, that the existence and intelligibility of all determinate forms of being have the same requirements or structure as "writing"; like generation, it presupposes not merely the separation of the
product from the producer, but the death of the originator. Nothing "is"
eternally. The "other" of the finite forms of existence is a negative infinity which has no characteristics or qualities of its own, no beginning
or end, not even mere presence. Plato did not, therefore, correctly understand the character of his own activity. He did not understand why, to
preserve Socrates' speeches, he had to write them down, even though, as
he himself emphasized in both the *Phaedrus* and the *Second Letter*, written records are always inadequate and lead to misunderstanding. Plato
did not perhaps understand fully why he himself denied any claim to
authorship and insisted, "there is not and will not be any written work

of Plato's own. What are now called his are the work of Socrates at the time of his beautiful youth."[58] Plato did not understand that if there is no Being, all we have or know are repetitions of images, each of which is incomplete or inadequate and thus has to be replaced or supplemented by another.

Rather than emphasize the recognition of the essentially heterogeneous and therefore imperfectly intelligible character of the whole in the Platonic dialogues like Strauss, Derrida insists on the logocentric character of the philosophic tradition Plato originated in the name of Socrates. In the first place, he sees, emphasis on the heterogeneity in the ends of human life as well as between the human and the non-human points back to an untenable metaphysical distinction between body and soul. (We do not know of any disembodied "souls." Moreover, if the soul has parts, as Socrates argues in the *Republic*, it cannot be immortal, according to the argument of the *Phaedo* concerning the necessary dissolution of composites.) Second and more fundamental, by insisting on the centrality of *logos* in the history of philosophy—the *logos* which entails not only differentiation, but also supplementarity—Derrida believes that he has found a way of rereading that tradition which makes it more open and inclusive (of Egyptian or mythical material, for example) and less supportive of authoritative or hierarchical institutions and structures.

Plato suspected that open recognition of the interminable play between opposites would endanger all order—intellectual as well as social. He thus had his major spokesman suggest that an investigation of the *logoi* would lead to knowledge of an eternally intelligible order of ideas and that those who acquired this knowledge would make the best rulers or guardians of the city "in speech."

Looking back at the two-thousand-year-old history of philosophy, Derrida observes that, rather than undermine established authority, philosophers following Socrates have shown rulers how to acquire power and impose order more effectively by showing them how to rationalize social relations. The greatest threats to the preservation of human life and society in the twentieth century have not come from the dissolution of traditional order or morals as a result of philosophic questioning; the greatest dangers have arisen from the imposition of total(itarian) orders with an ideo-logical justification. Derrida responds to the threat posed by attempts to "rationalize" everything—in both the philosophical and social sense—by showing that the *logos* by means of which philosophers from Socrates onwards have conducted their investigations has no eternal basis or origin; on the contrary, it proceeds by means of a continuous process of differentiation that does not produce any stable order or meaning.

Eight

Derrida's New [Hi]story

nsisting that there is no eternally present origin or Author, Derrida agrees with Nietzsche, in effect, that God is dead. And if "Being" is "known" only in its absence, as Heidegger argues, the word does not really have any meaning and should not be used. If there is no-thing simply or eternally present, everything should be regarded as a 'trace' of something that is no longer there that will itself be gradually erased or concealed by later marks. In contrast to Nietzsche and Heidegger, however, Derrida does not think this insight into the essentially transitory character of all things is the result of a lengthy historical development. On the contrary, as he showed in "Plato's Pharmacy," the traces of the essential in-decidability of all issue(s) are to be found from the very beginning. And if his-tory has no beginning or origin, he argues in his next two works on Plato, *The Post Card* and *Khora*, it does not have an end either.

RECONCEIVING "HISTORY": *THE POST CARD:* FROM SOCRATES TO FREUD AND BEYOND

The volume entitled *The Post Card* has two parts. The first half consists of a fictional preface, containing a series of *Envois* or sendings. These are messages written on postcards, parts of which have been burned, lost, or erased, by an author of somewhat variable identity or identities, to an addressee whose character and relation to the author is said to be unique and essential, but whose personal, sexual identity is emphatically undetermined and who is never named. Although the author often appears to be Jacques Derrida, a French scholar who visits Oxford and Yale and has friends named Paul de Man, Jonathan Culler, and J. Hillis Miller, he begins by observing:

You might read these *envois* as the preface to a book that I have not written. . . . Who is writing? To whom? And to send, to destine, to dispatch what? . . . I owe it to whatever remains of my honesty to say finally that I do not know. Above all I would not have had the slightest interest in this correspondence and . . . [its] publication, if some certainty on this matter had satisfied me.[1]

Derrida uses postcards rather than letters to suggest that the writings we receive from the past do not and cannot have any determined recipients. They can and will be read by people unknown to and unintended by the authors. The messages they bear may never reach their intended audience, transmit their intended meaning, or have the desired effect. Although the *envois* are reprinted in chronological order, there are gaps—both in the messages themselves and in the time that elapses between them. The writings that are saved are fragments. There is no clear, known principle determining which are selected or preserved. What remains may well be a matter of chance. Our historical heritage—the Western tradition that Derrida suggests here extends "from Socrates to Freud and beyond"—does not have the character of *a* sending or destiny *(Geschick)*, as Heidegger claimed.[2] As Derrida argues in his analyses both of the picture reproduced on the back of each of his postcards and of the Freudian legacy in the three essays that follow *Envois,* neither the beginning nor the outcome of this history can be determined.

All the *envois* are written on postcard reproductions of a medieval drawing which shows Socrates seated in a chair writing with Plato standing behind him. Derrida's first view of the Matthew Paris drawing in the Bodleian library at Oxford was an "apocalyptic revelation: Socrates writing, writing in front of Plato, I always knew it, it had remained like the negative of a photograph to be developed for twenty-five centuries—in me of course." The drawing represents an inversion of the usual understanding—of the sequence of time, influence, history.

Everything in our bildopedic culture . . . is constructed on the . . . axiom. . . : Socrates comes *before* Plato, there is between them—and in general—an order of generations, an irreversible sequence of inheritance. Socrates is before, not in front of, but before Plato, therefore behind him, and the charter binds us to this order: this is how to orient one's thought.[3]

Did the medieval artist get the names wrong? In a passage of the *Second Letter* he had cited in "Plato's Pharmacy," Derrida is reminded, Plato explained that

It is impossible for what is written not to be disclosed. That is the reason why I have never written anything about these things, and why there is

not and will not be any written work of Plato's own. What are now called
his are the work of a Socrates in the time of his beautiful youth.[4]

If, as Plato's Socrates argues in the *Phaedrus,* true writing is writing on
the soul (or what is learned by heart, according to the *Second Letter*), in
teaching Plato Socrates wrote (on) him, and Plato merely put down on
paper what Socrates initially wrote. Socrates had to pay a price for his
historical influence, however. What Socrates is writing, Derrida imagines,
is his own death sentence; as Plato indicates, Socrates arranged his own
execution. He had to die, so that Plato could immortalize him in writing.
Like other authors, Socrates had to pay for the immortality of his name
with his life.

Socrates' "writing" on Plato represents his attempt to convey his testimony, his patrimony, his will to future generations. But, what if future
generations are not content merely to receive? What if they have wills
of their own? What if Plato secretly resented Socrates' ascendancy over
him? Is not the Socrates of the Platonic dialogues Plato's creation? By re-
creating his teacher, did not the "son" make himself "father"? In the
picture, Plato seems to be directing Socrates' writing from behind.

> Plato behind Socrates. Behind he has always been, as it is thought, but not
> like that. Me, I always knew it, and they did too, those two I mean. What
> a couple. *Socrates* turns his *back* to plato, who has made him write what-
> ever he wanted while pretending to receive it from him.[5]

In writing a history of sorts, did Plato not overturn the order of generation and the generations? This is the "apocalyptic" inversion Derrida
takes the medieval print to emblematize.[6]

Historical influence is not and cannot be unidirectional. It is not
merely a matter of what is "sent" to later generations; it is also a question
of what they are willing to take or receive.

> Example: if one morning Socrates had spoken for Plato, if to Plato his ad-
> dressee he had addressed some message, it is also that p. would have had
> to be able to receive, to await, to desire, in a word to have *called* in a certain
> way what S. will have said to him; and therefore what S., taking dictation,
> pretends to invent—writes, right? p. has sent himself a post card (caption
> + picture), he has sent it back to himself from himself, or he has even
> "sent" himself S.[7]

Plato was no more able to determine or control the meaning and attribution of his writings than was his teacher. Although Plato explicitly signed
his letters and so indicated that he was their author in a way he claimed
not to be the author of the dialogues, Derrida observes, later scholars
have questioned the authenticity of the letters and accepted them as

Plato's own work only to the extent to which their form and content correspond to the writings "Plato" himself attributed to Socrates. Like Strauss, Derrida thus concludes that Plato and Socrates are ultimately impossible to separate. But, where Strauss argues that Plato presents himself or his teaching indirectly through the mouth of Socrates in order to conceal parts of his understanding from a popular audience, Derrida suggests that Socrates and Plato are united by a law of writing that connects them not only to each other but to us, their heirs, as well.

> I also feel them both diabolical, . . . indicting me for my unnameable treachery. . . . The . . . couple Plato/Socrates, divisible and indivisible. . . , [signing] the contract which binds them to us until the end of time. . . . The one who scratches and pretends to write in the place of the other who writes and pretends to scratch.[8]

Nietzsche was naive, when he described Socrates as he who does not write. Nietzsche

> understood nothing about the initial catastrophe. . . . Like everyone else he believed that Socrates . . . came before Plato who more or less wrote at his dictation. . . . From this point of view, N. believed Plato and overturned nothing at all.[9]

So long as a thinker like Nietzsche posits a beginning and a possible end to history, he assumes the existence of a stable, determined order. To overturn the history of Western philosophy or metaphysics, it is as necessary to undermine the notion that history has a set direction or end as it is to reject the existence of atemporal, non-material ideas.

Derrida uses the post card of Socrates and Plato to image the indeterminate reversibility of what has been called 'history'.

> What I prefer, about post cards, is that one does not know what is in front or what is in back, here or there, near or far, the Plato or the Socrates, recto or verso. Nor what is the most important, the picture or the text, and in the text. . . . Here, in my post card apocalypse, . . . reversibility unleashes itself, goes mad.[10]

According to Derrida, his post card thus

> naively overturns everything. . . . It allegorizes the catastrophic unknown of the order. Finally one begins no longer to understand what to come, to come before, to come after, to foresee, to come back all mean—along with the difference of the generations, and then to inherit, to write one's will.[11]

The dependency of the historical legacy upon the willingness of later generations to receive it points to another important characteristic of the relation between older and younger, teacher and student, Socrates and

Plato. It is erotic. At second glance, Derrida thus concludes that his post card is obscene: Plato is having an erection in Socrates' back. But as he later observes, "not just anyone buggers Socrates."[12]

Socrates had to seduce Plato into accepting his teaching; but Plato also had to seduce Socrates into taking him as his student.[13] The master did not accept anyone or all kinds of entreaties; in the *Symposium* Alcibiades relates his own failure to seduce Socrates. Socrates and Plato were united by a shared desire to have ideal progeny.

> Everything comes back to the child. Look at the discourse they address each other on the immorality of the soul. In truth they had nothing to say on immortality. By writing to each other they have made immortality the way we made love. This is our interminable symposium.[14]

But reading Plato in light of his ungrateful heir, Freud, Derrida suggests, this desire to reproduce has not been properly understood. Erotic attachments produce a certain amount of pleasure, perhaps the greatest or most intense pleasure of which human beings are capable; but as Plato himself indicated, they are not merely products of pleasure-seeking. Eros is not and should not, therefore, be understood merely as a want or lack that can be filled by an external object. Erotic desires also involve a certain impulse, whether or not it is immediately present or conscious, to reproduce, to copy, or to double oneself.[15]

In *Beyond the Pleasure Principle*, Freud explicitly inquired about the relation between this instinctive impulse to repetition and the search for pleasure, associated primarily with sexual relations, that psychoanlysts argued was at the root of all human behavior. But in the first of three chapters in which he considers "Freud's legacy," Derrida emphasizes, the father of psychoanalysis was not able to come to any definitive conclusion in his own "speculations." Like "Plato" or his text, "Freud" was compelled in to leave the question of the character of the fundamental drive or drives that both give rise to and definitively shape human existence open to further consideration by future generations. As Derrida would say, the "issue" is undecidable.

Freud wrote in a tradition founded by Plato—or Socrates—but he was an heir who refused to acknowledge his intellectual debt to any previous philosopher. Although he admitted that his psychological investigations produced theories very much like some articulated earlier by Nietzsche and Schopenhauer, Freud explicitly denied that their writings had any influence on him.

Like natural children, Derrida suggests, the intellectual progeny of authors like Plato and Nietzsche become separated from, and thus independent of, their "fathers" by virtue of the need to write them down, if they are to exist and be propagated in the future. Authors cannot control the future fate and reception of their works. They might be totally destroyed. (In his post cards, Derrida discusses the possibility of burning them and, by erasing all record, thus preserving the exclusive character of their authors' love in a self-inflicted "holocaust.") But, he also suggests in his analyses of the ambiguous family relations of Socrates to Plato, Plato to Freud, and Freud to Plato, "filial" connections are not easy, perhaps even possible to sever entirely.

Although Freud denies any philosophical interest or influence in chapter 1 of *Beyond the Pleasure Principle,* Derrida observes, he nevertheless finds it useful in the penultimate chapter to refer to a theory Plato "let Aristophanes develop" about the sexual drive having its origin in a desire to restore an earlier condition. Although he notes that it is a myth, Freud does not pay any attention to the literary form, the fact that Aristophanes is only one of the speakers, or that his is a tale told and retold by other narrators who admit that there are lacunae in their memories.

> Now, Aristophanes is not just anyone . . . for Socrates. Or for Plato. He is the other. In *The Clouds* he had violently attacked Socrates. In the *Apology,* Plato accuses him of . . . having been the first accuser of Socrates, or even his betrayer. . . . And Plato, in accusing Aristophanes, defends Socrates, is behind. Or in *front* of him, showing him with his finger as a lawyer presents the defendant: here is the innocent man, the martyr.

What is Plato doing by letting Aristophanes "'develop' what Freud calls the 'theory'"? Freud does not ask. Instead he erases Socrates. "Is it in order to trace a tradition back to Plato, and to constitute himself as its heir?" Freud once again denies any real debt. In a footnote twice as long as his summary of Aristophanes' "theory," Freud cites another Austrian scholar who claims to have found the origins of the Platonic story in earlier oriental sources. "Freud [himself] compulsively seeks . . . to displace the object and to restore an 'earlier state'."[16]

By analyzing the organization of Freud's own speculations, which are explicitly said to be neither philosophical nor scientific, Derrida brings out their repetitive and ultimately inconclusive character. More specifically, he shows that Freud's own text has the same obsessively repetitive character the analyst himself finds in the famous game his grandson invents, the game in which the boy first takes evident satisfaction in throwing his toys away, saying "o-o-o," which his grandfather translates as "*fort,*" and later modifies by means of a spool, pulling the toys back again with an "a-a-a" or "*da.*"

Freud does what he is describing; he recalls himself "and thereby makes what is called his text, [like Socrates he] enters into a contract with himself in order to hold onto all the strings/sons *(fils)* of the descendance. No less than of the ascendance."[17] Although he himself admits no debts to his philosophical forerunners, Freud is concerned about his own legacy—both within his immediate family and the psychoanalytic movement he has founded. The boy with the spool is his daughter Sophie's son; in Judaism descent is traced through the mother, but it is not accompanied by the family name. The boy's game may represent his way of overcoming his pain at his mother's absence by mastering it through repetition; it may also represent a desire for taking vengeance upon her for leaving and thus express a desire for her to be away, permanently. He does not cry when she leaves or when she dies the following year. When his father goes to war the next year, Ernst commands his toys *"fort*—to the front." The grandfather displays some of the same ambivalence toward both his son-in-law and his daughter; when Sophie dies he does not cry any more than his grandson did. He proceeds with his work and publishes *Beyond the Pleasure Principle* the next year. Freud cried only at the death of that second grandson who, he confided to Marie Bonaparte, on 2 November 1925, "was a kind of universal legatee, and bearer of the name according to the affect (the community's filiation assured by the woman. . . ; in certain Jewish communities the second grandson must bear the first name of the maternal grandfather; everything could be settled by a Judaic law)." A year earlier he had written Ferenczi, "I have survived the Committee that was to have been my successor. Perhaps I shall survive the International Association. It is to be hoped that psychoanalysis will survive me." "That he hoped for this survival of psychoanalysis is probable," Derrida comments, "but *in his name:* . . . he says that he *survives* it as the place of the proper name."[18]

It is the insight that his legatees—natural or intellectual—may die before he does that leads an author to write. Those who believe they can decipher the marks will make themselves "his" forever. The activity of writing thus presupposes an awareness of one's own impending death that leads one to separate a part of oneself, one's thought or work under one's "signature," to divide the intellectual "corpus," as it were, from the living body so that it will survive. But that separation or division within oneself represents a certain doubling of oneself, a repetition as it were. The division and the deferring involve an alterity, an involvement in and with the totally other, Derrida emphasizes, that is not one of opposition.

Freud repeated much more of Plato than he realized. Not merely did Freud find it necessary in the end to have recourse to a Platonic story; not merely did that story show, like Freud's own story of the spool and his investigation into what, if anything is *Beyond the Pleasure Principle* as a whole, that the origin is a speculation. Like Aristophanes' story,

Freud's analysis deals not only with the origin but also the variation in sexual drives. Without his recognizing it, Freud's analysis of what is "beyond the pleasure principle" follows (which is to say, is bound by and so repeats) the logical constraints of Socrates' *logos* concerning pleasure and its limits in the *Philebus*.[19] In chapter 1, Freud comments that he would be happy if some philosopher would tell him what pleasure is. Freud thinks he puts it aside, but the question is inescapable. By investigating what is beyond pleasure, Freud himself shows that it has two limits— the cessation of all pleasure in the end of life and hence of desire and the suppression of all pleasure in total desire without any satisfaction that would end in death as well. The "reality principle" that leads people at times to postpone pleasures so that they can continue to live and take pleasure in the future is not the opposite or the "beyond" of the pleasure principle so much as a self-limitation of pleasure that is the necessary condition of its future repetition and survival. What Freud reproduces in *Beyond the Pleasure Principle* is thus the mixture of the limited and the unlimited of which Socrates speaks at the beginning of the *Philebus*.

The unconscious repetition of Plato leads to a kind of return to Nietzsche as well.

> Freud has situated *Bindung* before pleasure and before sexual pleasure. . . . There would be, bound to stricture, and by means of it, a notion of mastery which would be neither of life nor of death. It would be even less what is at stake in a struggle of consciousness or a struggle for recognition. And sexuality would no longer determine it in the last analysis.[20]

As Freud's writing of the mastery *(Herrschaft)* of the pleasure principle and Ernst's getting pleasure from mastering his pain indicates, the drive which is irreducible to any other is a drive not for pleasure but for mastery. And that drive is essentially self-referential. "The drive to dominate must also be the drive's *relation to itself:* there is no drive not driven to bind itself to itself and to assure itself of mastery over itself as a drive."[21] Derrida thus concludes that "the motif of power is more originary and more general than the PP, is independent of it, is its beyond." He immediately qualifies that claim by insisting that

> It is equally the case that everything described under the heading of the death drive or the repetition compulsion, . . . no less overflows power. This is simultaneously the reason and the failure, the origin and the limit of power. There is power only if there is a principle or a principle of the principle. . . . Thus there is only *differance* of power.[22]

Reproductions are not necessarily exact copies; as Derrida suggests in his *envois*, they may have different messages addressed to different people on their backs. Whereas Plato's Socrates taught that all things are copies of eternal, unchanging ideas, his heir Derrida insists that there are only simulacra; there are no originals. Whereas Nietzsche taught that everything is a product of the will to power, Derrida argues that there is only *differance* of power. Authors seek to impress their will on subsequent generations, but they do not control the reception of their works. Playing on his own last name, Derri-da suggests that like Plato he stands behind Socrates. Like Plato in *"Envois"* he writes fragmentary, fictional "letters" and dialogues. In *The Birth of Tragedy*, Nietzsche claimed that the Platonic dialogues constituted the first novel; *The Post Card* explicitly belongs to the same genre.[23] In a play on his first name, Jacques *(j'accepte)* also claims to accept everything.[24] But does he? It is not possible, according to Derrida, to incorporate or reappropriate everything, because there neither is nor was ever anything complete, whole or "proper" in itself.

Just as Plato's (or Socrates') legacy can be disputed, so Derrida shows can and has Freud's. It is a continuation in more than one sense of the same and the different. In *"Le facteur de la vérité,"* Derrida himself disputes Jacques Lacan's claim to have recovered the truth of Freud's text, the meaning of the repetition compulsion of *Beyond the Pleasure Principle*, through a reading of Edgar Allen Poe's story, "The Purloined Letter." Lacan himself was trying to displace or replace an earlier psychoanalytic study of the story and its author by Freud's student Maria Bonaparte.[25] And in the transcript of the "confrontations" session Derrida had with representatives of the four major psychoanalytic schools in France entitled *"Du tout,"* with which he concludes *The Post Card*, he reminds them that the fact that each claims to represent the whole, the true form of psychoanalysis, means that the four together do not constitute parts of a larger whole. There is no whole at all—*"du tout."* If there is no whole, there is nothing clearly inside or outside. An "outsider" like Derrida, who is neither analyst nor analysand, may thus decide the character, fate, direction, or definition of the movement as well or as much as an explicit participant.[26] "Suppose that there were a founder, male or female, of psychoanalysis," Derrida suggests. "Let us take the name of Freud as the index . . . of such a function. . . . Freud had not had an analyst." There is, in other words, something unanalyzed which

> will have been that upon which and around which the analytic movement will have been constructed. . . ; everything will have been . . . calculated so that this unanalyzed might be inherited, protected, transmitted intact, suitably bequeathed. . . . It is what gives it structure to the movement.

To determine the character of the movement, it thus becomes necessary to analyze Freud.

The question then becomes: . . . Who will pay whom for Freud's *tranche*?
. . . The bidding has been opened—for some time. Let us say that what I
write or what makes me write . . . would represent . . . only one offer.[27]

In contrast to Freud, Derrida attempts to acknowledge his debts—first
and foremost to Socrates and Plato—but he is by no means sure that he
can free himself from them.

Whatever I say, whatever I do, I must paste on myself a stamp with the
effigy of . . . this royal, basilical couple, sterile but infinite in its ideal pro-
geniture. . . . They have signed our I. O. U. and we can no longer not acknowledge it. Any more than our own children. This is what tradition is,
the heritage that drives you crazy.

Even "those who liberate themselves better and more quickly, . . . those
who attempt to deal directly with them, as if this were possible. . . . Me,
for example." Those, too, have to pay. "The busier one gets liberating
oneself, the more one pays. And the less one pays, the more one pays."[28]

KHORA

Freud was not the only modern author to repeat Plato without recognizing it. In his most recent work on Plato, *Khora*, Derrida suggests that
Heidegger also reiterated a Platonic insight when he emphasized the difference between Being and the beings, that Being itself has no determinate qualities, and that it is known, therefore, only in its "absence" as
the "opening" that makes the emergence and intelligibility of the beings
possible. Indeed, Derrida suggests, the Platonic articulation of this insight
in the description of *khora* in the *Timaeus* is in some ways superior to
the later repetition, inasmuch as *khora* does not have the theological
overtones associated with Heidegger's Being or *Ereignis*. Whereas Heidegger argued that the history of philosophy represents the working out
of the implicit and therefore unrecognized limitations of the original experience of Being that become evident only at the end, Derrida contends
that those limitations are expressed at the very beginning in Plato's text.

Like Strauss, Derrida suggests in *Khora* that what becomes known as
"Platonism" or "metaphysics" is more Aristotelian than it is purely Platonic. Unlike Strauss, however, Derrida maintains that the dominant, traditional reading is legitimate, even necessary. What he seeks to show is
that in the *Timaeus* there is also a supplementary account of the cosmic
order which supports a more historical understanding of our "knowledge" as a series of incomplete stories. Derrida brings out not only this
particular alternative, but also the fact that there are alternative or com-

peting accounts of the tradition from its inception, because he thinks explicit recognition of the incomplete, nonnecessary character of any one account will have desirable political effects.

At the conclusion of his "Pharmacy," Derrida pointed out that Plato himself seemed to recognize the inadequacy of his description of the cosmos in terms of the eternal ideas and their sensible copies when in the *Timaeus* he suggested the need to posit an errant cause or third species. In *Khora*, he explains, "What Plato designated under the name of *khora* in the *Timaeus* seems to defy the 'logic of non-contradiction of the philosophers'. . . . *Khora* is neither 'sensible' nor 'intelligible'; it seems to be a 'third species' (*triton genos*, 48e, 52a)."[29]

In Timaeus's "likely story," *khora* names the place or receptacle occupied by the intelligible forms and their sensible images; it is introduced as a necessary condition for their existence. Not a part of the changeable world of becoming any more than of the eternal world of the ideas to which it also "gives place," *khora* cannot literally be said to generate anything. It does not, properly speaking, have a gender or sex.

Previous commentators have missed the singular importance of this "receptacle" which has no properties of its own. Most have described Timaeus's characterizations of *khora* as "mother" and "nurse" as well as "receptacle" and "stamp pad" as "metaphorical," without reflecting on the fact that the very concept of metaphor is a product of the metaphysical Platonic distinction between intelligible and sensible that *khora* is explicitly said to stand beyond. Although "Heidegger was one of the few never to speak of 'metaphor'," Derrida observes, he nevertheless "ceded to a certain teleological retrospection," when he suggested in his *Introduction to Metaphysics* that the Cartesian understanding of 'space' defined by extension is prepared for or by the Platonic *chora*. Both the Heideggerian transformation of *chora* into space and Aristotle's suggestion that *chora* is the equivalent of formless matter emphasize its absence of defining properties in abstraction from its positive function of "giving place."[30]

Previous interpretations of *khora* "consist always in giving form and thus determining it, that which however is only offered or promised in withdrawing itself from all determination."[31] Like Heidegger's Being, Derrida emphasizes, *khora* is not a being, although it is a necessary condition for, and inseparable from, the emergence of the beings.[32] But in Plato's *khora* there is no "risk of seeing the equivalent of an *es gibt*." Although Heidegger does not seem to intend such a reading, the grammatical structure of the phrase seems to point to an agent that "gives" to willing recipients. Unlike Heidegger's Being or *Ereignis*, *khora* will not "let itself be apprehended or conceived, according to anthropomorphic schemas of receiving or giving. *Khora* is not . . . a support or subject which will give place in receiving or in conceiving."[33] Nor is it the pure sensibility Kant determines as receptivity. It "does not *give* anything in giving place or in giving to think."[34]

Rather than function as a sign or name for an indeterminate origin, agency or cause, *khora* marks the site, a place or occasion for a series, an apparently unending series of admittedly partial, incomplete narratives—of the coming into being of the cosmos in Timaeus's likely story, for example, or of the *Timaeus* itself in the infinitely "rich and numerous" later readings it has provoked. Indeed, it is the inadequacy of each account that gives rise to the need and is thus the occasion for another. Insofar as each new account represents a re-telling of the old, it becomes a "receptacle" of or for it.

Derrida points out a series of formal analogies between elements of the setting or introduction and the later characterization of *khora* in the *Timaeus*. The dialogue begins with a summary of the results of an earlier conversation about the most desirable *politeia* (as described in the *Republic*). "Those who are elevated to be guardians of the city will not have anything of their own." Derrida asks, "Not to have anything *of one's own*, isn't that also the situation or site, the condition of *khora*?"[35] The more important parallel is, however, that between Socrates and *khora*. In explaining why he is unable to describe the city he has constructed in speech *(logos)*, in action or fact *(ergon)*, Socrates suggests that, like *khora*, he belongs to a *triton genos*. Like the poets, he deals only with words or images, not with actual deeds; like the sophists he lacks a proper place (his own city)—insofar as he is the founder of the "city in speech," he is no longer simply an Athenian, surely not an Athenian patriot. But he is neither a poet nor a sophist. By asking his practico-philosophical companions to compensate for his inadequacy, Socrates effaces himself to become the receptacle for their stories much the way *khora* does for the cosmos.

The impressions Socrates, *khora*, and we readers of the *Timaeus* receive constitute a series of stories, each of which reflects and reflects back on the previous one; each subsequent story thus contains and so becomes a receptacle for the previous. As indicated by Critias's re-telling of the story of the great victory of the ancient Athenians he heard from his grandfather, who had himself heard it from the great Athenian legislator Solon, who had in his turn heard it from an old Egyptian priest, who had read it in their written records of the deeds of the Athenians, the receptacle is like our memory. That memory is not the property of an individual or even a people; its contents need to pass through the external world, to be written down by other people in different places, to be preserved.

Because the receptacle itself is original or blank, there is a possibility with each new generation that the contents or archives may be partly, if not entirely lost, and have to be replaced with myth. Because they have no written records, the Egyptian priest points out, the Greeks have only mythical accounts of their own history. They are thus in their "infancy" compared to the Egyptians, even though the Athenians must have lived as long as the people who recorded the deeds of the Athenians. It becomes impossible in this account to determine which people is older, or which performed the more important task, the Athenian victory that saved the civilized world from destruction or the Egyptian records that saved the Athenian deed from oblivion. There is no unambiguous chronology in this history—oral or written; the order of the re-telling of the story in the dialogue is the opposite of the chronological order of the events re-told. Each narrative reflects the other as in a mirror, without any clear beginning or end of the series.[36] The written "beginning" of Athens's history is reflected by this "history" once again being written down in the dialogue, which like *khora* thus becomes the place of inscription. We readers become receptacles of the stories recorded just as Socrates is the "receptacle" of Critias's tale. In the *Timaeus*, we repeatedly see returns to the beginning, only to discover that there is no simple, identifiable origin.

The turn to the (his)story of ancient Athens occurs, because Socrates declares himself unable to describe the best city in action; the turn is presented, then, at least initially, as a turn from mere images, speeches, or ideas, which have no life, to action and fact. To show the city in fact means to show it not merely "in itself," in its domestic peace and order, but to show it in relation to, indeed, in conflict with, others—that is, at war. Bringing the city to life is not possible, Derrida observes, without incorporating the inevitability of death. That "incorporation" is linked, moreover, to the necessity of giving the city a specific identity or place. Human life, both individual and collective, is finite.

But, Derrida points out, the turn from "speech" or "poetic image" to "fact" is somewhat deceptive. The tale Critias tells is still a story. Its proximate source or origin is Solon. But who is Solon? He is presented as a poet who would have surpassed Hesiod or Homer (21a–b), if political urgency had allowed him time to develop his genius. Is there a fundamental difference between a legendary legislator and a poet?[37] What is the status and reliability of his source, the Egyptian priest, or of that priest's archives?

> From relation to relation, the author always becomes more distant. The myth told resembles then a discourse without a legitimate father. Orphan or bastard, it is thus distinguished from philosophical *logos* which, as is said in the *Phaedrus*, ought to have a responsible father.[38]

The story Critias tells is thus like the oneiric, "bastard" discourse Timaeus says must be used to describe the third genos, which belongs neither to the intelligible beings described by logos nor to the sensible objects of myth.

The most significant return to the beginning in the dialogue occurs, of course, in the midst of Timaeus's cosmology, when he suggests that "if one really wants to say how the world is born, it is necessary to insert a species of errant cause and the nature of its proper movement into the narrative" (48a–b). And to do this, it is necessary

> to retake all that one has been able to consider up to this point as the origin, to come back to the elementary principles, that is to say, the opposition between paradigm and copy; and then . . . to propose a principle of further division. . . . Then we distinguished two forms of being. Now it is necessary for us to discover a third kind. (48e)

We thus come back to a "pre-origin" which deprives us of the ability to proceed simply and exclusively according to the principled oppositions of philosophy—the distinctions between being and becoming, intelligible and sensible, word and thing. The "audacity" of the *Timaeus* consists in the recognition of such a necessity. In positing the need for a new beginning with what he calls *"khora,"* Plato points to the need continually to give a new account or the world, to tell the "likely story" anew, because each previous or received version is incomplete.

Does the re-discovery of this necessity mean that we should cease to refer to "the philosophy of Plato, the ontology of Plato, or of platonism"? "Not at all," Derrida concludes. What we call "Platonism" is an abstraction from the "fiction" written by "Plato." "Platonism is certainly one of the effects of the text signed by Plato, for a long time the dominant effect and for necessary reasons, but this effect is always found upon return to be contrary to the text."[39]

Unlike Strauss, Derrida does not return to the Platonic text to revive a full appreciation of the many layered teaching(s) conveyed by the poetic presentation—in contrast to the doctrines later abstracted by Aristotle, Kant, Hegel, and Heidegger—even though he thinks Plato's art deserves more attention.[40] In "How to Avoid Speaking: Denials," which contains a preliminary version of the argument of *Khora*, Derrida explains that he brings out the heterogeneity in the Platonic text in order to raise "deconstructive questions" about all teleological understandings of the Western tradition. (He thus pursues and generalizes the critique of Heideggerian *Geschichte* he began in *The Post Card* by emphasizing the ambiguous relation between Socrates and Plato.) By bringing out the elements or arguments in Plato's text that undermine the theory of the ideas, Derrida seeks to show that there is not and can never be a single reading of, or end to, the history of philosophy, from what has traditionally been taken to be the beginning. (As we know from "Plato's Pharmacy," Derrida does not think that Plato wrote on a blank slate or in the absence of a tradition any more than did his successors.)

In "Denials," Derrida describes three "moments" in Western history in which thinkers have faced the question of how to speak about "something" like God in so-called negative theology or *khora*, which is beyond being and therefore "is" not, which does not exist in the ordinary sense, and which can be defined only negatively in terms of what it is not. The first such moment is Greek—Platonic or Neoplatonic—and it has two different forms. The first is that announced in the *Republic* (509ff.) where the Idea of the Good is said to be "beyond being" *(epekeina tes ousias).* "Thus the Good is not, nor is it place. But this not-being is not a non-being." On the contrary, "from what is beyond the presence of all that is, the Good gives birth to Being or to the essence of what is . . . whence comes the homology between the Good and the sun." In making that comparison, Socrates alludes to "a third species *(triton genos)*" which "seems to disorient the discourse, because this is neither the visible nor sight nor vision."[41] But, saying that the Good has engendered this intelligible light in its own likeness, Socrates suggests that there is a resemblance between the Good and that to which it gives birth, Being and Knowledge. As becomes clear in the *Sophist,* this analogical continuity makes it possible for the "third species" to become the ground of a kind of mediation.

> In the *Sophist* (243b), this schema of the *third* also concerns Being. Of all the paired oppositions, one may say that each term *is.* The being of this *is* figures as a third that is beyond the two others. It is indispensable to the interweaving *(symploke)* or to the dialectical intersection of the forms or of the ideas in a *logos.*

According to Socrates in the *Phaedo, logos,* as the realm of the reflection of the ideas, which is neither simply intelligible nor simply sensible, thus becomes the locus of mediation.

> After having raised the question of non-being, which is in itself unthinkable *(adianoeton),* ineffable *(arreton),* unpronounceable *(aphtegkton),* foreign to discourse and to reason *(alogon;* 238c), one arrives at the presentation of dialectic . . . [which] receives the thinking of non-being as *other* and not as absolute nothingness or simple opposite of Being (256b, 259e). This confirms that there cannot be an absolutely negative discourse: a *logos* necessarily speaks about something.[42]

The Platonic teaching concerning the Idea of the Good and its relation to *logos* can thus been seen to point forward to the Gospel of John. But in his characterization of the second, Christian "moment," Derrida points out, there are two decisive differences: in Plato that which is beyond Being does not promise to reveal itself fully in a future event; nor does it create the material into which it impresses the eternal forms.

There is, however, a second Platonic characterization of a third species "beyond being," which cannot be theologized or historicized in the same manner—*khora*. In describing the two different kinds of "third species," Derrida suggests, Plato uses two concurrent languages. One allows the reappropriation of *khora* into the dominant Platonic ontology.

> Since it "receives all," *[khora]* makes possible the formation of the cosmos. As it is . . . neither intelligible nor sensible, one may speak of it as *if* it were a joint participant in both. *Neither/nor* easily becomes *both . . . and. . .* , the . . . multiplication of figures which one traditionally interprets as metaphors: gold, mother, nurse, sieve, receptacle.

Aristotle established a tradition of reading the *Timaeus* in this fashion.

> Since his *Physics* (bk. 4), this passage on the *khora* has always been interpreted as being *at the interior* of philosophy, in a consistently anachronistic way, as if it prefigured, on the one hand, the philosophies of space as *extensio* (Descartes) or as pure sensible form (Kant); or on the other hand, the materialist philosophies of the substratum or of substance which stands, like the *hypodokhe, beneath* the qualities or the phenomena.[43]

Such anachronistic readings are structurally inevitable, because of the a-chronistic character of *khora* itself.

But Derrida finds the "other language" that "would inscribe an irreducible spacing interior to . . . Platonism" more interesting. Once it becomes clear that the place named *khora* "belongs neither to the sensible nor to the intelligible, neither to becoming, nor to non-being (the *khora* is never described as a void), nor to Being," the inadequacy of all previous philosophical interpretations becomes evident.

> If the *khora* receives everything, it does not do this in the manner of a medium or of a container. . . . This is neither an intelligible extension, in the Cartesian sense, a receptive subject, in the Kantian sense of *intuitus derivativus*, nor a pure sensible space, as a form of receptivity. Radically nonhuman and atheological, one cannot even say that it gives place or that *there is* the *khora*. The *es gibt*, thus translated, too vividly announces or recalls the dispensation of God, of man, or even that of the Being of which certain texts by Heidegger speak. *Khora* . . . neither creates nor produces anything, not even an event, insofar as it takes place. . . . It is radically

ahistorical, because nothing happens through it and nothing happens to it.[44]

The re-discovery of Plato's "second language" thus enables him to avoid the theological underpinning and implications of the historical, "apocalyptic" views of philosophy—in Hegel, Marx, and Nietzsche, as well as in Heidegger.[45]

In his description of the second, Christian moment, Derrida emphasizes that "contrary to what seemed to happen in . . . the place called *khora*, the apophasis is . . . *initiated* . . . by the event of a revelation which is also a promise. This apophasis . . . opens up a history."[46] The historical views of philosophy in light of its end are thus shown to have not only a Greek but also a decidedly Christian, rather than strictly philosophical, origin.

Derrida explicitly remains silent about negative discourse in Jewish or Islamic traditions.[47] Following the dialectical form of thought he wishes to question, the third moment he describes is a mode of thought that is "neither Greek nor Christian" but "the most audacious and most liberated repetition" of both.

Heidegger's *What Is Metaphysics?* could be read "as a treatise on negativity." In this work, Heidegger argues that

> The experience of anguish puts us in relation to a negating which is neither annihilation, nor a negation or a denial [but which] . . . reveals to us the strangeness of what is as the wholly other. It thus opens up the possibility of the question of Being for *Dasein*, the structure of which is characterized precisely by what Heidegger calls transcendence.[48]

In *Vom Wesen des Grundes* Heidegger states that this transcendence is properly expressed by the Platonic expression *epekeina tes ousias*. But Heidegger immediately adds, "Plato could not elaborate the original content of the *epekeina tes ousias* as transcendence of *Dasein*." As we have seen, Heidegger "makes an analogous gesture with regard to the *khora*" in his *Introduction to Metaphysics* when he "suggests that Plato fell short of thinking of the place which, however, signaled to him." Seventeen years later on the last page of *What Is Called Thinking?* Heidegger again suggests that in locating the *khorismos* between Being and the beings, Plato points to the question of the wholly other place of Being—or the place of the wholly other—but again falls short.

In seeking the "place" of the "wholly other," Heidegger thus sees himself moving in and beyond the Platonic and the Neoplatonic traditions. But, Derrida suggests, Heidegger is also moving in and beyond the Christian tradition as well, although Heidegger himself does not seem to un-

derstand this. According to Heidegger, philosophy and theology are opposites which cannot be combined.

> "A Christian philosophy . . . is a squared circle." It is necessary to distinguish
> between . . . onto-theology [or philosophy, which] . . . concerns the supreme
> being or *causa sui* in its divinity . . . and [theology, which] is a science of faith
> or of divine speech, such as it manifests itself in revelation.[49]

When questions concerning revelation, the promise, the gift or event
progressively displace the question of Being and its transcendental horizon, time, in Heidegger's own thought, Derrida observes, it is hard to see
how this distinction between philosophy and theology is maintained.

In an interview with students at the University of Zurich in 1952,
Heidegger insisted that Being and God are not the same. "If I were yet
to write a theology, as I am sometimes tempted to do," he stated, "the
word 'being' ought not to appear." And yet, Derrida observes, Heidegger
proceeded then to refer his auditors to Luther who recognized that "even
if Being is 'neither the foundation nor the essence of God', the experience
of God—that is, the experience of revelation—'occurs in the dimension
of Being'."[50] As in the work of the negative theologian Meister Eckhart,
to which Derrida refers in describing his second moment, and to which
Heidegger himself referred positively on several occasions, Being or the
thinking of Being becomes the threshold.[51]

Does Heidegger's work represent a form of negative theology? Derrida
refuses to say. In *"Post-Scriptum"* Derrida suggests that negative theology occurs at the intersection of Platonic philosophy with Christian revelation; it could be represented like Heidegger's understanding of Being,
with a 'X'.[52] But he also observes that Heidegger's work lacks the prayer
which seems to constitute an essential moment or passage "between the
theological movement that speaks and is inspired by the Good beyond
Being or by light and the apopathic path that exceeds the Good," characteristic of all negative theology.

The three moments of negative discourse he has linked, as in a fable,
do not necessarily fit together, Derrida insists. That nonnecessity is, indeed, the primary reason for, and outcome of, his re-discovery of the
heterogeneity of Plato's text. If there is no simple beginning or origin of
philosophy or Western history in the dialogues of Plato, there is no necessary or inevitable end. Everything was and remains irreducibly open-
ended.

THE POLITICAL CONSEQUENCES

Plato understated the literally nonexistent character of the "foundation"
of all "being" and "knowledge," Derrida argued in "Plato's Pharmacy,"

because he feared this insight would undermine all order—moral, political and intellectual. Derrida himself is also concerned about the political effects of this insight. In his deconstructive readings of Plato, he brings out the second language, the arguments that undermine the official "Platonic" teaching, because he thinks recognition of the essentially ambiguous, undecided character of the Western philosophical tradition provides the basis for a freer, more open form of politics. Philosophical arguments that presented the development of scientific rationality in Europe as the end of history had been used in the nineteenth and twentieth centuries to justify imperialistic and racist policies, he reminds his readers in "The Other Heading: Memories, Responses and Responsibilities."[53]

With the collapse of the communist regimes in the East, Derrida observes, the possibility of European reunification looms once again on the horizon. The question thus arises, what "Europe" signifies. What do Europeans have in common? What constitutes European identity or culture?

Both the question and the answer appear to be quite old. Europe has long been defined not merely as the geographical promontory of the Asian continent, but as the spiritual head of humanity as a whole. "From Hegel to Valéry, from Husserl to Heidegger," Europe has been seen as the advanced point, signifying both the beginning or moving force and the end or completion of world civilization. This was, indeed, the view of history and "man" Derrida began criticizing in his very first work on Husserl.

But the historical view that privileges Europe—or a few select white European men—as the locus of the intellectual achievement and leadership of mankind is dated. "It dates from a moment when Europe sees itself *on the horizon*, that is to say, from its end (the *horizon*, in Greek, is the limit.)" Following Nietzsche (without mentioning his name or *Of the Use and Disadvantage of History for Life*), Derrida suggests, this historical discourse is the discourse of *epigones*, of those who look back rather than forward, of those who worry not so much about growth as decay.[54]

The question "we" Europeans face today is how to respond to this tradition—with an eye to the future! How do or should we regard the history of Europe from the perspective not of its end, but in light of what is to come, of what lies beyond the horizon and thus is unknown? "Like every history, the history of a culture no doubt presupposes an identifiable heading toward which the movement, the memory, the promise . . . dreams of gathering itself," Derrida observes. "But history also presupposes that the heading not be *given*, that it not be identifiable in advance and once and for all. The irruption of the new . . . should be awaited . . . *as* the unforeseeable, the *unanticipatable*, the non-masterable." Openness to the new does not and should not, however, entail simply forgetting or even destroying the old.

> Our old memory tells us that it is *also* necessary to . . . keep the heading, for under the banner . . . of the absolutely new, we can fear seeing return the phantom of the worst. . . . We must thus be suspicious of *both* repetitive memory *and* the completely other of the absolutely new.[55]

Conditions in Europe at the end of the Cold War resemble those between the two world wars insofar as the disintegration and withdrawal of the hegemonic powers give rise once again to the specter of outbursts of virulent nationalism, racism, and xenophobia. But the danger of the re-establishment of hegemonic centralized control does not arise now in the form of a single nation attempting to impose its rule on the others by force. That danger is emerging more surreptitiously, not so much in explicitly political as in economic and cultural form, in the concentration of the means and control of communication. Since the same communication technologies contributed greatly to the overthrow of the old, totalitarian systems and the consequent democratization of Eastern Europe, we would not want to repress or destroy them, even if we could. But we can "learn to detect, in order then to resist, new forms of cultural takeover."

If the threat is primarily cultural, so, too, should be the response:

> To say it all too quickly, I am thinking about the necessity for a new culture, one that would invent another way of reading and analyzing *Capital*, both Marx's book and capital in general; a new way of taking capital into account while avoiding not only the frightening totalitarian dogmatism that some of us have known how to resist up until now, *but also* . . . the counterdogmatism that is setting in today, . . . to the point of banning the word "capital," indeed even the critique of certain effects of . . . the "market" as the evil remnants of the old dogmatism.[56]

In responding to the modern discourse depicting Europe as the end of history, Derrida concentrates on the work of Paul Valery, who explicitly linked capital in the sense of accumulated goods with intellectual capital or ability to use them that Valery feared was being dissipated, and the rise of a capital city, a place in which both these kinds of goods were concentrated.

"We bear the responsibility for this heritage, right along with the capitalizing memory that we have of it. We did not choose this responsibility; it imposes itself upon us." It is, in fact, almost impossible not to respond to the historical circumstances in which one finds oneself, the "traces" of past actions and thoughts. Derrida emphasizes the "response" at the root of "responsibility," to suggest that our stance toward the past need not be confined to the either/or of acceptance or denial. At first glance, the responsibility European intellectuals have toward their history would appear to be contradictory, because it involves them in a kind of "double bind":

> It is necessary to make ourselves the guardians of an idea of Europe, . . . *but* of a Europe that consists precisely in not closing itself off in its own identity and in advancing itself in an exemplary way toward what it is not. . . . Will this have to consist in repeating or in breaking with, in continuing or in opposing?[57]

But, Derrida urges, all truly ethical, all truly political decisions arise from just such "impossible" aporias. "When the path is clear and given, when a certain knowledge opens up the way in advance, the decision is already made, . . . one simply applies or implements a program." When decisionmaking becomes merely an application of "know-how," ethics and politics become technological—and irresponsible. Since there is always a disproportion between any general rule and the particular circumstances to which it is applied, merely routine, unthinking "application" tends to produce one-sided, unjust results.[58]

We cannot, in fact, take a stance outside, above, or beyond our own history. We stand, rather, in the midst of it, looking both backwards and forwards. As a result, we continually have to ask what old maxims or conclusions mean under new circumstances. For example: Europe has taken itself to be "a promontory, an advance—the avant-garde of geography and history." And Derrida observes:

> To advance oneself is, certainly, to show oneself, thus to identify and name oneself. [But t]o advance oneself is also to rush out ahead, looking in front of oneself. . . , to launch oneself onto the sea or into adventure, to take the lead in taking the initiative, and sometimes even to go on the offensive. To advance (oneself) is also to take risks.[59]

Is it not possible, then, to understand "Europe" as

> the opening onto a history for which the changing of the heading [*cap,* which includes direction, intelligence, leadership, as well as protective covering] . . . is experienced as always possible? An opening and a nonexclusion for which Europe would in some way be responsible?[60]

Such an interpretation of the meaning of "the new Europe" would preserve the spirit of scientific discovery, the rigorous intellectual engagement with the world that has been Europe's pride in the past, while freeing it from parochial nationalism and racism. Those writers who have taken the achievements of European men to constitute the end of history have attributed universal significance to the works of particular people(s).

The necessity for such an inter-play between the universal and the partic-ular, the same and the different, ought to be recognized not merely as desirable but as a matter of principle—in the future.

If such an understanding of Europe and her responsibility were gener-ally adopted, it would entail a series of other duties as well:

1. "Opening Europe . . . onto that which is not, never was, and never will be Europe."

2. "Welcoming foreigners in order not only to integrate them but to recognize and accept their alterity."

3. "*Criticizing* . . . a totalitarian dogmatism that, under the pretense of putting an end to capital, destroyed democracy and the European heritage . . . [b]ut also . . . a religion of capital that institutes its dogmatism under new guises."

4. "Cultivating . . . such *critique*, . . . but also submitting it . . . to a deconstructive genealogy."

5. "Assuming the . . . *uniquely* European heritage of an idea of democ-racy, while also recognizing that this idea, like that of international law, is never simply given, that its status is not even that of a regulative idea in the Kantian sense, but rather something that remains to be thought and *to come*: . . . a democracy that must have the structure of a promise."

6. "Respecting differences, idioms, minorities, singularities, but also the universality of formal law, the desire for translation, agreement and univocity, the law of the majority, opposition to racism, nationalism, and xenophobia."

7. "Tolerating and respecting all that is not placed under the authority of reason. . . , different forms of faith, . . . [as well as] thoughts that, while attempting to think reason and the history of reason, necessarily exceed its order, without becoming . . . irrationalist."[61]

Derrida recognizes that his understanding of responsibility differs sig-nificantly from that commonly used in Anglo-American moral, legal, and political discourse, where to be responsible generally means to make oneself answerable or liable for the results of an action. As he points out in "Force of Law: The 'Mystical Foundation of Authority'," this notion of responsibility involves highly questionable concepts of identity and causation.[62] To take responsibility for one's acts, one has to be self-conscious. But, as Derrida began arguing in his critique of Husserl's *Ori-gins of Geometry*, such self-consciousness presupposes a division within the "self." There is, strictly speaking, no such "thing" as personal "iden-tity," at any moment, much less over time. Nor, Derrida stresses, can an "author" control all the effects of his or her deeds. How then can anyone justly hold him or her responsible for them?

Because his critique undermines the dominant "moral" understand-ing, some people believe they "have found in Deconstruction, . . . a mod-

ern form of immorality, of amorality or of irresponsibility." Other readers "better disposed towards so-called Deconstruction . . . discern . . .
increasing attention, to those things which one could identify under the
fine names of 'ethics', 'morality', 'responsibility', 'subject', etc."[63] But,
although Derrida clearly prefers the latter reading, he would

> break with both these . . . restorations of morality, including, therefore the
> remoralization of deconstruction which . . . risks reassuring itself in order
> to reassure the other and to promote the consensus of a new dogmatic
> slumber. . . . I know that, in saying that. . . , one gives ammunition to the
> officials of anti-deconstruction, but . . . I prefer that to the constitution of a
> . . . community of complacent deconstructionists, reassured and reconciled
> with the world in ethical certainty, good conscience.[64]

Like Heidegger, Derrida is willing to forego any claim to have an ethics, not only because he thinks that our notions of ethical behavior presuppose highly questionable metaphysical concepts, but also because he
wants to encourage his readers to question all forms of philosophical
morality—unremittingly. He stresses difference, criticism, and conflict
rather than sameness, affirmation, and agreement, because he wants,
above all, to avoid a smothering self-satisfied consensus that would constitute the end, although not the culmination of the European heritage
of critical discourse and democratic politics.

Derrida explicitly admits his is not the only or even the correct interpretation of the heritage of Europe. In "Interpretations at War: Kant, the
Jew, the German," he implicitly contrasts his own emphasis on the divisions or differences within the tradition with the older view that the disparate elements come together in a grand, philosophical-moral synthesis.
Curiously enough, like Strauss, he presents Hermann Cohen as *the* representative of the synthesizing interpretation he contests.

Introducing a talk he was giving in Jerusalem, Derrida indicated that
he shared some of Cohen's pacifist, socialist political goals.[65] He affirmed
his "solidarity with all those, in this land, who advocate an end to violence." He wanted to see the rights of both the Palestinians and the Israe-
lis respected. The success of the negotiations necessary to put an end to
the conflict would depend very much upon the "self-interpretation" of
these peoples. Speaking as a Jew to a predominantly Jewish audience,
he was concerned primarily with the self-interpretation of the Jewish
people—a self-interpretation, he reminded his audience, that had not
only been a subject of ongoing controversy, but had also changed over
time.

Early in the twentieth century two well-known Jewish philosophers
had articulated a self-understanding very different from that incorpo-

rated in the state of Israel. Franz Rosenzweig and Hermann Cohen had explicitly affirmed their Judaism, but opposed Zionism, partly because they were both neo-Kantians. Both lived through the First World War, but died before Nazism cast "a revealing and at the same time a deforming light" on the past.

Derrida begins with Rosenzweig's reaction to hearing Cohen speak, because it helps set the context.

> At last, here is a philosopher who is no longer a professional from academia: he thinks in front of us, he speaks to us of what is at stake in existence, he reminds us of the abysmal risk of thought or existence.[66]

Certain points of the encomium recall the experience some have described of their encounter with Heidegger's teaching during the years right after the First World War, Derrida observes, when Heidegger succeeded Cohen in his Marburg chair. "It is too often forgotten, . . . this neo-Kantian sequence has largely determined the context *in* which, . . . *against* which, Husserl's phenomenology, later the phenomenological ontology of the early Heidegger . . . in a way arose."[67] By drawing Cohen, Husserl, and Heidegger together, Derrida reminds his readers that all three philosophers put forward different versions of the end of history thesis *and* that this discourse is, as he stated in "The Other Heading," dated. It expressed hopes and justified political actions that appear "mad" in the retrospective light shed by World War II and the Holocaust.

Rosenzweig's praise of the combination of fiery passion, depth and clarity of thought in Cohen makes the latter's attempt in *Deutschland und Judentum* (first published in 1915, republished in 1924 with an introduction by Rosenzweig) to persuade American Jews to convince the U.S. Congress not to enter the war all the more troubling. If America entered the war, Cohen thought, Germany would lose; and Germany was the true, spiritual home of Judaism.

Cohen based this claim on an interpretation of Western history in which Jewish principles were first explicitly made universal by the Jewish Platonist Philo, who combined them with Greek philosophy. The logos, which acts as a mediator between God and man in Philo's philosophy, paved the way for the Christian notion of the Holy Spirit. And Christianity, in turn, spread this logocentric understanding worldwide. The Protestant Reformation in Germany initiated the third and culminating stage in this development. By means of its appeal to the integrity of the individual conscience over and against all external institutions, the Reformation introduced a new understanding of the ground of both science and religion or morality—truthfulness.[68]

Cohen's history of the West bears a striking resemblance to Heidegger's, Derrida comments:

> What happens . . . is nothing less than an interpretation of the sense of being. At a level and in a style that are not Heidegger's . . . but that could call for some cautious analogies, Cohen . . . *too* (for the same may be said of Heidegger), does so through an interpretation . . . of the instituted interpretations of Platonism, of the Platonic logos, *eidos*, and especially the *hypotheton*.

Cohen brings Plato together with modern astronomy and physics by means of Kepler (who once attempted to give an account of the world in terms of the five "Platonic" solids described in the *Timaeus*). But Cohen could achieve such a synthesis, only by displacing the dominant interpretation of Plato. According to Cohen:

> Idealism is no mere theory of ideas in contrast with the sensible or with matter. . . . Plato did not determine the idea with complete clarity. If he asked the question of Being, . . . he used terms among which privilege was mistakenly given to those that referred to vision *(Schauen)* or to intuition *(Anschauung)* in accordance with the etymology of the word *eidos*. The most fundamental determination, however, one which is to be found in Plato but has nevertheless been covered up and neglected throughout the renewals of Neoplatonism and the Renaissance, the one which founded idealism as a scientific project and a method, is the *hypothesis*.

The true conception of the Idea as hypothesis was rediscovered by German philosophers. As a result, "Being is not grasped as an immediate datum . . . but it is thought as a universal project, as a problem that scientific research must solve and whose reality it must prove." (This is the project, Derrida notes, that Husserl had called "philosophy as a rigorous science.")[69]

Derrida draws two other "cautious analogies" between Cohen and Heidegger. Both philosophers insisted upon a special connection between Greece and Germany; both also advocated a certain form of "national socialism." Although Cohen thought that "Fichte's philosophy of the Self is a theoretical regression in relation to Kant," he nevertheless urged his readers not to forget, "not only . . . Fichte's great 'discovery' that the Self is social, but also that the social Self is in its origin and essence a national Self." Cohen was too much a Kantian not to be suspicious of excesses of nationalist enthusiasm, so he also insisted on the consequent obligations or duties: mandatory military service, the right to vote, compulsory education. "While taking care not to give way to misleading analogies," Derrida comments,

One might be tempted to recall here the three "services" deduced by Heidegger, in his Rectorate Speech (1933). . . . The content of these two times three duties is undoubtedly not exactly the same. . . , Heidegger does not mention the right to vote. . . , but in both cases all of these obligations or services are deduced from national self-affirmation.[70]

Although the differences between Heidegger and Cohen are considerable, they both write "within the common web of a tradition that should never be forgotten." Both Heidegger and Cohen regarded the university as the guardian of the German spirit; neither defined what was distinctively "German" in terms of biology or "race."

Both Cohen and Heidegger claimed that their people was exemplary because of the tradition it incorporated; both argued that this exemplary status justified a world war.[71] Neither thinker seems to have recognized the fact that every nation is founded in and by an act of violence. But, Derrida emphasizes, this violent origin raises questions about the justice of every established political system in itself, much less its imposition on other peoples. By uncovering this originary violence, he argues in "The Force of Law," deconstruction serves the cause of justice—itself an impossible goal to achieve—by undermining the legitimacy of the presumed justification of enforced conformity.[72]

One could give a synthetic account or interpretation of the Western tradition in the late twentieth century, Derrida admits.

If the process of things becoming worldwide, if the homogenization of planetary culture involves techno-science, rationality, the principle of reason (and who can seriously deny this?), if the great family of *anthropos* is being gathered together thanks to this general hybridization—through the greatest instances of violence, no doubt, but irresistibly—and if it becomes unified and begins to gather itself . . . not as a genetic family but as a "spiritual" family, trusting in this set called science and the discourse of human rights, . . . then humanity does indeed unify itself around a Platonico-Judeo-Protestant axis. . . . This unification of *anthropos* in fact involves what is called European culture—now represented, in its indivisible unity, by the economic-technical-scientific-military power of the United States.

In that case

Cohen's hypothesis concerning the Platonic hypothesis and its lineage would not seem quite so mad. If it is mad, this is because it translates the "real" madness, . . . this logocentric psychosis which presumably got hold of humanity over twenty-five centuries ago, confusing or articulating science, technique, philosophy, religion, art, and politics all together within the same set.

But, Derrida asks, "from what external location can one claim to pronounce upon this truth of the truth? . . . Here is the entire question of what some people call deconstruction."[73] It is possible to continue telling the same "logocentrico-Judeo-Protestant" story; it is important to remember it. But it is also important to remember the lacunae, the omissions and the unanticipated consequences of that story; history both does and does not repeat itself.

From the "beginning" in "Plato," Derrida argues, there has been no single story. What we have—or what has been passed down to us—is a series of different accounts that have some common elements, but all of which leave something out. We should beware of taking any version of the story to be simply authoritative. Standing in the midst of our own [hi]story, looking both backwards and forwards, we cannot be sure that it or any other set of possibilities is complete.

Just as Cohen had to displace the dominant interpretation of Plato in order to put forward his synthetic interpretation of the Western tradition, so Derrida deconstructs the received reading of Plato in order to shake the still dominant self-understanding of the West and thus to counter its homogenizing political effects. By showing that there is an ineradicable instability of meaning from the very beginning—in the interrelations of its founders, Socrates and Plato, with each other and their "progeny" as well as in Plato's texts—Derrida seeks to show that there is a certain "space" at the interior of the tradition which provides an opening to that which lies beyond it, to that which is "to come." On the one hand, Derrida thus clearly and explicitly works within the tradition on an inherited set of received readings and texts. Deconstruction does not mean destruction, he repeatedly insists.[74] Deconstruction is inconceivable without Hegel, Nietzsche, Husserl, and Heidegger, and these philosophers all look back, in turn, to Plato. On the other hand, Derrida just as explicitly denies that any of these authors, texts, or approaches has any integrity or value in itself. He certainly does not attempt like Strauss to preserve them as sources or representatives of irreducibly different, alternative understandings of the whole.

In "The Other Heading," Derrida makes clear, his stance toward the Western heritage is not simply critical or negative.[75] On the contrary, he puts forward not only a new self-interpretation of Europe, but a positive program of political action. But, if we ask, why we should take the direction he indicates, why we should not merely tolerate, but be positively open to different peoples, cultures, or ways of thinking, when these "others" are not themselves open or tolerant, why we should continue to expose violations of human rights and international law, when he himself has shown that the concepts of both humanity and law or right have problematic foundations, or why we should hold onto the promise of democracy, when it is conceded like justice to be impossible to attain, we do not find very powerful reasons to accept the duties he would impose. Tolerance, openness, respect for rights, the rule of law, and the value of intellectual criticism—to say nothing of the promise of democracy—*are* all parts of the Western tradition and can be affirmed as such. However, the suggestion that we reaffirm our commitment to such principles simply because they are traditional seems less than compelling, especially on the part of an author who repeatedly and emphatically reminds us that we do not have anything, strictly speaking, "proper" or of our own.

Derrida is much better at pointing out the difficulties in other positions, arguments or texts than he is at articulating a positive alternative or "direction," which is to say, way of life.[76] He himself occasionally admits as much. For example, in "The Principle of Reason," he concedes that it is not certain that the questioning of first principles he advocates "can bring together a community or found an institution in the traditional sense."[77] And in *"Post-Scriptum"* he notes that "community [is] a word I never much liked, because of its connotation of participation, indeed fusion, identification; I see in it as many threats as promises."[78] If all forms of order have inherently questionable foundations, Derrida urges, the most important thing is to remain vigilant in the face of any and all attempts to articulate and impose any that would exclude other alternatives.

Nine

The Three Paths from Nietzsche and Heidegger

What, then, do we make of this series of reinterpretations of the philosophic history of the West, beginning with Plato? First, we observe, they are all somewhat tentative, if not, strictly speaking, hypothetical. Convinced for different reasons that it was impossible to attain the knowledge of the whole both Aristotle and Hegel claimed to possess, Nietzsche and Heidegger went back to Plato to discover what sort of human experience had generated the search for this unattainable goal. More specifically, they went back to Plato to discover the implicit and hence hidden limitations of philosophy as it had traditionally been understood so they could overcome those limitations. Once philosophers recognized the impossibility of attaining wisdom, both Nietzsche and Heidegger saw, they would no longer be able to proceed as they had before. Since both Nietzsche and Heidegger regarded philosophy as the highest and most spiritual form of human existence, they concluded that degeneration was inevitable, unless a new, even greater possibility was uncovered. But because Nietzsche and Heidegger came to have very different understandings of the character of Western philosophy, both its origins in Greece and its historical development, the new possibilities they announced were also very different—in some ways, even diametrically opposed. Whereas Nietzsche called for the emergence of philosopher-legislators who would impose their own order on the cosmos and so determine the meaning of human existence, Heidegger urged his readers to await the revelation of a new god or dispensation of fate. Neither Nietzsche nor Heidegger had or gave any assurance that the new dispensation would come. The only thing they claimed to know with certainty was that philosophy as it had traditionally been practiced was no longer possible. The history of philosophy had come to an end; whether that end would result in mere degeneration or would give rise to a new order, they could not be sure.

Gadamer, Strauss, and Derrida all challenge this Nietzschean-Heideggerian contention that philosophy has come to an end. What a thinker claims has come to an end depends upon what he thinks it was from the beginning. Gadamer, Strauss, and Derrida thus all return to Plato to show, in different ways and for different reasons, that philosophy never was or ever will be the kind of activity that has an end or completion. But where Gadamer and Strauss try to revive and perpetuate philosophy on the basis of a new understanding of what it was, Derrida attempts to bring it to "closure" by showing that nothing has a set meaning and that there is no necessary direction or order to history.

Gadamer and Strauss both argue that Plato's depiction of Socrates shows that philosophy did not originally consist nor was it expected ever really to consist in knowledge of eternal truths or ideas so much as in a certain form of human existence, the way of life constituted by an unending search for knowledge. Gadamer and Strauss offer very different accounts, however, of the grounds and results of this search.

In the *Republic*, Socrates suggests that philosophy consists essentially in the search for knowledge of the Idea of the Good. The need or desire to know what is truly rather than only apparently good arises, Gadamer emphasizes, out of the concerns of everyday human existence. Because most people believe or at least act as if they believe they know what is good, Socrates has to show them in elenchtic arguments that they do not know what they think they do. Such a critical showing is necessary to convince people that they must not merely "compare notes," but that they need to join together in an ongoing dialogue to discover what is truly good. According to Gadamer, philosophy thus forms the basis of a truly human community. As Plato shows in the *Republic*, philosophy also provides the education rulers need to free them from the desires for wealth or fame that lead most human beings in power to be unjust.

To understand why the search for knowledge is necessarily ongoing and open-ended, Gadamer suggests, we need to reread the Platonic dialogues in terms of the Christian conception of the "word" that mediates between the finite and the infinite. Plato's works led later thinkers like Leibniz to posit the existence of an independently existing, eternally intelligible order which could be replicated or copied by means of words or signs in the human mind. In fact, there is no intelligible order or integration of the whole apart from human inquiry into it. Because human life is finite, human knowledge is always limited. Not merely new generations, but all individuals constantly have to integrate new experiences into the general understanding they have inherited from the past and so gradually change that general understanding. They do this every day by means of language. Language is not merely the means, but the structure of similarities and differences whereby we comprehend the organization of the whole. That is why Socrates turned from a "scientific" study of things to an ongoing examination of the *logoi*. In language and only in language do we see how the parts—letters, syllables, and words—not merely acquire meaning, but become what they are only in the context of a whole that is more than the sum of its parts. Since that whole gradually changes over time as different individuals apply it to changing historical circumstances, we constantly need to reexamine the conclusions we come to about the world articulated in it. Although Plato himself did not explicitly elaborate an historical understanding of philosophy, his depiction of Socratic dialogue remains the best expression of such an understanding.

Strauss agrees that the philosophy represented by the Platonic Socrates constitutes a way of life rather than a doctrine or set of doctrines, but he challenges all of Gadamer's other major contentions. He agrees with Nietzsche and Heidegger in opposition to Gadamer that it is impossible to have an historical understanding of human life or philosophy without claiming to see the direction in which history is moving and thus its end. Absent such a claim, "history" becomes merely the record of what has happened, of events which often appear to be the results of mere chance or circumstance, and which do not therefore prove anything about the grounds, limitations or character of human knowledge. According to ancient philosophers, the most we can know is the overall structure of the cosmos, that is, the enduring general order or articulation of the different kinds of beings; we cannot know, predict, or determine particular outcomes. So little does Strauss think Platonic philosophy is fundamentally compatible with an historical understanding of human life, he presents it as *the* alternative to "radical historicism."

Philosophy arose, according to Strauss, when people began asking which of the ancestral ways was best on the basis of the difference observed between what comes into being on its own or by nature and what is produced by human art. Viewed in light of the distinction between nature and art—or convention—both gods and the laws they are said to support appear to be human fabrications, imposed by some who were cleverer and/or stronger on others. Because philosophers make such suggestions, the comic poet Aristophanes charged, they threaten to undermine the necessary foundations of the city, which secures the family and so the preservation of the human species. As Socrates' students Xenophon and Plato saw, philosophy had to defend itself from the charge of corruption; it needed to show that it served, rather than undermined, the requirements of political community. Like Gadamer, Strauss argues on the basis of his readings of all three original accounts of the life of Socrates, philosophy is a way of life that arises out of the concerns of everyday life, that is, from asking the question what is the best way of life. But, in direct opposition to Gadamer, Strauss maintains that, so far from providing the foundation or basis of a truly human community, philosophy exists in necessary tension with politics, not merely at the beginning in Greece, but in the twentieth century as well.

The tension between philosophy and politics first becomes evident through the questioning of received opinions, mores, or laws. But, if philosophical questioning led to the replacement of fallacious or unjust opinions by truer, philosophical education of its youth, it would benefit a city. This is the first way or guise in which Plato presents Socrates in his *Apology*—as a man who urges his fellow citizens to care for truth, justice, and the good of their souls rather than reputation, wealth, and bodily safety. In contrast to the philosopher Aristophanes lampoons in *The Clouds*, in the *Republic* Plato's Socrates explicitly defends justice. But in the course of the construction of the "city in speech" in the *Republic* Socrates shows that a just regime is almost impossible to achieve in fact. Philosophers must become kings, not only because philosophers do not have the desire for wealth or honor that makes most rulers unjust. Philosophers like Socrates who examine the opinions of each of their interlocutors individually in order to discover what they most deeply desire (or the character of their souls) are also the only human beings who have a chance of learning what would be good for each, the prerequisite for doing it or ruling justly. As Socrates states in his exchange with Meletus in the *Apology* and the Athenian reiterates in the *Laws*, such individualized instruction is the only way truly to educate or correct a human being. But, precisely because the instruction must be tailored to each and every individual and there are very few philosophers, such an improvement or education of the citizen body as a whole—which is as much as to say just rule—is impossible. The best practical solution, Plato shows in the *Laws*, is a combination of intelligent direction with popular consent. Because laws are always general, whereas individuals and their circumstances are singular, the rule of law is never simply or completely just. Those who administer the law also have to be educated, and if that education is to be more than indoctrination, it not only has to be individualized. It also has to lead future rulers to see the limitations of the law, both in itself and in their own regime. But philosophers who undermine the unquestioning loyalty young people have to their country are apt to be denounced as traitors. The love of one's own that Socrates shows in the *Republic* is the root of injustice cannot be eradicated without eradicating the reasons human beings join political associations in the first place, their desire to preserve themselves and their kind. This love of one's own is, indeed, essential to political life, because without it, no one would risk his or her life to defend the community from aggression.

"The city is completely intelligible because its limits can be made perfectly manifest," Strauss concludes in his study of the *Republic;* "to see these limits, one need not have answered the question regarding the whole; it is sufficient for the purpose to have raised the question."[1] In emphasizing the essentially limited character of human social life, Strauss ironically comes closer to Heidegger than either of his announced students, Gadamer and Derrida, who both stress the essential openness of human historical existence. But, where Heidegger argued that both human existence and knowledge are spatially and temporally limited, Strauss draws a distinction between politics and philosophy. Human beings have to form political associations in order to preserve themselves, and these associations are organized on the basis of certain authoritative opinions which will not be able to function as such, if philosophers openly and regularly expose their limited, only partial justice and truth. Political societies are and always will be essentially closed; unlike ancient polities, modern states are based on philosophically derived doctrines, but the philosophical basis does not prevent them from being popularly held as opinions. We recognize the dogmatic character of these opinions when we call them "ideologies." (In the past, Strauss agrees with Heidegger, the authoritative opinions on the basis of which a society was organized were usually traced to gods. Because philosophy always involves rationalistic questioning and criticism, such poetical-theological beliefs provided a firmer foundation for social order than modern philosophically derived dogmas.) But, Strauss insists in opposition to Heidegger, philosophy is not spatio-temporally limited the way the bodily existence of the individual and the political associations formed to secure it are. As Plato shows in the *Republic,* once human beings obtain what they need to survive, their desires immediately extend beyond the requirements of mere subsistence. The "limits" of the city are constituted by the irreconcilable requirements of *human* life. On the one hand, human beings cannot continue to exist without taking some account of the requirements of their physical self-preservation; if they are not to devote all their time and effort to providing for their own subsistence, they must cooperate with and thus to a certain extent attend to the needs of others (Socrates' friends, for example) who provide them with support. This is the reason philosophy must become political philosophy, if it is to take account of its own preconditions. But, on the other hand, Plato also shows, human beings are never satisfied merely with what is necessary to keep them

alive. We all want to live well; and the quest for the truly good or satisfying life leads those who are able to question the authoritative opinions
in their time and place and so to transcend these limits.

Although no actual polity can be perfectly just, Strauss argues, Plato
shows that an individual human being can be. In Book VI of the *Republic*
Socrates points out that those rare creatures whose love of truth is so
strong that it overcomes the fears and desires that make most people
apprehensive in the face of death, illiberal, greedy, and unjust, display all
the major forms of human excellence without actually possessing knowledge. It suffices that they seek it.

Like Gadamer, Strauss concludes that love of knowledge or philosophy
literally speaking is the greatest perfection of which human beings are
capable. We can never really or entirely possess wisdom per se. But, although Strauss agrees with Gadamer that human knowledge is essentially limited, the ground or source of the limitation he sees is fundamentally different. According to Gadamer, the limitation is essentially
temporal; we will constantly have to reconsider and reinterpret what we
think we have learned from the past in light of presently unknown future
developments. According to Strauss, the limitations on human knowledge do not arise simply or even primarily from the finitude of human
existence. Scientific knowledge can be additive; one generation can pass
on its learning to the next. Whether there is ever enough time to learn
everything depends ultimately on the character or quality of what there
is to know.[2] This is where the difficulty lies; the irreducible heterogeneity
of the cosmos, in particular the difference between the heterogeneous
ends of human life and the homogeneous mathematical knowledge that
can be applied to productive tasks, makes it impossible for us to know the
whole. And without knowledge of the whole, Strauss agrees with Gadamer, we do not have knowledge properly speaking.

Admitting that it does not represent knowledge strictly speaking,
Strauss nevertheless privileges the knowledge we have of the heteroge-
nous ends of human existence over the knowledge mathematics and the
productive sciences provide us of the homogeneous aspects of the cosmos.
The former is superior to the latter, he argues, because

> As knowledge of the ends of human life, it is knowledge of what makes
> human life complete or whole; it is therefore knowledge of a whole. Knowl-
> edge of the ends of man implies knowledge of the human soul; and the
> human soul is the only part of the whole which is open to the whole and
> therefore more akin to the whole than anything else is. But this knowl-
> edge—the political art in the highest sense—is not knowledge of *the*
> whole.

Strauss thus explicitly adopts the stance he attributes to Socrates:

> Socrates was so far from being committed to a specific cosmology that his knowledge was knowledge of ignorance. Knowledge of ignorance is . . . knowledge of the elusive character of the truth of the whole. Socrates . . . held . . . that we are more familiar with the situation of man as man than with the ultimate causes of that situation. We may also say he viewed man in light of the unchangeable ideas, i.e., of the fundamental and permanent problems.[3]

The irreducible division Strauss sees in human knowledge is reflected in the series of dichotomies he presents between reason and revelation, ancients and moderns, poetry and philosophy. As Maimonides showed in his *Guide of the Perplexed,* we cannot determine whether the cosmos had a beginning or whether something has existed eternally; there are insuperable difficulties either way. Nor is it clear whether we should organize our common life in order to enable a few human beings to achieve the highest possibilities, with the knowledge that it will always be at most a few, as the ancient political philosophers suggested, or whether we ought to lower our sights and secure the best possible conditions of life for most, as modern philosophers urge. It is not clear whether human life is essentially and necessarily tragic, because human desires can never be completely and lastingly fulfilled, or whether there is a form of human life truly worth living. The Platonic dialogues are, Strauss reminds us, works of art; it is not clear that we have another example besides Socrates of such a life. In Strauss's work, philosophy often appears to represent a goal more than an achievement. For example, in "What Is Liberal Education?" he declares:

> Plato . . . suggest[ed] that education in the highest sense is philosophy. Philosophy is quest for wisdom or quest for knowledge regarding the most important, the highest, or the most comprehensive things; such knowledge, he suggested, is virtue and is happiness. But wisdom is inaccessible to man, and hence virtue and happiness will always be imperfect. In spite of this, the philosopher, who, as such, is not simply wise, is declared . . . to possess all the excellences of which man's mind is capable, to the highest degree. From this we must draw the conclusion that we cannot be philosophers. . . , but we can love philosophy; we can try to philosophize. This philosophizing consists at any rate primarily . . . in listening to the conversation between the great philosophers. . . . But here we are confronted with the overwhelming difficulty. . . . Since the greatest minds contradict one another regarding the most important matters, they compel us to judge of their monologues; we cannot take on trust what any one of them says. On the other hand, we cannot but notice that we are not competent to be judges.[4]

Strauss seems to accept the classical rationalist alternative. But, since that alternative has become eclipsed in modern times, he may simply be trying to revive it in order to right the balance and so to reopen the fundamental questions. Strictly speaking, he repeats, neither he nor any one else knows—or can know.

What Strauss denies is the possibility of a synthesis or mediation—between human being and nature or human being and god—by means of *logos*, the great "fruit" of the combination of Platonic philosophy with Christian revelation, according to Gadamer. What the fact of language testifies to, according to Strauss, is the original, "naive" human perception of the differences among things—a perception we moderns threaten to lose as a result of the reductive, homogenizing character of scientific analyzes.[5]

Like Strauss, Derrida denies that *logos* has the mediating, synthesizing role both Gadamer and the dominant Neoplatonic tradition have attributed to it. Following Ferdinand Saussure, Derrida describes language as a system of differences.[6] But unlike Strauss, Derrida does not see language as a reflection or expression of the human perception of the essential heterogeneity of "things." He explicitly challenges both the humanizing and the holistic, "totalizing" tendencies of the Western philosophical tradition, tendencies that are reaffirmed, in different ways, by both Gadamer and Strauss when they argue that philosophy consists in a way of life, rather than in the promulgation of doctrines, and that knowledge, properly speaking, must be knowledge of the whole.

For Derrida "philosophy" refers primarily to an understanding or organization of everything that exists in terms of the logical, "Platonic" oppositions between intelligible and sensible, being and becoming, logos and mythos, etc. By showing that such distinctions are not simply tenable, even in Plato's own works, Derrida seeks to bring the Western philosophical tradition or metaphysics to closure by showing its limits. If there is something that always goes beyond these oppositions, that is "left over," unaccounted for, knowledge of the whole is not, never was, or will ever be possible. As Nietzsche argued, the activity previously called philosophy must be understood in different terms.

According to Derrida, however, philosophy should not be reconceived as a "way of life" or specific form of human existence. If we do not know that a natural order exists independent of our cognition, as Kant pointed out, it no longer makes sense to talk about a part of that order as "human nature."[7] As Heidegger argued in his *Letter on Humanism*, our notion of "man" or "human being" as the rational animal is a product of, and thus dependent upon, traditional metaphysics or cosmology. Beginning with Kant, Derrida observes in his essay on "The Ends of Man," a series of modern philosophers have thus sought to redefine the character and locus of intelligence as transcendental ego, spirit, consciousness, and *Dasein*. None of these philosophers entirely succeeded in freeing his thought of the residue of the metaphysical heritage, however, because they all continued to conceive of man in terms of his two "ends," as traditionally defined, his death as an individual and his overcoming that end through the attainment of undying knowledge. Even Heidegger, who insisted that all knowledge was finite and imperfect, ended up reverting to a rather traditional conception of "man" as distinguished by language and a special relation to "Being."

By freeing the notion of "trace" from the untenable theological or metaphysical concepts with which it was still associated in the works of Levinas, Heidegger, Nietzsche and Freud, Derrida thought he had developed the first real alternative to the traditional philosophical understanding of the world in terms of ideas or beings-in-themselves. Hegel and his successors had proposed an historical understanding of both the development of intelligible order and human life in place of "traditional" natural cosmology. But, Derrida observed, history for Hegel, Husserl, and Heidegger was simply and solely the history of reason. As such, it pointed back to the old metaphysical distinction between the finite body, subject to decay, and the mind able to transcend its spatio-temporal limitations. By reconceiving all forms of existence or being as traces of someone or something no longer present, Derrida could claim to have found a way of understanding everything to be finite, without a set, enduring order and necessity or a mysterious, inexplicable origin and apocalyptic end. If every "thing" is constantly losing some of its old content, becoming erased by the superimposition of other impressions or acquiring new significance from an ever-changing context, the world never was or will be entirely "logical" or calculable. The alternative to technological power-seeking and the consequent destruction of all distinctions or differences is not, as Heidegger thought, recourse to a mysterious dispensation of Being or "Gift." The alternative to the modern scientific "rationality" that makes everything into a source of power is a deconstructive reading of the tradition, that is, the traces left for us, which shows that there is no necessary, predictable, hence manipulable order.

The ironic result of Derrida's analysis of the preconditions for self-reflective or conscious thought as well as for the existence of ideas that can be reiterated or "recollected" over time—self-differentiation and deferral *(differance)*—is that it erases the basic difference between intelligent and other forms of existence. Everything becomes a "trace," separated or distinguished from others only by "spacing" or "margins." Derrida presents what has been called a "transcendental" analysis of the self-differentiating, deferring conditions necessary for people to be self-conscious and have ideas, but he does not retain a sense of the original, "naive" experience presupposed by his analysis. Rather than return "to the things" like Husserl, Derrida explicitly chooses to write on previously written texts. (According to Derrida, there isn't really anything else.) Why should the naive be preferred or thought to be more fundamental than the analyzed, than what has been shown to be the necessary precondition for the naive experience? The answer to that question would appear to be that, if human life is the only form of intelligent existence to which we have immediate access and of which we thus have at least potential knowledge, all knowledge must ultimately be or rest on self-knowledge. By deconstructing the concepts of "self" and "ego" along with the "human," Derrida destroys the basis of any hope we might have of acquiring any knowledge at all.[8] That destruction is not accidental or unintended, of course. Like Heidegger, but in a much more de-mystified manner, Derrida seeks to show that we do not know any single or singular origin, arche, foundation, or final cause.

Derrida does not claim to possess a "science" any more than he claims to provide people with a "method" of reading. More emphatically than the other "postmodern" thinkers we have surveyed, he denies that knowledge of the whole, that is, knowledge properly speaking, is possible. Since the other thinkers admit that human knowledge is, at best, partial, it seems that the merits of their respective positions cannot be decided on purely theoretical grounds. The relative advantages and disadvantages of their different understandings of the character and history of Western philosophy depend upon their practical effects as well.

Although Derrida denies philosophy constitutes a way of life, he repeatedly states that the deconstructive readings with which he would "supplement," that is, partly supersede and partly erase, the tradition are not purely theoretical. They have and are intended to have "practico-political effects."

If everything is as contingent, essentially undecided and undecidable as Derrida contends, the question arises, how do we take our bearings? How should we live? In *The Other Heading*, he urges, we should hold ourselves open, ready to respond to, before, and for "the Other." We would thus actively admit the undetermined, non-self-contained character of our existence.

Derrida takes the term "other" from Levinas, but he gives it a somewhat different meaning. Levinas argues that the experience of a face-to-face encounter with another human being constitutes an ethical relation that is more fundamental than the abstract ontological relation to Being Heidegger suggested was the distinctive characteristic of *Dasein*. (Like

Heidegger and Strauss, Levinas's study of Husserl led him back to concrete, everyday human experience as the foundation of all thought.) According to Levinas, the encounter with another prompts a man to ask himself, in an adaptation of Alexandre Kojève's analysis of the "master-slave" relation in Hegel, why he deserves to live rather than the other. Only by taking responsibility for the other, who has as much right as he, does a person establish his own right to live. Because that responsibility is infinite, it breaks through the limitations of human life and opens us up to that which lies beyond our experience, the positive Infinite. Although Derrida also emphasizes our "responsibility" to the "other," he denies that we can know any positive infinite. (This denial distinguishes his thought from negative theology as well.) He explicitly eschews ethics, and he criticizes Levinas, as he does Heidegger, for not taking a sufficient account of the sexual difference between human beings. (By reducing both women and men to the "human" Levinas reduces the "other" to the same—just the reductive philosophical tendency Levinas wants, above all, to avoid.)[9] In contrast to Levinas, Derrida does not seek to revive the essentially moral and hence free understanding of human existence Strauss suggests achieves its purest expression in the Hebrew Bible (because a moral view of the universe ultimately requires an omnipotent and omniscient God to enforce it) in opposition to the less anthropocentric, but more rational "Greek" philosophical view of "nature" or "being." On the contrary, Derrida argues that the two major components of the Western tradition necessarily (!) came together in their insistence on the mediating function of *logos*. But, where Gadamer celebrates the "fusion of horizons" that is constantly occurring in language and brings out its moral purpose or goal, the search for a good life which can be achieved only in cooperation with others, Derrida seeks, above all, to deconstruct this "phallo-logo-centrism" and so undermine the hierarchical organization of society he sees follows from it.

Like Heidegger and Levinas, Derrida thinks that the attempt to rationalize the world by redescribing it in "logical" terms (i.e., binary oppositions like those used in computers) inexorably leads to homogenization. As Kojève argued, the Western Neoplatonic tradition points toward the desirability of establishing a homogeneous world state. Does not the "good will" presupposed by the attempt to come to a mutual understanding, agreement or "fusion of horizons" remain a form of will, indeed, will to power, he asks Gadamer.[10] Derrida does not oppose "rational" homogenization with an analysis of the essential heterogeneity of purpose or ends in human life, summarized by the tension between politics and philosophy, like Strauss, because he thinks that such an analysis not only rests on an outdated understanding of "nature" but also because he sees that *any* substantive definition of the character or ends of "man," any moral or ethical distinction between good and bad, is inherently inegalitarian. Some people will have more compassion, regard for others, intelligence or . . . than others. Derrida's initial objection to the end or completion of history Husserl described as philosophy's becoming a rigorous science was that it is exclusive—limited, in effect, to "normal" European white men. (Derrida's second objection, which could be applied to Gadamer as well as to Husserl, was that the prospect of achieving such knowledge presupposed everything could be named, a contention Husserl himself was forced to deny at a very fundamental level.)

Rather than oppose the modern tendency to rationalize with an analysis of the human or an appeal to individual freedom (which, as Heidegger points out in his response to Ernst Junger in *Seinsfrage*, involves an assertion of the will that is at the root of the homogenization—or nihilistic denial of the intrinsic value of anything "in itself") Derrida attempts to go to the "root" of the difficulty by analyzing or deconstructing *logos* itself. *Logos* is not the property of any individual, "ego" or "identity," he emphasizes. It manifests itself only in particular languages, which are interpersonal and hence essentially indicative. No person can simply or purely perceive the inner thoughts and intentions of another; in light of the "unconscious" springs or sources or our thoughts and actions, no one can be sure about his or her own motives and meaning. The languages people use have common elements; as Gadamer argues in opposition to Heidegger, different languages do not articulate mutually exclusive worlds. It is possible to translate, although neither the structure nor the words are ever entirely the same. Because language is indicative, Derrida reminds his readers in his analyses of the "signature," there is always a play between the singular application of a word (even a proper name) and its general or collective meaning over time. The general meaning is affected by each application, and in the process, the distinctive character of each singular manifestation tends to become lost.

In "Force of Law: The 'Mystical' Foundation of Authority," Derrida argues that the same interminable play between general and singular that makes it impossible for any single term to retain exactly the same meaning over time produces an insoluble problem of justice at the social level as well. Political societies are organized on the basis of an understanding of right (or justice) which finds expression in their laws. If one asks what the source or basis of these laws is, however, one always comes back to an act of force. The basis of the law cannot itself be legal; and any agreement must, like the laws themselves, be enforced. The original violence is repeated, in a way, each time a particular case under law is decided. If the law is not merely applied to particular circumstances mechanically, which would almost surely be unjust, the gap between the general principle embodied in the law and the singular facts of the case ought to lead the decision-maker to reopen the question of the justice of the general principle. This moment of suspension or deliberation, the back-and-forth during which all the considerations known to be relevant are in play, before some are decided to be weightier than others, which then become subordinated, is *the* moment of justice, which is lost as soon as a decision is reached. That decision is not only necessarily partial—in favor of some at the expense of others. It is also necessarily made on the basis of less than full knowledge of all the relevant or possibly relevant considerations, because these considerations are, in principle, infinite, and decisions have to be made expeditiously; they cannot be infinitely postponed. The process of applying general principles or laws to particular circumstances does not simply represent an example of the fusion of horizons, as Gadamer argues, through which general principles or understandings are gradually modified as a result of the interaction or interplay between the general and the particular.[11] In each decision, Derrida emphasizes, there are winners *and* losers; some people and things are found to be less important than others—or even totally ignored. By showing the partial character of every decision, by reminding us who or what was silenced or repressed, deconstructive critiques of past legal decisions reveal the difference between law and its purported goal, the achievement of justice.

Don't such deconstructive critiques undermine the legitimacy of the rule of law by showing not only how but also that it is always different from justice? The answer to that question depends, Derrida suggests, on our understanding of the source and character of "legitimacy." The rule of law may depend ultimately upon force, but the rule of law is also obviously different from mere force. If we inquire into the difference, we discover that it lies not merely in the regularity or generality of law as opposed to whim, but in popular acceptance or consent. Since human beings always lack full knowledge of each other, to say nothing of their origins, ends, and circumstances, the basis of that consent is not simply reason or calculation so much as inferences drawn from past experience or the "received wisdom" which gradually but only gradually changes over time. "Custom is the sole basis for equity," Montaigne observed, "for the simple reason that it is received; it is the mystical foundation of its authority." Thus he concluded, "whoever traces it to its source annihilates it."[12]

Derrida questions Montaigne's conclusion by observing that our tradition—the Western philosophical tradition, as a whole, as well as the more particular Franco-American political tradition concerning the social contract—includes precisely that kind of questioning about the origins or source. As in *The Other Heading,* Derrida concludes that our heritage calls for a double, even contradictory, response. On the one hand, we must try to preserve that heritage. As an accumulation of the traces of past efforts, both intended and unintended, woven together into a narrative, that heritage may represent only a "legitimizing fiction," but it is, in fact, all we have. On the other hand, in the process of trying to preserve that tradition, of acting within it, we necessarily confront the fact that it contains disparate, even contradictory elements. In the face of these contradictions, it is impossible simply to affirm *the* tradition as if it were a unity. A Gadamerian attempt to come to agreement or fuse horizons covers over the fundamental differences. Only by making these differences thematic do we discover the reasons why all previous attempts to achieve our common goals—justice, if not truth and knowledge—have necessarily failed. By bringing out the limits of past endeavors, we also discover the need to invent new ways and means of seeking these same impossible, but nonetheless desirable goals.

Beginning from what would appear to be diametrically opposed politico-philosophical stances, radically historicist and anti-radically historicist, we thus see, Derrida and Strauss arrive at a remarkably similar understanding of the problematic character and foundation of our common life. Lacking full knowledge of the intentions and character of each and every human being as well as the bearing of the particular circumstances, human beings cannot and will never be able to establish a fully just order. As Gadamer also suggests, the best we can do is to try to come to some kind of working agreement on a set of generalizations or laws that encapsulate the "received wisdom" or reflections on the results of past experience. But, because the inferences drawn and agreed to rest on imperfect knowledge and do not, in practice, always produce desirable results, they are necessarily brought into question. There is an enduring, inescapable tension, therefore, between the need to maintain tradition and the destruction of that tradition by the questioning it itself provokes.

Derrida and Strauss draw diametrically opposed practical conclusions, however, from the insight into the problematic foundations of our common life they both trace back to the Platonic dialogues. The fundamental questions that give rise to philosophical inquiry remain open, because they are, in fact, insoluble, Strauss argues; but political societies must be closed. If the members of such societies are not to come to blows, they must agree on the way of life they wish to foster. Since these agreements are not based on knowledge, they will be partial. They will not be based simply on reason, but partly on a poetic appeal to the desires of the dominant parts of the society and partly on force. Because the law never represents direction by pure intelligence, it needs to be based on superhuman or divine authority. Modern philosophers thus undermined the most effective, popular basis of human self-restraint (or self-government) when they waged an unremitting attack on revelation. Nietzsche brought modern philosophy to its logical conclusion with his declaration that "God is dead." He and Heidegger both indicated the unsatisfactory character of that solution when toward the end of their careers they both looked forward to the revelation of a new god.

Strauss's emphasis on the need for a public, religiously based teaching he and other philosophers recognize is not based on reason has led critics to accuse him of nihilism, if not outright deception and manipulation.[13] Strauss responds to the charge of nihilism, I have argued, with his praise of Socratic philosophy. He does not urge would-be philosophers to engage in moral teaching, however, whether in the form of propaganda or proselytizing. On the contrary, as a result of his discovery of the esoteric art of writing practiced by medieval Islamic and Jewish Platonists, he emphasizes the need for philosophers to restrain the extent to which they openly and explicitly question popularly salutary beliefs in the gods and the immortality of the soul. Unlike Farabi's Plato, Strauss does not suggest that philosophers can gradually improve or reform public opinion over time. If knowledge of the whole is unattainable, all human beings will ever have are opinions, and most people's opinions will be reflections of their circumstances and traditions as well as their hopes and fears. Popular enlightenment is as impossible as a completely rational or rationalized politics.

As we have seen, Derrida draws the opposite conclusion from a similar insight into the partial character of all laws and governments. The self-restraint Strauss urges philosophers to exercise would leave many examples of injustice unidentified and unopposed. The incomplete justice of any law is, for Derrida, a reason to deconstruct it; the partial character of every regime is a reason why its violent origins should be exposed, and why it should be encouraged, if not forced to pay attention, to open itself to, those who have been silenced, oppressed and excluded.

It is no accident, Derrida suggests, that deconstruction has been adopted and practiced primarily in the United States. American history during the last two centuries can be described in terms of the deconstruction of the tradition Derrida recommends. In his classic study of *Democracy in America* in the early nineteenth century Alexis de Tocqueville argued that liberty was preserved in the United States not simply because of geography (isolation and the open frontier) or law (federalism and the constitutional separation of powers). The most important reason why Americans retained their liberties was to be found in their "mores," and these mores consisted in a combination of empirico-rational skepticism about practical, political affairs with generalized Protestant Christian moral and religious beliefs.[14] The arrival of "waves" of immigrant groups in the late nineteenth and early twentieth centuries with different beliefs and customs both diluted and challenged the reigning consensus. Following the Civil War, there have been repeated attempts to reiterate and revive this moral consensus. (American associates of Derrida are apt to see Ronald Reagan, William Bennett, and Allan Bloom as the leaders of the most recent revival.) But with each generation, the tradition has become more inclusive. What appeared to be fundamental divisions among Protestants, Catholics, and Jews as late as the 1950s no longer seem serious. The United States has been *the* society that has, in theory and to a great extent in practice, been "open" to "the other" in the way Derrida recommends. Neither Derrida nor his American associates have embraced America, in its aspiration or its achievements, however; consistently following their own principles, they have engaged rather in an unremitting critique.[15] Americans claim to believe in the rights of all human beings to life, liberty and the pursuit of happiness, but America has not, in fact, secured the rights of all. America claims to be open to all peoples and views, but neither the people nor their government actually are or have been.

Derridean analyses can only be critical, they cannot generate positive principles or a picture of a desirable way of life, because of the denial of the existence of any identity—personal, intelligible, or political—involved in the initial discovery of *"différance."* If all we "know" is that we are not and can never become aware of all the forces working upon and within "us" except that they will change over time in an essentially unpredictable way, it is difficult, if not impossible to articulate a vision of a desirable way of life for an individual or a people, much less to embrace and work for it enthusiastically.

The incapacity of Derridean deconstruction to generate a positive view of human life or direction makes the tack Heidegger and Strauss took from Husserl, attempting to recapture the prescientific understanding upon the basis of which human beings organize their lives rather than further analyzing or "reducing" fundamentally philosophical concepts, appear to be more promising, with regard to questions of practice as well as of theory. But, on the basis of their studies of the origins of the West, both Heidegger and Strauss conclude that human societies must be closed. As citizens of a liberal democracy, we might be tempted to see Gadamerian hermeneutics as an optimal compromise.[16] Following Nietzsche and Heidegger, Gadamer denies that we have knowledge of an independently existing, eternal intelligible order. Like Derrida, he insists, what we have is a heritage or tradition. We cannot and should not try merely to preserve that heritage, however. What we have received from the past will continue to live only if we reexamine and reevaluate it in light of new developments. Rather than a closed society or understanding, Gadamer advocates ongoing dialogue and openness.

The problem with Gadamerian hermeneutics, both Strauss, and Derrida point out in different ways, is that it does not take account of the enduring conflict and irrationality we encounter in the world. According to Gadamer, everything can in principle be articulated, that is, there is nothing in itself or necessarily *alogos*. According to Gadamer, all "horizons" or understandings can in principle be fused; there are no unbridgeable rifts or differences. If Gadamer were correct, wars would not be necessary. They would merely be products of historical misunderstandings that can, in principle, be overcome. *Political* associations would no longer be necessary. As Gadamer himself points out, in the *Republic* Plato shows that *political* associations first arise because of the need to fight wars. There would be no expansive drive(s) or need to resist them, if there were no fundamental, irresoluble conflicts of interest.

As both Strauss and Derrida point out, Gadamer does not provide an adequate account of the infinite expansion of the horizon he expects. The mere passage of time does not explain why differences cannot ultimately be resolved, why or how ever new perspectives will be generated.

Because they argue there is an irreducible conflict at the heart of things, Nietzsche, Heidegger, Strauss and Derrida all provide more adequate accounts of the reasons human beings will never possess knowledge of the whole and why we will therefore continue to disagree and fight. These thinkers also provide penetrating critiques of the other positions.

According to Nietzsche, everything is a manifestation of the Will to Power that strives always to increase itself; that is the reason, conscious or unconscious, Plato argued that philosophers should become kings. As the most spiritual or intense form of the will to power, philosophy consists in the attempt to impose order and meaning on the inherently meaningless stream of becoming, although previous philosophers did not admit or understand this. Heidegger objected that Nietzsche's doctrine of the Will to Power constitutes a prime example of the leveling tendency inherent in the metaphysical understanding of Being as a common, propertyless substratum. He had merely defined Being as Becoming. Because he did not perceive the temporal character of the traditional definition of being as what is present, he did not recognize the ontological difference between Being and the beings. Had he taken account of this difference, he would have seen that Being itself is never present. Rather than "being" anything, Being gives rise to an 'e-vent', the emergence and articulation of beings in a world, only by withdrawing into oblivion. Nietzsche did not see that the grounds of our existence are, therefore, ineluctably mysterious. Rather than urge his readers to "think" as they had never thought before, with wonder and thankfulness at the world they had been "given," Nietzsche encouraged them to transform it entirely. He thus denied, in effect, that the given had any value. Rather than overcome the nihilism he argued was inherent in the Western tradition, Nietzsche himself thus carried it out to its completion. To Nietzsche, the passage of time—the past—appeared to be *the* aspect of the world most beyond human control. Just as he claimed previous philosophers had posited the existence of an in-finite, im-mortal Being out of an unacknowledged desire to overcome the spatial-temporal limitations of their own existence and knowledge, so Nietzsche himself articulated the doctrine of the Eternal Return in an attempt to overcome *the* limitation he saw on the human desire to reorder the world. Because he did not distinguish Being from the beings, Nietzsche did not understand that, rather than merely constituting limits on our knowledge, space and time are, as Kant pointed out, the necessary, enabling conditions for the articulation of an intelligible world. Because he did not understand the significance of the ontological difference, Nietzsche did not recognize the real, qualitative difference between human beings and animals, that human beings are distinguished by their ability to respond to the "call of Being" by asking what each of the beings, disclosed by the "lighting" of "being" in the "open space" or *Zeitraum* in which they happen to find themselves, is. Nietzsche continued, rather, to understand "men" metaphysically merely as kinds of animals that had developed a rational faculty they were now in danger of losing. Whereas Nietzsche thought the conflict in the world was a result of an ongoing struggle for power in which everyone or thing attempts to master everything else, lest it itself be mastered, controlled and destroyed, Heidegger understood the conflict at the "essence" of things in a very different way. Because nothing exists in itself, he argued, things "are" and can be known only in relation to others. In his early works, he thus urged the need to tear violently through the layer of ossified, empty traditional concepts that had led philosophers to try to come to know things-in-themselves in order to recapture the original understanding of being-in-the-world which constitutes the basis not merely of human knowledge, but of human life or existence. And in his later works he beseeched his readers not merely to recapture a sense of "things" as distinct entities and parts of a larger whole, but to cherish them as such, lest everything be devoured in and by an essentially violent technological process that would transform everything and everyone into indistinguishable "standing reserve." To preserve the world, to preserve "man," it would be necessary for people to become aware of the fundamental tension or conflict between the concrete immediacy of what appears to be "ready-at-hand" and the thoughtful realization that there is no reason or necessity for it, us, or anything "to be" at all.

As we have seen, Derrida explicitly attempts to take the Nietzschean-Heideggerian critique of metaphysics even further. Although Heidegger showed that we did not and could not know anything eternal or in itself, Derrida argues, his use of the traditional ontological term 'Being' as well as his later evocation of the 'event' obscured the radically untraditional character of his analysis. By freeing *difference* from ontology and explicitly arguing that nothing has any identity in and of itself, Derrida can claim to have shown more clearly than his mentor why nothing has any stable meaning or existence in itself. By redescribing the things we encounter as traces of a *differance* in power, Derrida moves back toward Nietzsche; there is no longer a world or *Zeitraum* with a temporal horizon. But, using Freud, Derrida also argues that there is no "will" either. No one has or can have the power to impose or create an unshakable order. Everything happens both within and outside "human beings" through an invisible and essentially uncontrollable process of differentiation and deferral that has no beginning or end. One finds its traces in Plato as well as in Nietzsche. However, as a consequence of his dropping the ontological aspect of the difference Heidegger emphasized—a seemingly technical move—Derrida loses the contrast between the apparent self-evidence of the immediate world and its uncertain, unknowable foundations or roots, the difference Heidegger himself thought was essential.

Without any familiarity with Derrida, Strauss objected to this radical historicism, so to speak, root and branch. Insofar as historicism leads to an understanding of everything in terms of a struggle for, or difference in, power (or energy), it ignores the difference, to be found on the surface, between the human and the non-human things. As Heidegger's phenomenology shows, it is not necessary to posit the existence of an eternal species to give an account of the distinctively human; it *is* necessary to keep the difference between the human and the non-human, both the sub-human and the supra-human in view. Because modern scientific theories tend to be reductive, Strauss agrees with Heidegger, we have to try to free ourselves from the traditional understanding of the history or "progress" of philosophy and seek to recapture the experience out of which theory first arose. Strauss's studies of Socrates showed him that this pretheoretical experience included not only a discovery of the importance of distinguishing the human from the non-human things; it also included a recognition of the existence of a variety of human ends or goals, a variety more extensive than the two "ends" in death and/or the overcoming of death with knowledge that Derrida emphasizes, *and* that these goals conflicted with one another. People disagree, necessarily, about what the best way of life is, and these disagreements lead them into violent confrontations. *The* source of violence in the world is not to be found in a universal struggle for power; animals fight battles, but they do not wage war. Nor does the violence result merely from the difference between the security of our immediate world and its essential contingency. Violent conflict is distinctively human, but it is not simply or even primarily intellectual.

As Plato shows in the *Republic,* people come into violent conflict with one another, because they cannot and do not limit their desires to what is necessary for their own subsistence. They want something more and better. To get it, they band together by coming to some working agreements about the best way of achieving their common aims. These utilitarian agreements or conventions have the character of "justice among thieves," however. There is no reason for an individual to continue to abide by any such agreement the moment it is no longer in his interest to do so; in themselves these agreements and the partial, temporarily peaceful relations they establish among individuals are inherently weak. The realization on the part of the individual that he or she may die at any moment that Heidegger emphasized does not necessarily lead a person to see his or her fate as indissolubly tied to the destiny of his or her people. As Hobbes argues, a soldier may reasonably flee a battlefield in order to save his own life. As Derrida argues, there is always a potential conflict between the singular interest of the individual and the general interest of the community, a gap that makes justice itself impossible to achieve.

The source or reason for the recurrence of violent conflict is, in other words, the insoluble problem of justice. Heidegger recognizes this, in a way, in his discussion of *dikē* and *Gerechtigkeit* in his lectures on *Nietzsche.* But, Strauss objects, justice is not simply a question of intellectual order or power; it is the problem of what we usually call morality. Because Nietzsche, Heidegger and Derrida all claim to be beyond morality, they cannot and do not adequately address the problem, which is as much as to say, they do not provide an adequate explanation for the recurrent outbreaks of violent conflict in the world.

Nietzsche, Heidegger, and Derrida all claim to be beyond morality on the basis of an historical understanding of the Western tradition that combines Greek rationality with scriptural morality. Although all three of these thinkers claim to have purged their own thought of theology, the residue is still evident—in Nietzsche's last virtue, probity, for example.

Honesty is not one of the four cardinal Platonic virtues. Heidegger uses 'guilt' and 'conscience' as existential categories in *Being and Time*. As Derrida points out, Heidegger's later writings about the 'event' and *es gibt* also have a theological cast.[17] Derrida's own evocation of the Advent, his insistence on the need to be open to what is "to come," has prophetic or biblical overtones as well.[18] In response to Levinas's call to separate the scriptural from the rational, Derrida points out that the two parts of the Western tradition have been brought together in fact and with reason. It is necessary, therefore, to take account of the coupling as well as the difference.

> If one calls this experience of the infinitely other Judaism (which is only a hypothesis for us), one must reflect upon the necessity in which this experience finds itself . . . to occur as logos. . . . Are we Jews? Are we Greeks? We live in the difference between the Jew and the Greek, which is perhaps the unity of what is called history. . . . Does the strange dialogue between the Jew and the Greek . . . have the form of the absolute, speculative logic of Hegel. . . . Or . . . does . . . [it] have the form of infinite separation. . . ? Can it account for the historical *coupling* of Judaism and Hellenism?[19]

Strauss responds to Derrida's challenge, in effect, by arguing that the modern historical synthesis does not combine Greek rationalism and scriptural morality so much as it destroys them. There is a certain conjunction, he admits, between the teachings of the Greek philosophers and the Bible, especially about the requirements of maintaining a decent human society. But he argues that it is just this mixture of Greek philosophy with Scripture, a mixing he admits has occurred for a variety of reasons, that has prevented these radical historicists as well as their early modern predecessors from seeing the problem of morality in its original or stark form.

Although Greek philosophy and Scripture concur on certain moral teachings, for example, the necessity of preserving something like the nuclear family, the two component parts of the Western tradition nevertheless present two very different, incompatible visions of human excellence. Aristotle's magnanimous man, who habitually claims high honors for himself, because he knows he is worthy of them, lacks the shame and humility of the prophet Isaiah. And these two contradictory visions or understandings of human excellence point, in turn, to the two different, incompatible sources of morality. On the basis of rational calculation, one can deduce a set of rules, proscribing murder and theft, for example, that are necessary, more or less everywhere, for communities to survive. The problem is that it is not rational for individuals to follow these prohibitions, if and when they conflict with individual desires, unless the community is able to enforce a penalty; and it is impossible to police everyone all the time. On the grounds of rational calculation alone, Plato shows, only philosophers are just. They do not want anything that cannot be shared equally with everyone. They do not want power, wealth, or prestige; therefore, they only seek friends. If all human beings could become philosophers, they could and would live in peace. Circumstances, the requirements of self-preservation, and differences in native disposition and talent conjoin, however, to make this impossible. Most people have to spend most of their time providing food and shelter for themselves and others; they do not have the time or inclination to seek wisdom. Even when they use their intellects to develop technological means of relieving themselves from the pain of physical labor, they still concentrate on amassing the means of securing their own existence. They do not ask what the best form of human existence really is. Philosophers recognize that their own lives and activity depend upon the existence of a political community to provide them not only with food and protection but also with fellow seekers or students. Since they cannot fundamentally improve or reform their fellow citizens, because to do so they would have to change not merely their opinions, but their very natures, philosophers try at least not to harm their fellows by undermining the basis of their common life. The irrational fear of death and hope for an afterlife that lead most people to seek wealth, and some to want reputation or glory as well, are the seeds of religion; and in his studies of Thucydides, Strauss suggests, no community can last long without it, even though piety or faith alone is relatively weak. The difficulty is that these two sources of morality, reason and piety, are contradictory; reason leads human beings to doubt the claims of revelation, and the beautiful visions of revelation tempt nonbelievers like Nietzsche, Heidegger, and Derrida to articulate and embrace hopes that have no foundation in reason. (Modern philosophers tried to combine reason and revelation, Strauss suggested in his essay on "Jerusalem and Athens" because the scriptural view of human beings as essentially free and moral is nobler than the ancient, purely rationalist view. But when reason and revelation are synthesized, we see at the end of the Western philosophical tradition in the works of Nietzsche and Heidegger, reason, faith, and morality are all destroyed.)

Socrates first perceived the singular character of the human things, Strauss suggests in his study of Xenophon's *Oeconomicus*, when he asked, What is noble? The noble is neither simply useful (and hence calculable) nor is it simply pleasant (or beautiful to view). The noble is not visible; it exists only in opinion. As such, it is distinctively human. Indeed, Strauss suggests, there is no understanding of human life and hence of the world in which we live that does not begin, and in a sense end, with an examination of the problem of morality, that is, with the question of how we should live. As Nietzsche stated and Derrida reiterates, the end of morality is the end of "man."

Although Strauss's works are much less poetic or associated with the study of literary fiction than those of his competitors—Nietzsche, Heidegger, Gadamer, and Derrida—his concerns are, ironically, closer to those of the poets of old. As Homer says in the *Odyssey* VIII, ll. 25–35, the minstrel sings of the good and evil in human life. In the nineteenth century, literary artists like others turned to the study of "art for art's sake." As a result, we now tend to understand the difference between poetry and philosophy primarily as a difference in form. Plato was aware that poetry was more persuasive than discursive reasoning, Strauss points out; in the *Laws* the Stranger argues that legislators need to learn how to fit their speeches to the people from the poets. The ancient debate between the poets and the philosophers to which Socrates refers in Book X of the *Republic* concerns the question of whether there is a completely satisfying way of life. Since later poets like Lucretius and Dante conceded that philosophy was the best way of life, the substance of the debate became covered over. Nietzsche, Heidegger, Gadamer and Derrida could argue that poetry constitutes as good, if not a better vehicle for communicating "truth" or that poetry and philosophy are essentially the same only because they have forgotten *the* primary claim Plato's Socrates made in opposition to the politicians, poets, and artisans in his *Apology*—namely, that philosophy constitutes the only form of human life truly worth living. The only book Strauss devoted entirely to the study of poetry was *Socrates and Aristophanes*. But in this book he showed that, like Plato, he admired not only the artistry but also the wisdom of the ancient comic.

Aristophanes was a poet who suggested that piety is a necessary civic virtue, but who was obviously not simply pious himself. (In *The Birds* he celebrated a man's overthrow of the rule of the gods.) The tension between poetry and philosophy is related to, but it is not exactly the same as the tension between reason and revelation, according to Strauss.

By challenging his readers to reread the history of philosophy in terms of a strict disjunction between reason and revelation, Strauss asks them to study that history in a most untraditional way. All his own readings of individual philosophers, including preeminently his reading of Plato, have proven to be extremely controversial. That is, they invite debate and rebuttal. But if the purpose of the contemporary return to Plato is to show that philosophy has a future, he may have succeeded in fulfilling that purpose by demonstrating the need for an untraditional reading of the tradition better than anyone else.

Abbreviations

FW	Die Fröhliche Wissenschaft
GD	Götzen-Dämmerung
GM	Zur Genealogie der Moral
GT	Die Geburt der Tragödie
JGB	Jenseits von Gut und Böse
M	Morgenröte
MA	Menschliches, Allzumenschliches
NN	Vom Nutzen und Nachteil der Historie für das Leben
PTAG	Die Philosophie im tragischen Zeitalter der Griechen
WP	The Will to Power

LEO STRAUSS

AAPL	The Argument and the Action of Plato's "Laws"
CM	The City and Man
CR	The Rebirth of Classical Political Rationalism
HPP	The History of Political Philosophy
LAM	Liberalism: Ancient and Modern
NRH	Natural Right and History
OT	On Tyranny
PAW	Persecution and the Art of Writing
SA	Socrates and Aristophanes
SPPP	Studies in Platonic Political Philosophy
WIPP	What Is Political Philosophy? and Other Essays
XS	Xenophon's Socrates
XSD	Xenophon's Socratic Discourse

Notes

INTRODUCTION

1. Some question has been raised about Nietzsche's status as a postmodern in *Nietzsche as Postmodernist: Essays Pro and Contra*, ed. Clayton Koelb (Albany: State University of New York Press, 1990). The most questionable or controversial use of the term is, however, to describe the work of Leo Strauss. But, as Stanley Rosen has pointed out, "according to Strauss, modern thought in all its forms is determined by the idea of progress, . . . and hence is rooted from the outset in Enlightenment. Strauss's critique of modernity is thus a critique of the Enlightenment, similar to that of Nietzsche, but also entirely typical of what has frequently been called 'post-modernism'." "Leo Strauss and the Quarrel between the Ancients and the Moderns," in Alan Udoff, ed., *Leo Strauss' Thought: Toward a Critical Engagement* (Boulder and London: Lynne Riemer, 1991), p. 166. I am using the term "postmodern" to mean literally "after the modern," as applied specifically to philosophy, and not as the literary critic Iban Hassan suggests, to describe "an antinomian moment that *assumes* [!] a vast unmaking of the Western mind. . . , epistemological obsession with fragments, and a corresponding ideological commitment to minorities in politics, sex and language," although I recognize that the term often carries such connotations with it. Cf. Richard J. Bernstein, "An Allegory of Modernity/Postmodernity: Habermas and Derrida," in Gary B. Madison, ed., *Working through Derrida* (Evanston: Northwestern University Press, 1993), p. 204.

2. Heidegger's reading of Nietzsche has, of course, been contested—by Strauss and Derrida among others.

3. Two other students of Strauss provide eloquent testimony concerning the difficulty of the undertaking. In his beautiful memorial statement on "Leo Strauss," published in *Political Theory* 2, no. 4 (November 1974), Allan Bloom observes that "the books of his ripeness are almost as alien to us as are the books with which he dealt" (pp. 390–91). And in his account of "Leo Strauss: The Recovery of Political Philosophy," Eugene Miller point outs "The person who sets out to discover Strauss's own philosophical views is confronted with a task of

almost overwhelming complexity. He is obligated, in the first place, to understand all that Strauss has said about the principles of philosophical speech and writing. . . . Moreover, he must carefully compare Strauss's expositions in each case with the original sources under consideration." *Contemporary Political Philosophers*, ed. Anthony de Crespigny and Kenneth Minogue (New York: Dodd, Mead, 1975), p. 69.

4. *Truth and Method*, trans. revised by Joel Weinsheimer and Donald G. Marshall (New York: Crossroad, 1990), xxi.

5. "Correspondence concerning *Wahrheit und Methode*," *Independent Journal of Philosophy* 2 (1978): 5–6.

6. *Derrida and "Différance*," ed. David Wood and Robert Bernasconi (Evanston: Northwestern University Press, 1988), p. 5.

7. Cf. "Violence et Metaphysique," in *L'Ecriture et la différence* (Paris: Seuil, 1967), pp. 117–18; *Writing and Difference*, trans. Alan Bass (Chicago: University of Chicago Press, 1978), pp. 79–80: "That philosophy died yesterday, since Hegel or Marx, Nietzsche, or Heidegger . . . or that it has always lived knowing itself to be dying. . . ; that beyond the death, or dying nature, of philosophy, . . . thought still has a future. . . , these are problems put to philosophy as problems philosophy cannot resolve. . . . Nevertheless, these should be the only questions today . . . of those who are still called philosophers; and called such in remembrance, at very least, of the fact that these questions must be examined unrelentingly."

8. "Preface to the English Translation," *Spinoza's Critique of Religion* (New York: Schocken Books, 1965), p. 12.

9. Eric Vögelin, Emmanuel Levinas, and Hannah Arendt have also been concerned about the character and fate of the Western tradition and have presented new interpretations of its origins in Plato. But, in contrast to the thinkers included in this volume, Vögelin, Levinas, and Arendt have been more concerned about saving religion or politics from philosophy than with uncovering the original character of philosophy itself.

10. In *Beyond Good and Evil* (14), Nietzsche asks when people will begin to understand that physics is merely another interpretation. In *The Question concerning Technology*, trans. William Lovitt (New York: Harper and Row, 1977), pp. 3–35, Heidegger explains that techno-science is *the* modern way in which truth is disclosed. Gadamer explicitly writes about *Reason in the Age of Science*, trans. Frederick G. Lawrence (Cambridge, Mass.: MIT Press, 1983). Both in *Philosophy and Law*, trans. Fred Baumann (Philadelphia: Jewish Publication Society, 1987) and *Natural Right and History* (Chicago: University of Chicago Press, 1953), Strauss attempts to revive ancient rationalism, particularly with regard to politics, explicitly in light of the theoretical superiority of modern physics to Aristotelian cosmology. And in *Of Grammatology*, trans. Gayatri Chakravorty Spivak (Baltimore: Johns Hopkins University Press, 1976), p. 9, Derrida includes cybernetic programming as one of the kinds of writing with which he is particularly concerned.

11. Xenophon, *Memorabilia* 1.1.11–15.

CHAPTER ONE

1. *Nietzsche* (Pfullingen: Neske, 1961), trans. David Farrell Krell (New York: Harper and Row, 1979).

2. Recent critics like Gilles Deleuze and William Connelly recognize the affirmative character of Nietzsche's new conception of truth, history, and philosophy, but reject his conclusion on political grounds. Deleuze sees that the solitude of the Nietzschean philosopher makes community impossible; Connolly objects to Nietzsche's anti-democratic politics, although he urges his readers to take a nuanced stance toward Nietzsche's critique. See Gilles Deleuze, *Nietzsche* (Paris: Presses Universitaires de France, 1965), pp. 32–41; "Active and Reactive," in David Allison, *The New Nietzsche* (New York: Dell, 1970), pp. 85–113; *Anti-Oedipus*, with Felix Guattari (Minneapolis: University of Minnesota Press, 1983), xxiii. William E. Connolly, *Political Theory and Modernity* (New York: Basil Blackwell, 1988), pp. 137–67; *Identity/Difference* (Ithaca: Cornell University Press, 1991), pp. 190–92. Alasdair MacIntyre, *After Virtue* (Notre Dame, Ind.: Notre Dame University Press, 1981), pp. 239–40, also emphasizes Nietzsche's honesty and the radical solitude of the *Übermensch,* but he does not draw out the apolitical consequences of the combination.

3. *Einleitung in das Studium der platonischen Dialoge,* in *Nietzsche's Werke* (Leipzig: Kroner, 1913), III; trans. Olivier Berrichon-Sedeyn as *Introduction à l'étude des dialogues de Platon* (Combas: Eclat, 1991), p. 6.

4. *"Die Geburt der Tragödie,"* in *Werke,* I, 78, 74; trans. Walter Kaufmann, *The Birth of Tragedy* (New York: Random House, 1967), sec. 13, p. 89; sec. 12, p. 85.

5. Ibid., I, 81; sec. 14, p. 91.

6. Ibid., I, 76; sec. 13, p. 83.

7. Ibid., I, 77; sec. 13, p. 88.

8. Ibid., I, 77–78; sec. 13, pp. 88–89.

9. Ibid., I, 82; sec. 14, p. 93.

10. Ibid., I, 87; sec. 15, p. 98.

11. Ibid., I, 79; sec. 14, p. 90.

12. Ibid., I, 85; sec. 15, p. 96.

13. Ibid., I, 79; sec. 14, p. 90.

14. *Die Philosophie im tragischen Zeitalter der Griechen,* III, 361–64; *Philosophy in the Tragic Age of the Greeks,* trans. Marianne Cowan (Chicago: Regnery, 1969), sec. 3, pp. 39–43.

15. See Werner Dannhauser, *Nietzsche's View of Socrates* (Ithaca: Cornell University Press, 1974), p. 86; Walter Kaufman, *Nietzsche: Philosopher, Psychologist, Antichrist* (New York: Random House, 1968), p. 396.

16. *PTAG,* III, 358–60; sec. 2, pp. 34–38.

17. *Vom Nutzen und Nachteil der Historie für das Leben,* in *Werke in Drei Bänden,* ed. Karl Schlechta (Munich: Carl Hanswer Verlag, 1960), I, 229–30; *On the Advantage and Disadvantage of History for Life,* trans. Peter Preuss (Indianapolis: Hackett, 1980), sec. 3, p. 22.

18. See Catherine Zuckert, "Nature, History, and Self: *The Untimely Considerations* of Friedrich Nietzsche," *Nietzsche-Studien* 5 (1976), 55–81.

19. *NN,* I, 279–80; sec. 10, pp. 60–61.

20. *Menschliches, Allzumenschliches; Erster Band,* I, 451; *Human All Too Human,* trans. Alexander Harvey (Chicago: Charles H. Kerr, 1908), p. 26.

21. *Morgenröte,* "Vorrede," I, 3; *Daybreak,* trans. R. J. Hollingdale (Cambridge: Cambridge University Press, 1982), sec. 3, pp. 2–3.

22. *Die Fröhliche Wissenschaft*, II, 116–18; *Joyful Wisdom*, trans. T. Commons (New York: Frederick Ungar, 1964), pp. 153–76.

23. Sarah Kofman's claim that Nietzsche returns to the pre-Socratics, "Metaphor, Symbol, Metamorphosis," in *The New Nietzsche*, pp. 209–21, is based too much on his early writings.

24. *FW*, II, 118; p. 156.

25. *MA*, I, 102; pp. 509, 126.

26. Friedrich Nietzsche, *Die Wille zur Macht; The Will to Power*, trans. Walter Kaufmann and R. J. Hollingdale (New York: Random House, 1967), aph. 428. (As I have followed Kaufmann rather than Schlecta's numbering, I have simply cited the aphorism number in Kaufmann.)

27. "'It is through madness that the greatest good things have come to Greece,' Plato said, in concert with all ancient mankind" (*M*, I, 1023; aph. 14).

28. Ibid., 1246; aph. 496.

29. *Götzen-Dämmerung*, "Das Problem des Sokrates," II, sec. 9, pp. 954–55; *Twilight of the Idols*, in *The Portable Nietzsche*, trans. Walter Kaufmann (New York: Viking, 1954), sec. 14, p. 477.

30. *Jenseits von Gut und Böse*, II, 576; *Beyond Good and Evil*, in *Basic Writings of Nietzsche*, trans. Walter Kaufman (New York: Random House, 1966), sec. 14, p. 212.

31. Ibid., II, 211; sec. 211, p. 326.

32. *WP*, aph. 972.

33. *Zur Genealogie der Moral*, II, 876–77; *On the Genealogy of Morals*, in *Basic Writings*, III, 18: 572.

34. Cf. Robert Pippin, "Irony and Affirmation in Nietzsche's *Thus Spoke Zarathustra*," in Michael Allen Gillespie and Tracy B. Strong, ed., *Nietzsche's New Seas* (Chicago: University of Chicago Press, 1988), p. 47.

35. *Also Sprach Zarathustra*, "Das Nachtlied," II, 363; "Thus Spoke Zarathustra," in *The Portable Nietzsche*, trans. Walter Kaufmann (New York: Viking, 1954), p. 218.

36. "Nachtlied."

37. In listing the virtues of the philosopher of the future at the end of *Beyond Good and Evil* (aph. 284), Leo Strauss points out, Nietzsche thus replaces justice and moderation with compassion and solitude. *Studies in Platonic Political Philosophy* (Chicago: University of Chicago Press, 1983), p. 191.

38. *ASZ*, II, 443–44, Part III, "On Old and New Tablets," sec. 2, p. 309; II, 383–85; Part II, "On Poets," p. 239.

39. *Ecce Homo*, II, 1153–54; "Why I Am a Destiny," sec. 3, pp. 782–85.

40. *GM*, III, 857; III, 10: 551–55.

41. *WP*, aph. 141. Cf. Laurence Lampert, *Nietzsche's Teaching: An Interpretation of "Thus Spoke Zarathustra"* (New Haven: Yale University Press, 1986), pp. 100–200, 268–71.

42. *GD*, "Die 'Verbesserer' der Menschheit," sec. 5; II, 982.

43. *WP*, aph. 142.

44. Ibid., aph. 304.

45. *ASZ*, II, 437–38; Part III, "The Three Evils," pp. 301–2.

46. *GD*, II, 963; "How the 'True World' Finally Became a Fable," p. 485. Stanley Rosen brings out the similarities between Nietzsche and Plato—as well as

the crucial difference—in his gloss on this passage in *The Question of Being: A Reversal of Heidegger* (New Haven: Yale University Press, 1993), p. 159. He also brings out some of the difficulties in Martin Heidegger's interpretation in *Nietzsche* (Pfullingen: Neske, 1961), I, 231.

47. Nietzsche indicated that he did not think Plato presented his full teaching on the nature of philosophy in the *Republic*, when he reiterated his judgment in *GT*, I, 78; sec. 13, p. 89, that Socrates is "the true eroticist" in *GD*, II, 954; "Problem of Socrates," sec. 8, p. 439.

48. *JGB*, II, 648; aph. 190, p. 293.

49. *EH*, II, 1116; sec. 3, p. 736.

50. *JGB*, II, *"Vorrede,"* 566; p. 193.

51. *GM*, II, 860; III: 12, p. 555.

52. *JGB*, II, 805; aph. 5, p. 202.

53. *WP*, aph. 972.

54. *GM*, II, 849; III: 7, pp. 543–44.

55. Kaufmann, *Nietzsche: Philosopher, Psychologist, Antichrist*, p. 398.

56. *GD*, II, 956; "The Problem of Socrates," sec. 12, p. 479.

57. *JGB*, II, 648–49; aph. 191, pp. 193–94.

58. Cf. Tracy Strong, *Friedrich Nietzsche and the Politics of Transfiguration* (Berkeley: University of California Press, 1988), pp. 184–85; Leo Strauss, "Note on the Plan of Nietzsche's *Beyond Good and Evil*," in *SPPP*, p. 183.

59. Steven E. Aschheim, *The Nietzsche Legacy in Germany 1890–1990* (Berkeley: University of California Press, 1992).

60. Cf. the summary of Heidegger's early lectures in Theodore Kisiel, *The Genesis of Heidegger's "Being and Time"* (Berkeley: University of California Press, 1993), pp. 21–68.

61. Martin Heidegger, *Platon: Sophistes*, in *Gesamtausgabe* (Frankfurt: Vittorio Klostermann, 1992), secs. 1–2, 39, 56 (cc).

62. *"Nietzsches Wort 'Gott is tot',"* *Holzwege* (Frankfurt: Vittorio Klostermann, 1952); trans. William Lovitt, *The Question concerning Technology and Other Essays* (New York: Harper and Row, 1977), pp. 53–112.

63. Heidegger began his lectures on Nietzsche by observing that, "For a long time it has been declaimed from chairs of philosophy in Germany that Nietzsche is not a rigorous thinker but a 'poet-philosopher.' Nietzsche does not belong among the philosophers, who think only about abstract, shadowy affairs, far removed from life. If he is to be called a philosopher at all then he must be regarded as a 'philosopher of life'. . . . These common judgments about Nietzsche are in error." *Nietzsche* (Pfullingen: Neske, 1961), Band 1, pp. 13–14; trans. David Farrell Krell (Harper and Row, 1979), vol. 1, p. 5.

64. *Platos dialektische Ethik*, in *Gesammelte Werke* (Tübingen: J. C. B. Mohr, 1986), Band 5; trans. Robert M. Wallace (New Haven: Yale University Press, 1983).

65. "Plato's Educational State" (1941), trans. P. Christopher Smith (New Haven: Yale University Press, 1980), pp. 73–92; *Gesammelte Werke* 5: 246–61.

66. Leo Strauss and Hans-Georg Gadamer, "Correspondence concerning *Wahrheit und Methode*," *The Independent Journal of Philosophy* 2 (1978): 5–12; *Dialogue and Deconstruction: The Gadamer-Derrida Encounter*, ed. Diane P. Michelfelder and Richard E. Palmer (Albany: State University Press of New York, 1989), p. 25.

67. *Philosophy and Law,* originally published in German as *Philosophie und Gesetz* (Berlin: Schocken Verlag, 1935); trans. Fred Baumann (Philadelphia: Jewish Publication Society, 1987), pp. 18–19; "Preface to the English Translation," *Spinoza's Critique of Religion* (New York: Schocken Books, 1965), pp. 1–31.

68. *SPPP,* pp. 168, 174.

69. *The Rebirth of Classical Political Rationalism,* ed. Thomas L. Pangle (Chicago: University of Chicago Press, 1989), pp. 40–41. In this chapter I have argued, however, that Nietzsche was more aware of the overlap than Strauss seems to have thought.

70. *La dissémination* (Paris: Seuil, 1972), pp. 133–97; *Dissemination,* trans. Barbara Johnson (Chicago: University of Chicago Press, 1981), pp. 117–71.

CHAPTER TWO

1. *Nietzsche,* Band 2 (Pfullingen: Neske, 1961), p. 222; trans. Frank A. Capuzzi, *Nietzsche: Nihilism* (New York: Harper and Row, 1982), vol. 4, p. 164; "The End of Philosophy," trans. Joan Stambaugh in *On "Time and Being"* (New York: Harper and Row, 1972), p. 57.

2. *Nietzsche,* Band 1, pp. 180–87, 231–42; trans. David Farrell Krell, *Nietzsche: The Will to Power as Art* (New York: Harper and Row, 1979), vol. 1, pp. 154–60, 200–210.

3. Heidegger emphasized the need to return to the beginning in Greece in order to achieve a new beginning in Germany in his inaugural address as Rector of the University of Freiburg in 1933: "The Self-Assertion of the German University," trans. Karsten Harries, *Review of Metaphysics* 38 (March 1985): 471–73. Since this speech has often been dismissed as a politically charged aberration, the philosophical importance of the argument has generally been missed. Heidegger continued to emphasize the need for a return to the first beginning in order to make a new beginning in the sketch he drew for a second major work to follow *Being and Time,* entitled *Beiträge zur Philosophie,* in *Gesamtausgabe* (Frankfurt: Vittorio Klostermann, 1989), Band 65, pp. 106–66, and in his lectures on *Parmenides, GA* (Frankfurt: Vittorio Klostermann, 1982), Band 54, pp. 201–2, 242.

4. Following Otto Pöggeler, *Philosophie und Politik bei Heidegger* (Freiburg: Alber, 1972) and *The Path of Martin Heidegger's Thought* (Atlantic Highlands: Humanities International Press, 1987), I divide Heidegger's thought into three periods. The way in which Heidegger began each new stage of his thought with a rereading of Plato has become clear only with the publication of his lectures. The lectures he gave on Plato's *Sophist* just before he wrote *Being and Time* were published in his *Gesamtausgabe,* Band 19 (1992); those he gave on the *Republic* and the *Theatetus* in a course *Vom Wesen der Wahrheit* in 1931 in *GA,* Band 34 (1988); the course he gave on *Parmenides* in 1942–43 (which included a lengthy discussion of the myth of Er) in *GA,* Band 54 (1982), trans. Andre Schuwer and Richard Rojcewicz (Bloomington: Indiana University Press, 1992). For a useful summary of Heidegger's statements on Plato, see Alain Boutot, *Heidegger et Platon* (Paris: Presses Universitaires, 1987).

5. "The wish to understand a thinker in his own terms is something else entirely than the attempt to take up a thinker's quest and to pursue it to the core of his thought's problematic. The first is and remains impossible. The second is

rare, and of all things the most difficult." *What Is Called Thinking?*, trans. J. Glenn Gray (New York: Harper and Row, 1968), p. 183. Cf. also pp. 70–72, 76–77; "Plato's Doctrine of the Truth," trans. John Barlow, in William Barrett and Henry D. Aiken, ed., *Philosophy in the Twentieth Century* (New York: Random House, 1962), vol. 3, p. 251; *Introduction to Metaphysics*, trans. Ralph Manheim (New Haven: Yale University Press, 1959), pp. 122, 126. Although in introducing the reading of the "Ode on Man" in *Antigone* he gave in *IM*, p. 148, Heidegger suggested that it is necessary not only to read each part of a text in the context of the work as a whole but also to read each work in the context of the author's entire corpus, as David Halliburton observed in *Poetic Thinking: An Approach to Heidegger* (Chicago: University of Chicago Press, 1981), Heidegger himself never followed such a procedure. Since it is impossible to read all the works of all authors, Heidegger suggested at the beginning of "Plato's Doctrine of the Truth," we must take another tack: we must investigate what was not said—what was only implicit and so hidden—in the text. In reading Nietzsche, for example, Heidegger concentrated on his unfinished *Will to Power* rather than his completed works, because he was particularly interested in what had remained "unthought," i.e., the thoughts or themes Nietzsche himself had worked on without being able to carry out or complete.

6. As Otto Pöggeler has pointed out in "The Topology of Being," reprinted in Joseph Kockelmans, *On Heidegger and Language* (Evanston: Northwestern University Press, 1972), p. 109, in *Being and Time* Heidegger even proposed to establish a "science" of Being!

7. *Platon: Sophistes*, in *GA*, Band 19 (Frankfurt: Vittorio Klostermann, 1992).

8. Descartes severed this connection, when he argued in his first Meditation that we should not like Socrates merely examine various opinions human beings have about the world, but that we should doubt our very senses, the *aisthēsis* which Aristotle argued was not in itself sufficient, but was nevertheless the basis of all knowledge.

9. "Aristotle strove to move from *logos* to *noein*, which is free from *legein*. But his definition of the last *archē*, what is *adiarēton*, is achieved only through the orientation to *logos*. That is shown by the fundamental definition of *on*, the *ousia*, as having the character of *hupokeimenon*, that which already lies before, the completely primary presence. . . . What is spoken about, that is *hupokeimenon* in a formal sense. The fundamental character of Being is brought out of its connection with speech" (p. 225).

10. "The question with regard to Being and Not-being is central to the question of distinguishing philosophy from its negative, the sophist." Although he goes on to observe, "The question of the statesman [is] the Being of man as he exists in the polis," Heidegger characteristically says nothing about the statesman. In these lectures, as in his later discussions of the *polis* in the *Introduction to Metaphysics* and his lectures on *Parmenides*, Heidegger takes the *polis* simply to be the place where truth is disclosed. Thus he continues, "If there is no philosophy, i.e., no *legein* in its real meaning, then there is also no human existence. The anthropological question is also the ontological question, and both are plainly questions of 'logic' in the Greek sense, i.e., *logos*" (pp. 577–78).

11. Contrary to most scholars, who think that Plato intended to write a third dialogue on the philosopher to follow the *Sophist* and *Statesman*, Heidegger argues that he did not, because such a work was not necessary.

12. Heidegger translates *genos* as *Stamm* or tribe to distinguish Plato's usage from the later logical concept of genus and species.

13. *Sophistes*, pp. 275–76.

14. Ibid., p. 485.

15. Plato does not distinguish *eidē* from *genē*, Heidegger points out; that is one of the reasons he is not able to analyze either being or *logos* as clearly as Aristotle. Whereas *genos* points to the principle or *archē* of a thing *in* the thing, that makes it what it is, *eidos* emphasizes the independent factuality of the perceived in the beings and is not the basis upon which the Being of the ideas themselves becomes clear.

16. *Sophistes*, p. 535.

17. Ibid., pp. 558–59.

18. Ibid., pp. 570–71.

19. Ibid., p. 580.

20. Ibid., pp. 580–81.

21. Ibid., p. 467.

22. In the lectures he gave on the *Basic Problems of Phenomenology*, trans. Albert Hofstadter (Bloomington: University of Indiana Press, 1985) shortly after he published *Being and Time*, Heidegger suggested that the original understanding of things in terms of their use could be seen in Plato and Aristotle's use of various *technai* as models of knowledge. In the account of the chair often used to illustrate the meaning of Aristotle's four "causes," the "final cause" in contrast to the material [wood], efficient [carpenter], and formal [idea of a chair] is, of course, the use [to sit on]. Unlike the "pragmatists" who wish to claim him, Heidegger thought the definition of things in terms of their use was *only* primary; it was not sufficient.

23. According to Heidegger, the "sleepy animal" Rousseau imagined living all by himself in "the state of nature" was just that—an animal, not a human being. One of the difficulties with Heidegger's later claim that the historical understanding of "man" is peculiarly German in his lectures on *Schelling's Treatise on the Essence of Human Freedom*, trans. Joan Stambaugh (Athens: Ohio University Press, 1985), pp. 1–2, and *Hölderlin's Hymnen*, in *GA* (Frankfurt: Vittorio Klostermann, 1980), Band 39, is that he ignores the origin of such an account in Rousseau.

24. Heidegger regularly insisted on the difference between "impersonal, natural thinghood" and human existence by arguing that the question should be "who," not "what" "man" is. Hannah Arendt draws the same distinction when she argues that human life should be understood in historical rather than in natural terms. *The Human Condition* (Chicago: University of Chicago Press, 1958), pp. 20–21.

25. In "*Geschlecht: différence sexuell, différence ontologique*," in *Les cahiers de l'herne*, ed. Michel Haar (Paris: Editions de l'Herne, 1983), pp. 419–30; trans. Ruben Berezdivin, "*Geschlecht:* Sexual difference, ontological difference," *Research in Phenomenology* 13 (1983): 65–83, Jacques Derrida emphasizes the asexual character of *Da-sein*, as part or reflection of Heidegger's attempt to define

human existence not in natural, but in essentially historical terms. The problem is the tension that then arises between the *personal* character of *Dasein* and its asexual, hence seemingly impersonal description.

26. "Possibility as an *existentiale* does not mean the free floating ability-to-be in the sense of the 'indifference of the will' *(libertas indifferentia)*. Dasein is, as essentially affective, in each case already caught up in determinate possibilities." *BT*, 144. Cf. Karsten Harries's critique of "democratic" and "existential" readings of *Being and Time* in "Heidegger as a Political Thinker," in Michael Murray, ed., *Heidegger and Modern Philosophy* (New Haven: Yale University Press, 1978), pp. 304–28.

27. There has been a good deal of critical debate about the relation between Heidegger's "existential" analysis of "Being-in-the-world" in Division I of *Being and Time* and the "ontological" analysis of temporality in Division II. Cf. Michael Gelven, *A Commentary on Heidegger's "Being and Time"* (New York: Harper and Row, 1970), pp. 137–42, 173–76; William D. Blattner, "Existential Temporality in *Being and Time*," in *Heidegger: A Critical Reader*, ed. Hubert Dreyfus and Harrison Hall (Cambridge, Mass.: Blackwell, 1992), pp. 99–129; Mark Okrent, *Heidegger's Pragmatism* (New York: Columbia University Press, 1988), p. 196; Frederick Olafson, *Heidegger and the Philosophy of Mind* (New Haven: Yale University Press, 1987), pp. 92–92. What I have tried to show here is that Heidegger's analysis proceeds in three stages—"Being-in-the world," "Being-towards-death," and historical temporality—each of which goes deeper to reveal the fundamentally temporal structure of *Dasein* that makes the phenomena described in the earlier stage possible.

28. "What Is Metaphysics?" In Martin Heidegger, *Basic Writings*, ed. David Farrell Krell (New York: Harper and Row, 1977), pp. 95–116.

29. In response to Rorty's contention that Heidegger's notion of Being is as empty as the traditional concept he criticizes and that Heidegger's history of Being is therefore fundamentally indistinguishable from a traditional account of the history of philosophy, Okrent points out that Heidegger's history is the history not of "Being" but of the "truth of Being," that is, of the gradual disclosure that Being itself is never present or knowable, that the ground of or reason for intelligible existence is and has always been hidden. That is hardly the traditional view! Cf. Richard Rorty, "Overcoming the tradition: Heidegger and Dewey," *Review of Metaphysics* 30 (December 1976): 280–303; Mark B. Okrent, "The Truth of Being and the History of Philosophy," in *Heidegger: A Critical Reader*, pp. 143–58.

30. Heidegger had already noted the privative structure of the Greek word and argued that *a-lētheia* referred "primordially" (originally) to uncoveredness both in his lectures on *Plato's Sophist*, sec. 3, and in *BT*, I.6.44 (b). That uncoveredness belonged in the first instance, however, to *Dasein*, not to the beings or Being itself. It had to be violently "wrested" from the covering of everyday speech. Inasmuch as it emphasized the disclosedness of the beings to man, the interpretation of *a-lētheia* Heidegger began to give in his 1931 lectures was less subjective. Cf. *Vom Wesen*, pp. 70–77.

31. *Vom Wesen*, p. 75. Heidegger did not emphasize the human location of the occurrence of "truth" in the essay he published a decade later "On the Essence of Truth"—he wrote instead of the "open space"—nor did he comment on

the "historicity" of Plato's vision in "Plato's Doctrine of the Truth." By that time he had become concerned about the Nietzsche-like "subjectivity" of his early position and wished to stress the difference, not the similarity between his understanding and that of Plato.

32. Cf. *Vom Wesen*, p. 76, and "Of the Essence of the Truth," *BW*, pp. 118, 126–30, 137–39; "PDT," pp. 258–60.

33. "PDT," pp. 253–55, 260.

34. *Republic* 519c.

35. *Vom Wesen*, pp. 79–91. In "PDT," p. 261, Heidegger suggests that Plato did not make it clear that philosophy proceeded only within the "open space" of the "cave."

36. Cf. William Galston, "Heidegger's Plato: A Critique of *Plato's Doctrine of Truth*," *The Philosophical Forum* 13, no. 4 (summer 1982): 371–84; Adriaan T. Peperzak, "Heidegger and Plato's Idea of the Good," in John Sallis, ed., *Reading Heidegger: Commemorations* (Bloomington: Indiana University Press, 1993), p. 269ff.

37. *Nietzsche* I: 193–94 (165–66).

38. Heidegger bases this contention primarily on the Anaximander fragment. He also refers to Heraclitus's statement that *dikē* consists in strife and observes that in Parmenides' poem the goddess "truth" opens the doors of "justice" to let the poet see the various "ways" he may and may not follow. Cf. *IM*, pp. 160, 165–67; *Early Greek Thinking* (New York: Harper and Row, 1975), pp. 41–43.

39. *Nietzsche* I: 223 (192). In the place cited, Socrates observes that only souls that have had a glimpse of the eternal ideas can be incorporated in human bodies; such a glimpse (and therein possibility for "recollection") constitutes the distinctive feature of *human* being.

40. Cf. Stanley Rosen, "Heidegger's Interpretation of Plato," *The Journal of Existentialism* 7 (summer 1967): 477–504.

41. "PDT," pp. 261–69; *IM*, pp. 180–96.

42. "PDT, p. 269.

43. From beginning to end, Heidegger observed, Nietzsche's work was shaped by his opposition to Plato. *Nietzsche* I: 180–88 (154–60); II: 220–21 (IV: 164). At first, that opposition took the form of a reversal. Whereas Plato had taught that sensible things were mere imperfect copies of eternally existing, completely intelligible ideas, Nietzsche argued that modern philosophy had shown that the "ideas" were merely self-negating projections of emphatically mortal, by no means entirely rational human "beings." In the only world of which human beings really had any experience, in the "physical" or "perceptible" world which Plato himself agreed was characterized by continuous change, any attempt to establish or preserve a lasting condition, enduring order or "true" proposition would not only necessarily fail, but every such attempt would also inevitably be shown to be false. Whereas Plato suggested in his famous critique of poetry in Book X of the *Republic* that, as a copy or imitation of things in the world that were themselves imperfect copies of the "ideas," art was three times removed from the truth, Nietzsche responded that, as the creation of new objects, visions, or perspectives, art was closer than "truth" to the essential character of "reality." Indeed, because continual change required the generation or creation of ever new and different forms of existence, art was more "valuable" than "truth." *Nietzsche*

NOTES TO PAGES 53–58

I: 189–231 (162–99). Platonic philosophy could not be overcome simply by reversing the hierarchy between sensible and supersensible, art and "truth," however. As Nietzsche himself observed in a section of *Twilight of the Idols* entitled "How the 'True World' Finally Became a Fable: The History of an Error," such a reversal perpetuated the same fundamental intellectual structure. If there were no supersensible "real" world, there could no longer be a merely "apparent" world of the senses either. *Nietzsche* I: 231–42 (200–210).

44. *Nietzsche* II: 199–202 (IV: 147–48). "The Word of Nietzsche: 'God Is Dead'," in *The Question concerning Technology and Other Essays* (New York: Harper and Row, 1977), pp. 53–112.

45. Cf. "The Age of the World Picture," *QCT*, pp. 115–54.

46. Heidegger repeatedly refers to note 715 of *The Will to Power* (dated 1888): "The viewpoint of 'value' is the viewpoint of *conditions of preservation* and *enhancement* with regard to complex constructs of relative life-duration within becoming." *Nietzsche* IV: 62.

47. Cf. *Nietzsche* II: 30–40 (IV: 9); "Nietzsche's Word," pp. 96–97; WCT, pp. 57–73.

48. *Discourse on Method*, as translated by Heidegger, *Nietzsche* II:188 (IV: 135).

49. *Nietzsche* II: 225–26 (IV: 169); also *IM*, p. 196, "PDT," p. 263. It is tempting to follow Krell and translate *tauglich* as suitable or fitting, because "good" would then refer to what was ap-propriate and could be ap-propriated—either by becoming transformed into a human possession or by "letting it be." Heidegger had not worked out that duality in the 1930s when he began insisting on the amoral translation of *agathon*.

50. "PDT," pp. 266–68.

51. *Nietzsche* II: 221 (IV: 165).

52. Heidegger publicly admitted his earlier analysis had been wrong in "The End of Philosophy and the Task of Thinking," a lecture first published in French in 1964. Cf. *Time and Being*, p. 70. He may thus have conceded Paul Friedländer's point, although on different grounds. *Plato: An Introduction* (Princeton: Bollingen, 1969), p. 229.

53. In Hesiod's *Theogony*, Heidegger noted, *lēthē* arises out of strife and night. *Parmenides*, p. 130. Heidegger had argued that it was necessary to define *a-lētheia* in terms of its opposite in his first lectures *Vom Wesen der Wahrheit*. At that time, however, he argued that the decisive "turn" occurred in the *Theatetus* when Socrates concluded that there could be no such thing as false opinion in itself; misperception of an object or idea resulted from an erroneous direction or some other form of interference with the observer's "glance." Heidegger made the same argument about the meaning of the cave scene in the *Republic* in "Plato's Doctrine of the Truth." In his lectures on Parmenides, he thus shifted not only the locus of the change in the essence of the truth from Plato to Rome but also the character of the change that had occurred. In an essay he later wrote "On Time and Being," Heidegger admitted that the understanding of truth as correctness could be traced all the way back to Homer. Plato completed, but did not fundamentally change, the original Greek understanding.

54. Heidegger plays on the obvious relation in German between the "true" *(wahre)* and the "secure" *(gewahr)*.

55. Heidegger often referred to a fragment of Heraclitus in which he observed, "The god at Delphi whose oracle is at Delphi neither reveals nor conceals, but only indicates."

56. Heidegger had given a similar account of the *polis* in *IM*, pp. 152–53. In his earlier description Heidegger had also suggested that polities were founded in violence and that the founders would eventually find themselves in conflict with the polities they had founded. As a result of his confrontation with Nietzsche, in the 1940s he dropped the emphasis on the need for violent confrontation with the world in order to disclose the truth he had emphasized in *BT* and *IM*.

57. In order to purify his account of all moral, "other-worldly" elements, Heidegger ignored both the judgment, rewards, and punishments of individual souls when they descended and their choice of (and hence responsibility for) their next way of life on the basis of the knowledge they had or had not obtained in their previous life. Although Heidegger emphasized the introductory play on words in *apologos alkinou*, he did not take account of the way in which Plato's "myth" obviously constitutes a reinterpretation of Odysseus's famous account of his trip to Hades to King Alkinoos. On his trip Odysseus not only learned what was truly valuable in life from the shades of his mother and former associates; he also witnessed the unending punishment of famous criminals.

58. By having individual "souls" assume different shapes and forms when they came forth again on the surface of the earth, Heidegger suggests, Plato showed that the Greeks did not understand human existence "biologically," beginning with the birth of a particular "rational animal" and ending with its death.

59. In the *Nichomachean Ethics*, Heidegger observed, Aristotle thus called the knowledge philosophers possessed, *"daimonic."* It did not have anything to do with the ordinary, everyday concerns of life, but with the extra-ordinary and was thus associated with wonder or the wonder-ful.

60. Without an accent, Heidegger points out, the ancient Greek word for "look" and "goddess" are the same.

61. Heidegger limited this "saying" of the Being of the beings to the Greek language. Other "gods" and "myths," e.g., in the Bible, had a different character.

62. Unlike his successors, Heidegger saw, Plato had recognized the ontological difference. "PDT," p. 263; *WCT*, pp. 227–28.

63. *Parmenides*, p. 208. Heidegger found another such "hint" in Plato's *Theatetus* 194d5, 195a3; *Vom Wesen*, pp. 307–8.

64. Cf. *On Time and Being*, p. 17.

65. Cf. David A. White, *Logic and Ontology in Heidegger* (Columbus: Ohio State University Press, 1985), pp. 174–93.

66. Heidegger equates his initial search for the "meaning" of Being with his later investigation of the "truth" of Being in his *Beiträge*, part 1, sections 34–35. There appears, nevertheless, to be a difference.

67. The subtitle of the *Beiträge* was *Vom Ereignis*. Cf. p. 512: In a note to his "Letter on Humanism," Heidegger observed that *"Ereignis"* had become the word for his major thought since 1936, the time at which he began working on the *Beiträge*. It does not appear in his published works until much later, after the war.

68. Cf. *Beiträge*, pp. 227–90, *Parmenides*, pp. 220–25. Even though Heidegger insisted on the "abysmal" (unbridgeable) difference between the certainty of

faith and the essential ambiguity, hence uncertainty of all conceptions of Being, philosophy or "thought" in *WCT*, pp. 177, 213 (where he also explicitly classifies Soren Kierkegaard as a "religious" as opposed to a "philosophical" thinker), his conception of *Ereignis* nevertheless appears to bear the marks of his earlier theological training as much as his analysis of *Angst* in *Being and Time*, which had explicitly Kierkegaardian roots.

69. *Time and Being*, p. 19.

70. In *De Anima* gamma 8, 431b21, Heidegger reminded the auditors of his lectures on *Parmenides*, Aristotle observed that as the essence of "life," soul was in a certain way, being; that is, in a certain way, the Being of beings was grounded in the understanding of understanding in the soul. Cf. Heidegger's discussion of *anima* and *animus* in *WCT*, pp. 148–49.

71. *Human* beings were distinguished from other forms of life or being by their *logos*, as the Greeks originally saw, because beings became intelligible as such only in word. Although they displayed some sense of their environment, Heidegger argued, animals lacked *logos* because they lacked words. Cf. *Hölderlin's Hymnen*, pp. 61–75; "Letter," 199–207; *Parmenides*, p. 100; *WCT*, pp. 16, 61; and Jacques Derrida's critique in *Of the Spirit* (Chicago: University of Chicago Press, 1989), pp. 47–57.

72. The German phrase for "there is" is *es gibt*.

73. *Eigen* has the same relation to *Eigentum* that proper does to proper-ty; both *eigen* (as in the *eigentlich Da-sein* Heidegger analyzed in *Being and Time*) and proper refer, fundamentally, to a sense of one's own.

74. Cf. Jacques Derrida's discussion of "The Principle of Reason," in *diacritics* (fall 1983): 3–20 in which he explicitly builds on Martin Heidegger, *Der Satz vom Grund* (Pfullingen: Neske, 1957).

75. "What has long since been threatening man with death, and indeed with the death of his own nature, is the unconditional character of mere willing in the sense of purposeful self-assertion in everything. What threatens man in his very nature is the willed view that man, by the peaceful release, transformation, storage, and channeling of the energies of physical nature, could render the human condition, man's being, tolerable for everybody and happy in all respects." "What Are Poets for?" in *Poetry, Language, Thought*, trans. Albert Hofstadter (New York: Harper and Row, 1971), p. 116. Cf. also *Parmenides*, pp. 124–28; *QCT*, pp. 4–6, 12–32.

76. For this reason, Heidegger suggested in *WCT*, pp. 66–67, that nothing fundamental had been decided by the defeat of Germany in World War II. The postwar world was still characterized by the competition of the "superpowers" for total, worldwide dominion, to be achieved primarily by technological means. In the lectures he gave as an *Introduction to Metaphysics* in 1935–36 Heidegger had argued that Germany was caught in a "pincers" between the two technological superpowers, the U.S. and the U.S.S.R. The urgency of their situation might lead the German people to save not only themselves but "mankind" from technological leveling, if Germany would develop an alternative way through a "creative" interpretation of her "metaphysical" tradition.

77. *Parmenides*, pp. 226–39. The difference between Nietzsche and Rilke, according to Heidegger, was that Rilke did not contemplate the emergence of a "superman." He thought unconscious animals were superior to human beings.

His denigration of man was a result of his retaining the biological interpretation of "man" as the rational animal handed down by the metaphysical tradition, in which animality is fundamental.

78. "What Are Poets for?," pp. 91–142.

79. The accuracy of Heidegger's reading of Hölderlin has, not surprisingly, been seriously questioned; cf. Beda Allemann, *Hölderlin und Heidegger* (Zurich: Atlantis, 1956). I have shown the connections between Heidegger's reading of Hölderlin and his political thought more fully in "Martin Heidegger: His Philosophy and His Politics," *Political Theory* 10, no. 1 (February 1990): 51–79. On this connection, see also Frank H. W. Edler, "Philosophy, Language, and Politics: Heidegger's Attempt to Steal the Language of the Revolution in 1933–34," *Social Research* 57, no. 1 (spring 1990): 197–238.

80. " . . . Poetically Man Dwells. . . ," "Building Dwelling Thinking," and "The Thing," in *PLT*, pp. 213–29, 145–61, 165–86.

81. *Hölderlin's Hymnen*, "Remembrance of the Poet" and "Hölderlin and the Essence of Poetry," in *Existence and Being* (Chicago: Henry Regnery, 1949); "Language," in *PLT*, pp. 189–210; "Words" and "Language in the Poem," in *On the Way to Language* (New York: Harper and Row, 1971), pp. 139–56, 159–98.

82. Heidegger announces this original "sameness" in explicit opposition to Plato in *WCT*, p. 10.

83. *Nietzsche* I. As he pointed out at the beginning of his analysis of "The Origin of the Work of Art," Heidegger was also disagreeing with Hegel who had argued that art was *no longer* a means of expressing *Spirit*. One of the most striking differences between Nietzsche and Heidegger's readings of Plato is that Heidegger, for all his praise of poetry, absolutely ignores the poetic form of Plato's philosophic writing. Nietzsche did not.

84. *WCT*, pp. 85–110.

85. *IM*, pp. 115–94; "Letter on Humanism," *BW*, p. 194. In *WCT*, p. 154, Heidegger refers readers to his lectures on "Logic," beginning in 1934.

86. Cf. *WCT*, pp. 11, 30–31, 138–51; *Hölderlins Hymne "Andenken,"* in *GA*, Band 52.

87. One might object that Plato's student Aristotle considered "use" to be the "final cause." Such an understanding applied, however, only to "made" objects and, according to Aristotle, Plato thought there were "ideas" only of natural, not of made entities. For the Greeks the related distinctions between nature and art, nature and convention were fundamental. As Heidegger understands "things," there is no fundamental difference between made and "natural" objects. Both become what they "are" only in "use," that is, in preserving a particular way of life in a given "world" of meaningful relations.

88. *Parmenides*, p. 103; the Greeks knew only differences of "words" or "tongue."

89. "The Thing," *PLT*, p. 168. Heidegger has the "mythical" account of the construction of the cosmos by a *demiourgos* in the *Timaeus* primarily in mind.

90. "What Is a Thing?" p. 168. Heidegger substituted this opposition between *Herstand* and *Geganstand* for that he posed between *Zuhanden* (ready-at-hand) and *Vorhanden* (present-at-hand) in *BT*, because understanding things *Zuhanden* was even closer to a technological understanding than ancient contemplative philosophy.

91. As Werner Marx points out in "Poetic Dwelling and the Role of the Poet," *On Heidegger and Language,* pp. 245–47, this "world" has yet to exist. Only a few solitary poets and "thinkers" are calling "men" to turn to it.

92. As Heidegger observes in his lecture on "Building, Dwelling, Thinking," life in this world "remains for man's everyday experience that which is from the outset 'habitual'" (*PLT,* p. 147). The German word for 'habitual' or 'customary', *Gewohnte,* is obviously a form of *wohnen,* translated as "to dwell" or "in-habit."

93. 'Country' here is intended to signify not only 'homeland' but also the 'country' as opposed to the 'city.' Heidegger's poetic landscapes are as emphatically nonurban as they are anticosmopolitan. Cf. Martin Heidegger, "Why I Remain in the Provinces," in Thomas Sheehan, ed. *Heidegger: The Man and the Thinker* (Chicago: Precedent, 1981), pp. 27–30.

94. It was no accident that he publicly endorsed Nietzsche's analysis of the modern predicament in his most, indeed, his sole, explicitly political statement as Rector of the University of Freiburg, or that he withdrew rather quickly from immediate political involvement and began emphasizing the differences as well as the similarities between his own thought, Nietzsche, and official Nazi ideology. Cf. especially the lectures translated into English in *Nietzsche* (New York: Harper and Row, 1987), vol. 3, and the *Beiträge* in passing.

95. Most recent work on Heiddegger's politics has concerned his involvement with the Nazis and the connection, if any between this and his philosophy. In "Martin Heidegger: His Politics and His Philosophy" *Political Theory,* pp. 51–79, I argued that he was never a racist like the official Nazi ideologists, but that there was a connection between his "thought" with its emphasis on the centrality of language and history in the definition of a people and his joining the National Socialist Party. Recent works on Heidegger's politics include Victor Farias, *Heidegger and Nazism,* trans. Paul Burrell and Gabriel R. Ricci (Philadelphia: Temple University Press, 1989); Hugo Ott, *Martin Heidegger: A Political Life,* trans. Allan Blunden (New York: Basic Books, 1993); Pierre Bourdieu, *The Political Ontology of Martin Heidegger,* trans. Peter Collier (Stanford: Stanford University Press, 1991); Richard Wolin, ed., *The Heidegger Controversy: A Critical Reader* (New York: Columbia University Press, 1991); Philippe Lacoue-Labarthe, *Heidegger, Art and Politics: The Fiction of the Political,* trans. Chris Turner (Oxford: Blackwell, 1990); Luc Ferry and Alain Renaut, *Heidegger and Modernity,* trans. Franklin Philip (Chicago: University of Chicago Press, 1990); Fred Dallmayr, *The Other Heidegger* (Ithaca: Cornell University Press, 1993).

96. When David Krell first attempted to show the fundamental importance of Nietzsche for Heidegger's thought, he encountered resistance, because Nietzsche did not appear to play a major role in Heidegger's first major work, *Being and Time.* At the end of *BT,* Heidegger admitted that Nietzsche had also identified the three essential parts or aspects of a temporal existence or history in his early essay on "The Uses and Disadvantages of History for Life," but Heidegger then argued, Nietzsche did not see the inherent connection of the three. Heidegger had changed his mind about the character of Nietzsche's insight into the essential temporality or historicity of human life by the time he gave his famous series of lectures on *Nietzsche.* In interpreting the significance of "The Vision and the Riddle" in *Thus Spoke Zarathustra, Nietzsche* I:293–97 (II:41–44), Heidegger emphasized Nietzsche's insight into the connection between past, present, and

future. Cf. David Krell, *Intimations of Mortality* (University Park: Pennsylvania State University Press, 1986), pp. 126–37.

CHAPTER THREE

1. *Platos dialektische Ethik* in *Gesammelte Werke* (Tübingen: J. C. B. Mohr, 1986), Band 5, p. 161; *Plato's Dialectical Ethics*, trans. Robert W. Wallace (New Haven: Yale University Press, 1991), xxxi–xxxii (my translation).

2. *Philosophical Apprenticeships*, trans. Robert R. Sullivan (Cambridge, Mass.: MIT Press, 1985), 38–39, 49.

3. Because Gadamer treats Hegel primarily as a means of attaining a more genuine understanding of dialectic from Plato, I will not be examining Gadamer's interpretation of Hegel per se. Although in *Truth and Method*, trans. Joel Weinsheimer and Donald G. Marshall (New York: Crossroad, 1990), Gadamer states that "whoever wants to learn from the Greeks always has to learn from Hegel first" (p. 460 [*GW* (Tübingen: J. C. B. Mohr, 1986), Band 1, p. 464]), both in *TM* and in his essay on "Hegel and the Dialectic of the Ancient Philosophers," in *Hegel's Dialectic: Five Hermeneutical Studies*, trans. P. Christopher Smith (New Haven: Yale University Press, 1976), pp. 5–34 (*GW* III: 3–28), Gadamer argues that Hegel is important primarily for insisting on the need to go back and recapture the Greek understanding. Hegel's own understanding of Greek philosophy was mistaken. In *TM* he writes, "Hegel's [attempt to revive Greek dialectic is] . . . a magnificent reminder, even if unsuccessful of what dialectic really was and is. Hegel's dialectic is a monologue of thinking that tries to carry out in advance what matures little by little in every genuine dialogue" (p. 369 [*GW* I: 375]). In "The Heritage of Hegel," *Reason in the Age of Science*, trans. Frederick G. Lawrence (Cambridge, Mass.: MIT Press, 1981), p. 44 (*GW* IV: 468), he observes, "What so formed my thinking was a personalized, dialogical Hegel behind whom there always stood the daily, thoughtful intercourse with the Platonic dialogues."

4. *The Idea of the Good in Platonic-Aristotelian Philosophy*, trans. P. Christopher Smith (New Haven: Yale University Press, 1986), p. 5 (*GW* VII: 130).

5. *TM*, pp. 293, xxxvii (*GW* I: 298, *GW* II: 447).

6. *IG*, p. 6 (*GW* VII: 130).

7. Robert R. Sullivan, *Political Hermeneutics: The Early Thinking of Hans Georg Gadamer* (University Park: Pennsylvania State University Press, 1989), pp. 88, 134, 141–42, admits the influence of Heidegger, but argues that Stefan Georg was more important.

8. In his lectures on Plato's *Sophistes* (p. 237), Heidegger explicitly told his auditors (of whom Gadamer was surely one) that they ought to identify Socrates with Plato. Heidegger did distinguish Socrates from Plato much later in *What Is Called Thinking?*, p. 17, when he suggested that Socrates was the "purest" thinker of the West, because he did not write, but that this purity did not make him a better thinker.

9. *PDE*, p. 2. (*GW* V: 5–6).

10. In support of this position, Gadamer cites the *Symposium* 175e where Socrates says that, because he is a bodily creature who necessarily changes, he must constantly strive to recapture the knowledge he once had.

11. *PDE*, pp. 4–5 (*GW* V: 6–7). In the more detailed analysis of the argument

of the *Philebus* Gadamer gives in part 2 of *PDE,* he also suggests that Socrates' analysis of anticipated pleasure and the possibility of its basis in erroneous judgment indicates that Plato also shared a Heidegger-like insight into the future orientation of human existence.

12. Ibid.

13. Cf. *Being and Time* I: 3, 15–16, pp. 95–107 (H67–76).

14. Ibid., Int. II, p. 47 (H25).

15. "Plato" in *Heideggers Wege, GW* III: 238–48; trans. John W. Stanley, *Heidegger's Ways* (Albany: State University of New York Press, 1994), pp. 81–94.

16. *PDE,* pp. 3–7 (*GW* V: 6–9).

17. *IG,* p. 60 (*GW* VII: 160).

18. Ibid., p. 16 (*GW* VII: 136).

19. *PDE,* pp. 52–54 (*GW* V: 39).

20. Without saying as much explicitly, Gadamer thus challenges Heidegger's contention in *Basic Problems of Phenomenology* (and elsewhere) that Plato and Aristotle based their understanding not only of knowledge but also, ultimately, of being on an analysis of *technē* (and that their thought was, therefore, the root of modern technology). Cf. *Basic Problems,* part I, ch. 2, 11(b)–12(a-b). "In technē," Gadamer emphasized, "the process of production is subordinated to utility, and this subordination sets a limit to technē which, as Aristotle points out (EN Zeta 4), excludes it from making any claim to be an arete" (*IG,* p. 80 [*GW* VII: 172]).

21. The so-called "platonic" virtues were traditional virtues, Gadamer points out. Plato radically reinterpreted, if he did not simply subvert, the tradition by arguing that they were at bottom all one, i.e., knowledge. *IG,* p. 64 (*GW* VII: 163); *Dialogue and Dialectic,* trans. P. Christopher Smith (New Haven: Yale University Press, 1980), p. 83 (*GW* V: 256).

22. Cf. Martin Heidegger, "Plato's Doctrine of the Truth," in W. Barrett and H. D. Aiken, eds., *Philosophy in the Twentieth Century* (New York: Random House, 1962), pp. 255–65.

23. The descriptions of the "sophist" at 229e–231a and 268b–c could easily be applied to Socrates. In emphasizing his "patricidal" difference from Parmenides at 241d–251a, the Stranger also indicates that neither he nor Plato was an Eleatic.

24. By maintaining the existential differences among the interlocutors, Platonic dialogues image not only the actual process whereby specific individuals come to an understanding, but also the problematic character of the intelligibility of the whole, which consists of an agreement (or sameness) in word *(logos)* that somehow penetrates and organizes the various deeds or facts *(ergoi)* of particular, bodily forms of existence. By way of contrast, Gadamer observes, the arguments in "scientific" treatises are addressed to readers with no particular or defining characteristics and who are, therefore, indistinguishable from the disembodied mind of the author. A consistent scientific argument is, therefore, self-sufficient; what convinces the author should, in principle, suffice to convince any reasonable reader. *PDE,* pp. 38–44 (*GW* V: 29–33). To the extent to which the Platonic dialogues depart from this "scientific" model by virtue of their literary form, Plato did not suffer from the "phonocentric" illusion Jacques Derrida argues was characteristic of philosophy from Plato through Husserl.

25. "In a famous passage in the *Metaphysics* (1004b.22b)," Gadamer observes, Aristotle thus declared that "the difference between dialectic and sophism consists only in the *proairēsis tou biou* (the choice or commitment in life)." *DD*, p. 6 (*GW* VI: 174); *IG*, p. 100 (*GW* VII: 183).

26. *PDE*, pp. 51–52, 55–57.

27. "Plato and the Poets," *DD*, p. 48 (*GW* V: 194); cf. also "Plato's Educational State," *DD*, pp. 73–76 (*GW* V: 249–51).

28. "PP," *DD*, pp. 54–55 (*GW* V: 198–99).

29. "PP," *DD*, pp. 56–57 (*GW* V: 199–200).

30. "PES," *DD*, p. 87 (*GW* V: 259).

31. "PES," *DD*, p. 90 (*GW* V: 261).

32. "PP," *DD*, p. 58 (*GW* V: 201).

33. "PP," *DD*, pp. 65–66 (*GW* V: 206–7).

34. "PP," *DD*, pp. 66–67 (*GW* V: 207).

35. "PP," *DD*, p. 71 (*GW* V: 210).

36. *PA*, p. 78. Cf. Fred Dallmayr, "Hermeneutics and Justice," in *Festivals of Interpretation* (Albany: State University of New York Press, 1990), pp. 95–105.

37. "PES," *DD*, p. 81 (*GW* V: 255).

38. "PP," p. 52 (*GW* V: 197).

39. Heidegger resigned as rector and withdrew from politics when he discovered how serious the differences were between him and the Nazi ministry of education. However, he never repudiated the party or his own past involvement. As rector, he organized a reeducation camp for students; Gadamer was later sent to such a camp. After the war, Gadamer was made chancellor of the University of Leipzig, partly because he had not had any involvement with the criminal regime; Heidegger was not allowed to teach by the denazification authorities.

40. *TM*, p. 263 (*GW* I: 268). Gadamer has in mind, I believe, the criticisms of Heidegger written by his former student Karl Löwith and Eric Weil in *Les Temps Modernes* 2, no. 14 (November 1946): 343–60, and 3, no. 22 (July 1947): 128–38.

41. Cf. Martin Heidegger, *Poetry, Language, Thought*, trans. Albert Hofstadter (New York: Harper and Row, 1971), xxii–xxiii.

42. "Heidegger's Later Philosophy," in *Philosophical Hermeneutics*, trans. David E. Linge (Berkeley: University of California Press, 1976), p. 216 (*GW* VI: 252).

43. Ibid.

44. Cf. n. 9. Just as Heidegger's Being has to withdraw so that the beings can emerge, Gadamer pointed out, so in the *Philebus* the Good itself has to withdraw so that it can show itself in the beautiful.

45. "The Origin of the Work of Art," *PLT*, pp. 71, 75.

46. As Robert Bernasconi observes in "Bridging the Abyss: Heidegger and Gadamer," *Research in Phenomenology* 16 (1986): 1, there has been little study of the relation between the two thinkers, much less the differences between them.

47. *TM*, xxxvii (*GW* II: 447).

48. *TM*, xxxvii–xxxviii (*GW* II: 447–48).

49. Francis J. Ambrosio, "Dawn and Dusk: Gadamer and Heidegger on Truth," *Man and World* 19 (1986): 21–53, also argues that Gadamer took his understanding of truth in *TM* from Heidegger (without explicitly saying so).

50. Gadamer characteristically does not make his difference with Heidegger

explicit. The difference becomes visible, however, if one compares Gadamer's defense of his own hermeneutics from the charge that "it lacks a critical principle in relation to tradition" in the foreword to the second edition of *Truth and Method* and his account of the argument of *Being and Time* in "Heidegger's Later Philosophy," pp. 215–17. Gadamer was well aware of the distinction between authentic and inauthentic, "idle chatter" and real communication, which figured so prominently in Heidegger's early work and which Gadamer silently dropped.

51. *TM*, p. 132 (*GW* I: 135).

52. Ibid., p. 114 (*GW* I: 119–20).

53. Ibid., p. 115 (*GW* I: 120).

54. In "The Happening of Tradition: The Hermeneutics of Gadamer and Heidegger," *Man and World* 2 (April 1969): 374–77, Theodore Kisiel also points out that the emphasis on the individual in Heidegger is dropped by Gadamer, but he does not see or draw out the political implications of the change.

55. As Tsenay Serequeberhan points out in "Heidegger and Gadamer: Thinking as 'Meditative' and as 'Effective-Historical Consciousness'," *Man and World* 20 (1987): 59, "Gadamer fails to bring out the element of resolute 'releasement' which is central to Heidegger's conception of thinking. For Heidegger, resolute 'releasement' requires what J. L. Mehta calls a 'metaphysical archaeology' that enables the interpreter to pierce through to the primordial experience out of which the text originated."

56. *TM*, p. 378 (*GW* I: 383). Emphasis in the original.

57. On the basis of his study of theology, Gadamer thus disputes, in advance as it were, Derrida's contention in *Speech and Phenomena* that the beliefs that human beings can share exactly the same understanding and that speech has priority over writing originate in the experience of the simultaneity of thought and expression when one hears oneself utter one's own thoughts as one thinks them.

58. Cf. "Man and Language," *Philosophical Hermeneutics*, pp. 59–68 (*GW* II: 147–54).

59. *TM*, p. 416 (*GW* I: 420).

60. Ibid., p. 458 (*GW* I: 462).

61. Ibid., p. 457 (*GW* I: 461).

62. Ibid., p. 474 (*GW* I: 478).

63. Joel C. Weinsheimer, *Gadamer's Hermeneutics* (New Haven: Yale University Press, 1985), p. 213, points out the echoes of Heidegger's discussions of language in Gadamer, but not the differences between them.

64. Heidegger would probably respond that by identifying Being with language, Gadamer has humanized and thereby subjectivized it. But paraphrasing the line from Hölderlin to the effect that we are a "conversation," which Heidegger himself often quoted, Gadamer points out that he has shown that language is not merely a human invention—individual or social—and its operation is not, therefore, subject to human will.

65. In "The Heritage of Hegel," *RAS*, p. 56 (*GW* IV: 477), Gadamer observes, "The hermeneutics I developed was also based upon finitude and the historical character of *Dasein*, and it tried to carry forward Heidegger's turn away from his transcendental account of himself, albeit not in Heidegger's direction of an inspiration from the poetic *mythos* of Hölderlin but rather in a return to the open

dialectic of Plato and in reliance upon that 'dampening down of subjectivity,' as Julius Stenzel called it."

66. Cf. "Über leere und erfüllte Zeit," *GW* IV: 476–83.

67. Gadamer identifies the need for integration in hermeneutics especially with Hegel; cf. *TM*, pp. 165–69. He criticizes Heidegger for not correctly perceiving the relation between his own thought and Hegel's, because he insisted too much on his own difference and originality. Cf. "Hegel and Heidegger," *Hegel's Dialectic*, pp. 100–116 (*GW* III: 87–104), as well as "The Heritage of Hegel," *RAS*, pp. 56–63, 65–68 (*GW* IV: 476–83).

68. *PDE*, xxix–xxx (*GW* V: 159).

69. "Plato's Unwritten Dialectic," *DD*, p. 125 (*GW* VI: 130).

70. Gadamer cites "Die griechische Logistik und die Entstehung der Algebra," in *Quellen und Studien zur Geschichte der Mathematik, Astronomie und Physik*, sec. B, 1934, vol. 3, no. 1, *DD*, p. 129 (*GW* VI: 133). A brief version of Klein's argument can be found in English in "The Concept of Number in Greek Mathematics and Philosophy," pp. 43–52, in *Jacob Klein: Lectures and Essays*, ed. Robert B. Williamson and Elliott Zuckerman (Annapolis: St. John's College Press, 1985), pp. 43–52. The longer and fuller version is to be found in his *Greek Mathematical Thought and the Origin of Algebra*, trans. Eva Brann (Cambridge, Mass.: MIT Press, 1968).

71. In all his later analyses of the *Phaedo*, Gadamer emphasized, Socrates is talking to Pythagoreans. Cf. "The Proofs of the Immortality of the Soul in Plato's *Phaedo*," *DD*, pp. 21–37 (*GW* VI: 187–200); *IG*, pp. 25, 29 (*GW* VII: 142, 144).

72. "Number," pp. 49–50.

73. The purpose of *Greek Mathematical Thought and the Origin of Algebra* was to show that in the transition from ancient to modern mathematics the concept of number had been gradually changed so as to cover over its commonsensical, experiential foundation in the act of counting. Not considering one or the unit a number, that original concept was emphatically *not* reductive.

74. "Unwritten Dialectic," *DD*, pp. 132–33 (*GW* VI: 135–36).

75. Ibid., p. 143 (*GW* VI: 143–44).

76. Ibid., p. 145 (*GW* VI: 145).

77. Ibid., p. 146 (*GW* VI: 146).

78. Ibid., p. 154 (*GW* VI: 152).

79. "The indirect tradition . . . articulates and confirms the limitedness of all human knowing and shows why the highest possibility of such knowing must be named not sophia but philosophia" (ibid., p. 155 [*GW* VI: 153]).

80. Cf. Leo Strauss and Hans-Georg Gadamer, "Correspondence concerning *Wahrheit und Methode*," *The Independent Journal of Philosophy* 2 (1978): 5–12; and Georgia Warnke, *Gadamer: Hermeneutics, Tradition and Reason* (Stanford: Stanford University Press, 1987), pp. 136–37.

81. "A Review of Gadamer's *Truth and Method*," in *The Hermeneutic Tradition*, ed. Gayle L. Ormiston and Alan D. Schrift (Albany: State University of New York Press, 1990), p. 236.

82. "Reply to My Critics," in *Hermeneutic Tradition*, p. 288 (*GW* II: 268).

83. Habermas, "Review of Gadamer's *Truth and Method*," p. 239.

84. "Reply," pp. 287–88 (*GW* II: 267–68).

85. Ibid., p. 277 (*GW* II: 255). In *Beyond Objectivism and Relativism* (Phila-

delphia: University of Pennsylvania Press, 1982), pp. 150–65, Richard Bernstein poses this question very forcibly when he asks not merely, along with Habermas, whether Gadamer makes sufficient room for criticism but also whether Gadamer shows what kinds of societies or social structures encourage the development of practical reason and, concretely, what sorts of practical norms are involved.

86. *RAS,* pp. 86–87 (*GW* IV: 227–28).

87. Cf. Leo Strauss, *What Is Political Philosophy? and Other Essays* (Glencoe, Ill.: Free Press, 1959), pp. 39–40; Jacques Derrida, *"Differance,"* in *Speech and Phenomena,* trans. David B. Allison (Evanston, Ill.: Northwestern University Press, 1973), pp. 145–60.

88. *RAS,* p. 37.

CHAPTER FOUR

1. Leo Strauss and Hans-Georg Gadamer, "Correspondence concerning *Wahrheit und Methode,"* *Independent Journal of Philosophy* 2 (1978): 5–12.

2. *Natural Right and History* (Chicago: University of Chicago Press, 1953), pp. 26–34. Cf. Richard Kennington, "Strauss's Natural Right and History," *Review of Metaphysics* 35 (September 1981): 61–62.

3. Cf. Hans-Georg Gadamer, *Philosophical Apprenticeships,* trans. Robert R. Sullivan (Cambridge, Mass.: MIT Press, 1985), pp. 17, 38, 40–42, 60–69. In the mid-1920s Gadamer, Löwith, and Krüger were Heidegger's chief assistants. Gadamer's book suggests that Klein was closer to the Heidegger circle than Strauss, perhaps in part because he left Marburg in the mid-1920s for Berlin. Strauss himself has recorded his impression of Heidegger (as well as of Klein) at the time in "A Giving of Accounts: Jacob Klein and Leo Strauss," *The College* (April 1970): 3: "One of the unknown young men in Husserl's entourage was Heidegger. I attended his lecture course from time to time without understanding a word, but sensed that he dealt with something of the utmost importance to man as man. I understood something on one occasion: when he interpreted the beginning of the *Metaphysics.* I had never heard nor seen such a thing—such a thorough and intensive interpretation of a philosophic text. On my way home I visited Rosenzweig and said to him that compared to Heidegger, Max Weber, till then regarded by me as the incarnation of the spirit of science and scholarship, was an orphan child." What Strauss "could not stomach was [Heidegger's] moral teaching, for despite his disclaimer, he had such a teaching. The key term is resoluteness . . . [which leads in] a straight line . . . to his siding with the so-called Nazis in 1933. After that I ceased to take any interest in him for about two decades."

4. "Correspondence," p. 5.

5. In a later exchange with Jacques Derrida, Gadamer stated that "Leo Strauss got to the heart of the matter in saying that for Heidegger, it is Nietzsche, while for me it is Dilthey, who forms the starting point for critique." "Text and Interpretation," trans. Dennis J. Schmidt and Richard Palmer, in *Dialogue and Deconstruction: The Gadamer-Derrida Encounter* (Albany: State University of New York Press, 1989), p. 25.

6. Karl Löwith and Leo Strauss, "Correspondence," *Independent Journal of Philosophy* 5/6 (1988): 183.

7. Berlin: Akademie-Verlag, 1930; trans. E. M. Sinclair, *Spinoza's Critique of Religion* (New York: Schocken Books, 1965).

8. Kenneth Hart Green, "'In the Grip of the Theological-Political Predicament': The Turn to Maimonides in the Jewish Thought of Leo Strauss," in Alan Udoff, ed., *Leo Strauss' Thought: Toward a Critical Engagement* (Boulder and London: Lynne Riemer, 1991), p. 63, note 15, points out that Strauss restructured the section and chapter or subsection numbers for the English translation to make his demonstration of Spinoza's failure to refute revelation the central section. (According to the rules of reading Strauss formulated almost two decades after he published his first study of Spinoza, the central chapter, item, or discussion is often the most important.) Cf. *Persecution and the Art of Writing* (Glencoe, Ill.: Free Press, 1952), p. 24.

9. Cf. *Spinoza*, pp. 136, 141, 143–44, 205–6; *Philosophy and Law: Essays toward the Understanding of Maimonides and His Predecessors*, trans. Fred Bauman (Philadelphia: Jewish Publication Society, 1987), pp. 10, 13 (originally published as *Philosophie und Gesetz* [Berlin: Schocken Verlag, 1935]).

10. *Gay Science*, sec. 125; cf. Martin Heidegger, "The Word of Nietzsche," in *The Question concerning Technology and Other Essays* (New York: Harper and Row, 1977), pp. 53–112.

11. *Spinoza*, "Preface to the English Translation," p. 30. This observation, coming so early in Strauss's own thought, would also seem to be fatal to Stanley Rosen's contention in *Hermeneutics as Politics* (New York: Oxford University Press, 1987), p. 111, that Strauss chose philosophy rather than revelation, ultimately, as an act of will. Cf. Christopher Colmo, "Reason and Revelation in the Thought of Leo Strauss," *Interpretation* 18, no. 1 (fall 1990): 145–58.

12. *Philosophy and Law*, p. 18.

13. Strauss devoted a large part of his later study of modern political philosophy to bringing out its sometimes hidden antitheological animus. "We have devoted what at first glance seems to be a disproportionately large space to Machiavelli's thought concerning religion," he observes in his *Thoughts on Machiavelli* (Glencoe, Ill.: Free Press, 1958). "This impression is due to a common misunderstanding of the intention, not only of Machiavelli but also of a whole series of political thinkers who succeeded him. We no longer understand that in spite of great disagreements among those thinkers, they were united by the fact that they all fought one and the same power—the kingdom of darkness, as Hobbes called it; that fight was more important to them than any merely political issue. This will become clearer to us the more we learn again to understand those thinkers as they understood themselves and the more familiar we become with the art of allusive and elusive writing which all of them employ, although to different degrees. The series of those thinkers will then come to sight as a line of warriors who occasionally interrupt their fight against their common enemy to engage in a more or less heated but never hostile disputation among themselves" (p. 231).

14. Cf. Strauss's later statement in *What Is Political Philosophy? and Other Essays* (Glencoe, Ill.: Free Press, 1959), p. 37: "The difference between the classics and us with regard to democracy consists *exclusively* in a different estimate of the virtues of technology." (Emphasis added.)

15. "Modern natural science could be the foundation or the means of the victory of the Enlightenment over Orthodoxy only as long as the old concept of truth, which the Enlightenment had already destroyed, still ruled. . . . But this was a delusion. One was forced to ascertain that the 'goal- and value-free' nature

of modern natural science could tell man nothing about 'ends and values'. . . . If, therefore, modern natural science cannot justify the modern ideal, and if, correspondingly, the connection between the modern ideal and modern natural science is unmistakable, then the question must be posed whether, on the contrary, the modern ideal is in truth not the ground of a modern natural science, *and whether it is not also precisely a new belief rather than a new knowledge that justified the Enlightenment.*" *Philosophy and Law,* p. 15.

16. In "The Modern World of Leo Strauss," *Political Theory* 20, no. 3 (August 1992): 448–72, Robert Pippin argues that Strauss did not take adequate account of the nobility of freedom as a goal in later modern philosophy, e.g., in the works of Kant and Hegel. He ignores Strauss's early statement in *Philosophy and Law,* p. 16: "Even the most believing adherents of [modern natural] science admit that the rise of a new ideal (a new representation of the correct life of man) was decisive for the victory of Enlightenment over Orthodoxy, even if it only followed the success of natural science. Indeed, according to their view, the ideal of Freedom, understood as the autonomy of man and his culture, has this significance. But this view can be maintained only if one confuses 'freedom', understood as autonomy, with the 'freedom' of conscience, the 'freedom' of philosophizing, political 'freedom' or the ideal of autarky of the philosophical tradition. Freedom, understood as the autonomy of man and his culture, is neither the original nor the eventual justification of the Enlightenment. Rather, this ideal was only viable during an interval . . . when . . . one could forget the state of nature that alone could legitimize civilization." Strauss explicitly recognized the nobility of freedom as the goal of late modern philosophy. (As he reminds readers of his posthumously published *Studies in Platonic Political Philosophy* [Chicago: University of Chicago Press, 1983], pp. 31, 167–73, 233–47, he began his philosophical studies under the inspiration of the neo-Kantian Hermann Cohen.) Strauss insisted, however, that the articulation of this modern goal masked the tension between the requirements of political independence and the requirements of intellectual inquiry (a tension Strauss emphasized in his subsequent studies of ancient political philosophy) *and* that the civilization erected to secure this goal still depended for its rationale on the need to escape from the state of nature.

17. "*Begriff,*" in *Spinoza,* pp. 346–47. Heinrich Meier documents the ways in which Schmitt admitted the accuracy of Strauss's critique and responded to it by making changes in later editions of *The Concept of the Political* in *Carl Schmitt, Leo Strauss und "Der Begriff des Politischen"* (Stuttgart: J. B. Metzlersche Verlagsburachhandlung, 1988), pp. 11–92, to bring out the "theological" foundations of his own antiliberal position.

18. "*Begriff,*" in *Spinoza,* p. 351. It seems important to emphasize Strauss's disagreement with Schmitt's definition of the political in light of Hannah Arendt's accusation, reported by Elisabeth Young-Bruehl, *Hannah Arendt: For Love of the World* (New Haven: Yale University Press, 1982), p. 98, reiterated by Luc Ferry, *Political Philosophy I: The Ancients and the Moderns,* trans. Franklin Philip (Chicago: University of Chicago Press, 1990), pp. 20–21, that Strauss supported positions taken by a party that had no place for him as a Jew. It is hard to find any basis for her accusation except his qualified sympathy for critics of liberalism like Nietzsche and Schmitt. Like many Jewish university students, Strauss had been a Zionist from the time he was seventeen years of age ("A Giving of

Accounts," p. 2); his study of Spinoza convinced him that a secular Jewish state was incapable of preserving that which made Jews distinctively Jewish. ("Introduction," *Philosophy and Law,* p. 19; "Preface," *Spinoza,* pp. 1–31.) During the 1920s all Strauss's publications were in "Jewish Studies"; he worked for a Jewish Institute. (As I have argued in "A Heideggerian Strauss?," *The Review of Politics* 53, no. 4 (fall 1991): 723–25, Ferry's analysis of Strauss as a Heideggerian suffers from his failure to take account of the role or place of the conflict between reason and revelation Strauss began emphasizing in his early studies of Jewish authors.)

19. *The Political Philosophy of Hobbes: Its Basis and Its Genesis,* trans. Elsa M. Sinclair (Oxford: Clarendon Press, 1936 [reissued by the University of Chicago Press, 1952]), p. 5. He later disavowed his claims with regard to Hobbes's status as the founder of modernity in favor of Machiavelli (whose thought was clearly not based on the emergence of modern natural science) in the "Preface to the American Edition," xix–xx. Perhaps for that reason, in his later writings on Hobbes, Strauss conceded natural science a larger role in the formation and articulation of his thought. Cf. *NRH,* pp. 166–202; *WIPP,* pp. 170–96.

20. *Hobbes,* p. 113.

21. "Preface," *Spinoza,* p. 31. Hillel Fradkin also emphasizes the importance of Strauss's studies of medieval Judaism in the development of his thought as a whole in "Philosophy and Law: Leo Strauss as a Student of Medieval Jewish Thought," *Review of Politics* 53, no. 1(winter 1991): 40–52.

22. *Spinoza,* "Preface to the English Translation," p. 31.

23. *Philosophy and Law,* p. 20.

24. In "Quelques remarques sur la science politique de Maimonide et de Farabi," in *Revue des Etudes Juives* 100 (1936): 1–37, trans. Robert Bartlett, *Interpretation* 18, no. 1 (fall 1990): 4–5, Strauss states that "it is not the Bible and the Koran, but perhaps the New Testament, and certainly the Reformation and modern philosophy, which brought about the break with ancient thought. The guiding idea upon which the Greeks and the Jews agree is precisely the idea of the divine law as a single and total law which is at the same time religious law, civil law and moral law."

25. *Persecution and the Art of Writing,* pp. 18–21.

26. *Philosophy and Law,* p. 83. The implicit contrast, I believe, is to the "son of God" who, according to the Gospel of John, enunciates the "Word" [*Logos*]). As both Gadamer, *TM,* pp. 418–28, and Jacques Derrida, "How to Avoid Speaking: Denials," Ken Frieden, trans., *Derrida and Negative Theology* (Albany: State University of New York Press, 1992), p. 103; "*Comment ne pas parler: Dénégations,*" in *Psyche* (Paris: Galilee, 1987), p. 565, point out, the word was the means or concept through which Greek philosophy and scriptural revelation were synthesized first in Christianity and later in Western philosophy.

27. To be sure, in the *Guide* (II: 35) Maimonides seems to suggest that, in contrast to all other prophets, Moses' prophecy did not proceed through his imagination; he received the law directly from God. In his later essay on "How to Begin to Study the *Guide for the Perplexed,*" in *Liberalism: Ancient and Modern* (New York: Basic Books, 1968), pp. 161–66, Strauss argues not only that Maimonides admits, in deed, by explaining the bodily images of God in the Torah, that Moses' prophecy *does,* in fact, employ images, but also that he suggests that

Isaiah and the postbiblical commentators represented an improvement on the Torah insofar as they gave a less corporeal account of the original revelation.

28. In his "Remarks," Strauss comments, "That Maimonides characterizes a law which aims at the perfection of the intelligence as a 'divine law' appears, at first glance, surprising: cannot a law of this sort be the work of a philosopher? was knowledge not the end in relation to which the Platonic legislator established his laws? Let us recall, however, that Plato began his dialogue on the laws with the word 'God'—this dialogue, and no other work—and that according to him the true law aims not only at 'human' good, i.e., at bodily goods, but also and above all at 'divine' goods, the first of which is knowledge. Maimonides is then in perfect accord with Plato in seeing as the trait characteristic of the divine law the fact that it aims at the perfection of knowledge" (p. 17).

29. Ibid., p. 6.

30. *Philosophy and Law,* pp. 109–10.

31. For a fine account of the development of Strauss's understanding of Maimonides and Farabi see Kenneth Hart Green, *Jew and Philosopher: The Return to Maimonides in the Jewish Thought of Leo Strauss* (Albany: State University Press of New York, 1993).

32. "Farabi's *Plato,*" in *Louis Ginzberg: Jubilee Volume,* ed. Saul Lieberman, Shalom Spiegel, Solomon Zeitlin, and Alexander Marx (New York: American Academy for Jewish Research, 1945), p. 359. I wish to thank Christopher Colmo for drawing my attention to the importance of this essay. Cf. "Theory and Practice: Alfarabi's *Plato* Revisited," *American Political Science Review* 86, no. 4 (December 1992): 966–76.

33. "Farabi's *Plato,*" p. 366.

34. As Strauss points out here and elsewhere, one of the rules of classical rhetoric was to place the points one least wanted noticed in the center of an argument, where most people, concentrating on the introduction and conclusion, would not be apt to notice them.

35. "Farabi's *Plato,*" pp. 369–72.

36. Ibid., p. 375.

37. Ibid., p. 381.

38. Ibid., p. 383.

39. The article "Persecution and the Art of Writing," *Social Research* (November 1941): 488–504, was included in the book of the same title published in 1952. He observes in the Preface that he "made free use of [his] article 'Farabi's Plato'" for the Introduction.

40. "Farabi's *Plato,*" pp. 390–93. Emphasis added. In analyzing what Farabi meant by the "science of the beings," Strauss points out that in one passage Farabi calls it the "science of the natural beings." In another passage summarizing the *Timaeus,* Farabi speaks of the science of "the divine and the natural beings," and Strauss notes that in the *Timaeus* "Plato applies such terms to the maker of the universe, the gods who manifest themselves so far as they wish [like] Zeus. . . , the visible universe, the heaven, the stars, the earth. Hence, one could also say that the divine beings referred to by Farabi are simply the most outstanding group of natural beings in the sense of beings 'which are bodies or in bodies', i.e. the heavens. The identification of the heavenly bodies with God is said to have been the esoteric teaching of Avicenna."

41. *Social Research* 13, no. 3 (September 1946): 350–51.

42. *On Tyranny*, ed. Victor Gourevitch and Michael S. Roth (New York: Free Press, 1991), pp. 196, 201–4; *NRH*, pp. 32, 35. Cf. Kennington, "Strauss's Natural Right," pp. 61, 67.

43. *Birth of Tragedy*, sec. 15. As Nietzsche observed, Lessing pointed out that it was thus the search itself and not the "find" that made philosophy a life worth living. Lessing also exercised a formative influence on Strauss's understanding of the nature of philosophy, because he first called Strauss's attention to the phenomenon of esoteric writing. Cf. "Exoteric Teaching," in *Interpretation: A Journal of Political Philosophy* 14 (1986): 51–59, reprinted in *The Rebirth of Classical Political Rationalism: An Introduction to the Thought of Leo Strauss*, ed. Thomas L. Pangle (Chicago: University of Chicago Press, 1989), pp. 63–71.

44. Cf. Strauss, *SPPP*, p. 50.

45. Cf. *Genealogy of Morals* and *The City and Man* (Chicago: Rand McNally, 1964), pp. 34–35: "an egalitarian society . . . looks up to such uncommon men as devote themselves to the service of the common man."

46. "It is not necessary to be or become Aristotelian," he thus wrote his friend Alexandre Kojève on 16 January 1934; "[it is] sufficient to become Platonist." *OT*, p. 224.

47. In "An Epilogue," reprinted in *LAM*, pp. 211–12, he thus observes that insofar as "science is in principle susceptible of infinite progress, [it] is itself tantamount to the belief that being is irretrievably mysterious."

48. *CM*, pp. 42–43.

49. René Descartes, *Discourse on Method*, VI: 58–64.

50. *WIPP*, p. 26.

51. *The Political Philosophy of Hobbes*, p. 34; *Thoughts on Machiavelli* (Glencoe, Ill.: Free Press, 1958), pp. 285, 289.

52. It was no accident, thus, that Strauss's first major study of the ancient understanding of politics led him into a debate with a self-described "Hegelian" or that he set his discussion of "natural right" in explicit opposition to "radical historicism."

53. Cf. "The Three Waves of Modernity," reprinted in Hilail Gildin, ed., *An Introduction to Political Philosophy: Ten Essays by Leo Strauss* (Detroit: Wayne State University Press, 1989), pp. 81–98.

54. In his exchange with Alexandre Kojève, Strauss thus admitted that in the universal and homogeneous state the self-declared Hegelian thought constituted not only the necessary but also the just outcome of history *might* be established. Inasmuch as it would constitute the worst, most thorough tyranny of all times, he insisted, such a state was *not* desirable, it did not satisfy the most fundamental human desires, and its institution *could* be resisted. Underlying their political disagreement, Strauss suggested, lay one of the insoluble problems with which philosophy is and will, so long as it exists, be concerned: whether there is an enduring intelligible order (which as such limits human action) or whether everything is subject to change. Since he considered this to be one of the insoluble problems, Strauss could not deny that the future Kojève foresaw was possible. He simply denied that it had been shown to be inevitable. *OT*, pp. 207–12.

55. In *WIPP*, p. 47, Strauss observes, "Machiavelli's scheme was open to serious theoretical difficulties. The theoretical or cosmological basis of his political

teaching was a kind of decayed Aristotelianism. This means that he assumed, but did not demonstrate, the untenable character of teleological natural science." Likewise in *NRH*, pp. 266–71, Strauss argues that Rousseau corrected Hobbes by pointing out that, if human beings were by nature asocial, as Hobbes maintained, they would not have socially produced characteristics like speech and reason in "the state of nature." Lacking foresight, they would not, therefore, be naturally fearful or hostile or concerned about their standing in the eyes of others; they would, rather, be peaceful and free.

56. "Farabi's *Plato*," p. 378; *PAW*, p. 15.

57. *OT*, pp. 183–84.

58. *Thoughts*, pp. 83–84.

59. In *Thoughts*, pp. 289–99, 12–13, Strauss argues that Machiavelli does not and cannot give a coherent account of his own activity as a philosopher—or, even simply as a great benefactor of later generations—on the basis of the principles of human action he articulates. As the would-be author of "new modes and orders," he gains neither the modest security for life and property desired by the many nor the fame that moves "the great" to risk their lives. To effect the revolution in morals (or opinion) required for the realization of his political project, he had to become—and become known as—a teacher of evil. Rather than receiving the reverence due the father of the constitution based on his principles, Strauss points out, his name is associated to this day with a kind of politics that may be effective, but is nevertheless still disreputable. He is, moreover, rarely, if ever credited with philosophic knowledge; most commentators regard him merely as a political thinker, not as a man who retains his equanimity because his knowledge of the whole enables him to judge what it is reasonable to expect.

60. *Spinoza*, pp. 173–76, 295.

61. Cf. *Guide* I: 23, and "How to Begin to Study the *Guide*," *LAM*, p. 167.

62. "Introduction" and "The Literary Character of *The Guide for the Perplexed*," *PAW*, pp. 7–21, 38–94.

63. Strauss quotes Macaulay's observation to this effect in the frontispiece of *OT*, p. 22.

64. *On Liberty* (Baltimore: Penguin, 1974); first published 1859.

65. *PAW*, pp. 34–35.

66. "On a New Interpretation," p. 349. "Only because public speech demands a mixture of seriousness and playfulness," Strauss observes in "Farabi's *Plato*," "can a true Platonist present the serious teaching, the philosophic teaching in a historical, and hence playful, garb" (p. 377). Since Maimonides "considered histories and poems to be frivolous writings," Strauss explains in *Persecution and the Art of Writing*, "he was compelled to conceive of the Biblical stories as 'secrets of the Torah'." But he suggested, it was possible to explicate the "parables and enigmas" and yet maintain the esoteric character of the teaching by substituting "obscurity and briefness of speech, i.e., by ways of expression which are suitable exclusively to scholars" (pp. 65, 76).

67. Cf. Farabi's introduction to his commentary on Plato's *Laws* in Ralph Lerner and Muhsin Mahdi, ed., *Medieval Political Philosophy* (Ithaca: Cornell University Press, 1963), pp. 83–85, and Strauss's interpretation of it in "How Farabi Read Plato's *Laws*," in *WIPP*, pp. 135–39.

68. *OT*, p. 196, *WIPP*, p. 116; *NRH*, p. 32. Nathan Tarcov emphasizes both the

unconventional or nontraditional and open-ended character of Strauss's arguments in his response to John Gunnell's *Myth of the Tradition, American Political Science Review* 72 (May 1978): 122–34, in "Philosophy and History: Tradition and Interpretation in the Work of Leo Strauss," *Polity* 16, no. 1 (fall 1983): 5–29.

69. "On a New Interpretation," p. 351.

70. 70. Strauss, "On a New Interpretation," pp. 349–50, quoting Plato, *Seventh Letter* 341d2–e3.

71. *Natural Right and History*, p. 26. In "Leo Strauss and Maimonides," in Udoff, ed., *Leo Strauss*, p. 105, Remi Brague suggests that, whereas Nietzsche and Heidegger chose the second way, Strauss himself took the first.

72. Cf. J. G. A. Pocock, "Prophet and Inquisitor," *Political Theory* 3, no. 4 (November 1975): 385–401; George Sabine, "Review of Strauss's *Persecution and the Art of Writing*," *Ethics* 63 (1952–53): 220–22; John Yolton, "Locke on the Law of Nature," *Philosophical Review* 67 (1958): 477–98; and responses to these critics in Michael P. Zuckert, "The Recent Literature on Locke's Political Philosophy," *Political Science Reviewer* 5 (fall 1975): 271–304; "Of Wary Physicians and Weary Readers: The Debates on Locke's Way of Writing," *Independent Journal of Philosophy* 2 (1978): 55–66.

73. *PAW*, p. 30. Emphasis added.

74. In "Truths for Philosophers Alone?" *Times Literary Supplement* (1–7 December 1989): 1319, Stephen Holmes thus criticizes Strauss for not treating the works of philosophers simply as historical objects of study but for trying to find "wisdom" in their pages.

75. Cf. *WIPP*, pp. 67–68; *CR*, pp. 209–10.

76. Cf. *PAW*, p. 77, "Maimonides' Statement of Political Science," *WIPP*, p. 165, and *Thoughts*, p. 70: "It would be foolish to apply this suggestion mechanically, for Machiavelli's devices would defeat his purpose if he had applied them mechanically. It would be almost equally foolish to try to establish the meaning of his teaching by relying exclusively or even chiefly on his devices."

77. *LAM*, p. 7. See Walter Nicgorski, "Leo Strauss and Liberal Education," *Interpretation* 13, no. 2 (May 1985): 233–49, for a fuller account of Strauss's argument.

78. Interestingly enough, Strauss goes on to admit, "The greatest minds to whom we ought to listen are by no means exclusively the greatest minds of the West. It is merely an unfortunate necessity which prevents us from listening to the greatest minds of India and of China: we do not understand their languages, and we cannot learn all languages." Strauss knew that Heidegger had argued that was what necessary, above all, was a dialogue between East and West. Cf. *The Rebirth of Classical Political Rationalism*, pp. 42–44.

79. *LAM*, pp. 7–8.

80. "Philosophy and Politics, I," *Review of Metaphysics* 22 (1968): 60–61.

81. Cf. Shadia Drury, *The Political Ideas of Leo Strauss* (New York: St. Martin's Press, 1988), xv, 170–81; Luc Ferry and Alain Renaut, "Ce qui a besoin d'être démontre ne vaut pas grand-chose," in *Pourquoi nous ne sommes pas Nietzscheens* (New York: St. Martin's Press, 1988). Like Farabi, Drury claims, Strauss used the immunity of an historical commentator to put forward his own views in the mouths of others. But, where Strauss showed that Farabi departed from the evident teaching of Plato by ignoring his statements about the ideas and

the immortality of the soul, Drury does not show that Strauss himself ignored obvious elements of the teachings of either Machiavelli or Nietzsche in his presentation of them.

82. "In our age it is much less urgent to show that political philosophy is the indispensable handmaid of theology than to show that political philosophy is the rightful queen of the social sciences, the sciences of man and of human affairs; even the highest lawcourt in the land is more likely to defer to the contentions of social science than to the Ten Commandments as the words of the living God." *CM*, p. 1.

83. "Jews of the philosophic competence of Halevi and Maimonides took it for granted that being a Jew and being a philosopher are mutually exclusive." *PAW*, p. 19.

84. *Philosophy and Law*, p. 18; *SPPP*, pp. 149, 188. Cf. Terence Marshall, "Leo Strauss et la question des anciens et des modernes," *Cahiers de philosophie politique et juridique*, no. 23 (1993): 35–36.

85. *PAW*, p. 137.

86. Cf. Werner Dannhauser, "Leo Strauss as Citizen and Jew," *Interpretation* 17, no. 3 (spring 1990): 433–87.

87. *PAW*, pp. 105, 137.

88. "Political Philosophy and History," *WIPP*, pp. 56–77.

89. *NRH*, pp. 23–24.

CHAPTER FIVE

1. "Positivism is no longer what it desired to be when Auguste Comte originated it. It still agrees with Comte by maintaining that modern science is the highest form of knowledge, precisely because it aims no longer, as theology and metaphysics did, at absolute knowledge of the Why, but only at relative knowledge of the How. But after having been modified by utilitarianism, evolutionism, and neo-Kantianism, it has abandoned completely Comte's hope that a social science modeled on modern natural science would be able to overcome the intellectual anarchy of modern society. . . . [It now] decree[s] that there is a fundamental difference between facts and values, and that only factual judgements are within the competence of science." *WIPP*, p. 18.

2. Because Strauss used the failure of social scientists to recognize the "dictatorships" of Hitler and Stalin to be "tyrannies" as examples in his introductions to *OT*, pp. 22–28, and *CM*, pp. 1–10, students and critics alike have been tempted to see his thought originating in, if not based upon, opposition to totalitarianism. John Gunnell, "The Myth of the Tradition," *American Political Science Review* 72 (1978): 123, levels such an attack; to show how political philosophy arises out of political life, Thomas Pangle and Nathan Tarcov also begin their account of Strauss's thought in *The History of Political Philosophy*, 3d ed. (Chicago: University of Chicago Press, 1987), p. 907, with the Cold War. As both his introduction to *Philosophy and Law* and his "Preface" to *Spinoza* show, however, Strauss had concluded that liberal democracy did not constitute an adequate answer to the political problem and that modern rationalism or science lacked a foundation *before* the rise of Hitler.

3. In *NRH*, pp. 35–80, Strauss presented a lengthy critique of the work of Max Weber in support of this general claim.

4. Ibid., p. 19.

5. Cf. Eugene Miller, "Leo Strauss: The Recovery of Political Philosophy," in Anthony de Crespigny and Kenneth Minogue, eds., *Contemporary Political Philosophers* (New York: Dodd, Mead, 1975), p. 96.

6. *NRH*, p. 33.

7. Ibid., pp. 30–31. Although Strauss does not mention Heidegger by name or cite *Being and Time*, he clearly summarizes the argument presented in that book in his restatement of the basic theses of "radical historicism" on pp. 26–28 and 30–31. On 26 June 1950, he wrote to Kojève: "I have once again been dealing with Historicism, that is to say, with Heidegger, the only radical historicist, and I believe I see some light." *OT*, p. 251. (Strauss delivered six lectures on *Natural Right and History* at the University of Chicago in October 1949. He published the first chapter on "Natural Right and the Historical Approach," in *The Review of Politics* in October 1950.)

8. For an excellent account of Strauss's analysis of this pretheoretical experience and its significance, see James F. Ward, "Experience and Political Philosophy: Notes on Reading Leo Strauss," *Polity* 13, no. 4 (summer 1981): 668–87.

9. *CR*, pp. 28–29.

10. *SPPP*, p. 31; *OT*, p. 192; *WIPP*, pp. 42, 47–55. In his 26 June 1950 letter to Kojève, Strauss observed, "Heidegger's position is the last refuge of nationalism: the state, even "culture," is done with—all that remains is language." *OT*, pp. 251–52. He criticizes this notion in his essay on "Kurt Riezler," *WIPP*, pp. 237–40. (People speaking different languages can be effectively united—think of the Swiss federation—whereas speaking the same language has never prevented peoples from fighting wars, especially civil wars, among themselves.)

11. Martin Heidegger, *The Basic Problems of Phenomenology*, trans. Albert Hofstadter (Bloomington: Indiana University Press, 1982), pp. 119–20.

12. *WIPP*, p. 71.

13. Cf. *NRH*, pp. 81–93.

14. Cf. Strauss's statement in "Farabi's Plato," p. 366.

15. *NRH*, p. 120. Strauss cites Cicero, *Tusc. Disp.* v, 10; and Hobbes, *De Cive*, Preface, near the beginning.

16. The fourth primary source is Aristotle, but since Aristotle's knowledge of Socrates was, unlike Aristophanes, Plato, and Xenophon's, derivative, Strauss treats his comments only in passing and often, if usually only implicitly, critically.

17. *Socrates and Aristophanes* (New York: Basic Books, 1966), pp. 7–8.

18. Ibid., p. 6.

19. Strauss published the Platonic response first—perhaps because he wanted to contribute the essay on "Plato" for the *History of Political Philosophy* he wrote with his students, perhaps because he was asked to deliver the Page-Barbour Lectures at the University of Virginia in the spring of 1962 (which he published two years later as *The City and Man*), perhaps because he thought that it was most important (and sixty years of age, he didn't know how much longer he would live).

20. *SA*, p. 314.

21. *Oeconomicus* XI.3; *Phaedo* 96a–97b.

22. Like Nikias in *The Knights*, human beings perceive the gods to be inimi-

cal, because the gods act to restrain, if not to frustrate human desires, especially the desires of the pious.

23. In light of Strauss's response to Heidegger, it is important to note that the comic poet pointed out this interdependency and the way philosophy threatened both poles at the very beginning. In the story of Peisthetairos, Aristophanes also dramatized the practical, political conclusion of the desire to overcome the limitations of the human condition—the institution of a universal or world state under the rule of one tyrant. (Peisthetairos's ambition or *hubris* is comic rather than outrageous, Strauss explains [*SA*, pp. 190–93], because the form it takes in the play—building a city in the sky between the heavens where the gods dwell and the earth [Heidegger's "geography" also]—is literally impossible.)

24. Like Socrates, in *The Thesmophoriazusae* Euripides is accused of atheism and threatened with prosecution. Unlike the philosopher, however, the tragic poet is able to defend himself, because he understands the erotic desires of the women (who, Strauss argues [*SA*, p. 212], also represent the pious part of the city), and is, therefore, able to appeal to their compassion.

25. His associate Euelpides, who actually wanted to live with the birds in peace and pleasure, leaves as soon as he perceives the true character of Peisthetairos's ambition. Cf. Strauss's analysis of Xenophon's depiction of the character of the tyrant in *OT*, pp. 69–77, 80–88.

26. The reasons that desire can never be completely satisfied emerge most clearly, Strauss suggests, in Aristophanes' three political "utopias." Unlike Peisthetairos, the protagonists of the *Lysistrata*, *Assembly of Women*, and *Plutos* do not act solely for their own benefit, but for the good of others as well. Their schemes are, therefore, patently more just. They represent the realization of three enduring human dreams—the overcoming of war with love, the eradication of class conflict through the establishment of a perfectly egalitarian society, and the end of the unjust distribution of goods through the abolition of need. Unfortunately, Aristophanes suggests, Lysistrata's scheme to overcome war with love will at most be temporarily effective. Persistent human hopes to the contrary notwithstanding, love cannot conquer war, because love or desire is itself the source of human conflict, as the traditional association between Aphrodite and Ares indicates. Likewise in the *Assembly of Women*, Praxagora's scheme to make all men good by abolishing private property and so eradicating the causes of evil—cheating, stealing, envy, and litigation—requires her to impose severe restrictions on the natural erotic attraction human beings have to the young and beautiful. It is impossible to satisfy the desires people have to be treated equally or justly, to be free, and to have beautiful things—simultaneously and universally. Chremylos's curing of Plutos's blindness, which results in the automatic rewarding of justice with wealth and injustice with poverty, does not require the explicit regulation of eros the way Praxagora's egalitarian community does. By eradicating need, however, his scheme removes all incentive for human beings to engage in the arts. The result is a humdrum society in which human life lacks beauty, nobility, knowledge—the aspects of life usually taken to be most distinctively human and in which human beings, therefore, tend to take pride.

27. *SA*, p. 173. On Strauss's understanding of Parmenides, see *WIPP*, p. 251.

28. *SA*, p. 171.

29. Aristophanes' critique of Socratic philosophy, both for threatening to de-

stroy humanity by reducing everything to a measurable element able to take multiple forms and, in destroying humanity, "covering over" and so forgetting its own origin, presages Heidegger's critique of modern science to a remarkable extent. There are, however, two very significant differences. In the first place, Aristophanes' critique rests on the primacy of nature or desire, whereas Heidegger associates the emergence of truth fundamentally with history and art. Second, as a consequence of their different evaluations of human making, the ancient comedian and the modern philosopher represent two significantly different understandings of poetry. Both see *logos*, the essential medium of poetic images or words, as both revealing and concealing. But, where Heidegger suggests that the gradual loss or concealment of the original meaning-experience occurs inexorably, outside of anyone's control, Aristophanes suggests that the essential ambiguity of poetic images makes it possible for the poet intentionally to speak to two audiences at once—to present a just speech to the many and to point out the not quite so salutary truth to the wise. Aristophanes' understanding of poetry thus enables him not merely to comprehend but also to act in politics in a way Heidegger could not.

30. Strauss points out that Xenophon claims Socrates studied only the human things at the beginning of his *Memorabilia*, when he is defending Socrates from the charge of impiety; people suspected philosophers who investigated the heavens and things under the earth of not believing the Olympian gods. Later (*Memorabilia* IV.6.1), Xenophon reports that Socrates was constantly inquiring with companions what each of the beings was. Socrates' investigations were not limited to things human; they could not have been, because it is not possible to know the human except in distinction from the non-human. Socrates was not, as Aristotle claims (*Metaphysics* A, 987b1–4), solely a moral philosopher.

31. *Xenophon's Socratic Discourse: An Interpretation of the "Oeconomicus"* (Ithaca: Cornell University Press, 1970), p. 149. For a good introduction, see Christopher Bruell, "Xenophon's Socrates," *Political Science Reviewer* 14 (fall 1984): 263–318.

32. *CM*, pp. 20–21. Strauss's emphasis on the priority of the question and the need to return to the beginning reminds one of Heidegger. The difference is that *the* question to which Heidegger insists we must return is the question of the meaning or truth of Being itself. Strauss suggests the question we need repeatedly to raise concerns the different kinds. It is the forgetting not of the question of Being generally, but of the essential differences among the beings that has led to modern scientific reductionism.

33. In "What Is Political Philosophy?" (pp. 39–40), Strauss observes, "Philosophy strives for knowledge of the whole. . . . The whole eludes us but we know parts. . . . The knowledge which we possess is characterized by a fundamental dualism which has never been overcome. At one pole we find knowledge of homogeneity: above all in arithmetic, but also in the other branches of mathematics. . . . At the opposite pole we find knowledge of heterogeneity, and in particular of heterogeneous ends; the highest form of this kind of knowledge is the art of the statesman. . . . The latter kind of knowledge is superior to the former for this reason. As knowledge of the ends of human life, it is knowledge of what makes human life complete or whole; it is therefore knowledge of a whole. . . . But this

knowledge . . . is not knowledge of *the* whole. . . . Philosophy is characterized by the gentle, if firm, refusal to succumb to either."

34. *CM*, p. 19.

35. *XSD*, p. 164.

36. Ibid., p. 83. Xenophon made some changes on the historical records in his restatement of the indictment of Socrates, Strauss observes, but those changes were, in contrast to the changes made by Plato, very slight. *Xenophon's Socrates* (Ithaca: Cornell University Press, 1973), pp. 3–4.

37. The philosopher had observed that in human beings beauty was not merely a matter of appearance; some very attractive people proved upon examination to be quite depraved. Seeing a horse greatly admired, Socrates had reflected that, if a horse could be good by nature without any external equipment or possessions (or being a citizen—the horse was owned by a foreigner), so could a man like himself, provided he had a good soul, without possessing wealth.

38. Just as Strepsiades first sought out Socrates to help him with a problematic son, so, Strauss suggests, Kriton may have asked Socrates for help with his son. However, where Strepsiades wanted Socrates to teach him the rhetorical skills that would enable him unjustly to escape the debts incurred because of his son's love of horses (or desire to look fine in the eyes of others), Kriton hopes Socrates will counteract the love of comedies that keeps Kritoboulos in the city by persuading him to return to the country and take charge of the family farm. Just as Aristophanes charged Socrates with corrupting the young in *The Clouds*, so in the *Oeconomicus* Xenophon accuses the comic poet. By appealing to his audience's desire for pleasure, the comedian keeps them in the city, caught up in the affairs of others, instead of returning to the country to mind their own business—the definition of justice Socrates proposes in Plato's *Republic*. The ascetic or continent philosopher has a better effect on the youth who listen to him or follow his example than does the amorous poet.

39. Xenophon's Socrates has obviously learned the need to speak differently to different people. In the *Memorabilia* (IV.6.13–15), Xenophon reports, Socrates addressed people in two different fashions: "When someone contradicted Socrates, Socrates brought back the subject matter to its basic presupposition, that is to say, he raised the question, What is? regarding the subject under discussion, and he answered with the participation of the contradictor. Thus the contradictor himself came to see the truth clearly. . . . But, . . . when Socrates discussed something on his own initiative, that is to say, when he talked to people who merely listened, he did not raise the question, what is? but proceeded through generally accepted opinions, and thus he produced agreement among the listeners to an extraordinary degree." Strauss comments, "This latter kind of dialectics, which leads to agreement as distinguished from truth, is the most important part of the political art. It is the art which Homer ascribes to Odysseus" (*CR*, p. 139).

40. "The suggestion that Ischomachos was in a manner the source of both Socrates' substantive knowledge of the human things and his 'method' is a deliberate exaggeration that is meant to counteract the amazing neglect of the *Oeconomicus* on the part of those who are concerned with 'the Socratic problem'" (*XSD*, p. 149). First and foremost was Nietzsche, who characterized Socrates in

The Birth of Tragedy as the embodiment of an absolute and unnatural rationalism and later contrasted Socrates' ignoble, utilitarian calculations of self-interest with Plato's noble, self-denying asceticism.

41. There is a joke here as well. In *Oeconomicus* VII–X Socrates is relating the way Ischomachos told him a man should educate his wife. Although it is not absolutely clear it is the same man—Xenophon does not give his patronym—there was an Ischomachos who had a notorious wife. As Socrates would have known by the time he related the speech to Kritoboulos, less than a year after her daughter married Kallias, the mother moved in with the young couple as her son-in-law's mistress and the daughter attempted suicide. Although Socrates also had a wife who was notoriously difficult to live with, as Xenophon reminds his readers in the *Symposium* (2.10), Socrates had no illusions about his ability to educate or persuade her. When his son Lamprokles complains about his mother's vile tongue in the *Memorabilia* (II.2), Socrates urges him to change his attitude and behavior; the philosopher does not even propose going to Xanthippe in order to persuade her to change her ways. *XSD*, pp. 157–58; *XS*, pp. 136–38.

42. The two modes of protecting oneself from envy parallel Socrates' two modes of speaking—the philosophical inquiry into what things are and the "political" attainment of consensus. As Strauss notes, in contrast to Plato, Xenophon never says anything about Socrates' military exploits. Cf. *XSD*, p. 89; *XS*, p. 126.

43. Cf. *Apology* 32; *XS*, p. 135.

44. Like Aristophanes, Xenophon suggests that farming is a particularly good way of satisfying human need, because it tends to produce a rough kind of justice—the harder you work, the more foresight and self-control you exercise, the more profit you reap.

45. *XS*, p. 63.

46. As Strauss reminds his readers, Cyrus and Socrates represent the two alternative ways of life in Xenophon's works as a whole. Unlike Ischomachos, Xenophon shows in the *Cyropedia* VIII.3.1–15, Cyrus understood the importance of "dressing up."

47. Cf. *CM*, p. 29.

48. *Memorabilia* IV.1.2; *XS*, p. 49.

49. In his review of *Xenophon's Socrates* in *The Classical World* 66 (May 1973): 470, Stanley Rosen observes that "the episode with Theodote (which must be compared with Socrates' praise in the *Symposium* of his art of procuring), forms the approximate center of Strauss' book."

50. That is the reason, I believe, Xenophon reports that Socrates castigated him (as he had Strepsiades in the *Clouds*) as a "fool" and a "wretch" when he defended Kritoboulos's kissing of Alcibiades' son; Xenophon did not perceive the dangerous consequences of mistaking physical attraction for intellectual friendship. The only other place Xenophon uses the vocative "you wretch" in his Socratic writings, Strauss points out, is when Virtue addresses Vice (dressed up as a whore) in the story of Prodicus Socrates retells. *XS*, p. 20. The primacy of the visible is also the reason Socrates loses the beauty contest he declares with Kritoboulos in the central chapter of the *Symposium*; Socrates' companions cannot be persuaded that his thick lips are beautiful because they are better for kissing. Strauss comments, "The beauty contest proves in fact that Socrates is guilty also in this respect, that his simple equation of the beautiful with the useful is untrue.

Taken literally, it leads to a crude, calculating utilitarianism [stressed by Nietzsche] for which friends are pieces of property. . . . The beautiful (noble) cannot be reduced to the good (useful) [as Heidegger insisted on translating it] in the first place because the city and its interests cannot be reduced to the self-interest of the individuals; what is good for the city, is frequently noble rather than good for the individual. . . ; and in the second place because the beautiful in a different sense is good for the beholder rather than for the user" (XS, p. 167).

51. "Since wisdom is concerned with the beings only, it would seem that wisdom is not concerned with the good and beautiful things as such. . . . For the good things are not good for everyone and always and the beautiful things are beautiful relative to their purposes, which vary, but the beings are beings simply. . . . The good and noble things are the objects, not of sophia (wisdom), but of phronēsis (good sense) (cf. IV.8.11)" (XS, pp. 119–20).

52. CR, p. 135; XS, pp. 7–8.

53. Although Xenophon reports late in the Memorabilia that Socrates raised the questions What is piety? and What is justice?, he shows that Socrates taught students like Euthydemos that the answers to those questions are to be found, as a practical matter, in the legal definitions. Xenophon's Socrates does not explicitly raise the more decisive questions What is a god? or What is law? Xenophon indicates that Socrates led his students to ask such questions, however, when he describes Alcibiades' interrogation of his uncle Pericles.

54. CR, p. 125.

55. "The political proposals of the Republic are based on the conceits underlying Aristophanes' Assembly of Women. The complete communism . . . is introduced in Plato's Republic with arguments literally taken from Aristophanes' Assembly of Women. There is this most important difference. . . . Plato contends that complete communism requires as its capstone or its foundation the rule of philosophy, about which Aristophanes is completely silent. . . . While the Republic makes important use of the Assembly of Women, it is at least equally much directed against, and indebted to, the Clouds. Thrasymachus represents the Unjust Speech, and Socrates takes the place of the Just Speech. And the Just Speech is in Plato, of course, victorious. . . . As for music, Socrates demands in the name of justice that the poet as poet be expelled from the city. As for eros, the tyrant, injustice incarnate, is revealed to be eros incarnate. The Socrates of the Republic reveals his kinship with the unerotic and the amusic Socrates of the Clouds." CR, pp. 125–26. In CM, p. 61, n. 15, Strauss provides a list of citations of the parallel lines in the Assembly of Women, Republic, Thesmophoriazusae, and Lysistrata.

56. In The Acharnians, Dikaiopolis, with whom the comic poet identifies himself, achieves a kind of individual happiness, but only by unjustly separating himself from his polity. Leaders who seek to achieve peace and justice, not merely for themselves, but for their fellow citizens as well, like Lysistrata and Praxagora find it necessary to impose strong controls on their fellow citizens' desires, or like Chremylos to abolish the grounds of individual greatness.

57. In his account of Xenophon's Anabasis Strauss points out the contrast between Xenophon's friend Proxenos, a student of the rhetorician Gorgias, who can only deal with gentlemen, because he is only willing to use persuasion, and Xenophon, the student of Socrates, who knows when to use persuasion and when to supplement it with force. But Strauss argues, the most important contrast in

the *Anabasis* is not between Xenophon and Proxenos, but rather that between Xenophon and Socrates. Xenophon went on the excursion against the advice of Socrates; unlike his mentor he desired both wealth and power. Had it proved possible, Xenophon would have founded a city. It does not appear that he was as convinced as Plato that the philosophic life is simply superior to the political. *SPPP,* pp. 109–14, 124–28.

58. *Beyond Good and Evil,* aph. 211; in *The Will to Power,* aph. 972, Nietzsche gave Plato as an example of such a legislator who blindfolded himself with regard to the character of his own undertaking. M. F. Burnyeat correctly asserts that Strauss's entire position depends upon his reading of Plato. Burnyeat is not correct, however, in thinking Strauss's reading can be dismissed in a sentence or two. Cf. Burnyeat's extremely negative and unsympathetic judgment in "Sphinx without a Secret," *The New York Review* (30 May 1985): 30–36, with Gadamer's judgment in *Truth and Method,* trans. Joel Weinsheimer and Donald G. Marshall (New York: Crossroad, 1990), pp. 532–41.

59. In his later works Strauss rarely refers to Plato's letters. He never mentions the Second Letter in which, as Strauss reminded his readers in his review of Wild, Plato says that he wrote nothing, he simply reported the sayings of a Socrates made young and beautiful (noble). Strauss refers to the Seventh Letter in a footnote on p. 63 of *CM* where he points out the differences between the discussion in the *Republic* and subsequent historical attempts to overthrow the Athenian democracy. But he never discusses Plato's account of the problematic results of his own political involvement.

60. "The Platonic dialogue shows us much more clearly than an Epistle Dedicatory could, in what manner the teaching conveyed through the work is adapted by the main speaker to his particular audience and therewith how that teaching would have to be restated in order to be valid beyond the particular situation of the conversation in question" (*CM,* p. 54).

61. Both Gadamer and Strauss not only were friends of Jacob Klein but also attribute some of their decisive insights to him. Whereas Gadamer explicitly relies on Klein's analysis of the Greek understanding of number for his own understanding of the relation between the whole and the parts, Strauss never mentions this part of Klein's argument. He praises Klein, e.g., *NRH,* p. 78, and "An Unspoken Prologue to a Public Lecture at St. John's," *Interpretation* 7, no. 3 (1978): 1–3, primarily for showing how modern doctrines covered over and finally led philosophers to forget the foundation and roots of their own ideas in ancient ideas, which were based on common or natural, naive experience.

62. *CM,* pp. 61–62. In opposition to what Socrates says about the character of poetry at the end of the *Republic,* Plato's own dialogues are not and should not be taken to be mere copies of copies. They are, Strauss emphasizes, works of art and *not* historical reports.

63. If Strauss is correct about the original character of Platonism, Nietzsche is wrong when he claims in the Preface to *Beyond Good and Evil* that Christianity is simply Platonism for the masses.

64. In the *Laws,* Strauss points out (*AAPL,* p. 9), the Athenian Stranger declares that death is the end of the *polis;* the "true" city in the *Republic* arises and exists to supply the needs of the body; it is the floor.

65. Indeed, Strauss argues that the distorted picture of the philosopher Plato

gives in the *Republic* is modified, in one respect, in the *Statesman*, and in another, in the *Symposium*. By showing that the Eleatic Stranger's diaretic method of discovering what something is by "division," that is, by showing how a "thing" like a fisherman or a sophist is similar and so belongs to a certain "tribe" or kind, in some respects, but is different in others, leads to the ridiculous definition of "man" as a featherless bi-ped, Plato indicates that philosophy is not and should not be solely concerned with separating out the ideas of things by means of *dianoia*, as Socrates suggests in his description of the highest segment of the divided line in the *Republic*. Like Socrates himself, the philosopher needs to study the sensible realm of ordinary experience and opinion; he can never simply go beyond it. Likewise, in the *Symposium* Plato indicates that the philosopher is literally that, a seeker rather than a possessor of knowledge *(mathema)*, when he shows that, in his most voluntary and sole conversation with poets, Socrates claims to know *only* erotic matters. *HPP,* pp. 69–70; *CR,* p. 68.

66. *CR,* p. 155.

67. The two, and only two, aspects of the dialogues that can unquestionably be attributed to Plato himself, Strauss argues, are the titles and the selection of the conversations to be depicted. *CM,* pp. 56–57. (Over the years, Plato indubitably heard Socrates converse with many more people on many more occasions.) Insofar as the dialogues are works of art, moreover, rather than products of nature or random conjunction, they are products of intention which abstracts from chance. *CM,* p. 60.

68. Strauss thus corrects the tendency to associate Socrates with the Thirty Tyrants, because of his association with Critias and Charmides. E. g., in Indra Kagis McEwen, *Socrates' Ancestor* (Cambridge, Mass.: MIT Press, 1993), p. 97. As Strauss pointed out in his review of Wild, neither Plato nor his Socrates was a member of a political party nor can their arguments be used to support one.

69. *CM,* pp. 62–63. Like Gadamer, Strauss thus suggests that the description of the just city in the *Republic* does not constitute a practical program for political reform. The lesson Strauss draws from the dialogue differs markedly, however, from that derived by his German acquaintance. Whereas Gadamer concludes that Plato shows human community is founded on an ongoing deliberation about what is good, Strauss argues that by showing its limits, as Cicero saw, in the *Republic* Plato reveals the nature of politics.

70. Ibid., p. 65. If we look back at Xenophon's account of Socrates' conversation with Glaucon in the *Memorabilia* (III.8), we discover that it is very different from the *Republic*. Whereas Xenophon's Socrates questions Glaucon in order to shame him into admitting that he knows nothing about politics and has therefore nothing of value to offer the Athenian people, Plato's Socrates gives his companions a lesson in "self-control regarding the pleasures, and even the needs, of the body" by substituting the conversation about justice, a feast of thought in which he conjures up "many grand and perplexing sights" like the city in speech and his famous images of the divided line and the cave for the dinner they were initially promised. This dual lesson in moderation—both physical and intellectual or political—constitutes *the* action of the dialogue. Both of Socrates' students thus show him teaching continence as the precondition for wisdom, but Plato's Socrates is much less austere. He gives his readers an indication of the sort of intellectual pleasure that, Xenophon's Socrates explained to Antiphon, pro-

duced his continence regarding bodily things. To do so, he has to become something of a poet himself by presenting them with "grand sights" or images.

71. Strauss later comments, "Socrates' procedure in the *Republic* can perhaps be explained as follows: there is a particularly close connection between justice and the city and while there is surely an idea of justice, there is perhaps no idea of the city. . . . The eternal and unchangeable ideas are distinguished from the particular things which come into being and perish. . . . Perhaps the city belongs so radically to the sphere of becoming that there cannot be an idea of the city. Aristotle says that Plato recognized ideas only of natural beings. . . . Yet if there is a strict parallel between the city and the human individual, the city would seem to be a natural being." Ibid., pp. 92–93.

72. Although these guardians are also said to be experts in one military art, Strauss points out (again like Gadamer) they, unlike the other citizens, are explicitly admitted not only to have but also to need a dual nature, containing two opposed drives or tendencies. The proposition that each human being is designed by nature to do one and only one thing is thus shown to be, at best, only partially true. Only when the city thus becomes divided into two potentially opposed factions, one armed and one unarmed, does its organization become political, properly speaking; only now are there rulers and ruled. Strauss does not agree with Gadamer, however, that the political is the historical. On the contrary, he points out, the premise of the description of the inferior regimes in Book VIII is that the best regime was once actual. The inferior regimes are decayed versions; there is no notion of progress gradually achieved over time. Ibid., p. 129.

73. *CR*, p. 157.

74. Strauss's use of the qualifying clause "what Adeimantus calls theology," *CM*, p. 98, suggests he does not think Socrates or Plato would call 'theology' anything that did not begin with the question What is god?

75. "Somewhat later in the conversation Socrates suggests that justice is a specifically human virtue (392a3–c3), perhaps because justice is rooted in the fact that every human being lacks self-sufficiency and hence is ordered toward the city (369b5–7) and therefore that man is essentially 'erotic' whereas the gods are self-sufficient and hence free from *eros*. *Eros* and justice would thus seem to have the same root" (ibid., pp. 99–100). For this reason in Book X of the *Nichomachean Ethics* Aristotle declares that, being self-sufficient, the gods are not just. What is clear is that Socrates' understanding of the gods is *very* different from Aristophanes who suggests that they are misanthropic. The existence of Socrates' gods would not seem to depend upon human beings believing in them. They are *not* poetic images or interpretations of natural phenomena; they are ideas. Cf. Ibid., p. 240, where Strauss observes that for classical political philosophy "concern with the divine has become identical with philosophy."

76. Both Socrates and Strauss seem to ignore or abstract from international relations. Does the city not need to deal justly with other cities? As Socrates suggests in explaining, first, why guardians become necessary and, then, why they must be carefully educated, the city that does not restrict its citizens' desires to what they need to survive will have to take things from others unjustly. The relations of a just city with others will be limited, therefore, to defense. Will a city that contains a sufficient number of people and variety of trades to provide for the necessities be large enough to defend itself from others? It is not clear. (In

Plato's *Laws* the Athenian Stranger thus suggests a good city needs to be founded in an isolated, but sufficiently fertile place.) The need for defense itself raises a problem, moreover. When the city asks some of its citizens to give their lives in its defense, it subordinates the good of the individual to the good of the rest. But such a subordination of the good of one to the good or advantage of others was the definition of injustice, according to the exchange between Thrasymachus and Socrates in Book I. The problem associated with defense points to the reasons Socrates has to abstract from the body or concerns with bodily preservation in the parallel he proceeds to draw between the individual and the city.

77. "A provisional consideration of the soul seems to . . . [show that it] contains desire, spiritedness or anger, and reason, just as the city consists of the money-makers, the warriors, and the rulers" (*CM*, pp. 109–10).

78. Like Gadamer, Strauss observes how strange it is that the answer to the question What is justice? should be given less than halfway through the dialogue. Like everything else in the dialogue, he argues, this anomaly reflects the political context or setting. Unlike philosophical inquiries, political questions have a certain urgency; they have to be answered, somehow, now. Since the answer Socrates gives here is defective, the difference between the apparently doctrinaire character of the *Republic* and the clearly elenchtic dialogues is more apparent than real. Ibid., pp. 105–6.

79. Ibid., p. 109. The parallel Socrates draws between the city and the soul is defective, not merely because it results in a problematic abstraction from the body; it also produces a distorted view of the character and relation of the parts of the human soul. "It is very plausible that those who uphold the city against foreign and domestic enemies and who have received a music education should be more highly respected than those who lack public responsibility as well as music education," Strauss observes. "But it is much less plausible that spiritedness as such should be higher in rank than desire as such." Just as "spiritedness" encompasses a "large variety of phenomena ranging from the most noble indignation about injustice . . . to the anger of a spoiled child who resents being deprived of anything. . . ," so desire includes "*eros*, which ranges in its healthy forms from the longing for immortality through offspring . . . to the longing for immortality through participation by knowledge in the things which are unchangeable in every respect" (ibid., p. 110). Socrates can maintain that spiritedness is unqualifiedly higher and more reasonable than desire only by abstracting from *eros*.

80. *CR*, p. 159. Cf. Seth Benardete, "Leo Strauss' *The City and Man*," *Political Science Reviewer* 8 (fall 1978): 9.

81. As in an Aristophanic comedy, Socrates' denial that the difference between the sexes has any more relevance to the organization of the polity than the difference between bald and hairy men produces some apparently ridiculous results—old women exercising in the nude.

82. According to Strauss, there is an important difference between Aristophanes' "female" drama and Socrates' corrected version, headed by philosopher-kings, which is "altogether of male origin." Aristophanes' utopia is egalitarian, whereas the *Republic* is an aristocracy. Cf. *SA*, p. 282, *CM*, p. 114.

83. As Strauss points out with regard to the final "proof" of its immortality, one cannot know what the order or good of the soul is without knowing what

the soul is. Like the question What is god? the question What is soul? is not raised in this or any other of Plato's dialogues. Strauss indicates the reasons these questions are not asked in his analysis of the *Minos,* the Platonic dialogue in which Socrates explicitly raises one of the questions Xenophon's Socrates did not, What is law? In that dialogue, Socrates utterly dismisses consent as an ingredient of law, which he defines solely as the dictate of the divine intellect. Most laws are, we realize, mixtures, as Plato's two philosophical "strangers" teach. So, I believe, are the concepts of 'soul' and 'god' mixtures—of life with intellect in the case of soul and, as Strauss himself shows in his analysis of Maimonides' arguments concerning the attributes of God in his *Guide,* agency that can punish injustice with intellect that can produce order. There is, in other words, no simple or adequate answer to the What is ... ? question in these cases. To show that there is no soul or god per se would have pernicious effects on salutary popular opinions. The unanswerability of these three questions is an expression, however, of the noetic heterogeneity of the whole. Cf. *Liberalism: Ancient and Modern,* pp. 65–75.

84. In *WIPP,* p. 39, Strauss suggests that Plato gave a similarly negative definition of the philosopher, not in himself, but only in contrast to the sophist and the statesman.

85. *SPPP,* p. 3.

86. *CM,* pp. 120–21, 98–99.

87. Their disagreement about the possibility of living an entirely satisfying way of life leads, however, to different views of the gods. Plato's ideas do not depend upon human believers for their continued existence, and they are certainly *not* misanthropic the way Aristophanes' gods are. Aristophanes' gods have to act to check human desires, because he does not see any way those desires can be satisfied.

88. *CR,* pp. 177–83.

89. *HPP,* p. 75.

90. For a good introduction, see Mark Blitz, "Strauss's Laws," *Political Science Reviewer* 20 (spring 1991): 186–222.

91. In the *Politics,* Strauss observes, Aristotle calls the Stranger, Socrates. Plato's greatest student did not see any significant difference between Socrates and the Athenian Stranger.

92. *AAPL,* pp. 10–11.

93. Cf. Ibid., p. 2, "How Farabi Read Plato's *Laws,*" *WIPP,* p. 154: Just as "Farabi invented Platonic speeches ... with ease," so "Plato invented ... Socratic and other stories."

94. Farabi points to such an opposition, Strauss observes, by remaining altogether silent about philosophy in his *Summary of Plato's "Laws"* and by attributing the *Laws* to Socrates in his *Philosophy of Plato,* but not mentioning law as the subject of the dialogue. "It is as if Farabi had interpreted the absence of Socrates from the *Laws* to mean that Socrates has nothing to do with laws, and as if he had tried to express this interpretation by suggesting that if *per impossibile* the *Laws* were Socratic, they would not deal with laws" (*WIPP,* p. 153).

95. In his account of "How Farabi Read Plato's *Laws,*" Strauss concludes that "Socrates' silence about laws ... must be understood in the light of the implicit

distinction [made in section 30 of the *Philosophy*] between the way of Socrates and the way of Plato." *WIPP,* p. 153.

96. Farabi's failure to use the word 'philosophy' in his *Summary* "must be understood in light of the implicit distinction . . . between the way of Socrates and the way of Plato. The way of Plato emerges through a correction of the way of Socrates. The way of Socrates is intransigent; it demands of the philosopher an open break with the accepted opinions. The way of Plato combines the way of Socrates which is appropriate for the philosopher's relations to the elite, with the way of Thrasymachus, which is appropriate for the philosopher's relations to the vulgar. The way of Plato demands therefore judicious conformity with the accepted opinions. If we consider the connection, stated in the *Summary,* between the vulgar and the laws, we arrive at the conclusion that the appreciation or legitimation of laws becomes possible by virtue of Plato's correction of the way of Socrates" (*WIPP,* p. 153). In the note Strauss appended to this statement, he observed, "The first half of the *Philosophy of Plato* ends with 'Socrates'; the second half ends with 'their laws,' i.e., the laws of the Athenians."

97. *AAPL,* pp. 42, 64.

98. In his account of Farabi's reading, *WIPP,* pp. 148–50, Strauss points out that, although the gods are frequently mentioned in his *Summary* in contrast to their complete absence in his *Philosophy of Plato,* they are not mentioned in Farabi's account of Book VI (although they appear both in Plato's text and in Strauss's).

99. *AAPL,* p. 6.

100. Ibid., p. 38.

101. *Laws,* 709e–710d; *AAPL,* pp. 56–57.

102. *AAPL,* p. 47. In other words, the argument of the *Laws* does not abstract from body the way the argument of the *Republic* does. This is the reason that the regime of the *Republic* is said in *Laws* Book V to be best, but to be suitable only for gods or demigods and not for human beings. In the *Laws* citizens are allowed to have private property and to select specific individuals to marry. Inequalities in wealth are strictly limited, however; members of the two sexes are treated as equally as possible; and family life is subject to a good deal of public supervision. The city is ruled, moreover, by a "Nocturnal Council" of wise old men who choose young men to join their secret deliberations and so to become educated. As Aristotle observes in *Politics* 1265a1, the institutions of the *Laws* finally become hard to distinguish from those of the *Republic.*

103. *AAPL,* pp. 86–87. Strauss emphasizes his own agreement with this analysis when he reiterates "the necessity . . . of diluting true proportionate equality *which for us is always the political right*" (p. 180).

104. Ibid., pp. 20–21, 33. This moderation is *the* quality Nietzsche lacked in contrast to Plato, according to Strauss. *SPPP,* pp. 174, 183, 191. It is, we might venture to suggest, *the* distinguishing quality of the political philosopher qua political philosopher. *Sophrosune* is also the only "cardinal" virtue Socrates does not claim himself in Plato's *Apology.* But, as Xenophon shows, at his trial Socrates wanted to provoke the Athenians to condemn him; he was not trying to persuade them to live with him in peace. "Moderation in the highest sense of the word" appears to consist in a kind of self-restraint, practiced by Strauss himself as much

as by Socrates and Plato, insofar as he, too, emphasizes the public or political presentation of philosophy and only mentions the theoretical questions to which philosophers devote themselves in passing.

105. *AAPL*, pp. 20–21, 33.

106. Ibid., pp. 63, 66, 165–66. Although he teaches that citizens must be led to honor their souls, second only to the gods, and to believe that, as the source of motion, soul is prior to matter and so presumably to believe in the gods as well, the Athenian does not, any more than Socrates, raise or answer the questions What is soul? or What is god?

107. Ibid., p. 185.

108. Ibid., pp. 114, 180.

109. The obfuscation is not accidental, however. The Athenian explicitly argues that the successful legislator must convince his people that the laws he has drafted just now have been in effect from ancient times. Because *nomos* consists of a kind of opinion, it never has or can have the status of knowledge and will not, therefore, be able to answer philosophical questions or critiques. It has the same defect, in other words, that Socrates attributes to writing in general in the *Phaedrus*.

110. *AAPL*, p. 2.

111. But cf. *SPPP*, pp. 49–50.

112. *AAPL*, p. 91.

113. Ibid., pp. 155–56.

114. Ibid., pp. 3, 7, 11. At the beginning of the dialogue Kleinias answered the Stranger's initial question about Zeus's being the origin of Cretan law by saying that this was the "just," i.e., the conventional answer mandated by law. Even after the Athenian convinced Kleinias that it would be necessary to inculcate certain beliefs about the gods, in Book X he did not exhibit any indignation against atheists.

115. Cf. *SPPP*, pp. 42–43. In his essay "On Plato's *Apology of Socrates* and *Crito*" Strauss argues that Socrates shows "the primary charge concerns his corruption of the young and that the other three charges [concerning his impiety] are pure inventions thought out in order to give some plausibility to the corruption charge" (ibid., p. 41).

116. Strauss indicates the extent to which *thymos* has been abstracted from in the *Laws* by rarely using the word in his summaries. Although Thomas Pangle lists more than seventy-seven instances in which the word 'spiritedness', 'spirit', or *thymos* occurs in the index to his translation of *The Laws of Plato* (Chicago: University of Chicago Press, 1988), p. 560, Strauss uses the English translation only twice—once in his account of the need for human beings to be both gentle and spirited in his presentation of the discussion of the soul in Book V, p. 68, and second in his commentary on Book X, pp. 141, 143, where he points out that, having urged his interlocutors that they need to try to persuade atheists of the existence of the gods without spirited anger, the Athenian then finds it necessary to arouse Kleinias' spirit. The Athenian's speech has apparently smothered the passion that led "fathers" like Kleinias to persecute Socrates. Strauss uses the Greek word only in his account of Book XI, p. 167, when he observes that the Athenian's critique of "the kind of madness that comes from a bad nature and training of spiritedness *(thymos)*" leads the Athenian by "logographic necessity"

to talk about "evil-speaking," ridicule, and hence comedy—a reference, no doubt, to Aristophanes, who warned Socrates about the danger he might encounter by arousing the spirited opposition of the fathers by teaching their sons to be impious. Observing that comedy, although not necessarily tragedy will be allowed in the city, Strauss concludes by noting that, "what one ought to stress is the corresponding devaluation of *thymos* (cf. 888a2–6)."

117. *SPPP*, p. 168.

118. For an analysis of the way in which the structure of Socrates' defense in the *Apology of Socrates* follows the organization of Aristophanes' *Clouds*, see Michael P. Zuckert, "Rationalism and Political Responsibility: Plato's *Apology* and *The Clouds*," *Polity* (winter 1985): 271–97.

119. *WIPP*, p. 39.

120. *CM*, p. 120. In a letter to Aron Gurvitsch, Alfred Schutz reports that when Heidegger's "Plato's Theory of Truth" appeared, Strauss said that it was "the most brazen thing he ha[d] run into." *Philosophers in Exile*, ed. Richard Grathoff (Bloomington: Indiana University Press, 1989), p. 97.

121. For clear evidence of this influence, see Friedrich Nietzsche, *Introduction à la lecture des dialogues de Platon*, trans. Olivier Berrichon-Sedeyn (Combas: Editions de l'éclat, 1991).

122. "A Giving of Accounts," p. 4.

123. *SA*, p. 314; citation to *The Philosophic Way of Life*, trans. Paul Krauss, *Orientala* (1935): 300–334.

124. *CR*, pp. 40–41.

125. *SPPP*, p. 175.

126. Ibid., p. 191.

127. *PAW*, p. 21.

CHAPTER SIX

1. Joseph Cropsey, "Foreword," *SPPP*, p. vii; Thomas Pangle, "Introduction," Ibid., p. 1; Thomas Molnar, "The Straussian Universe," *The Modern Age* 29, no. 1 (winter 1985): 82; M. F. Burnyeat, ""Sphinx without a Secret," *The New York Review* (30 May 1985): 34.

2. Seventeen was a number with significance for Strauss. In his essay on "Maimonides' Statement on Political Science" in *WIPP*, pp. 165–66, he observes, "The central section of Maimonides' *Heptameres*, the thematic discussion of 'the account of the chariot,' the secret of secrets, consists of 7 chapters. . . . It . . . is surrounded by two sections of 17 chapters each." Strauss also refers his readers to the *Guide* I: 17 where Maimonides explains that neither divine nor natural science should be taught to the people as a whole and that ancient philosophers like Plato concealed what they said about first principles by presenting riddles.

3. *SPPP*, p. 147.

4. Ibid., p. 168.

5. Although the pre-Socratic philosophers do not agree with Hesiod in teaching "that everything has come into being," they do suggest that "the gods as ordinarily understood have come into being, just as heaven and earth, and therefore will perish again." Even Aristotle, who represented philosophy at "the time when the opposition between Jerusalem and Athens reached the level of what one may call its classic struggle, in the twelfth and thirteenth centuries," conceived of

god "only as a thinking being who rules the world only by thinking and thinks nothing but himself. He surely does not rule by giving orders and laws. Hence he is not a creator-god. . . . Man is not his image; man is much lower in rank than other parts of the world." It is almost a blasphemy, according to Aristotle, to attribute justice to this god. *SPPP,* pp. 165–67.

6. Ibid., pp. 164–66.

7. As Plato's two strangers teach, human beings have to form or invent cities for themselves, because the gods no longer rule or direct their actions; that is, there is no divine providence. Cf. *AAPL,* p. 58.

8. "Being concerned with 'the social idea'," Strauss observes, "Cohen does not say a single word on Christianity in the whole lecture." *SPPP,* p. 167. Strauss himself follows Cohen's example in generally ignoring the role of Christianity, which was explicitly the basis of much German idealist philosophy. Rather than seek a mediator between the two realms of poles of the Western tradition, Strauss wants to separate them.

9. Ibid., p. 167. Emphasis added.

10. If we disregard the introduction Strauss did not live to write, we see that his "studies" are divided into two parallel sets of eight essays. (When so divided, "Jerusalem and Athens" stands as the conclusion of the first set of essays on Platonic politics; it ends with a critique of Cohen, which is paralleled by the concluding essay in the second set of essays on Cohen's *Religion of Reason.*) Each set of essays begins with a critique of one of the "radical historicist" thinkers, who brought the value of the Western tradition into question. The three chapters Strauss had planned to write on Plato for the first set of studies are paralleled by three chapters on Maimonides, the medieval Jewish Platonist, in the second. Discounting the introductory essays on radical historicism, the central essay in the first set on Thucydides is paralleled by an essay on Machiavelli in the second. The connection between the chapter on "Xenophon's *Anabasis*" that follows the chapter on Thucydides and the review of Macpherson's critique of 'possessive individualism' that follows the chapter on Machiavelli is not immediately clear; both could be seen to point out the power of the attachment to one's own in politics. Strauss's brief history of the doctrine of natural law in the first set of essays concerning the ancient understanding more clearly parallels his review of J. Talmon's *History of the Jewish People* in the second. For an example of such variable counting (or not) of introductions, see Strauss's account of "How Farabi Read Plato's *Laws,*" in *WIPP,* pp. 147–48.

11. "Heidegger's philosophy of history has the same structure as Marx and Nietzsche's. . . . But Heidegger is much closer to Nietzsche than to Marx. Both thinkers regard as decisive the nihilism which according to them began in Plato (or before)—Christianity being only Platonism for the people—whose ultimate consequence is the present decay" (*SPPP,* p. 33).

12. "One is inclined to say that Heidegger has learned the lesson of 1933 more thoroughly than any other man" (ibid., p. 34).

13. Strauss's interpretation of Heidegger here is unique, but may nevertheless be correct.

14. *SPPP,* p. 37.

15. Thomas C. Brickhouse and Nicholas D. Smith present such a view of *Plato's Socrates* (New York: Oxford, 1994).

16. As Farabi pointed out, Plato's Socrates converses only with members of the elite, if not the highest elite.

17. *SPPP*, pp. 50–51. The reason Socrates says he does not propose exile is that "in any other city . . . he would have the same troubles as in Athens. The young men would listen to his speeches; if he were to chase them away, they would persuade their elders to expel him; if he would not chase them away, their fathers and other relatives would" (*Apology* 37d–e; *SPPP*, p. 50). But, as Socrates reminded his audience in his first speech, he had survived in Athens for seventy years. As Strauss pointed out in his introduction to *AAPL*, the conjunction between the reasons "the laws" give in the *Crito* why Socrates should not run away with the setting of the *Laws* suggests the philosopher could have gone anonymously to Crete and continued philosophizing there, if he had been younger.

18. In presenting reasons why he should not escape to safety after he had been convicted in the *Crito*, Strauss points out, Socrates does not mention either the soul or philosophy—considerations both he and the Athenian Stranger argue should take precedence over concerns not only about one's bodily self-preservation but also one's forbears, one of the grounds "the laws" give for his obligation to obey. The reasons "the laws" give correspond to Kriton's, but not to Socrates' own concerns.

19. In *Hermeneutics as Politics* (New York: Oxford University Press, 1987), p. 123, Stanley Rosen wonders why Strauss says in his discussion of Plato in *CM*, p. 61, that the dialogues are only "slightly" more akin to comedy than to tragedy. Here we have one reason; in the *Apology of Socrates*, Plato seems to many readers to present a tragedy. The conflict between politics and philosophy appears comic only "from some perspectives," Strauss observes. (In his analysis of Aristophanes he points out, a comedy cannot depict a death, because it is too serious.) There is, however, something comic about Socrates' presentation of himself as a tragic hero. He does not "seem to notice the slight incongruity of comparing his dying in ripe old age with Achilleus' dying young." *SPPP*, p. 44.

20. "Deeds are more trustworthy than speeches: Socrates did stay in prison, he chose to stay, he had a *logos* telling him to stay. But is this *logos* identical with the *logos* by which he persuades Kriton? We have indicated why this is not likely. . . . Kriton is concerned above all with what the people of Athens will say if he has not helped Socrates to escape from prison: what Socrates tells Kriton, Kriton can and will tell the people" (*SPPP*, p. 66). Nietzsche also thought that Socrates arranged his own death. *Birth of Tragedy*, sec. 13.

21. In Plato's *Meno*, Socrates is shown to outrage Anytus by arguing that outstanding Athenian statesmen like Pericles have failed to educate even their own sons. In Xenophon's *Apology to the Jury*, Socrates makes a snide prediction about the future of Anytus's own son. In Xenophon's *Symposium*, Lykon is shown to be so enamored of his son that he sees little else.

22. Strauss argues that, although the authenticity of this dialogue has been put into question, in the *Theages* Plato shows the same relation between the *daimonion* and Socrates' *eros* that Xenophon did. *SPPP*, pp. 46–47. In Plato's *Symposium* 216c–219c Alcibiades suggests that Socrates only pretends to be attracted to young men; his purported *eros* is really a way of attracting them to him so that he can guide, if not dominate, their lives.

23. *SPPP*, p. 70.

24. Both dialectics and politics are disqualified, because they use materials—mathematical figures, in the case of dialectics, and men or wealth, in the case of politics—produced by other arts. The only kind of knowledge that would seem to satisfy the dual criteria of production and use would appear to be the only kind of knowledge Plato's Socrates ever claims, the knowledge of erotic things that enables him, first to arouse desire for knowledge on the part of his young interlocutors and then to use that desire to make them better. But neither Socrates nor Strauss mentions the positive side of the philosopher's *daimonion* or its relevance to the substance of the discussion.

25. In contrast to Xenophon's Socrates, Plato's hero does not want to spend even an afternoon telling a foolish young man how to become *kalos k'agathos*, conventionally understood.

26. Socrates responds to Dionysodoros's critique of the doctrine of beautiful things "participating" in the beautiful and yet being different from the beautiful-in-itself with an eristic argument concerning the same and the different that reminds of one of Plato's other philosophical spokesman, the Eleatic Stranger, who suggests in the *Sophist* that we define everything according to its similarities and differences with others.

27. *SPPP*, p. 88. Strauss thus cites the passage in which Socrates explains why he and other philosophers stay out of politics with no reference to his *daimonion* whatsoever.

28. This is the message Socrates gives both Gorgias and Protagoras in the dialogues named after the rhetorician and the sophist.

29. Kriton takes Socrates at his word when the philosopher tells his old friend that he wants to study with the eristic sophists; Kriton simply refuses to join him. Kriton thus shows he does not understand Socrates' irony or enjoyment of intellectual play; and readers of the *Euthydemus* learn from the action that the philosopher's dissimulation extends beyond his making up the story about the oracle to explain his philosophical investigations and the use of his *daimonion* to explain his refusing to engage in politics. Kriton does not believe in the *daimonion;* he does not think the *daimonion's* failure to warn Socrates away from court constituted an adequate reason for him to go to trial. And, Plato indicates, Kriton was right. As he demonstrates in the *Republic,* Socrates does not need a divine voice to tell him that he will be killed if he goes into politics. Nor does he refrain from political action simply to save his life. Like the philosophers in the *Republic,* he does not want to devote his attention to affairs of state, because he has experienced a better way of life. As Xenophon shows, Socrates used his *daimonion* as an excuse, so he would not have to insult people by explaining the reasons he did not want to concern himself with their affairs. Like Aristodemus and Kriton, people who associated regularly with Socrates saw through that ruse. To prevent them from importuning him, Plato suggests, Socrates thus had to dissimulate further.

30. Strauss begins his "Preliminary Observations" by noting that they "'repeat,' i.e., modify some observations made in the Thucydides chapter of *The City and Man*" (p. 89). The most explicit modification occurs in his presentation of Thucydides' stance toward the piety of the Athenian general Nicias. In *CM* Strauss claimed Thucydides "reveals himself above all in his remark about the

fate of Nicias: Nicias deserved least of all the Greeks of Thucydides' time his disastrous end because of his full dedication, guided and inspired by law, to the practice of excellence" (p. 150). In his "Preliminary Observations" Strauss declares, "It is easy for us to find that the reference to 'the divine law' in Thucydides' account of the civil wars (III.82.6 [which he shows "led to complete disregard of the sanctity of asylum and to utter disregard of 'the divine law'"]) and to the gods [who are said to acknowledge the right of the stronger] in the dialogue between the Melians and the Athenians are the most important or the most revealing statements occurring in his work so far as the gods are concerned" (*SPPP*, pp. 93, 96). In *CM* he observed that Thucydides' sympathy for Nicias was "in accordance with our first impression according to which Thucydides' horizon is the horizon of the city" (p. 153). But later in the chapter Strauss showed that Thucydides had as much sympathy for the Athenian drive for glory as he had for Spartan "moderation." Indeed, he concluded, "Nicias like the Spartans believed that the fate of men or cities corresponds to their justice and piety. . . . But this correspondence rests entirely on hope, on unfounded or vain hope. The view set forth by the Athenians on Melos is true" (pp. 208–9). In his *Studies* Strauss makes the implicit conclusion of his previous analysis of Thucydides explicit when he states, "Thucydides' theology—if it is permitted to use this expression—is located in the mean (in the Aristotelian sense) between that of Nikias and that of the Athenian ambassadors on Melos" (p. 101). Contrary to his explicit conclusion in *CM*, Thucydides' horizon is *not* simply the horizon of the city. On the contrary, as Strauss showed in his account of "Thucydides' War" (*CM*, p. 159), the historian follows the expansive tendency of the city to its limits in order to reveal those limits, which have their origins in internal divisions. Every city is divided by the demands of necessity and right, war and peace, the few and the many. Cities are divided in this manner, because human nature itself is split, so that human beings vacillate between what the Athenian Stranger calls their primal fear and what Thucydides describes as pious hopes.

31. A comparison of Thucydides' *History* with Plutarch's account of the lives of Perikles and Alkibiades will remind the reader that the historian does not even mention the philosophical education of the Athenian leaders, the education Plutarch emphasizes.

32. *SPPP*, p. 111.

33. Ibid., p. 113.

34. Ibid., p. 136.

35. Ibid., pp. 138–39.

36. Ibid., pp. 140–45. Emphasis added.

37. Ibid., p. 145.

38. Ibid., p. 149.

39. Strauss refers his readers to a place at the beginning of the *Sophist* [216b5–6] where Socrates asks whether the Eleatic Stranger might not be a god and to the place in the *Theatetus* [151d1–2] where Socrates compares himself to a god, who is never unkind [or harms] anyone. Ibid., p. 175.

40. Ibid.

41. As Strauss points out, "The will to power takes the place which *eros*— the striving for 'the good in itself'—occupies in Plato's thought." Plato distin-

guished the desire for knowledge (*eros*) from the intellect (*nous*), the faculty through which we acquire it; "in Nietzsche's thought the will to power takes the place of both. . . ; it consists in prescribing to nature what or how it ought to be (aph. 9); it is not love of the true that is independent of will or decision" (ibid., p. 176).

42. Ibid., p. 178.

43. Ibid., p. 179.

44. Ibid., p. 181. A translation of Reinhardt's essay by Gunther Heilbrunn is to be found in *Interpretation* 6, no. 3 (October 1977): 207–24. Reinhardt argues that after *Zarathustra* Nietzsche's thought enters a new phase in which the 'over-man' Zarathustra, who has struggled against himself in order to overcome himself and remains "nothing but an old atheist" (*Will to Power* 1038), is superseded by Dionysus as philosopher. Seeking to make man "stronger, more evil, deeper than he is. . . ; more beautiful, too," Dionysus tempts men, like the hero Theseus, with Ariadne. She tells him the "truth," how to find his way through the labyrinth of life. But "though he calls it his truth, it is what surrenders to him, what seduces him and leads him astray." Embodying the principle of life itself—or love—Ariadne herself becomes the labyrinth from which he seeks to escape. When Theseus casts her away for having deceived him, she suffers. So does the god watching the tragedy who, loving both, wants to improve them and so causes them both to suffer desertion and destruction as the necessary condition for their rebirth and striving anew. Like the Christian passion play, Nietzsche's mystery is the story not only of sacrifice and redemption through love, but also of three as one, i.e., of the essential unity of the parts. In his notes for the *Will to Power*, Reinhardt observes, Nietzsche announces that "This Dionysian world of mine, a world in which the self is eternally creating and eternally destroying itself, this mystery-world of ambiguous desires. . . . This world is the will to power—and nothing besides! And you yourselves are this will to power—and nothing besides!" (p. 218). The Christian God demonstrated his love of humanity by giving his only begotten son to save those who believe in Him—in the afterlife; Nietzsche's Dionysus demonstrates his love of human beings by tempting them constantly to destroy themselves as they are (the effect of education, we might recall, according to the sophist Dionysodoros) in an attempt to become something better or more beautiful. In the myth of the ancient mystery religion, "Dionysus is dismembered by the Titans; according to Nietzsche, he destroys and renews himself, becoming the symbol not only of the new human being, but in the literal sense the god of the future" (p. 219).

45. *SPPP*, p. 183.

46. Ibid., pp. 184–85. Emphasis added.

47. Ibid., p. 185. "By saying Yes to everything that was and is," Strauss observes, "Nietzsche may seem to reveal himself as radically antirevolutionary or conservative. . . . Remembering Nietzsche's strictures against 'ideals' and 'idealists' we are reminded of Goethe's words to Eckermann (November 24, 1824) according to which "everything idea-like (*jedes Ideelle*) is serviceable for revolutionary purposes" (p. 180). In other words, Plato's philosophy may foster change more than Nietzsche's; the difference between the best and the existent provides not only grounds for discontent with the present but also guidance for intentional

action to improve current conditions. That is perhaps as much as to say, Plato's philosophy is more political than Nietzsche's.

48. Ibid., p. 187.

49. Among other things, Nietzsche stated in *Twilight of the Idols*), "Plato is boring." ("What I Owe to the Ancients," no. 2.) Plato or his Socrates seems to say the same old things, repeatedly; this is one of the ways in which he distinguishes himself from the sophist Hippias. In contrast to Plato, "Nietzsche surely is never boring" (*SPPP*, p. 183). He has several different, perhaps even contradictory teachings; and he explicitly innovates. He presents himself as the herald of a new "philosophy of the future."

50. *SPPP*, p. 174.

51. "At the end of the seventh chapter [of *Beyond Good and Evil*]. . . , he questions the truth of what he is about to say by claiming that it expresses merely his 'fundamental stupidity deep down'" (ibid., p. 190).

52. Ibid., pp. 197–98.

53. He suggested that a wise man should be extremely moderate in the way in which he tends to his bodily needs and that he should not vaunt his wisdom. (That is, like Socrates, who is not named, the wise man should be ascetic and moderate.) But, Maimonides also observed that "the extreme humility demanded by the Torah does not preclude the sage's concern with being honored. . . , for that concern only reflects his concern with the Torah being honored" (*SPPP*, pp. 199–200). If the chief proponents of the law appeared to be too humble, he recognized, the law would not be respected. But if they used their position to enrich themselves or vaunted their superiority, the justice of the law would also be brought into question. The middle Aristotelian way was best.

54. Ibid., p. 207. As Strauss observed in a footnote to his earlier essay on "Maimonides' Statement on Political Science," "Military art . . . is certainly not a part of the Torah" (*WIPP*, p. 158). Maimonides recognized that, for the Torah truly to be honored, it had to be made into effective law. For the Torah to become effective law, the Jews had to regain their political independence; and to regain their independence, they would have to organize and maintain an army. According to the *Mishneh Torah*, "The restoration of Jewish freedom in the Messianic age is not to be understood as a miracle." Cf. *Book of Knowledge from the Mishneh Torah of Maimonides*, trans. H. M. Russell and Rabbi J. Weinberg (New York: KTAV Publishing House, 1983), treatise V, ch. 9, sec. 2: "In the days of the Messiah in this world things will go on as usual, except that Israel will have its own government."

55. In his earlier essay on Maimonides' *Treatise*, Strauss was "tempted to say that the *Logic* is the only philosophic book Maimonides ever wrote" (*WIPP*, p. 158). Here he points out that the *Logic* has fourteen chapters. In chapter 7, at the end of the first half, Maimonides describes the syllogisms proving that the heavens are created as analogical; these syllogisms are based on a disregard for the difference between natural and artificial things. In chapter 8 Maimonides then says "that it is the art of rhetoric as distinguished from the art of demonstration that uses analogical syllogisms." In the middle of his treatise (where readers are least apt to notice), Maimonides thus suggests that the teaching the heavens are created is rhetorical.

328   NOTES TO PAGES 191–92

56. In his earlier gloss on the *Logic,* Strauss pointed out that, according to Maimonides, "Whereas the *nomos* [ancient law] entails a religion that is in the service of government, the divinely revealed law . . . puts government in the service of . . . the true religion. . . . Hence it is exposed to dangers which did not threaten the pagan *nomoi.* For instance, the public discussion of "the account of creation," i.e., of physics, did not harm the pagans in the way in which it might harm the adherents of revealed laws. The divinely revealed laws also create dangers which did not exist among the Greeks" (*WIPP,* pp. 164–65). To maintain they were true, the revealed religions had to oppose—indeed, according to Maimonides' *Guide of the Perplexed* (III, 19), they had to drive out and eradicate even the memory of—not only the ancient Greek rationalist account of nature but also other religions. The emergence of the revealed religions thus made the world a more dangerous place—for both philosophers and nonphilosophers. Nevertheless, Strauss suggests at the conclusion of this "note," the political difficulties or wars that resulted from the spread of revealed religion might not have been simply bad. Maimonides' "expression 'the great nation or the nations,' as distinguished from 'the great nation or all nations' may indicate that there cannot be a great nation comprising all nations. This 'Averroist' view is best known to us from Marsilius of Padua's *Defensor Pacis* (I, 17.10)." At the place cited, Marsilius observes that the question of whether a world government would be better than a variety of nations, separated by different languages and customs, is not settled, but the heavenly cause inclines to the latter, because wars moderate the procreation of men and animals and so enable the earth to support them. According to Marsilius, the practical effects of the wars thus support Averroes's theoretical argument for the eternity of generation. More generally stated, in concluding his "note" Strauss suggests that the political disputes that arose as a result of the spread of revealed religion may have had a beneficent effect insofar as they prompted thoughtful individuals to reopen the question of the truth of ancient philosophy as opposed to Scripture.

57. Machiavelli amused himself and some of his readers, Strauss observes, "by using the word 'virtue' in both the traditional sense and his sense." The distinction he occasionally draws between *virtu* and *bonta* "had been prepared by Cicero who says that men are called 'good' on account of their modesty, temperance, and above all, justice. . . , as distinguished from courage and wisdom. The Ciceronian distinction within the virtues in its turn reminds us of Plato's *Republic* in which temperance and justice are presented as virtues required of all, whereas courage and wisdom are required only of some" (*SPPP,* p. 215). Machiavelli's distinction between the *virtue* of rulers and soldiers as opposed to the goodness, fear-bred obedience or even vileness of the people, prepared the way, in turn, for Nietzsche's denial that temperance and justice would be virtues of the philosophers of the future. In demanding that philosophers be legislators, Nietzsche took Machiavelli's contention that the greatest thing a human being can do is to found "new modes and orders" to its logical conclusion.

58. *SPPP,* p. 227. Strauss's account of Machiavelli and his significance in the history of political philosophy resembles that he presented in "What Is Political Philosophy?" and *Thoughts on Machiavelli* with one exception. In his previous works, Strauss suggested that Machiavelli's political teaching rested on a kind

of "decayed Aristotelianism." In this essay, he concludes that Machiavelli's chief ancient sources were the materialists, Aristippus and Diogenes. Ibid., p. 228.

59. In *The Theory of Possessive Individualism*, the standard on the basis of which C. B. Macpherson finds Hobbes's political philosophy defective is "'the idea of freedom as a concomitant of social living in an unacquisitive society' . . . which . . . transcends the boundaries of any 'single national state'" (*SPPP*, p. 229). But, Strauss objects, "if the rational society is not the universal socialist society, 'the political theory of possessive individualism' must be examined in the light of a different ideal" (p. 231).

60. Ibid., pp. 235–37.

61. Ibid., p. 242.

62. Ibid., pp. 244–45.

63. Ibid., p. 168.

64. Cf. "The Three Waves of Modernity," in Hilail Gildin, ed., *An Introduction to Political Philosophy: Ten Essays by Leo Strauss* (Detroit: Wayne State University Press, 1989), pp. 85–86.

65. *CM*, p. 9.

66. *Liberalism: Ancient and Modern* (New York: Basic Books, 1968), viii.

67. *SPPP*, p. 211. What is 'modern' is seeing biblical morality and Greek rationality as two competing and fundamentally incompatible visions of human excellence between which it is impossible to choose. What is untenable, according to Strauss, is (1) the attempt of the early moderns to "lower the sights" and (2) the attempt of the later moderns, especially the German idealists, to respond to the human desire for a nobler vision of the possibilities of human existence by combining rationalism and biblical morality.

68. Ibid., pp. 210–11; *Thoughts on Machiavelli* (Glencoe, Ill.: Free Press, 1959), p. 133: "I believe . . . that the Bible sets forth the demands of morality and religion in their purest and most intransigent form."

69. "Three Waves," p. 82.

70. In his essay "Progress or Return?" Strauss thus points out the extent to which ancient political philosophy and the Bible agree not only on the content and importance, but also on the *fundamental insufficiency* of morality: "Greek philosophy and the Bible agree . . . that the proper framework of morality is the patriarchal family, . . . which forms the cell of a society in which the free adult males, and especially the old ones, predominate. . . . Consisting of free men, the society praised by the Bible and Greek philosophy refuses to worship any human being. . . . The Bible and Greek philosophy [also] agree in assigning the highest place among the virtues not to courage or manliness, but to justice. And by justice both understand, primarily, obedience to the law. . . , not merely civil. . . , but moral and religious law as well." But once again, he emphasizes, they disagree about the basis of morality: "The Bible teaches divine omnipotence, and the thought of divine omnipotence is absolutely incompatible with Greek philosophy in any form. . . . In all Greek thought, we find . . . an impersonal necessity higher than any personal being; whereas in the Bible the first cause is, as people say now, a person. This is connected with the fact that the concern of God with man is absolutely . . . essential to the Biblical God; whereas that concern is . . . a problem for every Greek philosopher" (*CR*, pp. 246–47, 252).

71. "A Giving of Accounts," p. 4: "Mr. Klein and I differ regarding the status of morality. . . ; in your scheme of things morality has a higher place than in my scheme."

72. *CM*, p. 11.

73. "Three Waves," p. 98; cf. Gildin's commentary on this statement in "Leo Strauss and the Crisis of Liberal Democracy," in *the Crisis of Liberal Democracy: A Straussian Perspective*, ed. Kenneth L. Deutsch and Walter Soffer (Albany: State University of New York Press, 1987), pp. 91–103.

74. God gave human beings an opportunity to live as they wish, without evil, which is to say in innocence, in the garden of Eden. Adam and Eve were not denied knowledge per se; "without knowledge [Adam] could not have known the tree of knowledge nor the woman . . . nor could he have understood the prohibition. Man was denied knowledge of good and evil, i.e., the knowledge sufficient for guiding himself, his life." The Bible does not say that Adam and Eve rebelled "high-handedly against God; they rather forgot to obey God. . . . Nevertheless God punished them severely." Freedom to disobey and punishment, that is, suffering the evil consequences of bad judgment or memory, necessarily go together. But, "after the expulsion from the garden of Eden, God did not punish men, apart from the relatively mild punishment which He inflicted on Cain. Nor did He establish human judges. God as it were experimented, for the instruction of mankind, with mankind living in freedom from law. This experiment just as the experiment with men remaining like innocent children, ended in failure. Fallen or awake man needs restraint, must live under law." The law cannot simply be imposed, however. After the Flood God thus asked human beings to join in a covenant with Him, though not as equal partners. "The inequality regarding the Covenant is shown especially by the fact that God's undertaking never again to destroy almost all life on earth as long as the earth lasts is not conditioned on all men or almost all men obeying the laws promulgated by God after the Flood: God's promise is made despite, or because of, His knowing that the devisings of man's heart are evil from his youth." The covenant with Noah prepares the way for the covenant with Abraham. In the interim, we witness the first division among human beings into cursed and blessed races and the attempt to overcome that division at Babel. "God scattered them . . . by bringing about the division of mankind into groups speaking different languages." This division constitutes a milder alternative to the Flood: "well-nigh universal wickedness will no longer be punished with well-nigh universal destruction; well-nigh universal wickedness will be prevented by the division of mankind into nations" (*SPPP*, pp. 154–62).

75. As Strauss points out, "The second account [of the creation of man in *Genesis*] makes clear that man consists of two profoundly different ingredients, a high one and a low one" (ibid., pp. 154–55).

76. Both in his initial account of "Plato's *Apology of Socrates* and *Crito*," p. 66, and in his essay on "Niccolo Machiavelli," p. 211, Strauss explicitly takes issue with Hobbes's critique of Socrates for having undermined law-abidingness.

77. Cf. *Federalist* 10.

78. In *Hermeneutics as Politics*, p. 136, Rosen suggests Strauss did not and could not have believed his own arguments that Aristotelian gentlemen should rule, because they were reflections of the philosopher. By 'gentleman' Strauss

made clear in his articles on liberal education (*LAM*, pp. 3–25), he meant primarily the educated; in the ancient world, the opportunity to obtain an education required one to have wealth. These gentlemen were reflections of the philosopher insofar and only insofar as they studied things for their own sake, that is, pursued activities that were good and beautiful in themselves, as opposed to useful crafts, trades, or kinds of knowledge. Like the ancient philosophers he praised, Strauss explicitly recognized that in most cases these "gentlemen" or "aristocrats" were no more than oligarchs.

79. Nor did Strauss think modern democracies had successfully educated all their citizens. Cf. *WIPP*, pp. 37–38; *LAM*, pp. 15–25.

80. *Thoughts*, p. 299: "The difficulty implied the admission that inventions pertaining to the art of war must be encouraged is the only one which supplies a basis for Machiavelli's criticism of classical political philosophy."

81. *CM*, p. 138.

CHAPTER SEVEN

1. *De la grammatologie* (Paris: Minuit, 1967), pp. 31–33; *Of Grammatology*, trans. Gayatri Chalzravorty Spivak (Baltimore: Johns Hopkins University Press, 1976), pp. 19–24.

2. In "Like the Sound of the Sea Deep within a Shell: Paul de Man's War," trans. Peggy Kamuf, *Critical Inquiry* 14 (spring 1988): 648, Derrida declares, "I am Jewish, I was persecuted as a child during the war, I have always been known for my leftist opinions, I fight as best I can, for example against racism (for instance, in France or in the United States . . .), against *apartheid* or for the recognition of the rights of the Palestinians. I have gotten myself arrested, interrogated, and imprisoned by totalitarian police."

3. "La pharmacie de Platon," in *La dissémination* (Paris: Seuil, 1972), pp. 97–98; *Dissemination*, trans. Barbara Johnson (Chicago: University of Chicago Press, 1981, p. 86.

4. Cf. "The Principle of Reason: The University in the Eyes of Its Pupils," *diacritics* 13 (fall 1983): 3–20, and "No Apocalypse, Not Now," *diacritics* 14 (summer 1984): 20–31.

5. E. g., Stanley Rosen, *Hermeneutics as Politics* (New York: Oxford University Press, 1987); Susan Handelman, *The Slayers of Moses: the Emergence of Rabbinic Interpretation in Modern Literary Theory* (Albany: State University of New York Press, 1982).

6. Leo Strauss, "The Three Waves of Modernity," in Hilail Gildin, ed. *An Introduction to Political Philosophy: Ten Essays by Leo Strauss* (Detroit: Wayne State University Press, 1989), p. 98; *Studies in Platonic Political Philosophy* (Chicago: University of Chicago Press, 1983), p. 30; Jacques Derrida, *Otobiographies: L'enseignement de Nietzsche et la politique du nom propre* (Paris: Galilee, 1984), pp. 41–42, 90–96, *The Ear of the Other*, ed. Christie V. McDonald (New York: Schocken Books, 1985), pp. 7, 28–30; *De l'esprit: Heidegger et la question* (Paris: Galilee, 1987), pp. 53–73; *Of Spirit: Heidegger and the Question*, trans. Geoffrey Bennington and Rachel Bowlby (Chicago: University of Chicago Press, 1989), pp. 31–46.

7. Cf. Strauss's critique of modern social science and the probable results of the institution of a world state, as advocated by Alexandre Kojève in *On Tyranny*,

ed. Victor Gourevitch and Michael S. Roth (New York: Free Press, 1991), pp. 22–28, 177–212, and "Like the Sound of the Sea Deep within a Shell," in which Derrida states that what he "practiced under the name" of "deconstruction" was designed primarily "to free oneself of totalitarianism as far as possible. It is no doubt my principal motivation" (p. 648).

8. Gadamer himself suggests as much when, in characterizing his own differences with Derrida, he refers to his correspondence with Strauss: "In a letter that has since been published, Leo Strauss got to the heart of the matter in saying that for Heidegger it is Nietzsche, while for me it is Dilthey, who forms the starting point for critique." Like Heidegger and Strauss, Gadamer sees, Derrida, too, begins from Nietzsche. "Text and Interpretation," in *Dialogue and Deconstruction: The Gadamer-Derrida Encounter,* trans. Diana P. Michelfeldern and Richard E. Palmer (Albany: State University of New York Press, 1989), p. 25.

9. *Edmund Husserl's "Origin of Geometry": An Introduction,* trans. John P. Leavey Jr. (Boulder: Nicolas Hays, 1978), p. 67.

10. *Origins,* p. 79. The *Origins* is written, Derrida suggests (p. 120), to a certain extent in response to Heidegger. While it is a mistake to forget the prescientific experience out of which science emerges, Husserl emphasizes, it is also a mistake to forget the scientific end of the inquiry. To give up the aspiration to make philosophy into a rigorous science (universally valid knowledge) is to give in to relativism.

11. Ibid., p. 116.

12. Ibid., pp. 79–80.

13. Ibid., pp. 81–82.

14. The "Three Questions to Hans-Georg Gadamer," that Derrida later raised in *Dialogue and Deconstruction: The Gadamer-Derrida Encounter,* pp. 52–54, are much the same as the three objections he initially made to Husserl. Although he did not specifically question Gadamer's contention that everything can be named, Derrida did raise questions about the willfulness of the "good will," the problems of incorporating psychological insights or findings about the "unconscious," and the recourse to the experience of the "living present."

15. *La voix et le phénomène* (Paris: Presses Universitaires de France, 1967), p. 3; *Speech and Phenomena,* trans. David B. Allison (Evanston: Northwestern University Press, 1973), p. 5.

16. *Speech,* p. 6 (*Voix,* p. 4).

17. Ibid., p. 53 (59).

18. In *"Différance,"* trans. David B. Allison, in *Speech and Phenomena,* pp. 129–30, Derrida explains he coined the word with the silent 'a' to signify the two meanings, to differ and to defer, a double signification which *only* appears in writing, not in speech.

19. *Speech,* p. 74 (82–83).

20. *Of Grammatology,* p. 70 (102–3). In *Philosophy as/and Literature: Nietzsche's Case* (New York: Routledge, 1993), pp. 11–16, Bernd Magnus, Stanley Stewart, and Jean-Pierre Mileur suggest that Derrida's departure from Heidegger reflects the influence of Saussure. Although I agree that Derrida's thought has a structuralist element that distinguishes it from Nietzsche and Heidegger by making it less historical, I think we should take Derrida's own use of the term "trace" instead of "sign," beginning with *"Differance,"* seriously.

21. Rather than responding to a "call of Being," Levinas argued, human beings respond first to the mute signs of distress in the face of another. Speech is initially vocative rather than indicative; our understanding and articulation of the world in language presupposes this first, *personal* appeal or demand and the consequent development of speech or language. This demand gives rise not only to our fundamental understanding of "self" but also to an infinite and inescapable responsibility for the other. Cf. "La trace de l'autre," *Tijdschrift voor Filosofie* (1963): 605–32; trans. Al Lingis, "On the Trail of the Other," *Philosophy Today* (1966): 40–41.

22. "Violence et métaphysique: essai sur la pensée d'Emmanuel Levinas," in *L'écriture et la différence* (Paris: Seuil, 1967), pp. 144–46; "Violence and Metaphysics," in *Writing and Difference*, trans. Alan Bass (Chicago: University of Chicago Press, 1978), pp. 97–98.

23. E. g., in the title of his book on *Psyche ou l'invention de l'autre.* Cf. Levinas, "Trail," p. 46, with Derrida, "Violence," p. 102.

24. "Violence," pp. 102–8 (150–60).

25. "L'Ontologie est-elle fondamental?," *Revue de Métaphysique et de Morale* 56 (1951): 88–98, trans. Peter Atterton, "Is Ontology Fundamental?," *Philosophy Today* 33 (1989): 121–29).

26. *Margins of Philosophy*, trans. Alan Bass (Chicago: University of Chicago Press, 1982), pp. 31–67.

27. "The Ends of Man," in *Margins*, pp. 124, 126–28, 130.

28. Ibid., pp. 131–32.

29. In an article on *"Geschlecht"* in *Research in Phenomenology* 13 (1983): 65–83, Derrida thus argues that Heidegger was justified in ignoring the sexual difference or choosing explicitly to make *Dasein* neutral initially as part of his attempt to break free of the anthropological or natural view of man.

30. *Spurs/Eperons: Nietzsche's Styles/Les Styles de Nietzsche*, trans. Barbara Harlow (Chicago: University of Chicago Press, 1979), p. 51.

31. Ibid., p. 103.

32. *Ear of the Other*, p. 20 (74–75).

33. "Interpreting Signatures (Nietzsche/Heidegger): Two Questions," in *Dialogue and Deconstruction: The Gadamer-Derrida Encounter*, pp. 52–54.

34. "Rather than protect Nietzsche from the Heideggerian reading, we should perhaps offer him up to it completely, underwriting that interpretation without reserve . . . up to the point where, the content of the Nietzschean discourse being almost lost for the question of being, . . . his text finally invokes a different type of reading, more faithful to his type of writing." *Grammatology*, p. 19 (32).

35. "Freud and the Scene of Writing," in *Writing and Difference*, pp. 196–231 (293–340).

36. Ibid., pp. 202–3 (300–301).

37. Ibid., p. 206 (306).

38. Ibid., p. 212 (314).

39. Ibid., p. 226 (335).

40. Ibid., p. 229 (339).

41. Ibid., p. 197 (294).

42. Critics sometimes take Derrida's argument about writing in the *Phaedrus* too literally, as if it concerned merely the merits of expressing things on paper

rather than vocally in speech. E.g., Yoav Rinon, "The Rhetoric of Jacques Derrida I: Plato's Pharmacy," *Review of Metaphysics* 46 (December 1992): 360–86. Jasper Neel, *Plato, Derrida, and Writing* (Carbondale: Southern Illinois University Press, 1988), represents a partial, but only a partial, corrective, because he treats Derrida's argument in the context of teaching composition.

43. "Pharmacy," pp. 66–67 (74–75). For this reason, some concluded it is an "early" work.

44. Quoted in "Pharmacy," p. 170 (197). The bracketed phrase is my translation of words Derrida himself supplies in Greek which are left out of the English translation. Rosen's criticism of Derrida in *Hermeneutics as Politics*, p. 56, for not taking any account of the way in which Plato wrote is thus not entirely justified. The difference between Rosen and Strauss, on the one hand, and Derrida, on the other, concerns the extent to which they think Plato intended and controlled the ambiguity.

45. Plato indicates as much, Derrida suggests, when Phaedrus describes the story of Boreas and Oreithyia as a *"mythologema"* (229c). Although Derrida does not take account of this, Socrates himself characterizes the "sayings" about the immortality of the soul discussed in the *Phaedo* (61d) the same way.

46. "Pharmacy," p. 85 (96).

47. Ibid., p. 115 (132).

48. Derrida cites *Meno* 80a–b where the young man accuses Socrates of "bewitching" *(pharmattein)* his interlocutors and the *Symposium* 194a where Agathon accuses Socrates of wishing to bewitch him (again *pharmattein)*, followed by Alcibiades' description of Socrates as a bewitching satyr who uses only a few words to have such an effect.

49. "Pharmacy," p. 117 (134).

50. Ibid., p. 119 (136).

51. Ibid., p. 130 (148).

52. Ibid., p. 134 (153).

53. Derrida cites the discussion in the *Cratylus* (432b–c) to show that, according to Plato, a perfect imitation would no longer constitute a mere imitation or copy. Although Derrida acknowledges that Plato does not always speak of imitation *(mimesis)* in disparaging terms, as in the *Sophist* where he distinguishes the *eidolon* from the *phantasm,* he nevertheless concludes that Plato must fundamentally view all "images" as defective "copies" of some original "truth." Cf. also "The Double Session," pp. 183–93 (203–9).

54. As the embodiment of *logos* or *spoken* dialectic, Socrates is not "the father." He is not the origin of the *logoi* he examines or gives. "In the dialogues, [Socrates] plays the role of father, *represents* the father." As he himself states in the *Apology* (31a–d), he admonishes his countrymen as a result of a divine voice. "As the bearer of this sign from God. . . , Socrates thus takes voice from the father; he is the father's spokesman" ("Pharmacy," pp. 146, 148 [169–70]). The voice which "pushes Socrates to take the place [*suppleer*] of the father or elder brother toward the Athenians" only dissuades. That is, the voice is essentially negative. And because the Socratic voice (or dialogue) is only negative, it itself is essentially sterile. As Socrates himself admits in the *Theatetus* (150c–d); he himself does not give birth to wisdom. He can only facilitate or abort the births of others.

55. Ibid., p. 154 (178).

56. Ibid., p. 155 (180).

57. In this respect his readings of Plato differ significantly from those he later gives of Edgar Allen Poe or Baudelaire. "*Le facteur de la vérité,*" in *La carte postale* (Paris: Flammarion, 1980), pp. 441–524 (*The Post Card,* trans. Alan Bass [Chicago: University of Chicago Press, 1987], pp. 413–96; and *Given Time,* trans. Peggy Kamuf (Chicago: University of Chicago Press, 1992), pp. 84–172.

58. "Pharmacy," p. 170 (197). I have adjusted the translation.

CHAPTER EIGHT

1. *PC,* pp. 3, 5 (7, 9). The variable identity of the author and his or her correspondent images Derrida's argument that there is nothing and no one that has a singular identity. "You do not know who you are nor to whom precisely I am addressing myself. But there is only you in the world" (p. 69 [77]). And p. 143 (155): "Beyond everything that is, you are the one—and therefore the other." On p. 147 (160): "You are my only double. . . . you are . . . the title of everything that I do not understand. That I never will be able to know, the other side of myself, eternally inaccessible, not unthinkable at all, but unknowable, unknown—and so lovable." Thus on p. 178 (193) he writes, "They will believe that we are two. . . , that we are legally and sexually identifiable, unless they wake up one day." On p. 185 (199–200): "I no longer know to whom I am speaking. . . . The worst mistake of our expert bloodhounds will consist in naming you, something I would never have dared to do." And on p. 199 (214): "I also thought that upon reading this sorted mail they could think that I alone am sending these letters to myself."

2. "This is serious because it upsets perhaps Heidegger's still 'derivative' schema . . . by giving one to think that technology, . . . let us say even metaphysics do not overtake, do not come *to determine* and to dissimulate an '*envoi*' of Being . . . but would belong to the 'first' *envoi*—which obviously is never 'first' in any order whatsoever, for example a chronological or logical order, or even the order of *logos*. . . . If the post . . . is announced at the "first" *envoi,* then there is no longer A metaphysics, etc. . . . , nor even AN *envoi,* but *envois* without destination" (ibid., pp. 65–66 [73–74]).

3. Ibid., p. 20 (25).

4. Ibid., p. 58 (65). This time Derrida does not add the Greek, and the English translation is somewhat different.

5. Ibid., p. 12 (16).

6. Ibid., p. 52 (59). In *d'un ton apocalyptique adopté naguère en philosophie* (Paris: Galilee, 1983), pp. 11–12; "Of an Apocalyptic Tone Newly Adopted in Philosophy," trans. John P. Leavey Jr., *Derrida and Negative Theology* (Albany: State University of New York Press, 1992), Derrida observes, "As Andre Chouraqui recalls in his short 'Liminaire pour l'Apocalypse' of John. . . , the word *gala* recurs more than one hundred times in the Hebrew Bible and seems in effect to say *apokalupsis,* disclosure, . . . the veil lifted from . . . man's or woman's sex, but also their eyes or ears. . . . Nowhere does the word *apocalypse.* . . . have the sense it finally takes on in French and other tongues: fearsome catastrophe" (pp. 26–27).

7. *PC,* p. 30 (35).

8. Ibid., p. 98 (107–8). "Scratch" here seems to refer both to erasure and to

sexual stimulation. Derrida's relation to his "other" in the *Envois* is also sexual. E. g., pp. 183–84 (198).

9. *PC*, p. 20 (25).

10. Ibid., p. 13 (17–18).

11. Ibid., p. 21 (26).

12. Ibid., p. 202 (217).

13. Derrida indicates that the principle is generalizable, when the author of the *Envois* observes, "In the last analysis I do nothing that does not have some interest in seducing you, in setting you astray from yourself in order to set you on the way toward me, uniquely—nevertheless you do not know who you are nor to whom precisely I am addressing myself. But there is only you in the world." *PC*, p. 69 (76–77). No author knows all his or her potential readers; but the relation to these readers defines his or her "world."

14. Ibid., p. 117 (128). Cf. p. 135 (147): "Just as for us, the problem of the child posed itself for them only in a second, at the very second when they accepted their homosexuality."

15. They also entail a certain lack of completeness or self-sufficiency. In "Heidegger's Ear: Philopolemology (*Geschlecht* IV)," trans. John P. Leavey Jr., in John Sallis, ed., *Reading Heidegger* (Bloomington: Indiana University Press, 1993), pp. 179–86, Derrida observes that in *What Is Philosophy?* Heidegger thus contrasted the eroticized character of the search for knowledge initiated by Socrates and Plato with the wonderful experience of "Being" to be found in the fragments of Heraclitus and Parmenides.

16. *PC*, p. 372–75 (394–400).

17. Ibid., pp. 320–21 (341–42).

18. Ibid., p. 334 (355).

19. Ibid., pp. 398–99 (425–26).

20. Ibid., p. 402 (429).

21. Ibid., p. 403 (430).

22. Ibid., p. 405 (432).

23. Richard Rorty's suggestion that *The Post Card* ought to be read simply as a novel or fiction that has no general philosophical doctrine may be supported by the message on the card dated 24 August 1979, "some will think, rightly or wrongly, that there is not one true word, that I am writing this novel to kill time in your absence (and is that untrue?)" (p. 252 [269]). Rorty's further contention that the fiction has only a private meaning is contradicted, however, by the comment reported from 15 March 1979, "I do not believe in propriety, property, and above all not in the form that it takes according to the opposition public/private" (p. 185 [199]). In *The Post Card* Derrida does explicitly take issue with the interpretation of his work Rorty opposes, namely, that *différance* constitutes a transcendental philosophical principle. 9 May 1979: "The postal principle is no longer a principle, nor a transcendental category" (p. 191 [206]). Cf. Richard Rorty, *Contingency, Irony, and Solidarity* (Cambridge: Cambridge University Press, 1988), ch. 6; "Is Derrida a Transcendental Philosopher?" in David Wood, ed., *Derrida: A Critical Reader* (Oxford: Blackwell Publishers, 1992), pp. 235–46; Rodolphe Gasche, *The Tain of the Mirror* (Baltimore: Johns Hopkins University Press, 1986), pp. 4, 8, 122–39; Christopher Norris, *Derrida* (Cambridge, Mass.: Harvard University Press, 1987), p. 156.

24. *PC*, p. 126 (138): "From you *j'accepte* everything, even what you do not know."

25. Both Bonaparte and Lacan read the story in terms of the Freudian notion of the castration of woman, Derrida observes. But where Bonaparte falls back on the unconscious of the author, Lacan finds a more general truth, the law of the signifier, which operates independently of any authorial intention. In his own reading, Derrida shares elements of both. Like Bonaparte, he emphasizes the doubles in the story, as well as its explicit connections to other tales, but he does not trace these to the author's unconscious. Like Lacan, he reads both Freud and Poe in terms of Heidegger; but where Lacan seeks the truth of "full speech" which occurs only through a dialectic of recognition, Derrida emphasizes the endlessly doubling character of this as all writing. If everything is a text, and a text is an interweaving of *traits* or traces, the elements can and perhaps inevitably will be rearranged. Nevertheless, one cannot escape the impression that Derrida thinks his reading is truer to the text—if not to "Poe"—than either of the others, because it is more comprehensive and because it takes better account of the literary form than either Freud or his students. An improvement on the original is not perhaps entirely true to the original?

26. It is never really clear who is a participant, Derrida suggests. He was confronted with a rumor he saw upon reflection that he could not disprove, that an unnamed person was in analysis with him.

27. *PC*, pp. 519–21 (548–49).

28. Ibid., pp. 100–101 (110–11).

29. *Khora* (Paris: Galilee, 1993), pp. 15–16.

30. In opposition to Aristotle, Derrida notes, Ibid., pp. 54–55, that Timaeus never uses the word *hyle* to qualify *khora*.

31. Ibid., p. 27.

32. "There is *khora*, but the *khora* does not exist. . . . We cite a word of Plato . . . [which refers] to something which is not a thing but which insists in its unicity, so enigmatic, as to allow or to make itself be called without response, without giving itself to be seen, conceived. Deprived of a real referent, that which in effect resembles a proper name is found also to call an X which . . . [has] nothing at all proper to it. . . . This very singular "im-propriety" . . . is that which *khora* ought, if one can say it, to guard . . . [and] what it is necessary *for us* to guard for it" (ibid., p. 30).

33. Ibid., p. 29. *The* point of emphasizing that there is only a cleft or abyss at the "root" of all things, according to Heidegger himself in his *Nietzsche* lectures, is "preventing a 'humanization' of being in its totality. The 'humanization' carries with it a moral explication of the world starting from the resolution of a Creator, that has its technical explanation, starting with the activity of a grand artisan *(Handwerker)* (the Demiurge)." *Khora*, n. 4; Martin Heidegger, *Nietzsche*, vol. 1, p. 350.

34. In the foreword to the separate publication of *Khora*—it was first published in 1987 in *Poikilia, Etudes offerts a Jean-Pierre Vernant*, Paris, aux editions de l'EHESS—Derrida notes that it is coming out simultaneously in the Galilee edition with two other essays, *Passions* and *Sauf le nom*, "works that seem to respond and perhaps to be clarified in the interior of one and the same configuration." He describes the three essays as "*on one given name* or on that which can

arrive at a given name." As the titles of the other two essays indicate, the question of the name has theological or perhaps anti-theological overtones. "Save the name" indicates both all we can know and what we should do, according to a certain Christian tradition of negative theology, which encourages prayers to or calls upon God, whose character we cannot determine or know. *Sauf le nom* appeared first in English, translated by John P. Leavy Jr., under the title of *"Post-Scriptum,"* in a volume of essays on *Derrida and Negative Theology*, ed. Harold Coward and Toby Foshay (Albany: State University of New York Press, 1992), pp. 283–323. (In the form of a fictive dialogue, it constitutes Derrida's response to a series of papers given at a conference on negative theology sponsored by the Calgary Institute for the Humanities which he was unable to attend.) "Passions" is an essay Derrida was asked to contribute as an "oblique offering" to a collection of essays on his work edited by David Wood, *Derrida: "A Critical Reader"* (Cambridge, Mass.: Blackwell, 1992), pp. 5–35. In this essay he suggests that the "offering" involves a kind of sacrifice. On p. 16 he compares the colloquium in which he has been asked to take part, involving a critique of his work that might be said to represent a dissection of his corpus for the sake of the reintegration or reincorporation of it by others, to the Last Supper, only to deny it. The point of the (anti)theological references is apparently to bring out the family resemblance—in particular the difficulties involved in naming something that does not exist—and yet to maintain the difference between his work and the tradition of negative theology. In "How to Avoid Speaking: Denials," a translation of "Comment ne pas parler: Dénégations," in *Psyche: Inventions de l'autre* (Paris: Galilee, 1987), pp. 535–95, trans. Ken Frieden, which appears along with *"Post-Scriptum"* in *Derrida and Negative Theology*, p. 77, Derrida flatly denies that he is engaged in negative theology. Although there seem to be clear references to the Father and the Son in *Sauf le nom* and *Passions*, in "Denials," he emphatically states, "this 'third species' that the *khora* is does not belong to a *group of three"* (p. 108). It is *not* the equivalent of the Holy Spirit or the *Logos;* it does not mediate between the two. It is more like the *chorismos*, which Heidegger says toward the end of *What Is Called Thinking?* Plato thought existed between Being and the beings—that is, a chasm or abyss.

35. "One is able to say the same about the remark that follows immediately (18c) and touches the education of women, marriage, . . . and the community of children, all these measures ought to be taken so that no one will be able to know and recognize as his or her own the children which come to be born. . . . One is still able to follow the thread of a formal analogy . . . of *khora* with the mother and, supplementary sign of expropriation, with the nurse . . . (it does not engender anything and does not otherwise have any property at all)" (pp. 50–51).

36. Derrida describes the same mirroring "operation" in the analysis of Mallarmé he gives in "The Double Session," the essay following "Plato's Pharmacy," in *La Dissémination* (Paris: Seuil, 1972).

37. In the *Symposium* 208c–209e, Diotima suggests that legislators and poets are engaged in essentially the same mode of seeking immortality. And in Book X of the *Republic*, the second and therefore center of the three arguments Socrates gives to show that he and his companions were right to expel poets from their city is that Homer and his kin have not proved to be effective legislators or educators.

38. *Khora*, p. 90.

39. Ibid., pp. 81–82.

40. In *Khora*, pp. 40–43, Derrida points out that Hegel's understanding of the inferiority of myth to thought can be traced back to Aristotle's *Metaphysics*. Indeed, Hegel seems to vacillate between two interpretations of myth; on the one hand, he takes myth to be evidence of an inability on the part of a people or author to ascend to the concept, but, on the other hand, he suggests that use of myth may indicate the didactical power of a serious philosopher. The two evaluations only apparently contradict each other, Derrida concludes; in both cases, the myth, as discursive form, is subordinated to the content of the concept signified.

41. "Denials," pp. 101–2 (563–64).

42. Ibid., p. 103 (565–66).

43. Ibid., pp. 104–5 (567–68).

44. *Khora*, pp. 105–7.

45. "Of an Apocalyptic Tone Newly Adopted in Philosophy," pp. 48–49 (59–60).

46. "Denials," pp. 117–18 (580).

47. In a remarkable footnote, he observes, "Despite this silence, or in fact because of it, one will perhaps permit me to interpret this lecture as the most 'autobiographical' speech I have ever risked. One will attach to this word as many quotation marks as possible. . . . But . . . for lack of capacity, competence, or self-authorization, I have never yet been able to speak of what my birth, as one says, should have made closest to me: the Jew, the Arab." "Denials," n. 13, p. 135. In 1981 Derrida told Richard Kearney, "I often feel that the questions I attempt to formulate on the outskirts of the Greek philosophical tradition have as their 'other' the model of the Jew. . . . And yet the paradox is that I have never actually invoked the Jewish tradition in any 'rooted' or direct manner. Though I was born a Jew, I do not work or think within a living Jewish tradtion. So that if there is a Judaic dimension to my thinking. . . , this has never assumed the form of an explicit fidelity or debt to that culture." This self-description raises serious questions about the validity of Jürgen Habermas's contention that Derrida's thought is a form of "Jewish mysticism." *Philosophical-Political Profiles*, trans. Frederick G. Lawrence (Cambridge, Mass.: MIT Press, 1983), p. 33. Cf. Michael J. MacDonald, "Jewgreek and Greekjew," *Philosophy Today* 35 (fall 1991): 215–27.

48. "Denials," p. 122 (584–85).

49. Ibid., p. 123 (586).

50. Ibid., pp. 126–27 (590–91).

51. Cf. Ibid., p. 121 (584).

52. "Post-Scriptum," pp. 305–22.

53. *The Other Heading: Reflections on Today's Europe*, trans. Pascale-Anne Brault and Michael B. Naas (Bloomington: Indiana University Press, 1992), pp. 4–83.

54. One of the works by Paul Valéry to which Derrida refers in this talk is entitled "Notes on the Greatness and Decline of Europe."

55. *Heading*, pp. 17–19.

56. Ibid., p. 56. The French title, *L'autre cap*, points to the complex play on the word signifying peak, head, heading, direction, brain, protective headgear, as well as the multiple means of "capital" in the contents of Derrida's talk. In *Specters of Marx*, trans. Peggy Kamuf (London: Routledge, 1994), pp. 14–15, Derrida

observes that intellectuals with left political sympathies had a sense of déjà vu, when at the end of the Cold War Francis Fukuyama reaffirmed Alexandre Kojève's thesis, first articulated at the end of World War II, concerning the end of history. Kojève himself had combined the claims of Hegel, Marx, Nietzsche, and Heidegger about the end of history. The idea was hardly new. *The* question was how to respond to the idea, specter, and/or event.

57. *Heading,* pp. 28–29.

58. Cf. "Force of Law: The 'Mystical Foundation of Authority'," in *Deconstruction and the Possibility of Justice,* ed. Druscilla Cornell, Michel Rosenfeld, and David Gray Carlson (New York: Routledge, 1992), pp. 17, 24–26.

59. *Heading,* pp. 48–49. Derrida observes that the very term "avant-garde" combines the looking forward to the new while retaining or guarding the old that he is advocating.

60. Ibid., p. 17.

61. Ibid., pp. 77–79.

62. "Force of Law," p. 25.

63. Examples of such would surely include Richard Kearney, "Derrida's Ethical Re-Turn," in Gary B. Madison, ed., *Working through Derrida* (Evanston: Northwestern University Press, 1993), pp. 28–50, and Christopher Norris, "On the Ethics of Deconstruction," in *Derrida* (Cambridge, Mass.: Harvard University Press, 1987), pp. 194–237.

64. "Passions," pp. 13–15.

65. "Interpretations at War: Kant, the Jew, the German," *New Literary History* (1992): 39–93. In "Denials," p. 83 (546), Derrida emphasized the significance of the location of the lecture by referring to the hope repeatedly expressed in the Haggadah used during the Seder, "Next year in Jerusalem!"

66. "Interpretations," p. 42.

67. Ibid., p. 41. In his "Preface to the English Translation," *Spinoza's Critique of Religion,* trans. E. M. Sinclair (New York: Schocken Books, 1965), which he dedicated to his friend Franz Rosenzweig, Strauss stated, "The new thinking . . . originated above all by Franz Rosenzweig, who is thought to be the greatest Jewish thinker whom German Jewry has brought forth . . . was counteracted by another form of the new thinking, the form originated by Heidegger. It was obvious that Heidegger's new thinking led far away from any charity as well as from any humanity. On the other hand, it could not be denied that he had a deeper understanding than Rosenzweig of what was implied in the insight or demand that the traditional philosophy, which rested on Greek foundations, must be superseded by a new thinking" (p. 9).

68. Strauss also argued that this scripturally based notion was the core of Cohen's thought and our last virtue, according to Nietzsche. *Studies in Platonic Political Philosophy* (Chicago: University of Chicago Press, 1983), pp. 186–88, 246.

69. "Interpretations," pp. 55–58. In joining Judaism to Hellenism and Protestantism, Derrida observes, again like Strauss, that Cohen also had to depart from the word of the Bible: "Judaism begins by the self-presentation of God in the burning bush. . . . In translating the Hebrew Formula into German, Cohen notes that the tense of the original version is marked by the future. . . . But . . . Cohen goes on to translate the '*Ich bin der ich bin*', into the Platonic idiom: God is being,

he alone. . . . Like the Good, God escapes any image. . . . The purely intuitive thought relating to him is not a thought of knowledge, but a thought of love. . . . Love is presumably the authentic word for faith in reformed biblical language. This is the Greco-Platonic Eros" (p. 65). In order to bring Judaism together with philosophical rationality and Protestant morality, as represented preeminently by Kant, Cohen also had to slight the Law. This was, indeed, the point, Derrida observes, at which Rosenzweig eventually rebelled. (Cohen was not alone in pointing out a special connection between Kant and Judaism, Derrida notes. "Hegel [also] saw in him a shameful Jew," a connection Derrida himself explores at greater length in *Glas* [Paris: Galilee, 1974, trans. John P. Leavey Jr. and Richard Rand, Lincoln: University of Nebraska Press, 1990].)

70. "Interpretations," pp. 79, 81.

71. Derrida emphasizes the question of the "exemplary" in his preliminary abstract of the lecture that is reprinted at the end of the translation.

72. "Force of Law," p. 21.

73. "Interpretations," p. 61.

74. For example, in "Letter to a Japanese Friend," in David Wood and Robert Bernasconi, ed., *Derrida and "Différance"* (Evanston, Ill.: Northwestern University Press, 1988), pp. 1–5.

75. In "An Allegory of Modernity/Postmodernity: Habermas and Derrida," in *The New Constellation: The Ethical-Political Horizons of Modernity/Postmodernity* (Oxford: Polity Press, 1991), reprinted in *Working through Derrida*, pp. 204–51, Richard J. Bernstein also argues that the political implications of Derridean deconstruction are not simply nihilistic.

76. For a fuller discussion of this point see Catherine H. Zuckert, "The Politics of Derridean Deconstruction," *Polity* 23, no. 3 (spring 1991): 335–56.

77. "Principle," p. 16.

78. In *Derrida and Negative Theology*, p. 292. Talking about his experiences with persecution as a Jew in Algeria and his studies later in France, Derrida once stated in an interview that he "felt as displaced in a Jewish community, closed unto itself, as [he] would in the other. . . . At nineteen [he] naively believed that anti-Semitism had disappeared. . . . A paradoxical effect, perhaps, . . . was the desire to be integrated into the non-Jewish community, a fascinated but painful and distrustful desire. . . . Symmetrically, oftentimes, [he] felt an impatient distance with regard to various Jewish communities. . . . From all of which comes a feeling of non-belonging that I have doubtless transposed." (*Derrida and "Différance*," p. 75).

CHAPTER NINE

1. *The City and Man*, p. 138.

2. Derrida makes a similar point when he rigorously distinguishes the "to-come" of which he speaks "from the future that can always reproduce the present." To argue that things necessarily change, one needs more than the passage of time. "Force of Law: The "Mystical Foundation of Authority," in *Deconstruction and the Possibility of Justice*, ed. Drucilla Cornell, Michel Rosenfeld, and David Gray Carlson (New York: Routledge, 1992), p. 27.

3. *What Is Political Philosophy? and Other Essays* (Glencoe, Ill.: Free Press, 1959), pp. 38–39.

4. *Liberalism: Ancient and Modern* (New York: Basic Books, 1968), pp. 6–7.

5. Cf. *WIPP*, p. 38.

6. *"Différance,"* in *Margins* (Chicago: University of Chicago Press, 1982), pp. 1–29.

7. Derrida has, therefore, been criticized for his "antihumanism." E. g., Joel Schwartz, "Anti-humanism in the Humanities," *The Public Interest*, no. 99 (spring 1990): 29–44.

8. For a related argument, see Charles L. Griswold Jr., *Self-Knowledge in Plato's "Phaedrus"* (New Haven: Yale University Press, 1986), pp. 239–41.

9. "At This Very Moment in This Work Here I Am," trans. Ruben Berezdivin, in *Re-Reading Levinas*, ed. Robert Bernasconi and Simon Critchley (Bloomington: Indiana University Press, 1991), pp. 40–47.

10. "Three Questions to Hans-Georg Gadamer," in *Dialogue and Deconstruction*, ed. Diane P. Michelfelder and Richard E. Palmer (Albany: State University of New York Press, 1989), pp. 52–53.

11. *Truth and Method* (New York: Crossroad, 1990), pp. 307–40.

12. Quoted in "Force of Law," pp. 11–12.

13. E. g., Shadia Drury, *The Political Thought of Leo Strauss* (New York: St. Martin's Press, 1988).

14. *Democracy in America*, vol. 1, part 2, ch. 9; vol. 2, part 1, ch. 1, 2, 5; part 3. This "deconstructive" sketch of American history is very *broadly* drawn. Thomas Jefferson, the author of a "rationalized" version of Christianity, and from whose *Notes on Virginia* Tocqueville drew heavily in writing *Democracy in America*, would not have agreed that his philosophical or political principles were "Platonic." On the contrary, he thought Platonism was ridiculously outdated.

15. Derrida himself has deconstructed the Declaration of Independence in *Otobiographies* (Paris: Galilee, 1984), pp. 13–32.

16. Gary B. Madison presents such an argument in "Coping with Nietzsche's Legacy: Rorty, Derrida, Gadamer," *Philosophy Today* 36, no. 1 (spring 1992): 3–19.

17. In *The Genesis of Heidegger's "Being and Time"* (Berkeley: University of California Press, 1993), pp. 69–115, Theodor Kisiel draws out of the religious roots of Heidegger's thought, especially his central concept of "care."

18. In the interview he granted Richard Kearney in 1981, Derrida stated that "It is true that I interrogate the idea of an *eschaton* or *telos* in the absolute formulations of classical philosophy. But that does not mean I dismiss all forms of Messianic or prophetic eschatology. I think that all genuine questioning is summoned by a certain type of eschatology, though it is impossible to define this eschatology in philosophical terms. . . . The prophetic word reveals its own eschatology and finds its index of truthfulness in its own inspiration and not in some transcendental or philosophical criteriology." But, when Kearney asked if Derrida thought his own work was prophetic, he responded, "Unfortunately, I do not feel inspired by any sort of hope which would permit me to presume that my work of deconstruction has a prophetic function. But I concede that the style of my questioning as an exodus and dissemination in the desert might produce certain prophetic resonances. It is possible to see deconstruction as being produced in a space where the prophets are not far away. . . . The fact that I declare it 'unfortunate' that I do not personally feel inspired may be a signal that deep down I still hope. It means

NOTES TO PAGE 274   343

that I am in fact still looking for something. So perhaps it is no mere accident of rhetoric that the search itself, the search without hope for hope, assumes a certain prophetic *allure*. Perhaps my search is a twentieth century brand of prophecy? But it is difficult for me to believe it." *Dialogues with Contemporary Continental Thinkers* (Manchester: Manchester University Press, 1984), p. 119.

19. "Violence and Metaphysics," in *Writing and Difference*, trans. Alan Bass (Chicago: University of Chicago Press, 1978), pp. 152–53.

Index